Reshaping Globalization

Multilateral Dialogues
and New Policy Initiatives

CPS BOOKS

Andrea Krizsán (ed.) (2001) *Ethnic Monitoring and Data Protection.*
The European Context. Published jointly with
the Human Rights Information and Documentation Center (INDOK)

Forthcoming

Miklós Sükösd and Péter Bajomi-Lázár (eds.) (2003) *Reinventing Media.*
Media Policy Reform in East Central Europe

Daniel Smilov (ed.) (2003) *Party Funding,*
Campaign Finance and Corruption in Eastern Europe

Judit Sándor (ed.) (2003) *Law in the Genetic Era*

Reshaping Globalization
Multilateral Dialogues
and New Policy Initiatives

Edited by

ANDREA KRIZSÁN
and
VIOLETTA ZENTAI

CEU PRESS

CENTRAL EUROPEAN UNIVERSITY PRESS

303.482
R 433

The publication of this volume was made possible by a grant from the Open Society Institute.

© 2003 Central European University

Copyeditor: *Arton Vidal*
Cover design and typesetting: *József Pintér*
Production: *Tamás Dombos*

English edition published in 2003 by
Central European University Press
An imprint of the
Central European University Share Company
Nádor utca 11, H-1051 Budapest, Hungary
Tel: +36-1-327-3138 or 327-3000
Fax: +36-1-327-3183
E-mail: ceupress@ceu.hu
Website: www.ceupress.com

400 West 59th Street, New York NY 10019, USA
Tel: +1-212-547-6932
Fax: +1-212-548-4607
E-mail: mgreenwald@sorosny.org

ISBN 963 9241 63 6
ISSN 1587-6942

Printed in Hungary by
Open Art Nyomda és Kiadói Kft., Budapest

Library of Congress Cataloging-in-Publication Data

Reshaping globalization : multilateral dialogues and new policy
initiatives / edited by Violetta Zentai and Andrea Krizsán.
p. cm. — (CPS Books, ISSN 1587-6942)
Includes bibliographical references and index.
Papers from a conference organized by the Central European University
in Budapest in October 2001.
Includes bibliographical references and index.
ISBN (pbk.)
1. International economic relations—Congresses. 2.
Globalization—Economic aspects—Congresses. 3. Globalization—Social
aspects—Congresses. 4. Globalization—Political aspects—Congresses.
5. Free trade—Congresses. 6. International trade
agencies—Congresses. I. Zentai, Violetta. II. Krizsán, Andrea.
III. Series.
HF1352.R465 2003
303.48'2—dc21
                                        2003005778

Contents

Acknowledgements

The Center for Policy Studies at the Central European University is grateful to the Open Society Institute for providing a Presidential Grant to the conference entitled "Reshaping Globalization: Multilateral Dialogues and New Policy Initiatives", which was held at the Central European University in Budapest on October 17-19, 2001. The grant also made possible publishing this volume. A special thank should be given to George Soros, the president of the Open Society Institute, for drawing the Center's attention to outstanding issues of globalization and encouraging the University to organize the conference. The Center for Policy Studies is indebted to the Centre for the Study of Globalisation and Regionalisation at the University of Warwick, in particular to its director Professor Richard Higgott, for being a devoted co-organizer of the conference and bringing excellent scholars to the larger community of the Central European University. Also, we would like to thank Karin Lissakers, the former US executive director of the IMF for her contribution in shaping the agenda of the conference. The editors of the volume owe a great deal to Zsuzsa Gábor and Lilla Jéri, colleagues at the Center for Policy Studies, for their unselfish and competent assistance at different stages of editing and publishing this volume.

About the Authors

LÁSZLÓ CSABA Professor, International Relations and European Studies Department, *Central European University*, Budapest, Hungary, and Chair, Committee on Economics of the *Hungarian Academy of Sciences*, Hungary

BOB DEACON Director of the Globalism and Social Policy Programme (GASPP), *National Research and Development Centre for Welfare and Health* (STAKES), Helsinki, and Professor of Social Policy, *University of Sheffield*, the United Kingdom

DANIEL DOR Lecturer, Department of Communications, *Tel Aviv University*, Israel

JONATHAN T. FRIED Senior Assistant Deputy Minister of Finance and G–7 Deputy for Canada

SUSAN GEORGE Associate Director of the *Transnational Institute*, Amsterdam and Vice-President of the *Association for the Taxation of Financial Transactions for the Aid of Citizens* (ATTAC), France

CHO KHONG Chief Political Analyst, *Global Business Environment Group*, *Shell International Limited*, London, the United Kingdom

IVAN KRASTEV Chairman of the Board and Research Director, *Centre for Liberal Strategies*, Sofia, Bulgaria

ANDREA KRIZSÁN Research Fellow, *Center for Policy Studies*, *Central European University*, Budapest, Hungary

JEAN-PIERRE LANDAU Financial Minister, *French Embassy*, London, the United Kingdom

JEAN-PIERRE LEHMANN Professor of International Political Economy, *International Institute for Management Development (IMD)*, and Director, *Evian Group*, Lausanne, Switzerland

ANDREW MACK Director, *Human Security Centre, University of British Columbia*, Canada, and former Director, *Strategic Planning in the Executive Office of the Secretary General, United Nations*

VIRA NANIVSKA Director, *International Centre for Policy Studies*, Ukraine

SHALINI RANDERIA Chair and Professor, *Department of Sociology and Social Anthropology, Central European University*, Budapest, Hungary and member of the working group on "Civil Society: Historical and Comparative Perspectives", *WZB, Social Science Research Centre*, Berlin, Germany

BRUCE RAYFUSE Director, *International Finance and Development Division, Department of Finance*, Canada

JAN AART SCHOLTE Professor of Politics and International Studies and Research Fellow, *Centre for the Study of Globalisation and Regionalisation, University of Warwick*, the United Kingdom

DIANE STONE Reader in Politics and International Studies and Principal Research Fellow, *Centre for the Study of Globalisation and Regionalisation, University of Warwick*, the United Kingdom

JOHN WHALLEY Professor of Economics and Co-Director, *Centre for the Study of Globalisation and Regionalisation, University of Warwick*, the United Kingdom

VIOLETTA ZENTAI Acting Director, *Center for Policy Studies, Central European University*, Budapest, Hungary and Project Manager, *Local Government Initiative, Open Society Institute*, Budapest, Hungary

List of Abbreviations

AIDS	Acquired Immune Deficiency Syndrome
AILA	Association Internationale de Linguistique Appliquée (International Association of Applied Linguistics)
APEC	Asia-Pacific Economic Cooperation
ASEAN	Association of South East Asian Nations
ASP	Application Service Provider
ATTAC	Action pour la Taxation des Transactions Financières pour l'Aide aux Citoyens (Association for the Taxation of Financial Transactions for the Aid of Citizens)
BCBS	Basel Committee on Banking Supervision
BIA	Built-in Agenda
BINGO	Business Initiated Non-Governmental Organization(s)
BIS	Bank for International Settlements
Both ENDS	(Environment and Development Services) for Non Governmental Organizations
CAS	Country Assistance Strategies (World Bank)
CEPR	Centre for Economic Policy Research
CEU	Central European University
CGIAR	Consultative Group on International Agriculture Research
CIDA	Canadian International Development Agency
CNN	Cable News Network
CoFaB	Convention of Farmers and Breeders
COSATU	Congress of South African Trade Unions
CSGR	Centre for the Study of Globalisation and Regionalisation
CSO	Civil Society Organization(s)
Development GAP	Development Group for Alternative Policies
DfID	Department For International Development
DPC	Derivatives Policy Group
DSB	Dispute Settlement Body

DSE	Deutsche Stiftung für Internationale Entwicklung (German Foundation for International Development)
EBRD	European Bank for Reconstruction and Development
ECOSOC	Economic and Social Council
EMEPG	Emerging Markets Eminent Persons Group
ETA	Euzkadi ta Azkatasuna (Homeland and Liberty)
ETC Group	Action Group on Erosion, Technology, and Concentration (formerly named RAFI)
EU	European Union
EURODAD	European Network on Debt and Development
FAO	Food and Agricultural Organization
FATF	Financial Action Task Force
FIBV	Federation Internationale des Bourses de Valeurs (World Federation of Exchanges)
FSF	Financial Stability Forum
FSU	Former Soviet Union
FTAA	Free Trade Agreement of the Americas
GASPP	Globalism and Social Policy Programme, Helsinki, Finland
GATS	General Agreement on Trade in Services
GATT	General Agreement on Tariffs and Trade
GAVI	Global Alliance on Vaccines and Inoculation
GDP	Gross Domestic Product
GNP	Gross National Product
GRAIN	Genetic Resources Action International
HIID	Harvard Institute for International Development
HIPC	Heavily Indebted Poor Country
IAIS	International Association of Insurance Supervisors
IASC	International Accounting Standards Committee
ICESCR	International Convention on Economic, Social and Cultural Rights
ICFTU	International Confederation of Free Trade Unions
ICSA	International Council of Securities Associations
IF	Integrated Framework
IFAC	International Federation of Accountants
IIF	Institute of International Finance
ILO	International Labour Organization
IMF	International Monetary Fund
IMFC	International Monetary and Financial Committee

INGO	International Non-Governmental Organization
IO	International Organization(s)
IOSCO	International Organization of Securities Commissions
IPMA	International Primary Market Association
IRA	Irish Republican Army
ISMA	International Securities Market Association
IT	Information Technology
ITC	International Trade Centre
JCIF	Japan Center for International Finance
MAI	Multilateral Agreement on Investment
MDB	Multilateral Development Bank(s)
MERCOSUR	Mercado Comun del Cono Sur (Southern Cone Common Market)
MFA	Multi-Fiber Arrangement
MFN	Most Favored Nation
MIT	Massachusetts Institute of Technology
NAFTA	North American Free Trade Agreement
NASDAQ	National Association of Securities Dealers Automated Quotation System
NATO	North Atlantic Treaty Organization
NBA	Narmada Bachao Andolan (Save Narmada Movement)
NBER	National Bureau of Economic Research
NePAD	New Partnership for Africa's Development
NGO	Non-Governmental Organization(s)
NIE	Newly Industrialized Economy(-ies)
NORRAG	Network for Policy Review Research and Advice on Education and Training (formerly Northern Research Review and Advisory Group)
NTPC	National Thermal Power Corporation
ODA	Official Development Aid
ODC	Overseas Development Council
ODI	Overseas Development Institute
OECD	Organization for Economic Cooperation and Development
OSI	Open Society Institute
OTC	Over-the-Counter
Oxfam	Oxford Committee for Famine Relief
PAYG	Pay As You Go
PINGO	Public Interest Non-Governmental Organization(s)

PRSP	Poverty Reduction Strategy Paper(s)
PUMA	Public Management Programme (OECD)
RAFI	Rural Advancement Foundation International (now named ETG group)
SAARC	South Asian Association for Regional Cooperation
SACU	Southern African Customs Union
SADC	Southern African Development Community
SADCC	Southern African Development Coordination Conference
SAPRI	Structural Adjustment Participatory Review Initiative
SDR	Special Drawing Rights
SES	Socio-Economic Security Programme (ILO)
SIGMA	Support for Improvement in Governance and Management in Central and Eastern Europe
SOFRES	Société Française de Recherches et Etudes par Sondage (French Company for Research and Polling Studies)
STAKES	Sosiaali-ja terveysalan tutkimus-ja kehittämiskeskus (National Research and Development Centre for Welfare and Health), Helsinki, Finland
SWAps	Sector-Wide Approaches
SWIFT	Society for Worldwide Interbank Financial Telecommunications
TCDC	Technical Cooperation between Developing Countries (UNDP)
TNC	Trans-National Corporation
TPRM	Trade Policy Review Mechanism
TRIM	Trade-Related Investment Measures
TRIP(S)	Trade-Related Aspects of Intellectual Property Rights
UN	United Nations
UNCTAD	United Nations Conference on Trade and Development
UNDP	United Nations Development Program
UNDPTCDC	United Nations Development Program Technical Cooperation among Developing Countries
UNESCO	United Nations Educational, Scientific and Cultural Organization
UNFPA	United Nations Family Planning Agency
UNICEF	United Nations Children's Fund (formerly United Nations International Children's Emergency Fund)

UNRISD	United Nations Research Institute for Social Development
UPOV	International Union for the Protection of New Varieties of Plants
USAID	United States Agency for International Development
WB	World Bank
WEB	World Economic Brainstorming
WEF	World Economic Forum
WHO	World Health Organization
WTO	World Trade Organization
WWF	Worldwide Fund for Nature (formerly World Wildlife Fund)

B K Title:

Introduction

Andrea Krizsán and Violetta Zentai

F02
F35

The concept of globalization has by now generated a vast array of critical and analytical writings all over the world—enough to occupy a whole room in the newly built Bibliotheca Alexandrina; the library, which strives "to become a non-profit center of learning and research at the national, regional, and international levels, with a view to reviving the glory of the ancient Library of Alexandria, which for six centuries was the center of world learning, and promoted universal knowledge. It was a beacon of science, rationality, tolerance, and philosophical diversity in a world of bigotry and superstition."[1]

Many critical interpreters of contemporary social affairs have stopped reading new volumes on globalization because they contend that the notion of globalization has emptied itself as the meaning of the term is endlessly stretched. The other part of the public engages itself in the debates on globalization even more intensively than before. Social theorists, policy advisors, media commentators, non-governmental activists, and business gurus express their own understandings of global issues by reflecting upon, but sometimes erroneously neglecting, each other. Authors of this volume, with other professionals and activists, came together to a conference organized by the Central European University (CEU) in Budapest in October 2001 with the assertion that critical commentaries on globalization still have a genuine place in intellectual and policy debates. Resonating with the title of the conference, identical with that of this volume, the authors believe that multilateral dialogues and policy initiatives could and should contribute to reshaping the course of globalization.

1. From Transition to Globalization

CEU is a young graduate educational and research institution that has a strong transnational identity and constituency. In the first ten years of its oper-

1. See Ismail Serageldin's presentation at http://www.serageldin.org/frameBibAlex.htm. Website accessed on January 19, 2003.

ation, the University focused on explaining the wholesale social changes in Central and Eastern Europe and the Newly Independent States triggered after the *annus mirabilis* of 1989. By the end of the 1990s, this regional focus became challenged by the growing conscience that social and political forces behind post-socialist transformations could not be purely explicated by and within the history of the region. The enduring interest in the legacy of the recent past could not prevent the CEU community from acknowledging that the hopes for fast, relentless, and peaceful social and economic progress, embracing the entire humanity following the Cold War, is fading away. The wind of transnational processes, which due to their unprecedented intensity and complexity in the 1990s deserve the distinctive term 'globalization', is also sweeping through this part of the world, often with chilly gusts.

Since the much publicized demonstrations against the WTO in Seattle in 1999 and subsequent street protests against high-powered meetings of international financial institutions, citizens, activists, and public intellectuals form the right and claim the space for expressing their critical views on globalization. Discontents with the outcomes of globalization in the 1990s, proposals for more pluralistic forms of decision-making, and radical solutions to global inequalities are discussed through clashes and dialogues among different actors. In post-socialist countries, the public media and critical debates did start to reflect upon these clashes and dialogues after the Seattle debacle, yet major social discourses are still dominated by the discrepancy between the high hopes of leaving state socialism behind and the often disappointing outcomes of embracing capitalism. It is primarily the antagonistic viewpoints in the globalization debates that have reached the public in this part of the world. Advocates of free market liberalism and local chapters of transnational civic movements have already stood up to voice their views. In the mainstream currents, however, global issues are restricted to EU accession and NATO enlargement as if those transnational creatures were self-contained realms. The disappointment with the post-1990 transformations seems to draw a veil on the public conscience over issues of extreme poverty, debt relief, and environmental protection on a global scale, as if those problems belonged to another planet.

The academic community of CEU realized that there was much more to scrutinize even from within the post-socialist world about the enhanced interconnectedness of the world in the 1990s. For example, it is impossible not to notice that the European Union accession process creates new divides among countries formerly tied together by oppressive regimes and reconfigures economic and political alliances across Eastern Europe, Asia, and even the Middle East. The discovery of the Central Asian countries by the multinational companies, extracting natural resources through relying on authoritarian local political regimes, generates new obstacles to turning these countries to truly democratic and progressing societies. The aftermath of the terrorist attack on September 11 raises concerns with the way in which issues of civil liberties and global security are posited against each other in transnational political debates and practices. All these changes are embedded into a 'new world order', in which only one, basically uncontested, superpower prevails.

CEU's growing conscience of global issues was intensified by the encounter with the sophistication and depth of the scholarly work done by the Centre for the Study of Globalisation and Regionalisation (CSGR) at the University of Warwick,[2] and also with the compassionate and provoking thoughts of George Soros, Chairman of the Open Society Institute and Soros Fund Management, and the founder of CEU, on crucial currents of global capitalism. In the spring of 2001, the decision was made that the 10th anniversary of the University should be celebrated by a conference addressing outstanding issues of globalization. The original and modest aim was that, in a joint effort, CEU and CSGR bring together scholars, international policy makers, from both the public and private domains, and significant players from within the transnational civil society to look at how a constructive dialogue between advocates and opponents of globalization might be developed.

As discussions on the conference program advanced, organizers learnt that George Soros, with the assistance of Karen Lissakers, the former US Executive Director of the IMF, was working on his own 'white paper' on globalization. The destruction of the World Trade Center towers in the attacks on September 11 added a new and dramatic dynamic to the debate about globalization. It became evident that multilateral dialogues are necessary but insufficient conditions to halt radical, often violent, resistance to globalization and to turn its benefits to the service of the many. Therefore, the conference program ventured more daringly to combine critical and policy thinking in distinctive areas of the global agenda. Organizers invited the former Mexican President Ernesto Zedillo to introduce his paper *Recommendations of the High Level Panel on Financing for Development* prepared for the United Nations in 2000, Catriona Laing, the representative of the UK Department for International Development (DfID) to bring the Department's white paper *Eliminating World Poverty: Making Globalisation Work for the Poor* for a critical scrutiny of the conference, and George Soros to present his white paper on globalization, which since then has been writ-

2. See the rich website of CSGR at http://www.csgr.org. Website accessed on January 19, 2003.

ten up to a book.[3] Organizers also commissioned a paper from Susan George, a highly respected figure of the transnational civil movement called ATTAC,[4] who drafted her *Planetary Contract* specifically for the conference. The diverse convictions, styles of reasoning, and target audiences of these key texts brought about provoking yet inclusive discussions at the conference and in this volume.

Recently published textbooks offer thorough reviews of the conceptual— sometimes confusing—thickness of the notion of globalization, and the way in which it becomes intertwined with interpretations on late modernity, post-modernity, and new currents in post-colonial critique.[5] Captivating theories have been developed to shape media commentaries and class-room discussions on shifting power relations and changing distribution of sovereignty in world polity (Held, 1995), on global risk society and its ubiquitous uncertainties (Beck, 1999), network society in the information age (Castells, 1996), cultural hybridization (Hannerz, 1996), civilization clashes (Huntington, 1996), just to name a few. Powerful binaries such as 'global wealth vs. local poverty', 'transnational capital vs. local labor', 'society of winners vs. losers' are promulgated by social theorists, anti-globalist movements, and high-powered political meetings as well. Intriguing discussions unfold on how the globalization process in the last two decades of the 20th century has changed the concept of the cosmopolis, originally imagined as an extra-territorial space to be experienced from different localities. It is a favorite subject of inquiry how the idea of internationalism, driven by the common matters of nation states, has become challenged by actors above and under the level of the nation state. It also generates major intellectual anxiety on how globalization changes the production of universal and local claims on good society.

With due respect to these endeavors, organizers neither sought a new interpretation of the concept of globalization, nor did they intend to provide a critical catalogue of already applied interpretations. Instead, they agreed on pursuing an approach best described by Richard Higgott, Professor and Director of CSGR, in his comprehensive report on the conference: "... 'globalization' has become one of the most normatively charged and politically contested concepts in day-to-day usage across the range of the contemporary policy process. For some it is the source of all that is modern, progressive and good in the post-

---

3. All these documents are available on the website of the conference: www.ceu.hu/cps/globconf. See also Soros (2001).
4. ATTAC stands for Association for the Taxation of Financial Transactions for the Aid of Citizens.
5. See, for example, Held and McGrew (2000), Higgott and Payne, eds. (2000), Inda and Rosaldo (2001), and Scholte (2000).

Second World War political economy. For others it is the major source of inequality, poverty and indeed, general societal dissonance." Accordingly, if all the positive aspects of globalization were to survive other than by force, they must not only be effective, but legitimate as well. In order to be legitimate, globalizing processes must satisfy standards and expectations concerning social justice, respect for human rights, and the protection of local communities and cultures, especially in developing countries. Globalization must develop suitable institutions that are open and transparent while being capable of regulating according to acceptable standards (Higgott and Robotti, 2001: 8–9). The organizers of the conference followed Higgott's account in translating the catchphrase 'globalization with a more human face' to articulate concepts.

It is a commonly voiced argument by critical globalists that humanity witnesses the widening gap between the universalistic rhetoric of human development and the reality of uneven impacts globalization. "Both global opportunities and global risks have outpaced global policy," admits a key report on globalization by the World Bank, published soon after the CEU conference (World Bank, 2002: 1). Noticing the urgency of tone in addressing the adversaries of globalization, the CEU conference agenda was based on the conviction that new alliances and coalitions can be formed among the governments, the corporate sector, and civil society in new and inclusive ways. New combinations of players, building coalitions around a common good, may succeed in providing both the integrated thought and action necessary to shape the processes of globalization constructively, as well as ensuring that democratic institutions are strengthened at the global level. In the spirit of the conference discussions, this volume endorses an intellectual position, which resists apocalyptic imagery and upholds the quest for democracy, the rule of law, and prosperity in a global social space.

2. From a Conference to a Volume

To further the debates on globalization constructively, the conference program intended not only to reveal the dark sides of globalization and the perverse incentives it often generates, but to contemplate the possibilities of positive actions as well. Although relying on different styles of reasoning and intellectual backgrounds, keynote speakers of the conference, Ernesto Zedillo and the philosopher John Gray, spelled out that a new chapter in the history of globalization should be opened. In an explicit language, global capitalism needs a visible hand that corrects the misallocation of private and public goods and ensures that the benefits of global capitalism are more evenly distributed among localities. This account was welcomed by vigilant critics of globalization, represented at the conference by Susan George and Waldon Bello, as well as the international financier and philanthropist, George Soros. Gray went even further and also proposed that it is essential to sharply distinguish between the idea of the worldwide free market and the process of globalization. The global free market is a political project that is not much more than a decade old; globalization dates back at least to the 19th century, when transatlantic telegraph cables provided, for the first time, an instant link between markets in Europe and North America (Gray, 2002). This account resonates both metaphorically and conceptually with a report on global social development issued by the United Nations Research Institute for Social Development with an evocative title *Visible Hands*. The report stresses that "the invisible hand of the market may be able to keep the global economy turning. But it takes the human hand to guide it in the most productive direction and to fashion a world that is socially inclusive, transparent, and democratically anchored" (UNRISD, 2000).

Soros and Gray, in their critical writings published before and after the conference, like-mindedly condemn the belief in the omnipotent power of free market forces. In a article subsequent to the conference, Gray proposes that "Contrary to the cranky orthodoxies of market liberals, capitalism does not need a worldwide free market to thrive. It needs a reasonably secure environment, safe from the threat of major war, and reliable rules about the conduct of business. These things cannot be provided by the brittle structures of the global free market" (Gray, 2001). Soros argues that the magic of the marketplace is the dominant belief in Western societies, and therefore, the threat of *laissez-faire* ideology is more potent for transitional societies than that of totalitarian ideologies. Soros also criticizes the dominant view of market fundamentalism resulting in a misallocation of private and public goods (Soros, 2001: 4). As the discussions at the CEU conference powerfully revealed, for understandable reasons, those who work for international organizations and national governments are less concerned with the impact of market fundamentalism and neoliberal thrust, than are the social critics. Serving institutions that are designed by political will and human design, these people rightly feel that their activities are not driven by the blind forces of the market or a pure *laissez-faire* ideology. Nonetheless, views converged at the CEU conference that not all conceptual and practical tools controlling the market forces were proved successful in the 1990s, thus new ones are needed.

Revolving around distributive and governance aspects of global policy issues, the conference discussions put on the agenda the growing discontent with the international financial and developmental agencies. Not believing in active malice and willful negligence, participants tried to give an articulate response to the popular feeling that the three major international financial institutions (World Bank, IMF, WTO) are 'the three prongs of the Devil'. Although street protests of the anti-globalist movements have particularly targeted the WTO and the G–7 and G–8 meetings since 1999, refined accounts concentrate more often on the IMF. These views hold that the IMF tends to reinforce boom-and-bust cycles, and it pushes countries into recession by forcing them to raise interest and cut budgets. This is exactly an opposite economic strategy of what the US government and the British Labor government are following. Informed policy debates also address the major controversies that international trade organizations, in particular the WTO, generate. These organizations are not designed to deal with the social problems they create or neglect. They produce a legal system in which international trade and competition laws operate as a *de facto* constitutional order on a global scale—without having the spirit of constitutional arrangements.[6] There are diverging views, expressed at the CEU conference as well, whether to give a much broader mission to the WTO or empower other organizations instead to develop ways of striking a good balance between free trade and public goods, such as clean environment, social safety, and labor standards.

It is evident that market fundamentalism and neoliberal orthodoxy is not the only force to blame. Globalization debates shed light on the fact that central governments, particularly in the developing word, often cold-headedly divert public revenues and pass them into the hands of corrupt local elites. Paradoxically, these wrongdoings are frequently due to a lack of real state authority. These governments may seem to be too weak to abuse their power. But the case often is the opposite: weak states tend to neglect human rights and the public interest to ensure the shaky basis of their power. The experiences of post-socialist transformation in Central and Eastern Europe and the former Soviet Union could give important empirical evidences to prove this thesis. An omnipotent and, for this reason, ineffective communist state has been quickly replaced with a paralyzed and differently inefficient post-communist state. The state power remained strong in areas where it should not have been, and remained weak where its intervention would have been essential. Some governments of these countries faithfully followed IMF and World Bank policy advice in the 1990s, yet they did not promote more responsible and efficient governance. Far from that, some of them have become captured by monopolists and sometimes criminal groups of the new rich.

A balance sheet of the consequences of globalization calls for ideas for change. But the simple question arises if it is possible to change those forces that caused the harmful outcomes of globalization. The most pressing query is how

---

6. See for example a full-fledged discussion of this discrepancy by Alain Supiot (Supiot, 1999).

one could change policy convictions, in fact many times policy orthodoxies, having insidious impact on the general well-being of people? Following a streamlined agenda of the conference, this volume revolves around five major themes. The sequence of these themes elicits a course of thinking from a critical review of global exchange of knowledge, through outstanding issues of global redistribution of growth and assets, to ideas on governance innovations.

2.1 Production of Global Knowledge

Although the conference primarily highlighted some distinctive policy issues of globalization, it gave a forum for participants to comment on how globalization is paving the way for both domination and plurality in the domains of knowledge production. From the point of view of reasoned policy debates, it is crucial how technocratic knowledge, easily available for transnational exchange, encounters with different local understandings of social realities. It also deserves a critical scrutiny how the distribution of technological development creates differential access to the advantages of global knowledge production and exchanges. Studies in this section of the volume ask who has the authority to make truth claims, who has the capacity to distribute knowledge, and who controls the language of knowledge production in the global arena.

Diane Stone argues that the production of knowledge on globalization itself has become global through networks of institutions and groups of people using the same writings and documents as reference points. Global public policy networks have emerged around policy issues that necessitate transnational exchange of ideas. Stone illuminates the progressive potential of these networks: they encourage experiments and multi-stakeholder cooperation. Nonetheless, the local domains of global knowledge production deserve special attention. Tensions and competition often arise between international and local policy experts groups. Daniel Dor speculates on the legitimacy of fears from language extinction in the global era. He warns that the international marketing industry has become interested in preserving local languages and thus penetrating into new local markets by the means of information technology. The outcome is an imposed multilingualism, which takes over much of the control held previously by the nation-state over setting linguistic standards. Due to the process of technological standardization, written language becomes more authoritative than oral language, which is spoken by the majority of nonprofessionals.

2.2 Social Values and Public Goods

It is often voiced that globalization based on the march of free market and liberal economic policy does harm to the production and maintenance of principal public goods. As a matter of fact, few would argue that free market in itself promotes a smooth path towards material equality between classes, genders, and regions, or towards clean environment and respect for human rights. It seems that the nation states are not any more, transnational institutions are not yet powerful and resourceful enough to take on this stewardship. Many commentaries express the fear that globalization generates a race to the bottom in which governments curtail spending on education and social safety nets, which only higher taxation levels could support. It is debated what is the right size and shape of a public sector, which is efficient enough to tame the unwanted effects of globalization and consonant with local institutional traditions, and how the lessons drawn from restructuring the welfare state in the 1990s could be instructive in the new Millennium.

Bob Deacon's essay offers arguments and empirical evidence to prove that the universal welfare state is compatible with globalization. In the Nordic countries, high level of taxation goes together with global competition. Deacon also explicates North–South tensions in discussing how public goods are to be protected in global trade. Many Southern governments and NGOs oppose the messages and normative policies of Northern advocacy groups, especially in labor and environmental affairs, for having detrimental consequences on local employment and economic growth. Instead of promoting Western values disguised in global standards, Deacon proposes to investigate the policy potentials of new forms of universalism, different from those of the West. Discussing public security as a chief public good, especially due to the consequences of September 11, Andrew Mack suggests that conflict prevention should look beyond the national security paradigm in order to understand the causes of violent conflicts in the world. Local knowledge is needed to prove the validity of generalizations that international aid and developmental institutions make.

Shalini Randeria explores the effects of global policy trends in developing countries, where poor communities often survive on their free access to the public goods. National governments develop economic policies based on transnationalization and privatization of these public goods, as it happens in India, for example. Randeira's analysis suggests that one should contest the notion of the 'victim state' frequently echoed in globalization debates and introduce the concept of the 'cunning state'. In contrast to much of the globalization literature, which emphasizes the increasing marginality of the state in the face of the global capital, Randeria argues that the state and its policies continue to play a pivotal role in transposing and shaping neoliberal globalization. Ivan Krastev suggests that the prevailing policy thinking misunderstands the effects of anti-corruption campaigns in Eastern Europe and by this blurs the prospects for establishing a rule of law culture. The crucial reason for this misunderstanding is a misreading of the nature of the public's anti-corruption sentiments. Anti-corruption sentiments are driven not by the actual level of corruption but by the general disappointment with the social and economic changes, and rising social inequality. This deep disappointment undermines the legitimacy and trust in public institutions. Then policy choices will be embedded into moral discourses to the extent that politics is reduced to the choice between corrupt government and clean opposition. Corruption-centered politics is one of the explanations for the observable transformation of East-European democracies into protest-vote democracies.

2.3 The Global Trade System and Development

Although statistical data proves rather than undermines the thesis that free trade, economic development, and wealth creation went together in the last two or three decades, few would deny that free trade is an insufficient condition for growth. In addition, free trade invokes the fear that instead of yielding to planetary integration, globalization connects powerful centers to subordinate peripheries, reconstituting the dominance of the West. Experiences of free trade under the tutelage of WTO revealed the uncertainty of global trickle-down effects and the injustice of differential rules institutionalized towards rich and poor countries. The growing concerns with its close-door operation weaken, if not undermine, the trust in the WTO and its assistance to the less developed countries.

Jean-Pierre Lehmann argues that Third World countries could not gain much from free global trade in the age of globalization. Yet, for its part the nationalist protectionism, which often favors the local rich and poses sanctions to other developing countries, did not bring progress. Connecting the issues of trade and public goods, Lehmann's caveat warns of hypocrisy and double standards when imposing absolute labor and environmental measures on developing countries. These actions often help the developed countries to take advantage of free trade at the expense of less developed countries. It is high time to consider that the government subsidies to agricultural sectors in OECD countries amount to some 300 million annually, which is approximately the size of the GDP of Sub-Saharan Africa. John Whalley discusses the perplexities of opening a new WTO trade round in November 2001 at Doha. He portrays the debates over the results of the Uruguay Round (1986–1994) for the developing countries as failing to produce a clear, agreed-upon standard to tell good from bad path towards development. Due to growing political mistrust, the proposed agenda for Doha, although it gives numerous possibilities for introducing issues of development, does not seem to convince the developing countries. In particular, developing countries are reluctant to address trade issues together with the issues of environmental and labor standards. The debates also reveal that it makes little sense to initiate a multilateral negotiation if the majority of countries still lack the elementary resources to effectively participating in the negotiations.

László Csaba investigates the broader economic context of global trade relations and analyzes the homogenizing and differentiating effects of globalization. Among the homogenizing tendencies, he identifies the spread of new management and organizational techniques, the pressure for more transparent rules for the capital markets, the environmental concerns becoming endogenous to production costs, and the internationally accepted codes of conduct related to international economic transactions. Among the differentiating effects, Csaba describes corporate governance culture, labor market regulations, civil service orientation, and the ethos of competition. This 'divergence in convergence' opens up a wide space for policy goals and arrangements, he argues.

2.4 New Sources of Funding and Reforming the Aid System

Throughout the 1990s, a simple rationalistic philosophy had a stronghold in the International Monetary Fund and the World Bank, which imposed identical policies on countries with vastly different histories, problems, and circumstances. There was only one route to modernity, the one defined by the advisors of these international organizations. In these days, there are clear signs that internal critical debates have started in many of the major developmental organizations, among them the IMF and the World Bank. The critical currents on aid policy ponder the acceptable level of Western contribution to aid missions, the efficiency of aid programs, and the dead ends that foreign aid often runs in, instead of paving developmental paths. Both insiders of and outsiders to international financial and aid institutions propose alternative sources of funding.

Jonathan Fried and Bruce Rayfuse assert that despite the 50 years of development experience, donors and recipients alike still do not know a lot about what exactly promotes development. Poverty reduction is not possible by wealth redistribution alone; one needs economic growth as well. In addition to aid money, macroeconomic stability and a strong financial sector are also needed to mobilize domestic savings. Fried and Rayfuse argue that the infamous Washington Consensus is not wrong, but incomplete. In addition to free trade, one needs social investments, such as improvements in the health and education sectors. Vira Nanivska, by using the example of Ukraine, explains that charity-type western aid alone, without a systemic application of results-based management and incentives for structural transformation, leaves democratic institutions and rules fragile in the target country. Without rigorous control over the development program, the aid recipient country is unable to take advantage of globalization and risks losing public support for further democratic reforms.

Jean-Pierre Landau refers back to the problem of public goods and connects it to aid distribution. He draws the attention to the distinction between public goods and common goods. In strict economic terms, the use of public goods is non-rival and non-exclusive. As nobody is prepared to pay for their use and production, it is justified to finance them from public resources, including taxes. Some public goods are global by nature, therefore, it is reasonable to think of introducing international taxation on them. Landau reflects upon the much-debated idea of introducing a Tobin-type tax on transnational financial transactions and a carbon tax on the use of carbon related energy resources. The underlying assumption is the possibility of a double dividend, which would reduce harmful activities (speculation and pollution) and produce additional sources for international development. Landau also argues that common goods are rival, though non-exclusive: the overuse of open sea-lanes or air traffic space, for example, creates congestion. Therefore, despite the political and technical difficulties, it would be wise to contemplate taxing the use of these goods.

2.5 Need for a Global Governance?

Even if the global political space is unbounded in moral sense, devices of public decision-making should be established. Many critics impinge upon the much-echoed expression that the world needs 'global governance without global government'. In optimistic accounts, global governance could heal fissures in the breach of polity pertinent to late modern societies. The culture of legality, constitutionality, rights, and democracy still seems to speak mainly through the nation-state. Yet, the nation state is not the only domain of democratic politics and reasoned policy debates. International organizations are prime targets of anti-global sentiments and their democratization is a captivating challenge. Equally importantly, national governments should be monitored and brought to task by transnational civil society organizations and groups which themselves also have the propensity to become key actors in global governance.

Cho-Khong argues that despite the fears of the lack of democratic control over the global economy, nation states still play a crucial role in redistribution.

But they are not enough to ensure a democratic control. Then the question arises: how to develop global governance without state governance? One potential avenue is to set rules to govern international systems based on common and shared values. Another possibility is to build strong regional institutions. Cho-Kong assumes that multinational enterprises would be partners in establishing innovative forms of governance, for example, in setting up a global anti-trust authority.

Susan George's contribution embraces several issues that this volume touches upon. She unmasks the incorrect representation of the global citizens' movement in the mainstream media as a movement exploding with the Seattle affair and as being fascinated with defensive and destructive actions. She calls for introducing Keynesian interventionism into global economic affairs to achieve a Planetary Contract. In this frame of partnership, the global citizens' movement will monitor crucial objectives of planetary actions such as environmental damage recovery, anti-poverty measures, and democratic cooperation among different political actors. On behalf of the movement, George proposes: "Facing the despair that breeds hatred and terrorism, it is our responsibility to respond with a contract of hope and renewal. It is affordable and necessary. Citizens will stand behind. Another world is possible."

In Jan Aart Scholte's interpretation, globalization moves both upwards and downwards from state agencies, therefore, the territory-bound statist governance is weakening and authority becomes dispersed. Civil society organizations venture to raise normative issues of globalization such as human security, social justice, and sustainable environment. Entering more perplexed fields, civil society groups now also venture to scrutinize issues of global finance, international financial institutions, and their policies. Besides the well-known blessings, the dangers of the enhanced presence of transnational NGOs in the global polity are also evident. They may pursue privileges; could act ill-informed and misdirected; may dilute the critical elements of their activity; ensure arbitrary privileges to certain groups; act upon a narrow cultural base; and rely on undemocratic inner practices. Scholte warns of the potential adversities of civil society empowerment exactly in order to strengthen the blessings it could bring to global polity.

3. From Policy Debates to Policy Actions

Since the CEU conference, a number of high-powered meetings, policy forums and reports, supported or contensed by media and social campaigns, addressed the burning issues of globalization. With no intention to be comprehensive, it is worth drawing attention to some of them that revealed reasoned political dialogue, policy wisdom, or action plans towards more even prosperity in the globalized world.

Soon after the CEU conference, the World Bank released its report entitled *Globalization, Growth, and Poverty* summing up its account of the outcomes of globalization in the 1990s. The title mirrors a recent change in the rhetoric of the international development agencies by emphasizing that in addition to generate growth, poverty reduction is also a major global objective. According to the report, integration into the world economy is correlated with higher growth but one must be careful about drawing conclusions and causality (World Bank, 2002: 5). It is statistically proven that the more globalized group of developing countries (about three billion people) have produced the highest growth rates in the 1990s, higher than that of the developed countries. But the rest of the developing world produced little if any progress in the last twenty years and its two billion people are marginalized (World Bank, 2002: 5). World Bank analysts argue that while it is true that inequality has grown both in the more and in the less successfully developing countries, some of the largest developing countries (China, India, and Vietnam) demonstrated major achievements in poverty reduction. The report also acknowledges that global integration has short-term disruptive effects on the local labor markets. The report highlights the importance of complementary policies for social protection and education. This reasoning indicates a more refined approach to economic restructuring and development than that advanced previously by international financial institutions (World Bank, 2002: 14). It still causes widespread anger that international financial institutions do not respect the diversity of economic and political systems and promote 'one size fits all' policy actions. The language of the 2002 World Bank Report on globalization, however, demonstrates a readiness to depart from the idea of a single best institutional model for creating economic growth and stability.

In the arena of global polity, it is an interesting new trend that some World Bank experts try to develop a conscience and identity distinctively different from that of the IMF. In his recently published and celebrated book, Joseph Stiglitz, the former chief economist of the World Bank argues that the IMF is a public institution established by tax payers' money but reports to finance ministers and central bank officials controlled by complicated voting arrangements. Besides its shaky legitimation, its performance also warrants criticism. The IMF was originally created upon the belief that markets are imperfect, but the organization later shifted to promote market supremacy. Ultimately, the IMF failed to produce global stability in line with its global mission (Stiglitz, 2002: 12). If the United States had followed the IMF model, it would not have produced the boom in the 1990s (Stiglitz, 2002: 74).

In 2002 the foreign aid records of rich western governments show that despite the United Nations proposal to share 0.7 percent of their annual GDP with poor countries, very few Western governments fulfill their duties. Most conspicuous is the negligence of the US government that contributes a regrettably low percentage of the country's annual GDP for foreign aid. It was a much awaited move made at the high level developmental conference organized by the UN in Monterey, Mexico in March 2002 that President Bush announced to increase the US assistance to selected poor countries by 50 percent by the year 2006. This will amount to five billion USD per year from 2004. Many observers contend that this announcement was late and superficial as the result in absolute terms is very modest. With this new offer, the US will earmark 0.10 percent of its annual GDP for foreign aid, compared to the 0.39 percent delivered by Europe.

At the Monterey meeting, George Soros repeatedly advocated the idea of offering more money and ensuring better spending efficiency by Western and international donors, even if foreign aid remains a high-risk enterprise. Invoking the idea raised in his white paper presented at the CEU conference and his subsequent book, Soros proposed to use more effectively the already existing devices, for example the Special Drawing Rights (SDR) issued through the IMF. Accordingly, the US Congress should ratify USD 27 billion in SDR earmarked for infrastructure projects in the world's poorest regions (see Authers, 2002). The new SDR proposal envisions an overseeing authority over these funds that does not undermine the power of the nation state but saves the foreign aid enterprise from narrow state interests. Several developing countries have backed the SDR proposal of Soros but the potential donors so far have rejected it.

Later in the summer of 2002, an important cross-national initiative was announced to advance the reform of the international aid machinery. The proposal for establishing NePAD (New Partnership for Africa's Development) was put on the table of the G–8 summit in Kananaskis, Canada in June 2002. The project is the brainchild of five African leaders to enhance good governance, human rights, and working peace in the continent in return for increased aid, private investment, and reduction of trade barriers. The initiative envisages to donate 64 billion USD to African reforms and thus to achieve a seven percent annual economic growth rate in Africa. Unfortunately, against the hopes that this initiative may generate, in May 2000 President Bush signed a bill, which in the next ten years will provide an 80 percent increase of subsidies given to American farmers. This protectionist move demonstrates again the hypocrisy of Western countries in pressing developing countries to lift their barriers while keeping their own ones. One should not blame only the US in this respect; agricultural subsidies in Europe still surpass those provided on the other side of the

Atlantic. It is disappointing that in the ongoing debates on reforming crucial budget and governance issues within the EU, a substantial restructuring of agricultural subsidies was delayed by the 2002 EC summits. Thus, the European Union continues to support agricultural production and producers instead of shifting to rural development, social inclusion, and sustainable environment and by doing so, it keeps protecting its markets from the developing world.

At the end of the summer of 2002, the Rio Plus 10 World Summit on Sustainable Development started in Johannesburg against tremendous skepticism. The final political declaration of the summit resonates with some of the principal concerns of critical globalists. "We commit ourselves to build a humane, equitable, and caring global society cognizant of the need for human dignity for all," asserts the declaration. It also admits that "[t]he deep fault line that divides human society between the rich and the poor and the ever-increasing gap between the developed and developing worlds pose a major threat to global prosperity, security, and stability."[7] Stepping beyond the binary rhetoric of the declaration, the summit resulted in major government commitments to expand access to safe water, proper sanitation and modern, clean energy services, as well as to reverse the decline of ecosystems by restoring fisheries, curtailing illegal logging, and limiting the harm caused by toxic chemicals. In addition to these commitments, many voluntary partnerships were launched in Johannesburg by governments, NGOs, and businesses to tackle specific issues. It is yet to be seen how these noble initiatives will generate partnership among Western and developing governments, international organizations, civil society initiatives, and the business community and whether enough resources will be found for their implementation.

In contrast with the promising tone of the Johannesburg Declaration and some clear foci of action defined, there is a stalemate to further some key environmental conventions, in particular the Kyoto Protocol. The protocol envisioned a five percent reduction of greenhouse gas emissions by 2012, but several scientists talk about the need of a 60 to 80 percent cut. As it stands today, by 2012 the protocol might reduce the emissions by only one or two percent of their 1990 levels. As there is a huge difference between the energy consumption of the developed and developing countries, the protocol puts the moral and economic burden on the wealthier. It seems rightly so: from the stroke of the new year to their evening meal on January 2, an average American family will consume, per person, the same amount of fossil fuel as a Tanzanian family uses in a whole year.[8] The

7. See http://www.johannesburgsummit.org/html/documents/summit_docs/
1009wssd_pol_declaration.doc
8. See the webpage http://www.guardian.co.uk/analysis/story/0,3604,858298,00.html

poor countries will not move until the rich countries promise both to take action at home, and provide realistic funds for adaptation. The geographical accident of birth could not justify enormous carbon emission privileges. Shrugging off international conventions on clean environment and sustainable development warrants critical reactions even if environmental concerns behind the major international conventions are most recently challenged by new currents of thoughts, to which vigilant counter-thoughts are immediately offered.[9]

Many domestic and foreign critics voice political and moral outrage because the US government does not behave as the only superpower in the world should. Although performing better in the 'war against terrorism' than the darkest scenarios envisioned after September 11, 2001, the George W. Bush leadership is practicing an unacceptable unilateralism in its foreign policy. It is not willing to recognize important international conventions, such as the International Criminal Court; it provokes even its close allies with its machismo towards Iraq. In so doing, the American government adds to the tensions that economic globalization has brought about. It is a vicious circle that the US is seen as an arrogant superpower and is blamed for all troubles and miseries of the world, whereas, by alienating its international partners, it will be anything but a superpower capable of tackling problems that globalization creates or does not solve. Harsh anti-Americanism in much of the developing world diminishes the chances for consensual and concentrated policy actions for a much more fair distribution of the privileges and burdens of globalization.

Despite the glimmer of hope that the high-powered summits and meetings saw in 2002, it is of paramount importance that many societies that had just tasted the fruits of globalization in the 1990s, like most of Africa and Central Asia, never got a second bite. China is perhaps the only country that has benefited unambiguously from open markets in the 1990s. Turkey and Argentina are in deep financial crises and suffer outflow of capital (Kahn, 2002). All critical thinkers of global matters should remember that rich countries are still reluctant to open up their markets for agricultural and textile products of the less developed countries. The annual private capital flows to developing countries fell from 300 billion USD in 1997 to just over half of this amount by 2001. Stock and bond markets draw more money out of developing countries than they put in. As Marc Malloch Brown, the Adminstrator of the United Nations Development Program pointed out in one of his recent talks, over four-fifths of the money that did go to the developing world went to just ten countries. The rest, particularly poorest of the poor—the fifty Least

---

9. A Danish economist, Björn Lomborg has made one of the most provoking statements on global environmental affairs (see Lomborg, 2002). Lomborg criticizes many of the hyperbolic statements that environmentalists have made over the years. For a critical commentary on Lomborg's book, see Raven (2002).

Developed Countries—got almost nothing.[10] This latter data appears even more dramatic if one gives credit to Dani Rodrik's thesis that it is not free trade but investment and subsequent accumulation of physical and human capital that helped the successful ones among the developing countries in the 1990s. One should also add that Rodrik warns of capital flow fetishism. Countries with an established rule of law, civic and political liberties, effective social safety net, institutions for conflict management do much better in responding to economic hardship (Rodrik, 1999: 88).

As the economist, Martin Wolf cautions, although globalization is mainly to make the territorial confinement of life loose or even virtual, borders matter more than ever before. The potentials for the pursuit of happiness depend on the very location where one is born. For countries in the poverty trap the future is a vicious spiral of gloomy economic conditions, poor governments, low human capital, and scarce infrastructure. However fashionable and gratuitous it has become to refer to Botswana as a splendid example of success story, failure stories are more numerous (Wolf, 2002). Despite the guilty conscience that many Western-based social critics, like Wolf, have developed, several economists warn that it is doubtful if making the rich poorer would make the poor richer. This caveat may well be valid. But it is impossible to control the spread of destructive technologies, to create global security, and to tackle organized crime and terrorist networks without cooperation between the rich, the successfully developing, and the marginalized countries. To that end, it matters how the developed world expresses its willingness to share the privileges and assets of the global wealth, and more significantly, how the developed world implements real actions to eradicate extreme poverty in a more commited and efficient way.

4. Access to Knowledge

The Central European University, in close alliance with its sister institution,

---

10. See the webpage http://www.undp.org/dpa/statements/administ/2002/september/20sep02.htm
11. The numerous nonprofit foundations created by the philanthropist George Soros are linked together in a loose network called the Soros Network. At the heart of this network are the 'national foundations', autonomous organizations active in more than 50 countries around the world, principally in Central and Eastern Europe and the former Soviet Union but also in Guatemala, Haiti, Indonesia, and West and South Africa. All of the national foundations share the common mission of supporting the development of open society. The Open Society Institute (OSI) based in New York and the Open Society Institute–Budapest (OSI–Budapest) assist the national foundations by providing administrative, financial, and technical support, as well as operate initiatives ('network programs') to address crucial policy issues, more and more with a global scope. Currently a major geographical shift is occurring in the Network: human and financial resources are reduced in the EU accession countries and enhanced in other developing regions of the world. See more on the website of the Network: www.soros.org.

the Soros Network[11], is committed to articulate critical and policy views in the global public sphere. Stemming from its genesis and location, CEU has specific responsibilities and distinctive intellectual resources to contribute to reshaping globalization. In Central Asia and the Caucasus, the University, hand in hand with the Open Society Institute, advises the transformations of educational institutions sought to renew the human capital indispensable for economic and social development. The CEU has put on its research agenda the problem of state capture by key sectors of industry, often in monopolistic position, which creates a perplexed developmental path in different corners of the post-socialist world as well as other developing countries. The academic community of CEU is prepared to bring policy actors, critical thinkers, and scholars together to examine the subtle issues of creating new borders by the European integration. The recently established Convention for the Future of Europe will be a prime test case of inclusive transnational politics within the developed world. New comparative research projects designed by CEU scholars will uncover the possibilities of reasserting moral considerations in economic exchange and thinking, and pursuing universal human rights amidst the plurality of voices defining the concept of rights. The University is opening new windows to cooperate with international actors, who have the steely determination to embrace the Arab world in global democratic transformations. CEU is also open to share its critical thoughts on building good governance in societies where political culture is weak and the tradition of modern public service is sporadic at best. Finally, the University enters into the globalization debates with an undisturbed conviction in the 'open society' tradition of the broader Soros Network, which promotes the values of free speech, fairness, and human rights in any political discussion and policy action.

Some recent initiatives of the Soros Network cast light upon how the 'open society' tradition reverberates in new global engagements. For example, the imbalanced relations between international corporations and local societies of developing countries recently inspired a quickly emerging campaign. The capacity of the state to shape policies that serve the public good depends on revenues coming from major sectors of the economy. In countries where the exploitation of natural resources gives the bulk of central state revenues and the government has little democratic propensities, the revenues often become the honey pot of local elites and leaders. Few of these countries' citizens benefit from this financial windfall because of government corruption and mismanagement. The *Publish What You Pay* campaign, initiated by Global Witness and George Soros, aims to help citizens hold their governments accountable for how these natural resource-related funds are managed and distributed. A coalition of more than 60

NGOs, including the Open Society Institute, invites wealthy countries' governments to require transnational extraction companies to publish net taxes, fees, royalties, and other payments made so that the civil society could more accurately assess the amount of money misappropriated and lobby for full transparency in local government spending.[11]

The Information Program of the Soros Network has recently announced the *Budapest Open Access Initiative* to eliminate the dominance of expensive scholarly printed journals available only by subscription. The initiative is based on the conviction that internet should be a public good which makes available the worldwide electronic distribution of the peer-reviewed literature completely free for all scientists, scholars, teachers, students, and other curious minds. To support open access to international research and scholarship, the Network will provide funding to support the publication of articles by authors residing and working in countries where the Soros Network is active in open-access and peer-reviewed online journals. It is assumed that removing the barriers to access to this literature will accelerate research, enrich education, share the learning of the rich with the poor and the poor with the rich, make this literature as useful as it can be, and lay the foundation for uniting humanity in a common intellectual conversation and quest for knowledge.[12]

This latter initiative brings us back to a new global center of knowledge production, where we virtually placed the globalization literature at the outset of this preface. It is the Bibliotheca Alexandrina, which envisons itself as a new global center of learning. It signals an interesting move that Ismail Serageldin has been appointed as the first general director of the library. Serageldin previously served as the Vice President for Environmentally and Socially Sustainable Development at the World Bank for a long time. He is acknowledged as a devoted leader of major international research and consultative groups engaged in rural development, anti-poverty measures, micro-credit programs, water management. To the provision of these public goods globalization offered an ambiguous stewardship in the 1990s. It is fair to call him a critical globalist. With his new position, he could become a catalyst of transnational encounters between critical texts of the humanity and problem-solving proposals to foster a fair and sustainable global development. His message should bring a profound encouragement to those who are not afraid of the uncertainties and difficulties of building a new course of global development. "To dream and to act on those dreams is the key to a better future. But we must be hard-headed and pragmatic as well.

11. See more information on the campaign's website at http://www.publishwhatyoupay.org.
12. See the website of the initiative at http://www.soros.org/openaccess.

Let us hold up a mirror to ourselves and say: is our analysis of the issues adequate or not? So what is the agenda for action?" (Serageldin, 1999).

By publishing this book, the Central European University is pursuing a pivotal role in preparing young talented people to secure the tools of understanding the perplexed issues of globalization. As Rector Elkana pointed out in his foreword to the conference report, an ambitious educational aim must guide the university leadership: it is to raise young people so that they are able to adapt to the various forms of tension and contradiction they are likely to face when understanding globalization and the place of their own society in it. Young people should understand that there are no black-and-white solutions on the horizon. They have to learn to live with contradictory values, with tensions between their loyalties to nations, religions, and the concept of a global open society (Elkana, 2001: 5).

References

Authers, John (2002) "Soros Condemns Deceptive Way US Aid Is Packaged." *Financial Times*, March 20, 2002.

Beck, Ulrich (1999) *World Risk Society*. Cambridge: Polity Press.

Castells, Manuel (1996) *The Rise of the Network Society. The Information Age: Economy, Society and Culture*. Volume I. Oxford: Blackwell.

Elkana, Yehuda (2001) "Foreword." In Richard Higgott and Paula Robotti, *Reshaping Globalization. Multilateral Dialogues and New Policy Initiatives*. A Conference Report. Budapest: CEU Center for Policy Studies. See also http://www.ceu.hu/cps/eve/globconf/glob_report.pdf.

Gray, John (2002) "The Decay of the Free Market." *New Statesman*, March 25, 2002.

Gray, John (2001) "The Era of Globalization Is Over." *New Statesman*, September 24, 2001.

Hannerz, Ulf (1996) *Transnational Connections. Cultures, People, Places*. London: Routledge.

Held, David (1995) *Democracy and the Global Order*. Cambridge: Cambridge University Press.

Held, David and Anthony McGrew (eds.) (2000) *The Global Transformations Reader: An Introduction to the Globalization Debate*. Malden, USA and Oxford, UK: Polity Press and Blackwell.

Higgott, Richard and Anthony Payne (eds.) (2000) *The New Political Economy of Globalization*. Volume 1 and 2. Cheltenham, UK: Edward Elgar.

Higgott, Richard and Paula Robotti (2001) *Reshaping Globalization. Multilateral Dialogues and New Policy Initiatives.* A Conference Report. Budapest: CEU Center for Policy Studies. See also http://www.ceu.hu/cps/eve/globconf/ glob_report.pdf.

Huntington, Samuel (1996) *The Clash of Civilizations and the Remaking of World Order.* New York: Simon and Schuster.

Inda, Jonathan Xavier and Renato Rosaldo (eds.) (2001) *The Anthropology of Globalization: A Reader* (Blackwell Readers in Anthropology). Oxford: Blackwell.

Kahn, Joseph (2002) "Losing Faith: Globalization Proves Disappointing." *The New York Times*, March 21, 2002.

Lomborg, Bjorn (2002) *The Skeptical Environmentalist: Measuring the Real State of the World.* Cambridge: Cambridge University Press.

Raven, Peter H. (2002) Science, Sustainability, and the Human Prospect. *Science* 297 (August 9, 2002): 954–958.

Rodrik, Dani (1999) *The New Global Economy and Developing Countries: Making Openness Work.* Washington, DC: Overseas Development Council.

Scholte, Jan Aart (2000) *Globalization: A Critical Introduction.* Basingstoke: Palgrave.

Serageldin, Ismail (1999) *Poverty and Inclusion: Reflections on a Social Agenda for the New Millennium.* Lecture at Villa Borsig Workshop Series, 1999. http://www.dse.de/ef/poverty/serageld.htm.

Soros, George (2001) *On Globalization.* New York: Public Affairs.

Stiglitz, Joseph (2002) *Globalization and Its Discontents.* Harmondsworth: Penguin.

Supiot, Alain (1999) *Work, Law, and Social Linkages.* IILS Public Lecture. Geneva: International Institute for Labour Studies. Accessed online on January 19, 2003 at http://www.ilo.org/public/english/bureau/inst/papers/ publecs/supiot/.

The World Bank (2002) *Globalization, Growth, and Poverty.* Washington, DC: The World Bank.

United Nations Research Institute for Social Development (2002) *Visible Hands. Taking Responsibilities for Social Development.* Geneva: UNRISD.

Wolf, Martin (2002) "Location, Location, Location Equals the Wealth of Nations." *Financial Times.* September 25, 2002.

I.

Production of Global Knowledge

Policy Knowledge in the Global Agora

Diane Stone

1. Introduction

   This chapter focuses primarily on professional or scholarly knowledge and the manner in which research and analysis are deployed in global policy domains. The discourses of 'knowledge management' and 'knowledge sharing' within organizations; the desire for 'evidence-based policy' and 'cross-national lesson-drawing' to improve policy development; and broader public efforts to build the 'knowledge society' and 'knowledge economy' are articulated by governments, non-state actors and international organizations alike. These are relatively instrumental understandings of knowledge where it is a tool or technology in economic and social progress. However, the discourse of 'knowledge for development' will be discussed in relation to time-honored questions regarding the relationship between knowledge and policy making. The qualitatively new consideration is how knowledge plays in evolving structures of global governance.

   The Central European University conference from which the chapters in this volume are drawn raised the question as to what might be meant by "the rigorous application of *best thinking* and *best practices* to the management of global systems." The idea of 'global best practice' is discussed here with reservation, recognizing that knowledge—or more specifically codified knowledge in the form of research—represents one form of power. As will be argued, a critical component of the relevance of global thinking is the strength of national and local intellectual communities to re-interpret and adapt thinking to their cultural context and country conditions. At face value, global public policy networks—one type of the new alliances and coalitions discussed during the conference—do incorporate the major stakeholders and the perspectives of local researchers. Without local input and re-fashioning of global knowledge, its application can be inappropriate, misconceived, and perverse. This requires developing and transition states to be active in global knowledge production. First, however, is a discussion of how globalization complicates our understanding of policy making and the decision-making structures within which knowledge is created and utilized.

2. Knowledge Production
and the Widening Scope for Global Public Policy

Much has been written on the different types of organization that create knowledge or undertake research in the pursuit of policy aims. Think tanks, for example, are a form of research organization that directly seeks to influence policy (see, *inter alia*, McGann and Weaver, 2000; Stone, 2000; Stone, Denham, and Garnett 2002). There is an extensive literature on the activities of philanthropic foundations in both advancing knowledge and in its utilization (Parmar, 2002; Gemelli, 1998). Universities, in contrast, have often been portrayed as being engaged in the disinterested pursuit of knowledge. However, there are mounting pressures for them to demonstrate their social and economic relevance, while the 'internationalization' of universities has been evident for decades with growing numbers of foreign students. Consultancy firms are increasingly involved with public policy (Saint-Martin, 2000). Many have been instrumental in the international spread and application of ideas concerning "new public management" (Krause-Hansen *et al.*, 2002). Furthermore, there are many large and globally active non-governmental organizations (NGOs) such as Greenpeace and Transparency International which undertake research and attempt to use the findings to influence policy-making at national levels as well as in international policy communities. More select gatherings of experts and policy practitioners such as the World Economic Forum and the Evian Group engineer policy dialogue between corporate, government, and intellectual leaders.[1] Also important is the role of government research bureaus, both those within departments, and autonomous non-departmental public bodies in manufacturing knowledge.

These organizations, and the professionals within them, are active in more informal intellectual communities, professional associations and knowledge networks that cross borders and institutions and are sometimes referred to as the transnational 'invisible college'. For want of a better term these disparate organizations, networks and associations will be referred to under the umbrella term of 'knowledge agencies'. These agencies create 'codified knowledge'; that is, concrete intellectual and scholarly product that is found in publications, conferences and declarations of advisory groups. This kind of knowledge is most amenable to global production as it can be packaged for distribution. However, knowledge agencies also produce 'tacit knowledge'—shared understandings, on-the-ground knowledge and common identities—that cannot so easily be trans-

1. See their websites at www.weforum.org and www.eviangroup.org/about.htm.

lated into global discourse. These agencies contribute to our understandings of the dimensions of policy problems and develop the conceptual tools to help manage issues in what will be referred to here as the global agora.[2] The global agora "consists of a highly articulate, well-educated population, the product of enlightened educational systems . . . who face multiple publics and plural institutions" (Nowotny *et al.*, 2001: 204, 205).

Traditionally, policy making has been deemed the preserve of national and sub-national government. Relatedly, most 'policy knowledge' has been bundled at the nation-state level. Attempts by scholarly communities and policy researchers to inform policy are limited by time and funding, so activities have tended to focus on what is perceived as the crucial decision making level. In the past, and still so today, this is at the level of national government. Only when regional or local governments have significant powers (as in a federal system) do they act as a magnet for researchers and policy entrepreneurs. Local informal governance can also be strong, especially when war, ethnic conflict, or a lack of central state capacity has undermined the influence of national governments. Such circumstances provide opportunity for local knowledge agencies such as universities and think tanks, as well as for foreign NGOs, consultants and development agencies, to shape policy developments (see Mbabazi, McLean, and Shaw, 2002). Yet, as noted by the Open Society Institute of the situation in Central and Eastern Europe:

> The policy process in many countries in the region remains fairly closed. Where 'outside' influence on the development of legislation, regulations and government programs is found, it is likely to come from government-endorsed foreign experts, the European Union and other international institutions. Not many local independent non-commercial organizations actively participate in this process (OSI, 2001: 7).

The trend toward multi-level governance complicates the national policy scenario. Multi-level governance is "negotiated, non-hierarchical exchanges between institutions at the transnational, national, regional and local levels" as well as the "relationships between governance processes at these different levels" (Peters and Pierre, 2001: 132). New sources of advice are emanating through regional arrangements such as the European Union. For example, the Forward Studies Unit of the European Commission, in efforts to legitimize the European project outside the EU, convenes *Carrefours* or symposiums to "exchange ideas with other research institutes, government and political parties, business and

2. The term 'agora' is borrowed from Nowotny *et al.* (2001) to refer to a social or public space in which science interacts and is constituted. The term is appropriated to the global domain to describe a new public space.

interest groups" (Sherrington, 2000). Other regional developments are creating new policy spaces into which knowledge agencies focus their attention. During the 1990s the ASEAN framework provided a venue for discussions in the immediate post-Soviet period for information sharing and collaborative research on security cooperation among the regional intellectual community in conjunction with the policy community (Nesadurai and Stone, 2000). The Blue Bird project on the 'reinvention of Southeastern Europe' coordinated by the CEU is similarly based on "the assumption that the invention of the region requires the construction of a common regional vision and the emergence of a regional public debate."[3]

While regional associations clearly present new policy forums for knowledge agencies, less well understood is the manner in which global policy processes have emerged. As a result of governments, international organizations and a variety of non-state actors responding to transboundary policy problems—be it cross border movement of money, pollution or refugees—or common property problems concerning the oceans or the atmosphere, new governance structures are evolving. New forms of 'soft' authority in "global public policy networks" (Reinicke *et al.*, 2000) have emerged alongside private regimes which complement the 'hard' or formal authority of states and international organizations. Governance results from strategic interactions and partnerships of national and international bureaucracies with non-state actors in the market-place and civil society. Public policy, whilst still dependent on the state, is informed by a wider range of actors and structures.

'Global public policy networks'—composed of NGOs, government agencies, business groups and international organizations—are helpful in some issue areas to come to terms where governments and international organizations do not have the ability to design and/or implement effective public policies alone. Examples include the Consultative Group on International Agriculture Research (CGIAR), the Global Development Network[4], the Global Water Partnership and the "Roll Back Malaria Initiative" (Reinicke *et al.*, 2000). These networks have been applauded for delivering public goods and services at the global level.[5] They are creators as well as disseminators and consumers of research and policy analysis.

A key feature of a network is a shared problem on which there is an exchange of information, debate, disagreement, persuasion and a search for solutions and appropriate policy responses. Through collective action, networks become a

3. For the Bluebird Project, see http://www.ceu.hu/cps/res/res_bluebird.htm; website accessed on September 11, 2002.
4. See www.gdnet.org.
5. Greater detail on global public policy networks can be found at www.globalpublicpolicy.net.

mode of governance whereby the patterns of linkages and interaction are the means by which joint policy is organized. In short, there is a functional interdependence between public and private actors whereby networks allow resources to be mobilized towards common policy objectives in domains outside the hierarchical control of governments (Börzel, 1998). This tendency is particularly noticeable in global politics where governance structures and public institutions are more diffuse and lack the central coordination hierarchy and designation of authority that are characteristic of national polities. At the same time, the transnational character of policy problems establishes rationales for research collaboration, sharing of information and cooperation on other activities that creates a dynamic for the international diffusion of ideas and policy transfer. Global knowledge production is both constitutive of, and constituted by, these relatively fluid global policy networks.

A number of analyses have highlighted the progressive potential of networks. Due to their informal character, networks are often more effective at incorporating a wider range of stakeholders than public sector bureaucracies. Furthermore, networks are seen as an alternative mode of policy learning, encouraging dialogue and experimentation among similar or neighboring 'recipient' countries with donors concerning 'best practice' (de la Porte and Deacon, 2001). Additionally, networks can build trust, consensus, and what has been called "global social capital" helping to ameliorate the "democratic deficit" in the global agora (Reinicke, 2001: 45). In short, the positive attributes of networks are that they are responsive, flexible and non-bureaucratic and consensual, characterized by open-ended and inclusive decision-making.

Yet, participation in networks and private regimes can be limited. Transnational policy communities tend to be club-like, professional, and elite in character. Involvement is usually limited to recognized stakeholders and experts in the policy field. Participation and knowledge sharing is informally restricted and regulated by the network to exclude spiritual, peasant, or protest knowledge. "Indeed, people who construct knowledge in secular, anthropocentric, technoscientific, instrumental terms have generally exercised the greatest power in global spaces" (Scholte, 2000: 187). Moreover, participation can be costly. Access to global public policy networks requires time, commitment and resources. Many developing country knowledge agencies do not have sufficient resources to devote to national policy deliberations let alone global dialogues. Consequently, the dominance of OECD actors in regional and global policy debates is notable. These transnational policy communities and professional associations produce much of the knowledge about international standard setting and global best practice (Reinicke, 2001: 44). Accordingly, the negative features of networks are that they can be closed and secretive, exclusionary and elitist in character creating gate-keeping decision-making cliques.

Network efficiency, power and influence can thus only be the product of an erosion of democratic accountability and a cumulative process of de-democratization and an effective disenfranchisement of those excluded from the hallowed corridors of the 'web' (virtual or otherwise) (Hay, 2000: 41).

Networks have 'janus-faced' qualities in terms of representation and accountability. Research networks are composed of elites, yet these research networks also represent a potential counter to the dominant positions of the "knowledge bank" (Gmelin, 2001) better known as the World Bank.

In sum, the production of global knowledge cannot be considered in isolation from the impact of globalization upon governance and the emergence of new forums of policy deliberation such as global public policy networks. Growing global political inter-connection runs in tandem with knowledge utilization and incorporation of expertise. This is apparent in the dynamics behind the transfer of policy approaches from one country or region to another and the international spread of ideas that bolster these processes. However, the focus has been on horizontal transfers of best practice between countries, to the neglect of analysis of the vertical transfers in the global agora.

3. The Global Diffusion of Ideas and Policy Transfer

Knowledge production and utilization does not take place simply within the confines of a nation-state. Instead knowledge is diffused, ideas are spread and policies are transferred beyond territorial boundaries and legal jurisdictions. This phenomenon is an important contributing factor to global convergence. Convergence describes a pattern of increasing similarity in economic, social and political organization between countries that may be driven by industrialization, globalization or regionalization. The tendency for states to become more alike can result from voluntary acts of cross-national lesson-drawing as well as from 'imposed' policy lessons such as might occur with loan conditionality. A key role of knowledge agencies—as well as global public policy networks more generally—is not only to produce ideas, but also to facilitate their spread.

Great interest has emerged in development agencies and international organizations in the spread of knowledge about international standards/benchmarks and best practice. An example is the information disseminated by the OECD's Public

Management Programme (PUMA). It builds a number of mechanisms—publications, networks of senior officials, conferences, etc.—to spread information and provide 'forward thinking' on matters such as national accounting standards, human resources management, and "OECD Best Practices for Budget Transparency".[6] Similarly, SIGMA—a joint initiative of the EU and OECD—advises transition countries on improving public governance at the central government level.[7]

Standards setting via national regulation, loan conditions or the formation of international regimes promotes convergence.[8] It often results from 'policy transfer'. This is a process by which "*knowledge* about how policies, administrative arrangements, institutions and ideas in one political setting (past or present) is used in the development of policies, administrative arrangements, institutions and ideas in another political setting" (Dolowitz and Marsh, 2000: 5, my emphasis). The assumption is that transfer results from a rational process by decision-makers of a search for 'best practices' followed by imitation and modification. The emphasis is on the logic of choice in selection of policy ideas, the interpretation of circumstances or environment and (bounded) rationality in adaptation. Ideational actors and forces are predominant rather than economic factors.[9]

States alter institutions and regulatory policy as a consequence of an international consensus around a set of beliefs with sufficient normative power that political leaders fear they will appear as recalcitrants and poor international citizens. Convergence results from the power of abstract concepts, normative standards, policy paradigms, and models of the rationalized bureaucratic nation-state. Once an idea or policy model become dominant—for example, privatization, liberalization, and deregulation—other approaches lose their appeal and legitimacy. Rather than assuming that ideas simply percolate and diffuse gradually, a policy transfer perspective asks who or what is drawing policy lessons and emulating practice or even exporting knowledge and imposing policy ideas.

6. The PUMA web-site can be found at http://www1.oecd.org/puma/
7. SIGMA stands for Support for Improvement in Governance and Management in Central and Eastern Europe. The web-site is at http://www1.oecd.org/puma/sigmaweb/
8. For a discussion see Drezner (2001) who distinguishes between approaches that "diverge on whether the driving force is economic or ideational, and whether states retain agency in the face of globalization or are dominated by structural determinants" (Drezner, 2001: 55). Structuralist approaches identify a process of institutional isomorhpism. Laggard states emulate the practices of global leaders. Their behavior is led by the taken-for-granted aspects of political life where actors follow rules, shared interpretations, schema, and meanings. Agent-centered approaches do not dismiss structural forces but suggest that in varying degree, states and organizations can mediate, these dynamics.
9. The 'race to the bottom' of regulatory standards is one economic argument that considers convergence occurs due to threat of capital flight that causes non-converging states to modify their regulatory policies in order not to lose their competitiveness in the global economy. A criticism is the erroneous assumption that states ignore other constituencies—electorates, bureaucracies and interest groups—and do not have market power *vis-à-vis* global capital (Drezner, 2001: 58).

One important mode of policy transfer is through the elite networking of transnational policy communities or global public policy networks. These communities of experts and professionals share their expertise and information and form common patterns of understanding regarding policy through regular interaction such as through international conferences, government delegations, websites and sustained email communication (Bennett, 1991: 224–225). The ideas surrounding the 'new public management' is an example of a dominant discourse that has become institutionally embedded propelled by the professional interactions of OECD civil servants (Krause-Hansen *et al.*, 2002), consultants (Saint-Martin, 2000), professional associations, think tanks and others.

In addition to constructing dominant set of beliefs, experts and professionals potentially become a stronger causal factor in policy transfer when they become 'policy entrepreneurs'— "people who seek to initiate dynamic policy change" (Mintrom, 1997: 739). They help transfer the intellectual matter that underpins policies. They can provide the rhetoric, the language, and scholarly discourse to give substance and legitimacy to certain preferred positions. These entrepreneurs engage in a variety of strategies to win support for ideas: "identifying problems, networking in policy circles, shaping the terms of policy debates, and building coalitions" (Mintrom, 1997: 739). They operate alongside *official* actors such as bureaucrats, politicians and political appointees in transferring policy practices.

Of concern to a regional association, national polity or local community is the process of the knowledge exchange. Technical cooperation, overseas training and the role of international consultants in institutional development can be a "one-way transaction" (Tilak, 2001: 256) from aid organizations or developed countries to developing countries. Consideration also needs to be given to whether the technical knowledge that is 'shared' can be effectively utilized. Simple advocacy of 'best practice' does not confront deep-rooted asymmetries of power that exist in numerous developing and transition countries that may confound appropriate knowledge utilization (Tilak, 2001: 261). Moreover, understandings of 'best practice or thinking' are mediated by contractors and consultants who implement programs and who "add to the complexity to any message" about best practice (de la Porte and Deacon, 2001). Even so, the knowledge base of organizations and countries is highly uneven. The scope for interaction between knowledge agencies and decision-makers as well as the absorption and adaptive capacity of a political system to global knowledge on best practice varies significantly from one country to another.

Finally, 'lessons' and 'best practice' represent codified, formal, and technical knowledge to be found in reports, reviews, web-sites, and government and

OECD documentation centers. This codified knowledge can squeeze out tacit and practical knowledge.

> Meaningful and useful knowledge is produced and reproduced . . . not by re-inventing locally what can be gathered from scanning a central global knowledge bank or by replicating best practices. Local problem perceptions and solutions have to be part of the local settings and processes (Gmelin, 2001: 9).

Tacit knowledge is more ephemeral, recognizable in performance and usually deemed more subjective and procedural. In other words, traditional, 'grassroots' and practitioner knowledge is frequently less amenable to such transfer rooted as it may be in communal understandings or local practices. Indeed, the reviews of past programs necessarily reflect the evaluation requirements of donor agencies, government departments, and other funders/authorizers of policy programs and are less focused on what has been learnt or experienced by the recipients or subjects of the program (King, 2001: 3). It is necessary to address whose knowledge becomes globalized knowledge and to recognize the asymmetrical power relationships among knowledge producers and consumers in shaping and channeling what is diffused.

4. The Production of Global Knowledge

Universities have expanded in the western world and new universities—public and private—have proliferated in developing countries. University internationalization (as well as 'Europeanization') is apparent in the establishment of international offices, curriculum development, course credit recognition and transfer, discipline-based networks, collaborative links with foreign universities, multilingualism, and/or adoption of English as language of instruction in some courses (Callan, 1998). The internationalization of universities is manifest in the movement in foreign students. Academics have become more mobile, and finding more varied employment in think tanks, government advisory bodies and international organizations. In a number of countries, 'brain drain' represents a significant development problem.

International organizations have consolidated over the past half century and with this institutional development has been the establishment of in-house research departments (Squire, 2000). The 'development economics research group' of the World Bank is a strong hold of the economic examination of questions of development to the exclusion of other disciplines (Denning, 2001:

143). United Nations agencies such as UNESCO and UNRISD have a direct interest in building the knowledge base of society.[10] Moreover, these international organizations collaborate on, contract out or commission greater amounts of research with groups around the world. Their funding power has strong influence in structuring the supply of global knowledge and shaping research agendas.

Governments are also very important producers of knowledge. Needless to say, capacity for in-house research and policy analysis varies dramatically from one country to the next (see Stares and Weaver, 2001). It can not be claimed that all policy analytic units can project their thinking into regional and global debates in the same way that the DfID report on globalization has been discussed (DfID, 2000). The role of the British Council in promoting British education (and the more understated policy transfer role of the Centre for Policy and Management Studies attached to the British Cabinet) cannot be matched by the governments of Belarus or Mali. Similarly, other development agencies such as USAID, DSE (German Foundation for International Development), or CIDA have enviable resources at their disposal for the dissemination of their version of 'best thinking' on development.

NGOs are becoming influential knowledge providers. Their expert standing is derived from professional status and experience of their staff and capacity to gather data. The World Economic Forum and the Evian Group are private associations. Yet, the business and government leaders and high status intellectuals they are able to assemble bestow a patina of power and authority. Testimony to the perceived influence of WEF has been the creation of the 'Other Davos' meetings for alternative thinkers in the anti-globalization movement.[11] Scholarly associations and professional bodies also fall into this category of third sector organizations for the advancement of knowledge.[12] However, most notable among third sector organizations are the independent foundations such as Ford, Nuffield, Aga Khan, McArthur, Sasakawa, and Gates. These international foundations increasingly incorporate a global focus in their research funding.

10. United Nations Research Institute for Social Development (http://www.unrisd.org/) and United Nations Education, Scientific, and Cultural Organization (http://www.unesco.org/)
11. Information about the 'Other Davos' meetings can be found at www.otherdavos.net/.
12. These associations (such as for example, the International Institute for the Advancement of Science or the Third World Academy of Sciences) are too numerous to recount. An excellent overview of both official and independent organizations dedicated to building research capacity in developing countries can be found in a recent report to DfID (see Young and Kannemeyer, 2001). Of the 49 organizations covered, there were four foundations, seven research institutes, 11 international NGOs and nine regional NGOs. In other words, approximately two-thirds that could be categorized as 'third sector' or (global) civil society organizations.

The production of knowledge in the global agora is jointly constructed through the interactions of these agencies in 'international knowledge networks'. This is "a system of coordinated research, study (and often graduate-level teaching), results' dissemination and publication, intellectual exchange, and financing, across national boundaries" (Parmar, 2002). Governments, foundations and international organizations provide key financial resources for think tanks and universities to conduct research and investigate the viability of transmitting policies developed elsewhere. They feed into and help sustain global public policy networks like GAVI (Global Alliance on Vaccines and Inoculation) or the CGIAR. In these global networks, the distinction between knowledge producers based in the official domain and (global) civil society becomes very blurred.

5. Knowledge Production and Global Public Policy

In general, policy research is incorporated into policy making where and when it is demanded by decision-makers. Experts and their organizations acquire political credibility by performing scientific services for states and international organizations. They respond to demand for knowledge that performs one or a combination of five functions:
- instrumental use;
- cognitive explanation;
- ritualistic nourishment;
- legitimation;
- no use (adapted from Tilak, 2001: 260).

5.1 Instrumental Uses of Knowledge

Experts can provide a range of services for official consumers such as informed judgments and analysis of existing programs. Knowledge agencies are also useful acting as independent agents monitoring progress on adherence to international treaties and agreements. They also contribute to governance and institution building by facilitating exchange between official and other private actors via networks. Importantly, "the technologies of globalization have also enlarged the amounts and types of empirical evidence" (Scholte, 2000: 191) available not only to scholars but also to policy makers. The welter of information produces a requirement for knowledge sifters or editors to distinguish between poor and rigorous research, to find policy relevant knowledge or to synthesize, distill, and re-package knowledge into a manageable format.

The Public Policy Initiative of the Open Society Institute, for example, is a capacity building effort to promote policy centers across Central and Eastern Europe to "inform the policy community" (OSI, 2001: 7). Often, however, analysis is provided in response to official invitation. Those who demand and fund research usually set the research agenda even if there is a high degree of autonomy in how that research is conducted. Consequently, international organizations, foundations, aid agencies, governments, and corporations shape the demand for knowledge and stamp a character on the supply of that knowledge. A shift in the research paradigm with increasing emphasis on the utilitarian value of knowledge results. The current emphasis is on the value of research for 'user-groups', the production of graduates with skills that allow them to better understand the global political economy and the pragmatic concern for evidence-based policy.

5.2 Conceptual Frameworks and Interpretation

Knowledge production provides the conceptual categories and interpretative frameworks within which to find explanations and policy options for global as well as local problems. This is captured in the agenda of the Blue Bird Project to establish a "vision community of thinkers" to inspire regional policy debate (OSI, 2001: 51). In other words, think tanks, university institutes and researchers help develop the theories, discourse, methods, and models that shape policy understandings and potentially become ruling ideas.

There is a common theme in the ideational literature that ideas matter more (or at least their impact more observable) in circumstances of uncertainty where interests are unformed or some kind of crisis (war, environmental catastrophe, election swings) disrupts established policy patterns and provokes paradigmatic revision (see Haas, 1992). Ideational forces or knowledge agencies are presented with a 'window of opportunity' to compete to redefine the policy context. The global agora is a domain of relative uncertainty where interests are unformed, institutions underdeveloped, and political authority unclear.

5.3 Rituals and Symbols

Academic institutes and think tanks are used routinely by political leaders to announce policy initiatives or clarify positions. For example, most American Presidents and a host of distinguished international leaders have delivered presentations at the Council on Foreign Relations in New York as a prestigious platform from which to make policy announcements. Similarly, scientists are appointed to government committees to lend a scholarly veneer as well as provide advice. Other experts in civil society bodies—think tanks, foundations, scientific charities, professional associations—perform similar roles organizing seminars and closed discussions as well as hosting foreign delegations. Because of their professional image and scholarly aspirations, they are viewed as a more benign or cooperative alternative when compared to the relatively more critical stance, subjective knowledge, and occasionally disruptive lobbying of many NGOs. Accordingly, knowledge agencies have often built stable relationships with official actors in governments and international organizations. Individuals get access to information and entry to official policy communities while state agencies can legitimize their policy position by arguing that they are interacting with and consulting independent civil society organizations or experts. On the other hand, multilateral initiatives to commission research or establish international policy task-forces of experts may be less indicative of the power and influence of knowledge agencies and more symptomatic of circumstances where research and expertise is used to legitimate prior policy positions.

5.4 Legitimacy and Authority

Experts exercise some authority because of the scholarly legitimacy and scientific status they claim, or are perceived to, hold. They appropriate authority firstly, on the basis of their scholarly credentials and institutional location in quasi-academic organizations focused on the rigorous and professional analysis of policy issues; and secondly, their establishment as organizations independent from both the state and market that strengthens their reputation as civil society organizations. These endowments give experts some legitimacy intervening with knowledge and advice in global and regional policy processes. Their scientific image is reinforced by their institutional affiliations with universities and think tanks as well as the media exposure they sometimes acquire. Moreover, the companies and official agencies that employ this expertise have an interest in bolstering this perception (and perhaps discrediting other varieties of expertise). However, their scholarly legitimacy and rationalism is finely tuned and can be called into question by ideological advocacy and politicization. It undermines their reputation as providers of independent analysis or neutral expertise. Too close an affinity with government, political parties, or NGOs can damage their authority and legitimacy as objective (or at least balanced) knowledge providers.

An extensive body of social theory contests the scientific status of 'experts' and knowledge agencies as simply one kind of narrative that is no more legitimate than the knowledges of indigenous groups, practitioners, or religious revival movements. Postmodernist explanations regard knowledge as not only bound to time and place but the person or agency that created it. Cultural and historical context determine the character of truth. Rationalist understandings of scientific objectivity are not regarded as 'truth' but as contingent and contestable knowledge claims. "It is the social power relations—rather than any fundamental truth—that have elevated rationalism over other modes of knowledge in modern contexts" (Scholte, 2000: 191).

5.5 Irrelevant Knowledge

Whilst research and educational institutions, as well as private consultants and think tanks, may aspire to influence global thinking and shape policy agendas on global policy problems, the more frequent reality for those in policy-making milieux is not to use research rationally and comprehensively. Knowledge agencies may be ignored or patronized at will by governments. Furthermore, some developing countries do not absorb effectively either global or local knowledge. They lack governmental capacity in the form of in-house policy units or well-trained bureaucracy. Nevertheless, policy irrelevance does not necessarily mean social or cultural irrelevance.

The nature of influence exerted by knowledge agencies in the global agora reflects the knowledge function they perform. The instrumental value of knowledge agencies is to be found in the day-to-day deliberations of development agencies, international organizations, and global public policy networks. The conceptual influence of knowledge on policy is much more diffuse, incremental, and 'atmospheric' but can be powerful over the long term. The inclusion of experts in policy debates can be symbolic recognition of the importance of research. By contrast, acting as 'legitimizers' is perhaps a reflection of the lack of influence of knowledge agencies even though it may be a means to secure resources. The likelihood of the irrelevance of research makes a good counter factual point suggesting that interests rather than ideas shape policy and politics. There are many intermediary variables between knowledge production and subsequent policy design and implementation. Researchers and experts are one small and relatively unimportant group compared to vested interests of transnational corporations, governments, and other political actors seeking to shape policy. Consequently, rather than the agency of individual experts, think tanks or university institutes, it is their collective impact and development of common themes with other interests that institutionally embeds certain technical discourses as hegemonic within international organizations and global public policy networks.

Knowledge production in the global system tends to be based on a complex interweaving of network interactions. Sometimes, these are loose, ad hoc relationships with like-minded policy institutes, NGOs, university centers, and government agencies, in a given issue area to exchange information, ideas and keep abreast of developments. At other times, advisors and their institutes act as policy entrepreneurs within tighter networks such as an epistemic community. Networks are important both in embedding knowledge agencies in a relationship with more powerful actors, and in increasing their audience or constituency, thereby potentially amplifying their impact. The emergence of global knowledge elites consolidating in global policy networks raises new questions about inclusion and global access.

The growth in the supply and international spread of knowledge and expertise has impact not only on the character of knowledge but also on channels into and participation in global policy developments. Knowledge-based authority is one foundation behind the "enforceable societal relations" and sets of hegemonic ideas within what some identify as the emerging global polity (Ougaard and Higgott, 2002). Recognized standards and modes of verification are often generated under the canons of academic research and intellectual collaboration. This does not allow an even playing field for many NGOs and community organizations that do not have the expertise or resources to conduct the intellectually coherent and technically proficient studies that match the research capabilities of development agencies. Subjective perceptions, practitioner insights, grassroots knowledge, and communal voices do not have the same credence or value as 'expert' deliberations. Moreover, such knowledge cannot be up-rooted easily from its context and packaged in format to be transmitted upwards into global domains. Indeed, it may not make sense out of context. The character of global knowledge—technical, codified, elite, and homogenized language—produces new inequities. Those with elite knowledge skills and attributes—graduate degrees, professional experience in international organizations—are more likely to be able participate in global policy dialogues.

6. The Local Domain of Global Knowledge Production

Improving access to global knowledge and disseminating best practice are vitally important to many developing countries without strong university sectors or research capacity within government or civil society. This paper disputes neither the need nor the value of global sources of knowledges. For many in developing and transition countries, the opportunity to study abroad, to participate in OECD training programs and networks, or to access the databases of organizations like the World Bank represents the best available knowledge. Instead, the issue is more about participation in knowledge production—what knowledge is (re)produced and where it is disseminated. As noted of the role of consultants in EU social policy transfers to Central and Eastern Europe: "It is principally the [international] experts who are on the ground in the recipient country that have the possibility to shape policy issues through the projects they participate in" (de la Porte and Deacon, 2001, my insertion).

Universities, foundations, and think tanks play an important role as both regional/global knowledge interlocutors and as local/national knowledge repositories. Strong national and local capacity in knowledge creation is crucial not only in enhancing national policy learning and development of policy solutions but as a necessary base from which to engage in global policy debates and became effective interpreters and adapters of global knowledge. Strong local capacity not only provides a bulwark against the standard models and 'one-size-fits-all' application of global knowledge, it is a source of new data, fresh insights, and innovative synthesis.

This is contested terrain. In the local application of knowledge and implementation of policy global standards are most keenly felt by local communities. Tensions and competition often result between international experts with the national policy communities that are critical of the lack of knowledge of local conditions and cultures. Structural adjustment loans are often supplemented by technical assistance, frequently in the form of consultants (Larmour, 2001). The preference for foreign consultants, especially by donor agencies that tie technical assistance to the hire of donor-country experts is often regarded as a constraint on the development of in-country research capacity and policy expertise.

International cooperation in research, . . . which largely takes the form of research by consultants . . . tends to displace public funding of research. It also sets new research agendas. The short term needs and compulsions of international research also contribute to negating the value of long-term research on the one hand, and building of sustainable capacities of the universities and research institutions; and as a corollary to the research conducted or sponsored by international organizations, domestic research generally gets devalued (Tilak, 2001: 259).

In Sri Lanka, "This causes resentment among locals and discourages them from active participation" (Stanley Samarasinghe, November 2, 1999). Another cause for complaint has been the imposition of 'one-size-fits-all' development models and inappropriate application of 'world standards'. In Bulgaria ". . . it is quite difficult to argue with some foreign consultants in developing projects, especially with foreign donors, that not all research instruments that work in some part of the world also work in the others" (Lilia Dimova, November 17, 1999). These local experts question both the quality and utility of policy knowledge marketed by the consultancy industry and the interests of donors in demanding such knowledge.[13]

Foreign consultants and international experts are important in promoting the international exchange of knowledge. However, local universities, foundations, and think tanks are helpful in mediating between the local needs and experiences and the general knowledge available. They open up spaces for pluralistic dialogues across national and cultural boundaries and challenge mainstream thinking. In particular, local knowledge agencies can improve understanding of policy transfer processes. Specifically, they can identify the conditions under which policy transfer occurs, when policy transfer is either appropriate and will enhance 'best practice' or when it will lead to policy failures. In doing so, knowledge agencies are constitutive of the process and become propellers of transfer. This is apparent when academics, consultants or think tank staff are seconded to the World Bank or IMF; undertake consultancy work for aid agencies like Finnida, and engage in advocacy work for NGOs or consultancy that draws attention to overseas experience.

Also not to be neglected is the manner in which education and skills acquisition are major elements of the policy transmission process. For example, poorly understood is the manner in which the movement of foreign students contributes to policy diffusion. A significant proportion of graduate students are sponsored by their home governments, usually a specific ministry to undertake policy or economically relevant degrees in Europe and North America. Long-standing schemes of international student exchange such as the Columbo scheme, Rhodes scholarships, and Fulbright fellowships, and the more recent example of Soros scholarship scheme as well as Socrates in the EU, represent significant channels for the international movement of ideas, policy and practice. In the case of the USA,

> Its ability to spread ideas is further enhanced by the wealth and prestige of
> US universities which attract a growing number of foreign students. In

13. These comments were taken from an electronic dialogue initiated by the World Bank Institute, titled "Bridging Research and Policy," which was held between October 28 to December 2, 1999. Full statements are archived at www2.worldbank.org/hm/hmgdn/index.html; website accessed on September 11, 2002.

addition to being immersed in US culture, foreigners studying business, economics, law and public policy in the United States also receive an education that stresses the virtues of free markets, democratic institutions, and the rule of law. . . When it comes to US cultural hegemony, American universities may be as powerful a weapon as the American military (Walt, 2000: 40).

As universities internationalize, intellectual exchange and cross-national engagement via the 'invisible college' becomes routine. Yet, relatively few universities have global reputations and most of these are located in Europe and North America.

As the CEU grows, it can also be a mediator, editor, and interpreter of global knowledge. That is, to take global lessons and best practice assumptions and evaluate for inapplicable ideas or inappropriate transfer.

There is much to learn from other countries and organizations, but strong local knowledge agencies are also needed to modify 'best thinking and practice' to suit local arrangements and cultural expectations. For example, a small transnational liberal college like CEU can project regional thinking to an outside world and aspire "to improve the policy environment in the region by diversifying the sources of public policy input."[13] Think tanks, research networks, and home-grown experts in other regions can likewise act as mediators, editors, and interpreters of global knowledge. This may well lead to divergence and difference recognized more as a positive attribute and as a source for future innovations than as a sign of a lack of consensus, policy coherence or certainty. To be of social value in this context, universities and other knowledge institutions need to carve out their own space in the global agora to evaluate 'best practice'.

7. Conclusion: Think Local, Act Global?

Policy transfer and global knowledge sharing has at least two dimensions, but one dimension has received greater attention. It is easier to adopt the discourse of 'think global, act local' and develop 'knowledge sharing' and capacity building programs around this mantra. Valuable programs have been initiated to provide desperately needed support for local universities and policy institutes as well as to make global knowledge more accessible to developing countries for local

13. See the Center for Policy Studies home page www.ceu.hu/cps.

interpretation and application. However, there are clear asymmetries of power and capability inherent in 'knowledge for development'. It is a far more difficult enterprise to 'think local and enact it globally'. For example, the seventeen policy centers supported by the OSI have "obtained a significant degree of credibility and influence in their respective areas of practice." However, awareness of their activities and expertise is not "reflected outside national boundaries" (OSI, 2001: 7). The capacity to participate in global policy dialogues and networks is not as well developed. Greater focus on this side of equation not only requires recognition of the disparities in research capacity and therefore the inability of many countries to participate in global knowledge production, but also recognition of the great diversity of knowledge. Top-down knowledge sharing or the development of global databases that can be easily accessed are not so well structured to allow the reverse flow of knowledge from local knowledge producers into global knowledge production. University institutes and independent policy centers need not only to be policy entrepreneurs among their local communities and within national polities but to develop some capacity as policy entrepreneurs in the global agora.

References

Bennett, Colin J. (1991) "Review Article: What is Policy Convergence and What Causes It?" *British Journal of Political Science*, 21: 215–233.

Börzel, Tanja (1998) "Organizing Babylon. On the Different Conceptions of Policy Networks." *Public Administration*, 76(summer): 253–273.

Callan, Hilary (1998) "Internationalization in Europe." In Peter Scott (ed.) *The Globalization of Higher Education*. Buckingham, UK: The Society for Research Into Higher Education and the Open University Press, pp.44–57.

De la Porte, Caroline and Bob Deacon (2001) "International Consulting Companies and Eastern European Accession to Europe." Summary of Report. www.stakes.fi/gaspp/consultingcompanies.html.

Denning, Stephen (2001) "Knowledge Sharing in the North and South." In Wolfgang Gmelin, Kenneth King and Simon McGrath (eds.) *Development Knowledge, National Research and International Cooperation*. Edinburgh, Bonn, and Geneva: CAS-DSE-NORRAG, pp.133–152.

DfID—Department for International Development (2000) *Eliminating World Poverty: Making Globalisation Work for the Poor*. White Paper on International Development, UK, HMSO.

Dolowitz, David and David Marsh (2000) "Learning from Abroad: The Role of Policy Transfer in Contemporary Policy Making." *Governance*, 13(1): 5–24.

Drezner, Daniel W. (2001) "Globalization and Policy Convergence." *International Studies Review*, 3(1): 53–78.

Gemelli, Giuliana (ed.) (1998) *The Ford Foundation and Europe (1950s–1970s): Cross Fertilization of Learning in Social Science and Management*. Brussels: European University Press.

Gmelin, Wolfgang (2001) "Managing Which and Whose Knowledge for Development." In Kenneth King (ed.) *Knowledge, Research, and International Cooperation*. Northern Policy Research Review and Advisory Network on Education and Training, NORRAG News, 29(July). Edinburgh: Centre of African Studies, University of Edinburgh, pp.9–12.

Haas, Peter (1992) "Introduction: Epistemic Communities and International Policy Coordination." *International Organization*, 46(1): 1–35.

Hay, Colin (2000) "The Tangled Webs We Weave: The Discourse, Strategy, and Practice of Networking." In David Marsh (ed.) Comparing Policy Networks. Buckingham, UK: Open University Press, pp.33–51.

King, Kenneth (ed.) (2001) *Knowledge, Research and International Cooperation*. Northern Policy Research Review and Advisory Network on Education and Training, NORRAG News, 29(July), Edinburgh: Centre of African Studies, University of Edinburgh, pp.1–90.

Krause-Hansen, Hans, Dorte Salskov-Iversen, and Sven Bislev (2002) "Discursive Globalization: Transnational Discourse Communities and New Public Management." In Morten Ougaard and Richard Higgott (eds.) *Approaching the Global Polity*. London: Routledge, pp.107–124.

Larmour, Peter (2001) "Coercive Transfer? Conditionality and Policy Reform in PNG and the South Pacific." Unpuplished paper. Australian National University.

Mbabazi, Pamela, Sandra MacLean, and Timothy Shaw (2002) "Governance for Reconstruction in Africa: Challenges for Policy Communities and Coalitions." *Global Networks*, 2(1): 31–47.

McGann, J. and R.K. Weaver (eds.) (2000) *Think Tanks and Civil Societies: Catalysts for Ideas and Action*. Sommerset N.J.: Transaction Press.

Mintrom, Michael (1997) "Policy Entrepreneurs and the Diffusion of Innovation." *American Journal of Political Science*, 41: 738–770.

Nesadurai, Helen E.S. and Diane Stone (2000) "Southeast Asian Research Institutes and Regional Cooperation." In Diane Stone (ed.) *Banking on Knowledge: The Genesis of the Global Development Network*. London: Routledge, pp.183–202.

Nowotny, Helga, Peter Scott, and Michael Gibbons (2001) *Re-Thinking Science: Knowledge and the Public in an Age of Uncertainty*. Oxford: Polity Press.

Open Society Institute (2001) *Open Society Institute Related Public Policy Centers.* Activity Report, June. Budapest: OSI.

Ougaard, Morten and Richard Higgott (eds.) (2002) *Approaching the Global Polity.* London: Routledge.

Parmar, Inderjeet (2002) "American Foundations and the Development of International Knowledge Networks," *Global Networks,* 2(1): 13–30.

Peters, B. Guy and Jon Pierre (2000) "Developments in intergovernmental relations: towards multi-level governance," *Policy and Politics,* 29(2): 131–135.

Reinicke, Wolfgang H. (2001) "Walking the Talk: Global Public Policy in Action." In *Global Public Policies and Programs: Implications for Financing and Evaluation.* Proceedings from a World Bank Workshop. Washington D.C.: The World Bank, pp.43–48.

Reinicke, Wolfgang, Francis Deng, *et al.* (2000) *Critical Choices: The United Nations, Networks and the Future of Global Governance.* Ottowa: International Development Research Center.

Saint-Martin, Denis (2000) "The Formation of the New Entrepreneurial State and the Growth of Modern Management Consultancy." In Dietmar Braun and Andreas Busch (eds.) *Public Policy and Political Ideas.* Cheltenham: Edward Elgar, pp.82–97.

Scholte, Jan Aart (2000) *Globalization: A Critical Introduction.* Basingstoke: Palgarve.

Sherrington, Philippa (2000) "Shaping the Policy Agenda: Think Tank Activity in the European Union." *Global Society,* 14(2): 173–189.

Squire, Lyn (2000) "Why the World Bank Should Be Involved in Development Research." In G. L. Gilbert and D. Vines (eds.) *The World Bank: Structure and Policies.* Cambridge: Cambridge University Press, pp.108–131.

Stares, Paul and Weaver, R. Kent (2001) *Guidance for Governance,* Tokyo and Washington DC., Japan Center for International Exchange and Brookings Institution.

Stone, Diane (2000) *Banking on Knowledge: The Genesis of the Global Development Network.* London: Routledge.

Stone, Diane, Andrew Denham and Mark Garnett (2002) *Think Tanks Across Nations.* Manchester: Manchester University Press.

Tilak, Jandhyala (2001) "Knowledge Development and International Aid." In Wolfgang Gmelin, Kenneth King and Simon McGrath (eds.) *Development Knowledge, National Research and International Cooperation.* Edinburgh, Bonn, and Geneva: CAS-DSE-NORRAG, pp.253–264.

Walt, Stephen M. (2000) "Fads, Fevers, and Firestorm." *Foreign Policy,* 121(November-December): 34–42.

The World Bank (1999) *Knowledge for Development: World Development Report 1998–99*, New York: Oxford University Press.

Young, John and Natalie Kannemeyer (2001) *Building Capacity in Southern Research: A Study to Map Existing Initiatives.* London: Overseas Development Institute.

When Relativism Becomes
a Marketing Strategy: Globalization, Knowledge, and
the World Language System

Daniel Dor

F 0 2

> "Based in a conviction that all truth is socially constructed, today's con-
> sumer experts have set about redefining their goals: from uncovering the
> universal predictive laws of the market to understanding the multiple, over-
> lapping, and often contradictory identities of consumers themselves."
>
> Pat Wehner (2001)

Taking a glance at the remarkably ambitious list of topics which this book attempts to address—especially the one having to do with the 'production of global knowledge', which gives its name to this section—I feel that this paper requires a short introductory apology: it says nothing about 'global governance' or 'sources of funding for the aid system'; it does not include 'new policy initiatives'; and it definitely is not about the 'production of global knowledge'. Rather, it has to do with some of the *linguistic* parameters of the complex process of globalization and as such, at least on the face of it, it seems to deal with issues that are rather unrelated to the main topics of the book.

I believe, however, that there is a lesson to be learned from the linguistic issues I will discuss here, and an important lesson for that matter—as important for the central themes of this book as it is for the specific discourse on language and globalization. The lesson is that when discussing questions of knowledge in the context of globalization, the most fundamental issue that we have to keep in mind is not so much that of the insensitive imposition of *global, universal, Western, first-world* knowledge on the *problematiques* of the locale, but rather that of the insensitive imposition of *specific patterns of interaction* between global and local knowledge. These patterns, instead of meeting the needs of local people, actually enable the rapid transformation of the locale into a global consumer market, strip local people of the *means of production* of their own knowledge, and leave the control over the local means of production of knowledge in the hands of Western economic powers, especially transnational corporations.

In other words, the big divide—theoretically, practically, and morally—is not between agents (local or global) who understand the inherent variability of knowledge and those who do not. The simple fact is that by now virtually everybody understands something about the variability of knowledge. Instead, the big divide is between those agents who attempt to make use of this understanding to make quick profits at the expense of local people, and those who attempt to make use of this understanding to make the life of local people better. The challenge, then, is not so much that of finding better ways of understanding local knowledge on its own terms, and incorporating it into the global scheme of knowledge; the challenge is to find ways to help local people keep, or regain, control of the means of production of their own knowledge, in a world where the very idea of cultural relativism is gradually and rapidly becoming a marketing strategy, where knowledge itself is becoming a commodity, and where people are gradually finding themselves in the new role of being consumers of knowledge, i.e., paying for the use of knowledge that was supposed to be theirs in the first place. Today's true challenge, then, is to find new ways to put brakes on this process.

Let us take a look at some of the parameters of the intricate relationship between the process of globalization and the dynamics of linguistic change. Current debates on the possible linguistic consequences of the process of globalization concentrate on the complementary questions of *Englishization* and *language loss*. Englishization is the process of the global spread of English, the so-called language of globalization. Language loss is the process where speakers of local languages, all over the world, are forced to give up on their native languages and adopt what we call *a language of wider communication*, which today is in most cases English. These two questions—the question of Englishization and the question of language loss—are regularly formulated in literature in terms of the struggle between the *global* and the *local:* The driving forces behind the spread of English are equated with those pushing economic globalization; and the factors working against Englishization are equated with local resistance trends to economic globalization (cf. Philipson and Skutnabb-Kangas, 1999; Skutnabb-Kangas, 2000, and references therein).

Obviously, this formulation of the two questions raises yet a third question, this time of the *predictive* type, and this question, in turn, raises the level of globalization-related anxiety in the public discourse all over the world: if indeed the world is gradually becoming a universalized, borderless, flattened global market, does that imply the extinction of the very notion of linguistic variability? Will all local languages simply perish, together with their unique cultural perspectives and patterns of thought, and the historical memories associated with them? Will everybody simply speak English?

This formulation of the question is not without its merits. It is certainly relevant, for example, in the case of Tunisia, where a World Bank report recently offered suggestions for reforming the educational system. This would entail developing "tracks of study more in line with the demands of the global economy"—in other words, 'strengthening' higher education in English at the expense of Arabic and French (cf. Judy, 1999). It also helps recruit people for the very important task of language preservation. But on the global scale of things it is highly misleading. The arguments against this formulation are rather complex (cf. Dor, forthcoming), but for the moment two central points need to be considered.

First, contrary to common fears, I think we can safely predict that the great majority of speakers around the world are in no danger of losing their native languages. This, as we shall see later, is not all good news, but for the time being, let me be precise about what this prediction means: according to reasonable estimates (cf. De Swann, 1998; Skutnabb-Kangas, 2000), about 95 percent of the world's population speak about 5 percent of the worlds' languages, and the other 5 percent of the speakers speak the other 95 percent of the languages. So I do not in any way intend to imply that the great majority of *languages* around the world are safe—they obviously are not—I submit that the great majority of *speakers* around the world are.

Secondly, the fact that most speakers around the world will probably continue using their native languages in the future does *not* imply that local resistance forces to globalization will somehow manage to win the battle against the power of economic and cultural globalization. The opposite contention is actually closer to the truth: most speakers around the world will probably continue to use their native language *because* this is in the best interest of the beneficiaries of economic globalization. As opposed to the accepted view among academics and anti-globalization activists, the beneficiaries of economic globalization do *not* have a vested interest in the global spread of English. In fact, they have a greater interest in two different developments: as far as short-term objectives are concerned, the beneficiaries of economic globalization have an interest in harnessing local languages as tools for penetration into local markets. The long-range objective is that of *achieving maximal control over local languages*—and gradually transforming them from common goods, shared by the community, to commodities, controlled by western businesses and sold back to their users. In fact, major players in the global economy—most importantly the international marketing and software industries—are already aware of this and are working hard to achieve these goals.

The possible result of this process may turn out to be what I call *imposed multilingualism*: the global imposition of new patterns of linguistic usage, development, standardization, maintenance, and variability—those patterns which best match the needs of a global consumers' market. In a global linguistic system determined by such globally-imposed patterns of multilingualism, the great majority of speakers around the world may get to keep their languages, but the languages will no longer be *theirs*. The languages, as commodities and communication interfaces, will belong to the economic center—to be used, manipulated and *sold back* to their speakers.

Let us, then, take a look at the short-term developments: try searching the Internet for such key-word combinations as 'globalization, language', or 'globalization, knowledge'. You will find that more than 90 percent of the relevant websites belong to businesses, businesses that buy and sell *products of linguistic and cultural relativism*. Linguistic and cultural relativism is now a very popular commodity. Researching linguistic and cultural variability, and selling the results of this research, is a flourishing business. Companies sell directories, databases, reports, translation services, automatic translation software—and guidebooks for doing business away from home, which, in some cases, look very much like simplified textbooks for Anthropology 101. The World Bureau[1], for example, "produces databases, reports, directories, and other information services that give corporations a competitive advantage in the international marketplace." Uniscape, an Application Service Provider (ASP) specializing in translation services, recently unveiled its Globalization Infrastructure for eBusiness, a software platform aimed at creating multilingual, multicultural e-businesses in 42 languages. The platform includes the Global Content Manager, which monitors changes on corporate websites and triggers multilingual content-localization processes.

There are numerous companies of this type, and what they suggest makes sense. A recent study by Forrester Research Inc., which concentrated on *electronic commerce*, states that "shoppers are three times more likely to buy products in their own language." Waiting until consumers reach a sufficient level of proficiency in any language other than their own, including English, means losing them to the competition. Here is what Chris Potts, chief executive of e-commerce strategy specialist Citria, quoted in Gray (2000), has to say about the subject:

> As the Internet expands globally, users become less and less sophisticated technologically and in other ways. Their skills and patience are in short supply and they are not going to learn a foreign language just to use the web. To be global, to put it bluntly, you have to go down to their level. You have to provide easy screen navigation and local language.

If there ever was a perfectly sincere formulation of the neo-neo-colonialist's view of the neo-neo-colonized—those individuals which should be "controlled by means of ideas" (Phillipson, 1992)—this must be it: they are less sophisticated

---

1. See www.worldbureau.com.

("technologically and in other ways"), unskilled and impatient, and whoever wants to be able to make them into consumers should "go down to their level" and provide them with e-commerce technology in their *own language*. This strategic view is not without precedents: the reader is reminded of the Vatican's decision, in the 1960s, concerning the proper way to find more easy access 'to the minds and the hearts of men'. A major part of that decision was to approach people through their native language. In both cases, language is not the goal, but the means.

Quite obviously, this multilingual strategy works directly against the process of Englishization: it strengthens those languages other than English which are capable of sustaining a consumers' market, and *reduces the urgency*, on the part of local speakers, of learning English as a foreign language. It opens up opportunities for global communication, exchange of knowledge, commerce and consumption between center and periphery—where the translation function is handled and financed by the economic center (and, of course, by the economic elite of the peripheries), and not by the individual users. As the urgency of learning English is reduced, more non-native speakers of English around the globe may remain at the shallow proficiency level (cf. Graddol, 1999), which may prevent unstable states of *diglossia* from emerging. In this state of affairs, the prospect of a major English takeover seems to be dramatically reduced.

Which languages have a real chance of erecting this business-based fence and slowing down the penetration of English into their communities? As far as I can tell, the number of such languages may be, at least in principle, surprisingly large. As a first approximation, I would hypothesize that a language should be safe if it proves *capable of sustaining a virtual market*. This capacity, in turn, should probably be a direct function of the economic potential of the language community (the number of speakers and their economic status), and an inverse function of the financial investment needed for the establishment of the market. As far as the *inverse* function is concerned, it should be noted that the establishment of a virtual market for any language community is to a very large extent based on *universal technologies*, which are already in use elsewhere. This significantly reduces the investment needed for the establishment of virtual spaces for additional languages. Moreover, major software companies are currently investing hundreds of millions of dollars in researching and developing *machine translation* technologies. Most of the products which are currently on the market are not very accurate,[2] and I doubt whether we will ever get to a point where automatic translation will be able to handle literature or poetry. However, I do not see any

---

2. Cf. the special edition of *Wired*, dedicated to machine translation, www.wired.com/wired/archive/8.05/.

real reason to doubt that it will eventually reach a state in which it will easily and quite accurately deal with business and technical texts (probably with some human editing, fine-tuning conversational styles, cultural niceties, and so on). In this future state, the establishment of a virtual market for each additional language may, at least in principle, demand very little financial investment.

Consequently, such markets may be established for much smaller languages. As a matter of fact, one of the most effective future strategies that ethnic movements could adopt in their struggle for the preservation of their languages is establishing Internet presence—and this is exactly what many such movements are already doing. Obviously, this is not going to be possible for all languages: Many minor languages fatally wounded in the era of colonialism will not be able to make the necessary move. Many of them may eventually perish. I would, however, risk the following prediction: If my general assumptions are correct, the 150–300 major languages of the world, and possibly others, have a very good chance of survival. The reader is reminded that these languages are spoken by no less than 95 percent of the world's population.

In this scenario, then, market dynamics shall help preserve a significant degree of global linguistic variability, and this, in and of itself, is not something to complain about. However, the move towards a global market-based linguistic system seems to imply some very fundamental changes in the relationship between *languages*, *speakers*, *communities*, and *nation-states*—some of which seem to me potentially intimidating. In general, the post-modern condition is already making it more and more difficult for nation-states to play their traditional roles *vis-à-vis* their national languages. In the market-based linguistic system, I would like to claim that some of these roles will be taken over by the 'superpowers' of the software, marketing, and media industries—the future 'owners' of the linguistic commodity. In this state of affairs, these global agents may have the power to control linguistic change, set linguistic standards, and, eventually, supervise and manipulate the linguistic distribution of knowledge. As far as I can tell, we are already seeing significant precursors of this trend.

One of the most important traditional roles played by nation states with respect to their languages was that of *territorial unification*: national languages have well-demarcated territorial boundaries—the boundaries of the state. Territorial unification has traditionally been the key to national control over languages. It allowed nation-states to set linguistic standards, work out language-planning policies, control the language curricula in the education system, and use language as a major component in the construction of national identity. In the market-based linguistic system, however, territorial unification will probably not be possible—certainly not to the same extent as it used to be. As indicated, the chance of a language to construct its own virtual space is a direct function of the number of its speakers and their socio-economic status. Crucially, this function is 'interested', so to speak, in the aggregate of linguistic preferences of groups of individuals as such, *regardless of their physical whereabouts*. As the introduction to the statistics tables in Global Reach[3], demonstrate, territorial unification does not play a role in this state of affairs:

> Here are the latest estimated figures of the number of people online in each language zone (native speakers). We classify by languages instead of by countries, since people speaking the same language form their own online community no matter what country they happen to live in.

The notion of 'language zone' is an extremely significant element in the new market-based system. Speakers belong to a 'language zone' on account of their linguistic preferences *as such*, regardless of whether their language is or is not the national language of the nation state they live in. The Russian 'language zone', for example, includes Russian-speaking immigrants in the US, in Germany or in Israel, as well as citizens of the Russian state. This state of affairs makes life much harder for nation states not just with respect to their minority languages—but also with respect to their *own* national languages. The fact that most Russian speakers still reside in Russia loses its constitutive status—and becomes a contingent statistical generalization. In other words, languages will follow English and will no longer be, in Cochran's words, "linked exclusively to a demarcated territory" (Cochran, 1999: 62).

As the development of 'language zones' is a function of the economic capacities of the language communities, the actual evolution of the different 'language zones'—which languages and dialects will get to have their own zone—will to a large extent depend on the marketing considerations of transnational corporations. This is most clearly evidenced in the business of global media (cf. Parker, 1995). As Parker shows, the language of global broadcasting poses problems of "economic efficiency for advertisers":

> Satellites can deliver programming and advertising instantaneously and simultaneously across the more than two dozen languages spoken in Western Europe, but the viewers—as repeated market research shows—want their television delivered in local tongues (Parker, 1995: 68).

Faced with this fundamental problem, major players in the global media industry are already adopting a strategy which is based, according to Parker, on

3. Cf. Global Reach, www.glreach.com/globstats/index.php3.

"the recognition that for the time being global broadcasting will follow a pattern of multilingual corporate expansion and alliance, bringing with it the age-old questions about culture and property and ownership that have marked the capitalist world since its birth" (Parker, 1995: 86).

This strategy, in turn, may have far-reaching implications for the dynamics of language change, the patterns of language use, and even the control of linguistic standardization. Traditionally, setting linguistic standards has been one of the most important linguistic roles of nation-states. Standards were established on different levels: to be a proper speaker of a language, you had to have the proper accent, use the right type of syntax, spell correctly, and communicate according to a fixed code of politeness. These standards functioned as the demarcating line between the national language and its less favorite dialects, and played an especially crucial role in the establishment of an individual's social status. All this, quite evidently, is long gone. In recent decades, linguistic standards have played a much weaker role in the construction of social status, and Western nation states have gradually adopted a 'hands-off' policy with respect to standardization. For example, the literacy curriculum in the first years of grammar school in many Western states now puts very little emphasis on correct spelling and grammar—and concentrates on such issues as holistic literacy, general communication and interpretation skills, self-expression, creativity, clarity and logic, narrative construction, and so on.

At the same time, however, the traditional role of standard setting is gradually being taken over by the new designers of the emerging 'language zones'. The language of the media, for example, plays a very important role in the development of linguistic standards and patterns of usage, and as the control of media production in local languages is gradually concentrated in the hands of multinational corporations, their ability to develop linguistic standards is also increasing.

Even more importantly, the software industry has already provided a substitute for the standardization machinery of the nation state, such as the grammar and spell checkers in the word-processing software which we all use. In Modern Hebrew, for example, two spelling standards have been, for a long while, in competition: In the *partial spelling* standard, vowel letters corresponding to 'i', 'o' and 'u' are used sparingly; in the *full spelling* standard, they are used wherever possible. The default setting of my spell checker, however, is a rather arbitrary compromise between the two, which has created a new standard.

An even more dramatic example comes from Mandarin Chinese: computer keyboards cannot possibly handle the huge number of characters of the language, so the way you get characters to appear on your screen is by typing the words in Roman letters—sound by sound. The point is that the software developed for this purpose only recognizes the standardized pronunciation. If you are a speaker of a dialect, and your pronunciation is slightly different, you will not be able to get the right character on your screen. All this does what the national standardization project did not even try to accomplish: it forces speakers to learn the standardized pronunciation of the spoken language in order to be able to write. The same phenomenon may occur with the advancement of voice-activated software in other languages.

Strictly speaking, of course, none of these standards are unappealable: my Hebrew checker, for example, has non-default settings for the *full* and *partial* standards. The thing is, however, that standards were never *totally* unappealable, and default settings are *always* the single most determining factor. On the one hand, professional writers could always bypass their national standards, and they probably will be able to go on doing that. (Although, as editorial managers in major publishing houses are gradually coming to understand, implementing a different standard for great quantities of written materials, while working with Microsoft Word, is becoming more and more difficult.) On the other hand, linguistic standards, whether they are set by nation states or by software companies, have always targeted the millions of non-professional writers, and these do not even dream of 'arguing with the machine' when it comes to 'correct spelling' and 'proper grammar'. Quite crucially, moreover, professional modern writers had some impact on the standards of their languages: they could develop them, or at least push them to their limits. Non-professionals had at least some unmediated, personally acquired knowledge of the standard. In the currently evolving condition, on the other hand, professional writers may have very little influence on the evolution of the standards, and non-professionals will gradually get to the point where they will simply have to trust the software and let it do the standardization work for them—their own knowledge of the standard may be very limited. Although the great majority of the world's speakers may get to keep their languages (and use them for communication purposes) the languages will no longer be 'theirs' in the *agentive* sense; speakers (and their communities and states) will have much less influence of the dynamics of linguistic change, maintenance, and standardization. Control over languages will be taken over, on a global scale, by the software industry. Languages—as commodities and as communication interfaces—will belong to the economic center, to be used, manipulated, and 'sold back' to their speakers.

What all these examples seem to tell us is a story about what superficially seems to be the incorporation of local variability into a global system of knowledge, but is actually a façade for a business strategy that takes away the means of production of local knowledge from the people—and leaves them with a global commodity which is no longer theirs, but is nevertheless designed to cater to their local sensibilities. The battle, then, is not simply between the global and the local, or between the imposition of global knowledge and the incorporation of local knowledge. It is the battle between the use and the abuse of local knowledge, in a global state of affairs, which is first and foremost determined by the business strategies of multinational corporations.

References

Cochran, Terry (1999) "The Linguistic Economy of the Cosmopolitical." *Boundary 2*, 26(2): 59–72.

De Swaan, Abram (1998) "A Political Sociology of the World Language System (1): The Dynamics of Language Spread." *Language Problems and Language Planning*, 22(1): 63–73.

Dor, Daniel (forthcoming) "A Language Is a Dialect that Has a Search-Engine." In Wolf Lepenies (ed.) *Entangled Histories*. Berlin: Campus.

Graddol, David (1999) "The Decline of the Native Speaker." In David Graddol and Ulrike H. Meihof (eds.) *English in a Changing World*. The AILA Review.

Gray, R. (2000) "Make the Most of Local Differences." *Marketing*, April 13, 27–28.

Judy, Ronald A.T. (1999) "Some Notes on the Status of Global English in Tunisia." *Boundary 2*, 26(2): 3–44.

Parker, Richard (1995) *Mixed Signals: The Prospects for Global Television News*. New York: The Twentieth Century Fund Press.

Phillipson, Robert (1992) *Linguistic Imperialism*. Oxford: Oxford University Press.

Phillipson, Robert and Tove Skutnabb-Kangas (1999) "Englishization: One Dimension of Globalization." In David Graddol and Ulrike H. Meihof (eds.) *English in a Changing World*. The AILA Review.

Skutnabb-Kangas, Tove (2000) *Linguistic genocide in education—or worldwide diversity and human rights?* London: Lawrence Erlbaum Associates.

Wehner, Pat (2001) "Opinion: Ivory Arches and Golden Towers: Why We're All Consumer Researchers Now." *College English*, 63(6): 759–768.

II.

Social Values and Public Goods

The Prospects for Equitable Access to Social Provision in a Globalizing World[1]

Bob Deacon

(SADC, Mercosur, ASEAN)

FO2
I30
015 019

1. Introduction and Overview

There are three themes in this chapter. One concerns the place of universal social provisioning in the global discourse concerning desirable national social policy. A second concerns the response of Southern governments to a Northern imposed social policy agenda. The third concerns the prospects for the development of a regional dimension to Southern regionalism. Linked together the themes and the analysis associated will enable an assessment to be made of the prospects for equitable social provision in a globalizing world.

In sum the chapter argues, first, that the idea of universalism as an approach to welfare policy came to be seriously challenged in the context of neoliberal globalization. This challenge derived from an analysis of the inequitable impact of the partial welfare states of post-colonialism. However the World Bank and Northern donors in their understandable concern to focus on the poorest of the poor failed to appreciate the historical lessons of cross-class solidarity building which was the underpinning of European Welfare States. While focusing public provision on the poor the middle class were being seduced by global private markets in health, social care and social security thus breaking the basis upon which future equitable universal social provisioning

1. Earlier versions of parts of this paper were delivered at an United Nations Research Institute for Social Development (UNRISD) conference at the Geneva UN High Level Meeting on Social Development in June 2000; at a Seminar on Globalization and Equity convened by the Swedish Academy of Sciences in Stockholm in October 2000; at an UNRISD seminar convened in September 2001 in the context of launching its research program on Social Policy in a Development Context; at a UNDP Technical Cooperation between Developing Countries (TCDC) Seminar on Social Policy in the Globalization context held in Beirut in February 2001; at a UK Department for International Development (DfID) Seminar on March 30, 2001; at the ILO Socio-Economic Security Programme (SES) Advisory Board Meeting in Bellagio, Italy in May 2001; at the UK Social Policy Association Conference in Belfast in July 2001; and at the Warwick Centre for the Study of Globalisation and Regionalisation (CSGR) conference on Globalization and (In)equality in March 2002. The author is grateful for comments made at each of these events which both strengthened my conviction that the paper was worth publishing and enabled improvements to be made in the text. All errors and shortcomings remain my responsibility.

might have been built. There is some evidence that the intellectual tide is now turning. Not only is there empirical evidence that universal welfare states are compatible with globalization but also there are signs that important actors influencing the South may be rediscovering the importance of universalism.

Second, the Northern-driven socially responsible globalization agenda with which the UK government have been associated through, for example, the formulation of Chancellor Gordon Brown's Global Social Principles (see Ferguson, 1999) has run into the sand of Southern opposition. The social policy principles have joined the labor standards issue in the global North–South impasse. Two things are required to move beyond the impasse. One is much greater Northern commitment to either greater North–South transfers or to global taxation for global public goods and to the opening of Northern markets to the South. The other is for the idea of international social standards to be devised and owned by the South.

Third, constructive regionalism with a social dimension represents one possible future for world cooperation based on principles different from those of global neoliberalism. A key question is whether the European attempt to combine regional economic policy with a regional social agenda will be replicated in Southern trading groups. On the one hand, there is evidence of an advancing social dimension to Southern regionalism in MERCOSUR, ASEAN, etc. On the other hand, competing neoliberal inspired regional groupings—such as the Free Trade Area of the Americas (FTAA) or the Asia-Pacific Economic Cooperation area (APEC)—may undermine this. The Southern policy of the EU will be important: can it shift from being perceived by the South as part of the problem to being part of the solution?

Overall it is argued that the prospects for equitable social provision in a globalizing world depend on a greater Northern commitment to global social transfers, to a larger voice being given to the South in the articulation of international social standards and to the fostering in the South of a regional approach to social policy that echoes the model provided by the European Union.

The analysis and conclusions in this paper are derived largely from the results of the Anglo-Finnish Globalism and Social Policy Programme that was set up in 1997 specifically to examine the relationship between globalization and social policy and articulate a case for a socially progressive globalization.[2] That project has so far held five international seminars. The first in 1997, involving middle and high level participation from several UN agencies and the World Bank as well as scholars for several continents, focused on the governance of global social policy. The second in 1998, involving international trade union and social movements' spokespersons, focused on global trade and investment agreements and their implications for social

2. See www.stakes.fi/gaspp.

rights. A third took place in late 1999 and focused on the role of International Non-Governmental Organizations (INGOs) and consulting, companies as subcontractors in global social governance. The fourth was hosted in 2000 in India and focused on the globalization of social rights. This enabled the GASPP network to be broadened to include many Southern voices. A useful South–North dialogue on social policy emerged from this. A fifth took place in 2002 in Dubrovnik in cooperation with the International Labour Organization (ILO) and the World Health Organization (WHO) on the globalization of private health and social protection and the implications of this development for socio-economic security.

2. Globalization and the Threat to Equity?

A key question is whether, as is often presumed, the globalization process influences or indeed determines for countries what their social policies are. Does globalization limit the social policy choices available to governments in the North and the South?

In general terms I have argued elsewhere (Deacon, 1997; 1999a) that globalization:

- Sets welfare states in competition with each other. This raises the specter but not the certainty of a race to the welfare bottom. It raises the question as to what type of social policy best suits competitiveness without undermining social solidarity.
- Brings new players into the making of Social Policy. International organizations such as the IMF, World Bank, WTO and UN agencies such as WHO, ILO, etc. have become involved in prescribing country policy. Also relevant are regional organizations such as MERCOSUR, ASEAN, SADC, etc. International NGOs have substituted for government in this context.
- Generates a global discourse about best social policy. Because supranational actors have become involved the traditional within-country politics of welfare has taken on a global dimension with a struggle of ideas being waged within and between International Organizations (IOs) as to desirable social policy. The battle for pension policy in post-communist countries between the Bank and the ILO was a classic example (Deacon 1997).
- Creates a global private market in social provision. Increased free trade has created the possibility of mainly USA and European private health care and hospital providers, education providers, social care agencies and social insurance companies benefiting from an international middle class market in private social provision.

When we began the GASPP project there was a worry among those concerned with universal social provisioning as part of the struggle for social equity that these factors would push social policy in all countries in a residual neoliberal direction. In other words there was a worry that the neoliberal character of globalization would determine that social policy took on a neoliberal character too (Deacon, 1997; Mishra, 1999).

These fears have been partly allayed. In terms of the actual impact of economic globalization upon social policy in more Northern and more developed economies a new scholarly consensus is emerging that argues and demonstrates that:

- Globalization does not necessarily have to lead to the 'residualization' (and privatization) of social provision. In the North there are arguments and experiences that show that redistributive social policy with high levels of income taxation and high levels of public health, education and social security *are* sustainable in the face of global competition. In a comparative survey of Anglo-Saxon (e.g. the UK), Conservative Corporatist (e.g. Germany), and Social Democratic (e.g. Sweden) welfare states both the neoliberal and social democratic approaches remained competitive. The neoliberal approach of course risked creating increased inequity that compensatory social policy such as tax credits seeks to minimize. The most challenged were work-based welfare states funded on the basis of labor taxes with locked in inflexible labor contracts for industrial workers. So long as revenue for social provision was raised from citizens rather than capital and service jobs are high quality public ones, high level universal social provision is sustainable and does not undermine competitiveness and ensure full employment (Scharpf, 2000; Sykes *et al.*, 2001).
- At the same time the fears of social dumping in the South have been shown to be exaggerated (Alber and Standing, 2000). Moreover evidence from a recent global survey of the impact of globalization upon economies has shown that some governments in the South have chosen to increase their social spending during liberalization (Taylor, 2000).
- Moreover it is now recognized internationally that globalization and openness of economies generates the need for more not less attention to social protection measures (OECD, 1999).
- A response to globalization in some middle-income countries has indeed been to create universalistic forms of social policy. A good example is Korea (Huck-Ju Kwon, 2001).
- Some of the social policy responses adopted in Latin America and elsewhere in the hey-day of the neoliberal Washington Consensus—such as the full privatization of pension schemes—are now being shown by comparative policy

analysts to have questionable advantages in terms of net savings effects and other criteria (Mesa-Lago, 2000; Huber and Stephens, 2000). Mesa-Lago shows that neither old-fashioned state socialism (Cuba), nor new-fashioned neoliberalism (Chile) but socially regulated capitalism (Costa Rica) does best economically and socially.

This is reassuring but despite this evidence I have argued (Deacon, 2000) that certain tendencies in the globalization process and certain policy positions adopted by international organizations still give cause for concern especially with regard to social policy in more Southern and more underdeveloped economies. I examine these below.

Today we are not confronted by a global neoliberal Washington Consensus where belief in unregulated market reigns supreme. The dominant global discourse has shifted from a socially irresponsible neoliberal globalization to one that expresses concern about global poverty. A 'socially responsible' globalization discourse and practice has replaced the earlier one. It has had to because of the global social movements against the neoliberal form of globalization. This new consensus is not a truly global consensus. Many social movements in the South would not subscribe to it.

In an UNRISD paper (Deacon, 2000), I showed in some detail that the new consensus among Northern donor agencies and major international organizations consisted of the following elements:

- Global macro-economic management needs to address the social consequences of globalization.
- A set of social rights and entitlements to which global citizens might aspire can be fashioned based on UN conventions.
- International development cooperation should focus aid on meeting basic social needs.
- Debt relief should be speeded up so long as the funds are used to alleviate poverty.
- The globalization of trade generates a need for the globalization of labor and social standards.
- Good governments are an essential ingredient in encouraging socially responsible development.

There are, however, a number of disagreements as to how to proceed with this new orientation:

- Much of the South is understandably suspicious of even progressive social conditionality.

- How both world trade and world labor standards can coexist without the standards being reduced to minimal core standards or used for protectionist purposes is far from clear.
- Initiatives to empower the UN with global revenue raising powers which fund global social rights are firmly resisted by some.

My concern with this emerging consensus is that despite the apparent shift from global neoliberalism to global social responsibility the coexistence of four tendencies within the new global paradigm, if allowed to be pursued, will still undermine an equitable approach to social policy and social development. These tendencies are

- the World Bank's continuing belief that governments should only provide minimal or basic levels of social provision and social protection;
- the OECD's Development Assistant Committes's concern (subscribed to in Geneva 2000 by the UN as well as the Bank and IMF) to fund only basic education and health care with its new international development targets;
- the International NGO's continuing self interest in winning donor contracts to substitute for government social services; and
- the moves being made within the WTO to speed the global market in private health, social care, education and insurance services.

My concern is the following. Where the state provides only minimal and basic level health and social protection services, the middle classes of developing and transition economies will be enticed into the purchase of private social security schemes, private secondary and tertiary education, and private hospital level medical care that are increasingly being offered on a cross-border or foreign investment presence basis. The result is predictable. We know that services for the poor are poor services. We know that those developed countries that do not have universal public health provision at all levels and public education provision at all levels are not only more unequal but also more unsafe and crime-ridden. Unless the middle-class is also catered for by state provision, good quality social provision can not be sustained. This is the prospect for many countries that buy into this new development paradigm. Research is urgently needed into the welfare strategies now being adopted by the middle-class in developing countries.

How did the idea of social policy geared to securing greater equity through processes of redistribution and universal social provision get so lost in the context of globalization? Because in my view:

- Globalization in terms of the form it took in the 1980s and 1990s was primarily a neoliberal political project born at the height of the transatlantic

Thatcher–Reagan alliance. This flavored the anti-public provision discourse about social policy within countries and contributed to a challenge to the idea of regional trading blocks such as the EU which had a partly protectionist purpose.

- The collapse of the communist project coinciding as it did with the height of neoliberalism gave a further push to the rise of the myth of the marketplace.
- The perceived negative social consequences of globalization generated a new concern for the poor. In the name of meeting the needs of the poorest of the poor the 'premature' or 'partial' welfare states of Latin America, South Asia, and Africa were challenged as serving only the interests of a small privileged work force and elite state employees. A new alliance was to be struck between the World Bank and the poor (see Graham, 1994 ; Deacon, 1997). The analysis of the privileged and exclusionary nature of these provisions was accurate. However, by destroying the public state services for the middle-class in the name of the poor, the politics of solidarity—which requires the middle class to have a self-interest in public provision that they fund—was made more difficult. The beneficiary index measures of the Bank showing how tertiary education spending, for example, served the elite contributed in no small measure to this development. The Bank's technical expertise was ill-informed about the political economy of welfare state building.
- In the late 1980s and 1990s the self-confidence of defenders of the social democratic and other equitable approaches to social policy was temporarily lost. The critics of neoliberal globalization came to believe their worst-case prognosis.

Are there signs of a shift in the global discourse leading to a reassertion of the politics of social solidarity and universalism? There are a number of global initiatives that have the aim of re-establishing the case for, and finding ways of implementing, universal public provisioning as part of an equitable social policy in Southern countries. Among them are:

- A new UNRISD research program on Social Policy in a Development Context under the leadership of Thandika Mkandawire which has the stated objective to "move (thinking) away from social policy as a safety net . . . towards a conception of active social policy as a powerful instrument for development working in tandem with economic policy." This program held, with Swedish funding, its inaugural conference in October 2000 at which social policy scholars from most regions of the world were present (see www.unrisd.org).
- The rethinking presently being undertaken within the ILO concerning the sustainability of its traditional laborist approach to social protection, in par-

ticular the Socio-Economic Security In-Focus work program which is searching for new forms of universalistic social protection to complement the very limited coverage in the South of work-based social security schemes. Good practices being revealed within this program could inform Southern social policy making.[3]

- The ongoing activities of several UN agencies support this more universal approach. Such activities include the UN Commission of Human Rights and their increased focus on the convention on Economic, Cultural, and Social Rights, the continuing work by UNICEF to work for Basic Services for All, the activities following on from the UNESCO conference on Education for All in 2000, and the program of work leading to the high-level meeting on Finance for Development in 2002.
- Also important is the follow-up work from Geneva 2000 by the UN Social Policy and Social Development Secretariat including the codification of UN social policy. The work program of the Commission for Social Development, which included in 2001 a focus on social protection and in 2002 a focus on economic and social policy, is of especial relevance. Some comments on this are elaborated below.

The report of the UN Secretary-General (E/CN.5/2001/2) on "Enhancing social protection and reducing vulnerability in a globalizing world" prepared for the February 2001 Commission for Social Development is an important milestone in an attempt to articulate UN social policy. Among the positive features of the report are the following.

- It is the first comprehensive UN statement on social protection.
- The thrust of its argument is that social protection measures serve both an equity-enhancing and an investment function and such measures need to be a high priority of governments and regions.
- It defines social protection broadly to include not only cash transfers but also health and housing protection.
- It accepts that unregulated globalization is increasing inequity within and between countries.
- It argues that social protection 'should not (serve only) as a residual function of assuring the welfare of the poorest but as a foundation for promoting social justice and social cohesion" (Article 16).
- It argues that if equity is the goal then "tax-funded social transfers are highly effective if the fiscal situation permits" (Articles 89 and 95k).

3. See www.ilo.org/ses.

- While being rather vague on the nature of a public-private welfare mix in provision it does point out that "insurance markets are difficult to operate effectively" (Article 95c).

It has to be said that discussion on even this paper became bogged down at the Commission. While the EU was supportive, the G–77 wished again to link it to issues of global financing and governance arrangements (Langmore, 2001). The North–South impasse on global social standards to which this chapter turns below bedeviled even the Commission's work.

There is cautious room for optimism from the standpoint of those concerned to see the case for universal provision to secure an equitable social policy at a national level being reasserted in international social policy discourse. The point should not be overstated, however, for two reasons. The Bank is still powerful and not convinced about redistributive politics, and a North–South tension over social standards still complicates any global agreement on desirable social policy. On the first point, a recent Nordic evaluation of the new 2000–2001 World Bank Development Report on Poverty (Braathen, 2000) concluded that the Bank—at least at the discursive level—had shifted from its 1990 focus on social paternalism to a 2000 focus on social liberalism and even social corporatism—within which the poor are to be given a voice. It still has not embraced in any significant way the social radicalism approach that would involve redistributive policies, except perhaps in the sphere of land reform. It is to the second point that the chapter now turns.

3. The North–South Impasse and Beyond

Reaction against the worst excesses of global neoliberalism gave rise in the 1990s to a number of mainly Northern generated initiatives to begin to challenge this policy drift: to reinsert a social purpose into the global economy and to counter some of the more obvious negative aspects of partial global economic integration. These initiatives included:
- the suggestion to include a social clause in trade agreements;
- the proposition for a better than safety nets set of global social policy principles;
- the emergence of a discourse concerning global public goods;
- the increased emphasis given to social rights in the human rights agenda; and
- the placing of global tax regulation onto the UN agenda.

However, in terms of reaching a North–South agreement on a global approach to national social policy that goes beyond safety nets, there are real obstacles to be overcome. Concerning the desirable social policies to be implemented in an era of globalization, an impasse now seems to have been reached in the global dialogue. Northern-based global social reform initiatives—such as the 'social policies principles' initiative of UK's Gordon Brown that intended to modify the free play of global market forces with appropriate global social policies of international regulation—have met with understandable but frustrating opposition from many Southern governments and some Southern-based NGOs and social movements. The UN's 'Copenhagen plus Five' Social Summit in Geneva in 2000 saw a similarly characteristic debate when the proposal for a set of social policy principles was rejected. This was on the grounds that these might become a new conditionality imposed by the North and there was anyway no money forthcoming from the richer countries to help pay for the implementation of such principles. Moves beyond this impasse would seem to require two changes. One would be a greater commitment on the part of the North to support international resource transfers to pay for global public goods—such as basic universal education combined with an opening of trade opportunities in the North for Southern countries. The other is for the South to own and develop for itself any such social policy principles or standards based on a review of best practice in the South.

An interesting initiative that might point to a way beyond the impasse was a recent 2001 South–South conference on social policy in a globalizing era convened by the UNDP's TCDC unit. The aim of the conference and subsequent program was to develop—through policy dialogue, comparative research and exchange programs—an understanding in the South of ways in which an equitable and socially inclusive approach to social policy might be pursued within the context of globalization (see www.tcdcwide.net/SSPGnet).

At this conference it was argued that a South–South dialogue can and should learn from the Northern debates and experiences but also there is already a considerable body of knowledge about what policies in the South contribute most to sound human development. I articulated in an opening address that the South might learn from the North that:
- Neoliberal globalization does not mean countries have to adopt neoliberal social policies.
- A commitment to equitable social welfare, on one hand, and economic efficiency and competitiveness, on the other, are compatible.
- Social provision (education, health and social care, social protection) provided by the market works for some at the cost of equity.
- Social provision based on workplace entitlements used to work for some at the price of the exclusion of others. It is increasingly ill-advised as a strategy for welfare.

- Social provision based on citizenship or residence entitlement is the surest way of maximizing social inclusion and equity.
- Social policy in a globalized era requires not only national social policy but also regional and global social policy. Regulations at EU/MERCO-SUR/ASEAN/SADC and global level are needed to ensure the sound operation and equitable outcomes of the international market in labor, health, education, and social care.

The conference also cited examples of good Southern practice. Upon their review of the positive experiences that combined economic growth with conscious social development in Botswana, Mauritius, Zimbabwe, the Indian state of Kerala, Sri Lanka, the Republic of Korea, Malaysia, Barbados, Costa Rica, and Cuba, Chen and Desai (1997: 432) argued:

The key ingredients to successful social development appear to be responsive governance, socially friendly economic policies, and the universal provisioning of social services. In all these endeavors the role of the government is central.

These examples of good practice in the South have been reinforced in the recent UNRISD collection edited by Dharam Ghai (1999). Other best practice countries and policies that have already been identified from this earlier research and comparative evaluation include:
- In Asia, Korea—because of its extension of labor based benefits to a wider population as a result of the government increasing outlays for social expenditure from five percent of GDP in 1980 to 7.8 percent in 1997; in India, the state of Kerala—because of its tradition of sustained public expenditure despite globalization; Malaysia—because of its more restrictive approach to globalization; and Singapore—because of its investment in human capital and job creation.
- In Latin America, Uruguay and Costa Rica—because of their reform of PAYG pensions without a full privatization; Brazil—because of the experiments with a minimum income approach to socio-economic security; Colombia—because of the broadening of its tax base in the face of globalization; Argentina—because of the state subsidized an employment program in the health and education sectors, which enabled female workers to get jobs.
- In Southern Africa, Mauritius and Botswana—because of the introduction of universal pension entitlements.

Nonetheless, the UNDP conference also noted the significant differences between the experiences and prospects of some Southern countries from more developed ones. These included the observations that:

- Coverage by formal social protection schemes in many developing countries is tiny.
- Families and community networks contribute a large measure to social protection.
- Basic land reform and the redistribution of assets has not begun in some places; entrenched elites have not yet perceived that their interests might also be served in the long term by a more equitable approach.
- The fiscal and institutional capacity of many states has been severely hampered by former colonialization and subsequent globalization.
- The western concern with state-based rights and equity is not easily transferable to a Confucian-influenced 'Asian' discourse or a traditional African village practice of extended familial duties.
- The Islamic practice of *zakat* embraces the notion of redistribution but within a framework of obligations that may not extend to those who are not Muslim.
- Some governments perceive that in their countries, short term interests are being served by entering the unregulated global market on the basis of the comparative advantage of the absence of 'expensive' social protection measures.

All of these and more factors would need to be taken into account in a South–South dialogue, which would give more emphasis to new forms of universalism outside the work-based systems of social protection. It would involve articulating ways in which governments can support familial forms of welfare, as well. In my view, however, it may not be helpful if we exaggerate these differences. The lessons from one of the most developed parts of the South, namely Eastern and South-Eastern Asia, is interesting. It seems that the path of social welfare development promoted here may be somewhat different from that in Europe (a greater focus on regulating compulsory private provident funds rather than actual state provisions). All in all, these emerging welfare states are ahead of Europe when you compare the time when legislation was enacted for risk contingencies with the level of economic development in the country (Hort and Kulhne, 2000). Moreover, South-Eastern Asian states now face the same issue that Europe faces with regard to the sustainability of pension provisions (Gough, 2001). In its reform of the welfare state, China is addressing the same question faced by Germany or France: whether to move from workplace-based social insurance to individual unpooled private pension funds or to a resident-based (within cities at least), pooled public pension scheme.

4. The Social Dimension of Regionalism

The emerging South–South dialogue is also taking another form. Several emerging trading blocks and other regional associations of countries in the South are beginning to confront in practice the issues of the relationship between trade and labor, social and health standards and the issue of how to maintain levels of taxation in the face of competition to attract capital. In this context the potential advantage for developing countries of building a social dimension to regional groupings of countries are being considered. Such advantages may be summarized as having an external and internal dimension. In relation to the rest of the world, such an approach affords protection from global market forces that might erode national social entitlements and can create the possibility of such grouped countries having a louder voice in the global discourse on economic and social policy in UN and other fora. Internally through intergovernmental agreement, regionalism would make possible the development of regional social redistribution mechanisms, regional social and labor regulations, regional sectoral social policies in health, education, etc. They might also develop regional social empowerment mechanisms that give citizens a voice to challenge their governments in terms of supranational human and social rights. A regional approach could facilitate intergovernmental cooperation in social policy in terms of regional health specialization, regional education cooperation, regional food and livelihood cooperation, and regional recognition of social security entitlements. This in turn would facilitate the regulation of the *de facto* private regional social policies of health, education, and social protection companies.

Initial analysis of the extent to which SADC, MERCOSUR, and ASEAN have developed a regional dimension to social policy in their Southern regions is summarized in Table 1. This summary is taken from a report to UK DfID on this topic (Deacon, 2001).

Table 1. The Social Dimensions of Regionalism in Three Southern Regions.

Aspect of regional social policy	SADC	MERCOSUR	ASEAN
Regional redistribution	Customs duties in SACU eroding. No new initiatives.	Talk of a regional social fund. A few regionally funded project border areas.	Nothing significant. Some capacity building for new in members.
Regional social and labor regulation	No. Campaigned for by COSATU.	Important Labor and Social Declaration. Reciprocal Social Security entitlement. Joint Health and Safety inspection.	Recent Declaration on ASEAN and Caring Societies. No legal force.
Regional health policy	Yes and recently strengthened with equity concerns.	Little documented.	Yes but dependent on external funds. Recent trade and health initiative.
Regional education policy	Recent capacity review. Quality assurance and other measure.	Mutual recognition of qualifications.	ASEAN University scholarships and exchanges. Curricula design in schools.
De facto private regionalism	New initiatives by regional private health care companies.	Beginnings of cross border private provision.	Major lobbying of international health insurance companies.
Cross-border learning from best practice	Yes, especially pensions and grants to school attenders.	Yes. Chilean Liberalism argued for by World Bank and Uruguayian 'social democracy' seen by others as an alternative approach.	Recently through a safety-net working party.
Human, including social rights moves	SADC Gender Unit as model. Call for SADC court of rights.	Civil society lobby with regional focus. Possible new MERCOSUR Working Group.	Policy of strict non-interference. Little evidence of regional lobbies, but may be changing.

There are characteristic differences between the regional approaches to social policy. In each region, there are complicating factors associated with (a) the particular histories of the regions; and (b) the geopolitics of the region that are affecting the pace of social development in the regions. In the case of SADC, the era of the front-line state solidarity afforded to South Africa by the other countries is still waiting to be rewarded. In the case of ASEAN, the initial policy of non-interference in the internal affairs of member states is only being eroded slowly. In the case of MERCOSUR, the differential devaluation of Brazilian and Argentinean currencies and the diverse ways the economies are responding to globalization threatens unity. At the same time, a wider neoliberal regionalism with expectations of a lower level of concern for the social dimension is a competing alternative certainly in the case of Asia (APEC) and Latin America (FTAA).

An important factor in this global transatlantic struggle for and against global neoliberalism or global social democracy is the EU. Whether the EU is perceived as a model to follow or merely a self-interested Northern social protectionist block will depend on whether it opens its borders to Southern trade unilaterally and increases its support for North–South transfers (Deacon, 1999b). The UK government role is quite important here both in terms of arguing for easier trade access for the South that may benefit some countries but also for potentially undermining the European Social Democratic project in favor of neoliberalism. The ambivalence of the UK position in this crucial EU versus USA struggle for the social dimension of regionalism is rather important.

While an adequate assessment of the significance of the social dimension of Southern regionalism will have to wait upon further research and the passage of time, it can be concluded that:

- There is a social dimension to each of the three regional groupings studied. These range from the least developed in ASEAN to the most developed in MERCOSUR.
- Regional think tanks, regional NGOs, and to some extent the regional secretariats are more focused on advancing this dimension than national governments.
- Emerging social problems with a regional dimension may stimulate further intergovernmental cooperation. These include cross border labor migration, cross border AIDS infection, and cross border drug running.
- The imminent advancing of free trade arrangements within each region will either lead to increased concern with differential labor standards and other aspects of regional social policy or to the beginning of the erosion of the trading block.

- All regions need to face the political choice between either strengthening the existing regions, together with their emerging social dimension, or dissolving the existing regions in favor of entering neoliberal-inspired wider trading blocks.
- It is an important question whether Europe can present itself as a model of a socially regulated region and act as an agency that could help further a social dimension of regionalism elsewhere. For the countries within MERCOSUR, Europe is playing a role and is seen by some actors as a model. This is the case to a lesser extent in SADC. In the ASEAN countries, Europe is more often neither seen as a model nor are its attempts to influence regional policy accepted. If Europe wishes to extend its influence to help construct a world of regions with a social dimension (to counter global neoliberalism) then it will have to put its social development policy before its trade interests and it will have to match its moralizing about rights with resource transfers to enable these to be realized in practice.

The wider significance of the social dimension of Southern regions arises when the current North–South global social policy making impasse is brought into the picture. After Geneva 2000 Social Summit (see above), the need is to foster a set of North–South alliances so that the social dimension of globalization is thought through in ways that do not appear to threaten Southern trading interests. Fostering a South–South dialogue on the role of the social dimension of regionalism within the context of a greater commitment on the part of the North to greater resource transfers and/or global taxes may be one way of building such alliances.

5. Conclusions

This paper has argued and demonstrated that globalization is not incompatible with universal social provisions within the affected countries if the 'cross-class' alliances necessary for such a universalistic strategy can be built and sustained. Certain features of both the global discourse on social policy (the favoring of neoliberalism) and the emerging global private market in health and social care may, however, undermine the prospect for such solidarities being built in many developing countries. Attempts by Northern global social reformers to soften the harshest aspects of the global neoliberal project by injecting a social dimension into globalization have foundered on the rocks of Southern opposition born of past exeriences of colonialism and structural adjustment conditionality. The bat is now passing to the South to figure out ways of developing effective social policies in a globalizing context. Some Southern voices, those that are critical of the neoliberal features of globalization, are now beginning this job. A South–South dialogue on best practice in social policy from the standpoint of equity is being initiated. Within that emerging dialogue the role of the social dimension of Southern regionalism is likely to figure large.

At the Indian National Convention against Globalization on March 21–23, 2001, Walden Bello of the Focus on the Global South addressed the theme of the present Global Conjuncture (Bello, 2001). He noted the existence of the post-Washington-Consensus attempts to develop a softer approach to corporate globalization. He rejected, however, the strategies of bringing the social agenda to bear on the workings of the WTO, the Global Compact with transnational corporations (TNCs) initiated by the UN Secretary General and the increased cooption of INGOs into the business of the World Bank, among other things. He argued that instead of shoring up corporate globalization, we should seek to enter a period of "de-globalization" that would include reorienting economies for the local market and "carrying out long-postponed measures of income (and land) redistribution" (Bello and Bullard, 2001). Such a strategy would work for a plural world, would weaken the influence of the WTO, the World Bank and the IMF and "turn them into just another set of actors coexisting with and being checked by other international organizations, agreements and regional groupings. This strategy would include strengthening diverse actors and institutions such as UNCTAD, the ILO, and evolving economic blocs such as MERCO-SUR, SAARC, SADCC, ASEAN. A key aspect of 'strengthening' of course, is making sure these formations evolve in a people-oriented direction and cease to remain regional elite projects" (Bello and Bullard, 2001).

Therefore, even in a globalizing world, it is possible to achieve equitable social provisioning both in the North and South, if common purpose is found between Northern and Southern. There are such voices, both in the North and South, articulating the importance of both nurturing solidarities within countries and nurturing a social dimension to regionalism in the context of a cooperative world order based on negotiated inter-regional agreements rather than on unregulated market principles.

References

Alber, Jens and Guy Standing (2000) "Globalization and Social Dumping. An Overview." *Journal of European Social Policy*, 10(3): 99–119.

Bello, Walden and Nicola Bullard (2001) "The Global Conjuncture: Characteristics and Challenges." *Focus on Trade*, No. 60. March.

Braathen, Einar (2001) "New Social Corporatism. A Discursive-Comparative Perspective on the World Development Report." In *A Critical Review of the World Development Report 2000–2001*. Bergen: CROP, 31–42. www.crop.org

Chen, Lincoln C. and Meghnad Desai (1997) "Paths to Social Development: Lessons from Case Studies." In Santosh Mehrotra and Richard Jolly (eds.) *Development with a Human Face*. Oxford: Oxford University Press, pp. 421–434.

Deacon, Bob *et al.* (1997) *Global Social Policy: International Organisations and the Future of Welfare*. London: Sage.

Deacon, Bob (1999a) *Towards a Socially Responsible Globalization: International Actors and Discourses*. GASPP Occasional Paper No. 1. Helsinki: Stakes.

Deacon, Bob (1999b) *Socially Responsible Globalisation: A Challenge for the European Union*. Helsinki: Ministry of Social Affairs and Health.

Deacon, Bob (2000) *Globalization and Social Policy*. UNRISD Occasional Paper No.5. Geneva: United Nations Research Institute for Social Development (UNRISD).

Deacon, Bob (2001) *The Social Dimension of Regionalism*. GASPP Occasional Paper No.8. Helsinki: Stakes.

Ferguson, Clare (1999) *Global Social Policy Principles: Human Rights and Social Justice*. London: Social Development Division, Department for International Development.

Ghai, Dharam (1999) *Social Development and Public Policies*. London: UNRISD and McMillan.

Gough, Ian (2001) "Globalisation and Regional Welfare Regimes: The East-Asian Case." *Global Social Policy*, 1(2): 163–189.

Graham, Carol (1994) *Safety Nets, Politics, and the Poor*. Washington: Brookings Institute.

Hort, Sven E.O. and Stein Kuhnle (2000) "The Coming of East and South-East Asian Welfare States." *Journal of European Social Policy*, 10(3): 162–184.

Huber, Evelyne and John D. Stephens (2000) *The Political Economy of Pension Reform: Latin America in Comparative Perspective*. UNRISD Occasional Paper No. 7. Geneva: UNRISD.

Huck-ju Kwon (2001) "Globalization, Unemployment, and Policy Responses in Korea." *Global Social Policy*, 1(2): 213–234.

Langmore, John (2001) "The UN Commission for Social Development, February 2001: An Opportunity for International Political Evolution." *Global Social Policy*, 1(3): 277–280.

Mehrotra, Santosh and Richard Jolly (1997) *Development with a Human Face.* Oxford: Oxford University Press.

Mesa-Lago, Carmelo *et al.* (2000) *Market, Socialist, and Mixed Economies: Comparative Policy and Performance—Chile, Cuba, and Costa Rica.* Baltimore: Johns Hopkins University Press.

Mishra, Ramesh (1999) *Globalization and the Welfare State.* Cheltenham, UK and Northampton, MA: Edward Elgar.

Mkandawire, Thandika and Virginia Rodríguez (2000) *Globalization and Social Development after Copenhagen: Premises, Promises, and Policies.* UNRISD Occasional Paper No.10. Geneva: UNRISD.

OECD (1999) *A Caring World: The New Social Policy Agenda.* Paris: Organization for Economic Cooperation and Development.

Scharpf, Fritz W. and Vivien A. Schmidt (eds.) (2000) *Welfare and Work in the Open Economy.* Oxford: Oxford University Press.

Sykes, Robert, Bruno Palier, and Pauline M. Prior (2001) *Globalization and the European Welfare States: Challenges and Change.* Basingstoke: Palgrave.

Taylor, Lance (ed.) (2000) *External Liberalization, Economic Performance, and Social Policy.* Oxford and New York: Oxford University Press.

September 11, the Anti-Terror Campaign, and the Prevention of Violent Conflict

Andrew Mack

The horrific events of September 11, 2001 created both risks and opportunities for those committed to the promotion of sustainable and equitable development and the prevention of violent conflicts.

The risks are twofold. First, that resources intended for development and conflict prevention may be diverted to tasks that have little to do with either. In particular the large amounts of discretionary funds in aid agency budgets can look very tempting to politicians who are confronted by the political imperative to 'do something' about terrorism, but who have few resources to do it with. Second, there is an important opportunity-cost question. Counter-terrorism is clearly a form of conflict prevention; what is contested is the share of prevention resources that it should command.

The fact is that international terrorism kills relatively few people worldwide—fewer than one thousand a year on average over the past thirty years. This compares with an average of some half a million combat-related deaths a year in the 1990s from armed conflicts around the world, almost all of them in poor countries, and a majority of them civilian. And criminal violence in 1998 alone killed some 750,000 people.

To make the point more dramatically, consider the genocide in Rwanda. Here the death toll was the equivalent to a September 11 atrocity every day for some 200 days. The international community did nothing to even try and stop the killing. No one said "the world has changed." If the slaughter of innocents is the primary reason for our concern about political violence, we should resist pressure to transfer resources from war prevention to terrorism, which is a form of violence that kills relatively few people.

We can identify three types of response to the threat of international terrorism. What might be called the 'war' and 'criminal justice' response modes focus on destroying terrorist organizations and capturing and bringing to justice the terrorists themselves. The third type of response focuses on 'root causes'—addressing the conditions that create the 'fertile ground' for the emergence of terrorism in the first place. And it is here that the response to September 11 has the potential to contribute to the broader cause of conflict prevention.

The immediate—and wholly understandable—US reaction to the assaults on New York and the Pentagon was to attack and eliminate the perpetrators of terror. No one wanted to hear about underlying causes. American columnists wrote angry editorials condemning those who argued that, while the crimes were indeed horrific, it was also necessary to understand the conditions that give rise to them.

To many Americans any attempt to 'explain' terrorism seemed akin to blaming the victims. To talk about the need to 'understand' the root causes of terrorism sounded like empathizing with terrorists. This was at best naïve; at worst despicable. Nothing could excuse what the terrorists did. The problem was not to 'understand' Osama Bin Laden and his network of evil murderers, but to destroy them.

These critics argued that poverty, dispossession, and repression can no more explain terrorism than they can excuse it. Terrorists are found in rich countries as well as in poor ones. Sub-Saharan Africa, which is far poorer than the Middle East, is devastated by repression, poverty, and internal violence, but no sub-Saharan state has hosted an international terror organization. Moreover, the terror bombers of September 11 came from the middle classes, not the dispossessed, while Bin Laden himself is a multi-millionaire.

This line of criticism fundamentally misses the point. Seeking to understand the roots of political violence does not mean excusing it. But understanding causes is a necessary condition for long-term prevention. What is needed is a two-front strategy: one that attacks the perpetrators of violence but also addresses the conditions that allowed them to flourish.

Consider an apt medical analogy. If someone is struck down by a heart attack, swift diagnosis and aggressive intervention are needed. But no physician would argue that treating the symptoms of crisis, however important, is—on its own—an adequate response to the problem of heart disease. Effective prevention means addressing the preventable causes of that disease—inappropriate diet, smoking, and lack of exercise—as well as its deadly symptoms. The same logic applies to terrorism. Every effort must be made to penetrate the terror network and neutralize the terror organization, but this is not enough. Without also addressing underlying conditions that provide the 'fertile ground' on which terrorism thrives any counter-terrorism successes will be short-lived.

For terrorists to succeed in the long term they need a degree of popular support. Consider the case of middle-class European terrorism of the 1970s—the Red Brigades, the Baader–Meinhof Group, and the Angry Brigade. All of these organizations had a vision, an ideology, and an organization. But none had any real popular resource base and when their organizations were penetrated and their members arrested, there was no pool of new recruits to draw on. They simply ceased to be a significant threat.

In contrast, the Basque separatist movement, ETA in Spain and the IRA in Northern Ireland are organizations that have survived for decades. Here the elimination of individual terrorists does not stop the violence because the organizations that they served have deep roots in their respective communities.

Al Quaeda clearly fits in the latter category not the former. In Pakistan, many of its recruits were educated in radical Islamic schools, the *madrassas*, some of whose clerics indoctrinated students with a deep hatred of the US. Parents send their children to such schools because they have no choice—there are simply not enough places in state schools in Pakistan for poor children. American critics have recognized too late that this is indeed the case—in so doing they have embraced the 'root causes' explanations on which they previously heaped scorn.

Those who think that the idea of addressing the conditions that give rise to political violence is naïve and unworkable might think for a moment about the Marshall Plan—the huge effort by the US to assist the economic recovery of Europe in the wake of the Second World War. The *realpolitik* rationale for the plan was simple: if the economies of Europe failed to recover, the resulting poverty and misery would provide a fertile ground for the growth of communism. The program worked.

In the context of the September 11 crisis it is noteworthy that, in February 2002, the US Senate passed a bipartisan anti-terrorism resolution, which noted that . . . poverty, hunger, political uncertainty, and social instability are the principal causes of violence and conflict around the world." It resolved that ". . . the United States should lead coordinated international efforts to provide increased financial assistance to countries with impoverished and disadvantaged populations that are the breeding grounds for terrorism" and that "the United States Agency for International Development . . . should substantially increase humanitarian, economic development, and agricultural assistance to foster international peace and stability, and the promotion of human rights."[1] As one commentator noted, "[i]t took nearly 4,000 American deaths, the destruction of the World Trade Center and a war in Afghanistan to make it happen, but key members of Congress now want to share more of America's wealth with other nations."[2]

Few, however, believed that the Senate resolution would have much impact on the Bush Administration. But here too there has apparently been a seismic

1. See http://frwebgate.access.gpo.gov/cgi-bin/getdoc.cgi?dbname=107_cong_bills&docid=f:sr204is.txt
or http://www.usembassyjakarta.org/terrorism/senate204.html.
2. See e.g. Kiely (2002).

shift in attitude. Surprising many, the new Congressional commitment to aid was echoed in the promises made by President Bush on March 14, 2002 to increase US aid spending by some 5 billion dollars.[3] Bush's emphasis on the need for aid to address the root causes of violence as well as it perpetrators was surprisingly similar to a speech made by the Secretary-General of the United Nations, Kofi Annan. In his 1999 annual report to the General Assembly, Annan argued that in dealing with global violence, the United Nations needed to shift from a "culture of reaction" to a "culture of prevention"—to address the root causes of destructive conflicts rather than focusing only on their violent symptoms. And the need for greater stress on prevention is now conventional wisdom in the World Bank, among the G–8 leaders, and in the OECD. Development agencies are now routinely enjoined to view development through the conflict prevention lens. What this means in practice is far from clear.

To prevent conflict we need to understand its causes and for this we need the insights of the research community. Without a broad understanding of the causes of violent conflict, prevention policy becomes akin to prescribing medicine without any diagnosis. But what the research community produces and what the policy community needs are not the same thing.

First, the traditional security studies community—particularly in the United States—is still focused on what might be called the national security paradigm. These scholars still spend most of their time writing and arguing about the causes of interstate war—even though interstate wars are now extraordinarily rare and even though the theoretical frameworks used to explain interstate war are largely irrelevant for explaining more than ninety percent of the wars that are now fought primarily within, not between, states.

Second, scholars are not very good at communicating with policy-makers. Their professional rewards derive from the production of long theoretical treatises, not succinct and accessible policy briefs for busy officials. And the field of econometrics, which is producing some of the most interesting recent research, is virtually incomprehensible, not only to policy-makers, but also to other members of the research community who are not familiar with econometric methods.

Third, although it is widely agreed that the root causes of violent conflict are found in the socio-economic realm, security specialists and economic development theorists speak different and sometimes incommensurate languages and do not communicate well. There is a similar problem in the official world. In the United Nations, for example, the departments with a responsibility for security know little about development. Those in departments that deal with develop-

3. See http://usinfo.state.gov/topical/global/develop/02031402.htm.

98

ment have traditionally regarded conflict prevention as highly politically sensitive and best left alone. The United Nations confronts a further problem in that—unlike the World Bank—it lacks a research-oriented culture and simply does not have the resources to undertake in-house research.

Fourth, the new wave of quantitative research on civil wars associated with the World Bank uses statistical inference techniques to seek to distill certain general lessons from studying literally hundreds of cases. This type of research is akin to the work of epidemiologists studying the causes of diseases. It tells us about *probable* causes, it seeks to provide *general* lessons about risk—for example, heavy smokers are seven times more likely to succumb to lung cancer than non-smokers. This type of research—whether on disease or war—can provide some important, though qualified, *general* answers about the factors that increase the risk of war or disease.

Consider the following examples. A major study at the United Nations' World Institute for Development Economics Research on armed conflict argues that the so-called "horizontal inequality"—that is inequality of access by social groups to a range of political, social, and economic resources—is a major cause of violence.[4]

Let us assume, for the sake of argument, that this finding is correct. What then are the broad policy prescriptions? The first point to note is that development policies that are successful in meeting the traditional development goal of increasing economic growth may well also increase horizontal inequality—and hence the risk of war. Viewing development policy through the 'conflict prevention lens' would thus mean pursuing policies that sought to prevent 'horizontal inequality' from increasing—i.e. they imply the need for 'growth with equity' strategies. This might imply a less rapid rate of increase in GDP, but what is lost on the growth front may be compensated for by improvements on the security front.

Take another case. One of the strongest findings to come from the World Bank's research on violence is that poor countries whose exports are highly dependent on primary commodities are twenty times more likely to be involved in violent conflict than those that have no such dependency. Assume again that the findings are correct. The clear policy message here is that development strategies that seek to increase export diversification will reduce the risk of armed conflict. But protectionism in the North is a major barrier to poor country export diversification. So trade liberalization in the North should be seen as an important security-enhancing strategy for the South.

4. See Stewart (2001).

The policy measures that may be needed in the unique circumstances of a particular country cannot be determined in the abstract and policy makers need more than broad generalizations about risk. In addition to the broad prescriptions derived from the study of large numbers of cases, they also need to take into account local conditions. This requires country expertise and—above all—local knowledge. One size never fits all.

Conclusion

If we believe that policy should be determined by informed analysis based on good data, then the policy community needs the research community as policy-makers rarely have either the time or expertise to undertake research. But the research community also needs the policy community since policy *outcomes* are the most important test of policy *prescriptions*—including those that are derived from research.

References

Kiely, Kathy (2002) "Importance of Foreign Aid Is Hitting Home." *USA Today*, February 12, 2002.

Stewart, Frances (2001) *Horizontal Inequality, a Neglected Dimension of Development*. Helsinki: United Nations University, World Institute for Development Economics Research.

Between Cunning States and Unaccountable International Institutions: Social Movements and Rights of Local Communities to Common Property Resources

Shalini Randeria

F23 Q21 034
F02 013 F13
019

This essay delineates various trajectories of globalization and their contestation by examining the interplay between international institutions (the World Bank, IMF and WTO), civil society actors (social movements and NGOs) and the state. Using empirical material from India, two kinds of conflicts are analyzed: (1) the clash between environmental conservation and human rights; and (2) the collision between the right to livelihood of local communities dependent on common property resources and a model of economic growth based either on state-led development or on privatization managed by the state. The case studies focus on the constrained yet central role of the state in transposing processes of globalization into the national arena. They remind us that globalization as locally experienced involves the activities of multinational corporations; the impact of WTO rules and World Bank credit conditionalities; state (in)action in enforcing these regimes; the risks of displacement due to development projects; impoverishment and exclusion in the wake of market fundamentalism; global discourses of biodiversity and indigenous peoples' rights; as well as the local politics of transnationally linked social movements. Given its centrality to the neoliberal restructuring of governance both within and beyond the nation-state, law provides an important vantage point from which to study some of these facets of globalization and the resistance to it.

The case studies analyzed below show a diversity of supra-state and non-state actors at work in varying alliances with one another at the local, national and supranational levels. But they also demonstrate that the state is not merely a victim of neoliberal economic globalization as it remains an active agent in transposing it nationally and locally. The monopoly of the state over the production of law is certainly being challenged both by international institutions and by civil society actors, subnational as well as supranational (Günther and Randeria, 2002). However, in contradistinction to the widespread diagnosis of the consequent decline of the state and a dismantling of its sovereignty, I argue in the first section that it would be a mistake to take this self-representation of states at its face value. We are faced not by weak, or weakening, states but by cunning states[1] which capitalize on their perceived weakness in order to render themselves unaccountable both to their citizens and to international institutions (Randeria, 2001, 2002c).

The second section uses the successful struggle against patents on the Neem tree to illustrate six theses on the transnationalization of law, state sovereignty and the role of civil society actors from a post-colonial perspective. The paradoxical consequences of the World Bank supported biodiversity project for the protection of lions in Gujarat, western India are considered in the third part. The next section deals with the network 'Campaign for Peoples' Control Over Natural Resources' which is contesting the state-market nexus involved in privatization at the expense of the poor. The global success of the transnational movement against the Narmada dam which, however, failed to translate into local gains for those displaced by the project is the subject of the fifth part. Finally, I discuss the disappointing experience of civil society actors who filed claims on behalf of those adversely affected by World Bank projects before the Inspection Panel, an innovative transnational legal arena which has failed to realize its potential so far.

1. The Cunning State, Unaccountable International Institutions and the Paradoxes of Democratization

Due to its salience in domesticating neoliberal policies, the state remains an important interlocutor for civil society actors challenging these policies or seeking to mitigate their effects. However, grassroots NGOs and social movements in India are not only engaged in a struggle against the state and international institutions for the protection of the rights of indigenous peoples and other local communities over common property resources, but are proactive in formulating new norms weaving together traditional collective rights, national laws, and international standards. Their struggle for environmental justice is being waged through broad based political mobilization and media campaigns but equally through the increasing use of national courts and international legal fora. The latter includes the Inspection Panel at the World Bank whose very genesis owes a great deal to the transnational coalition against the Narmada dam in western India (Randeria, 2001; 2002a; 2002c).

An important dynamic in the local transposition of neoliberal globalization consists in a part transnationalization and part privatization of the state which

---

1. My thanks to Ivan Krastev for suggesting this term to me to describe the new strategies of the subaltern state in relation to supranational institutions.

increasingly effaces, on the one hand, the boundary between the national and supranational and, on the other, between state and civil society. Both contribute to what I have elsewhere described as the new pattern of 'scattered sovereignties' (Randeria, 2001). The resulting reconfiguration of the state includes the selective implementation by the state of norms and policies designed by supranational institutions like the World Bank and the IMF and imposed in the form of 'credit conditionalities' (Moore, 2000) or of 'project law' (Benda-Beckmann, 2001). The distinction between law and public policy becomes increasingly blurred as rule-making is increasingly placed outside the arena of legislative deliberation and democratic decision-making (Randeria, 2003). But an analysis of processes of *'glocalization'* needs to go beyond unpacking the state in terms of its legislative, administrative and judicial institutions each with their own logics. It must also include both an analysis of the decentralization of the state and devolution of powers to regional and local governments as well as to NGOs which have taken over many of the functions of the state. If the state at the national level has lost some of its powers, the regional governments have gained in influence as they now negotiate directly with the World Bank and try to implement investor-friendly policies in a bid to attract domestic and foreign capital. Therefore, the dynamics of glocalization are best studied at the level of the different regional governments in India. Two of the case studies in this paper will unravel some of these transformations, therefore, using empirical material from the province of Gujarat in Western India.

The new architecture of unaccountable global governance facilitates 'passing the power', a game in which international institutions claim themselves to be utterly powerless servants of their member states, and states in turn capitalize on their perceived powerlessness in the face of prescriptions from Washington DC or Geneva (Randeria, 2001). This creates dilemmas for civil society actors for whom the state is both an ally and an adversary depending on the context. On the one hand, they need the state in order to protect the rights of citizens *vis-à-vis* multinational corporations and international institutions. On the other hand, civil society actors increasingly use the international arena and transnational political spaces to bypass the state, as for example, in the case of the anti-Narmada dam movement discussed below, in order to directly address supranational institutions whose policies directly affect the lives of poor citizens.

Much of the literature on globalization emphasizes the increasing marginality of the state and its retreat in the face of inroads by global capital. In contrast, I have argued that the state continues to play a pivotal role in transposing and shaping neoliberal globalization at the national and local level. In order to grant multinational corporations licenses to exploit natural resources, the Indian state amended its laws and policies on mining and minerals under pressure from the World Bank to facilitate private investment, foreign and domestic, in sectors reserved exclusively for the state until recently. And it is the use by the Indian state of its land acquisition policy of colonial provenance to acquire land for industry which has led to forcible displacement on a large scale. The state has permitted the setting up of private industries in areas inhabited largely by indigenous communities and granted to corporations mining licenses, tax and labor law concessions, and favorable terms of operation in contravention of many of its own laws and policies (Kumar and Shivalkar, 2001).

While recognizing the new constraints on the freedom of the state to design and implement their own laws and policies, it would be a mistake to accept the self-representation of the cunning state about its own weakness. The government of India has definitely not implemented all the policy reforms demanded by the World Bank and the IMF nor enacted all the legal changes suggested by it. Invoking national sovereignty, it has refused to allow the Inspection Panel of the World Bank to investigate complaints by Indian citizens adversely affected by World Bank projects as we will see below. Nor has it agreed to the full convertibility of the Rupee, for example, and has complied only partially, selectively, or half-heartedly with other conditionalities like deregulation of the labor market or privatization of state enterprises. In contradistinction to weak states like Bangladesh or Benin, cunning states like India certainly have the capacity to decide which of the remedies prescribed in Washington for the ills of the national economy should be administered selectively to different sections of the population.

Contrary to the rhetoric of many globalization theorists and of political elites, the state is not being rolled back as a rule making or rule enforcing agency. In an age of scattered sovereignties, it has merely lost its monopoly over the production, adjudication, and implementation of law, if given the plurality of post-colonial legal landscapes it ever had such a monopoly (Randeria, 2002a; 2002b). The World Bank's 1997 World Development Report titled *The State in a Changing World* reflects the new role of the state as envisaged by international institutions. The post-structural-adjustment state is conceived of by them as an 'enabling state', as one arena of regulatory practice among others (Gill, 1999). The prescribed goal of 'good governance' entails restructuring of the state to ensure the "reliability of its institutional framework" and "the predictability of its rules and policies and the consistency with which they are applied" (World Bank, 1997: 4–5). The policies and rules themselves, however, are insulated from public deliberation and parliamentary decision-making resulting in a "democracy without choices" (Krastev, 2002). Elections in such a situation result merely in a change of parties or of leaders but the voters are unable to influence policy changes.

My argument will be that despite its decentering, and restructuring through the workings of international institutions and the market, the state remains an important albeit contested terrain in processes of globalization. So that all laments about the loss of state sovereignty to the contrary, legislative enactments, judicial decision-making and administrative (in)action will continue to affect the way processes of globalization are mediated, experienced, and resisted in India. By grounding the experience of globalization in an empirical study of resistance against forced displacement and an examination of local struggles over access to natural resources, I seek to link everyday life in rural India to transnational flows of capital and the policy discourses which travel with them. By analyzing the global as part of the local, such an exercise can contribute to an understanding of the specificities of local transformations and the power relations that shape them. As the case studies discussed here show, law is an increasingly important, if ambivalent, arena in which to contest interpretations of environmental standards, human rights and the public good, the regulation of the environment or access to common property resources.

2. NGOs Challenge US Patent on the Indian Neem Tree in Munich

On the 9th and 10th of May 2000, the fate of the Indian Neem tree hung in balance in Room 3468 of the European Patent Office in Munich. At issue was the legitimacy of a patent for a method of preparing an oil extract from the seeds of the tree to be used as a pesticide, one of 14 patents on products of the Indian Neem tree granted by the Munich authority. The American transnational corporation W.R. Grace and the US Department of Agriculture, joint owners of six of these patents, were represented by a lawyer's firm in Hamburg. Ranged against them was a transnational coalition of petitioners asking for the patent to be revoked: Vandana Shiva, Director of the Research Foundation for Science, Technology, and Ecology; Linda Bullard, President of the International Federation of Organic Agricultural Movements; and Magda Alvoet, currently the Belgian Health and Environment Minister. They were represented by a Swiss Professor of Law from the University of Basel.

The representatives of the American chemical concern remained silent throughout the two days of hearing. It was the silence of the powerful, of those who knew that time, money and the government of the Unites States of America were on the side of American corporate interests. The European Patent Office heard the powerful political arguments of Vandana Shiva on 'biopiracy' and intellectual colonialism as well as the testimony of the Sri Lankan farmer,

Ranjith de Silva, on the moral illegitimacy of a patent that disregards centuries of traditional local knowledge. But what ultimately counted for the Opposition Division Bench hearing the case were measurements of centrifugation, filtration, and evaporation in the testimony of Abhay Phadke, an Indian factory owner. His firm near Delhi has been using since 1985 a process very similar to the one patented by the American multinational corporation and the US Department of Agriculture to manufacture the same product in India. At the end of a five-year legal battle on May 10, 2000 the European Patent Office revoked the patent on the grounds that the process patented by the Americans lacked novelty.

The story of the struggle around the Indian Neem tree serves to illustrate six theses on the transnationalization of law, the role of the state as an architect but also a victim of globalization, and the role of civil society actors in mobilizing local protest as well as in creating alternative norms.

2.1 Hegemonic vs. Counter-Hegemonic Globalization

The European Patent Office in Munich was the scene of a conflict between two visions of globalization and over its future shape and direction. The battle lines were drawn here as in Seattle between proponents of a neoliberal globalization for profit and its globally-networked civil-society opponents. As actors in an emerging global civil society, transnationally networked farmers' movements and environmental NGOs in India are among the most ardent opponents of a new international legal regime of 'intellectual property rights' that provides transnational corporations (TNCs) in the North cheap and easy access to the natural resources of the South. They have argued that the increasing commercialization of common property resources turns common heritage into commodities, jeopardizing the biodiversity of agricultural crops, threatening the livelihood of poor primary producers and forcing consumers of seeds and medicines in the South into dependency and often destitution. They point out that the capitalist countries of the North industrialized without the constraints of a patent regime which they have now imposed on the developing world. Central to their struggles in the local, national, and transnational legal and political arena is the question: who sets the rules for the processes of globalization and according to which norms? These movements are raising issues of food security and farmer's rights but more generally of social justice, democratization of global governance and the legitimacy of international institutions and legal regimes.

For example, a public hearing was organized in September 2000 in the south Indian city of Bangalore by several NGOs, women's groups, agricultural worker's unions and farmer's movements on the effects of the WTO regime of intellectual

property rights on the lives of Indian farmers. At this 'seeds tribunal', many farmers testified to the destruction of biodiversity in their regions, to the sale of kidneys
by family members to meet the rising expenses of agricultural inputs, to suicides
by farmers caught in a debt trap due to the high price of seeds by multinational
corporations and subsequent crop failure—but also to the inadequate and poor
quality of the public distribution of seeds which facilitates the entry of foreign
multinationals in this sphere and to the resultant market dependency and indebt-
edness of small peasants. The farmer's organizations passed a resolution calling on
multinationals like Monsanto to "Quit India" echoing Mahatma Gandhi's slogan
coined in 1942 at the height of the national movement against British domination.
They called for a boycott of seeds by Indian subsidiaries of multinationals so long
as the former do not become independent of these foreign firms. They also vowed
to maintain the food sovereignty and seed sovereignty of farmers and protect it
from multinational companies while declaring that they will not obey any patent
law or plant variety protection law under the WTO regime which consider seeds
to be the private property of these corporations. They demanded that seeds and
food be excluded from the TRIPs (Trade Related Intellectual Property Rights)
regime of the WTO and advocated the reintroduction of the quantitative restrictions on agricultural imports removed recently by the Government of India in consonance with WTO provisions for trade liberalization.

2.2 Cunning Rather Than Weak States? Contesting the Limits to State Autonomy

At this public hearing, the jury, consisting of eminent jurists, intellectuals, and
activists, envisaged a central and active role for the state in the protection of the
livelihoods of farmers in India. It recommended improvement of the public distribution of seeds; the setting up of regulatory bodies to ensure good quality agricultural inputs; a ten-year moratorium on the introduction of genetic engineering in
food and farming; representation for farmers in the agricultural prices commission; and guaranteed minimum agricultural support prices. But the jury's diagnosis of the "silence of the state" on the issue of farmer's rights presumes a state
which is either unaware of or inactive on this issue. However, the Indian state has
been anything but silent as the introduction and passage of new legislation like the
Patents (Second) Amendments Act of 1999, the Protection of Plant Varieties and
Farmer's Rights Bill of 1999, and the Biological Diversity Bill of 2001 shows. A
harsh critique of the state coupled with an appeal to it to protect the rights of vulnerable groups reflects some of the ambivalence of civil society actors with respect
to the state, whom they view as both opponent and ally. Under conditions of economic and legal globalization the state is simultaneously seen as in collusion with

multinational corporate interests and as protector of national sovereignty. But can the Indian state be relied on to reform its policies in favor of its vulnerable citizens rather than in favor of global capital? This depends on whether the state has not only the capacity but also the will to do act in the interests of its citizens. My contention is that we tend to misrecognize cunning states as weak ones. Weak states can not protect their citizens whereas cunning states do not care to.

The global harmonization of differing national systems of patent law illustrates some of the complexities of legal globalization and the contradictory role of the state in it. There is no global patent law; the field is still regulated on the national level with the exception of the EU. But the WTO's TRIPs regime imposes powerful constraints on the sovereignty of nation-states both with regard to the content and timing of national laws which have to conform to the new WTO regime. The extent of national autonomy under the sui generis system available as an option under the TRIPs, which NGOs would like their governments to exploit, remains highly contested with mounting pressure against it from genetic technology exporting nations like the USA and Argentina. However, despite legal transnationalization and the growing importance of the WTO, the state remains an important arena of law production. Despite the fact that India had an elaborate and functioning legal framework in this area, it has had to amend its patent laws. In addition to patents on processes which were permitted earlier, the country has had to introduce patents on products in conformity with the TRIPs regime. In consonance with WTO requirements, it has had to enact laws on plant varieties and breeder's rights in order to permit for the first time the patenting of agricultural and pharmaceutical products. However, even within the WTO framework, there are some choices which states can make if they have the political will to protect the more vulnerable of their citizens. Instead of exercising these limited choices at its disposal, the Indian state chose to portray itself as utterly powerless to protect the interests of small farmers. It chose to lay all responsibility for the new national legislation on the constraints imposed by the supranational regulatory framework alone, thus absolving itself of any accountability towards citizens for its own political decisions.

As the Gene Campaign[2], an Indian NGO, has pointed out, the WTO requires member states to legislate either a patent regime or an effective *sui*

---

2. Gene Campaign, founded in 1992, is a research and advocacy organization based in New Delhi, India working on the issues of protection of genetic resources and indigenous knowledge as well as the rights of farmers, local communities and indigenous people to the use of these resources without hindrance. It is a combination of an expert NGO and a grassroots level organization working in 17 states in India and its work is focused on ensuring food and livelihood security for rural and indigenous communities. It has played a significant role in raising public awareness of these issues through media campaigns, and in influencing the formulation of national policies on international property resources, biodiversity, and international trade.

generis system to protect newly developed plant varieties. The new transnational regulatory regime does not enjoin states to follow the UPOV[3] model laid down in the International Convention for the Protection of New Varieties of Plants. The Indian state, therefore, had a choice to opt for a sui generis system more suitable to the Indian context, an option it did not exercise. The UPOV system is based on the needs of industrialized countries where agriculture is a commercial activity unlike in a country like India with a large majority of small and marginal farmers. The Gene Campaign argues that the UPOV model thus protects the rights of big companies who are the major producers of seed in the North in a context where seed research is conducted in private institutions for profit. It is thus at odds with Indian realities where not only is most research in the area done in public institutions but where farmers are seed producers and have individually and collectively conserved genetic resources. The Gene Campaign, therefore, advocates that instead of basing its new patent regime on the unsuitable UPOV system, the Indian state choose the *sui generis* option within the WTO framework to enact legislation of its own which would adequately protect the rights of its farmers as producers and consumers of seed.

Moreover, as many critics of the Uruguay Round in India have pointed out, contrary to its rhetoric of creating a level playing field, many WTO rules tilt the balance further against the countries of the South. Theoretically, it may be the case that the latter who are net losers from the TRIPs regime, could offset such losses by gains from textile or agricultural trade liberalization. However, most countries of the North, which have been very slow to comply with their commitments in this regard, can take recourse to the very extensive safeguard provisions for agricultural and textile trade. The TRIPs agreement lacks any such provision that would permit countries to reimpose tariffs temporarily in case losses to domestic producers are heavier than expected. So though the costs of implementing the TRIPs regime has turned out to be much higher than anticipated for most developing countries, the Agreement merely allows for a certain grace period for implementation. Many of the developing countries, including India, therefore, would like to reopen for negotiation those compromises which they made in the Uruguay Round under imperfect information and the threat of unilateralism by the USA.

3. The International Union for the Protection of New Varieties of Plants (UPOV) is an intergovernmental organization with headquarters in Geneva (Switzerland). It is based on the International Convention for the Protection of New Varieties of Plants, as revised since its signature in Paris on December 2, 1961. The objective of the Convention is the protection of new varieties of plants by an intellectual property right.

2.3 A Plurality of Conflicting Supranational Legal Regimes

Two of the strategies that have been adopted by subaltern states faced with structural adjustment conditionalities and several supranational legal regimes is to delay implementation at the national level and to exploit the existence of a plurality of international laws and treaties, which often contravene one another. India along with African and five Central and Latin American countries has called for a review and an amendment of the TRIPs Agreement of the WTO and a five-year moratorium on its implementation. The Organization of African Unity and India have demanded that the TRIPs regime be brought into consonance with the Convention on Biological Diversity and the International Undertaking on Plant Genetic Resources, which would result in the exclusion of life forms from patentability and the protection of innovations by local farming communities. The Indian government has pointed out that its obligations under the TRIPs run counter to some of its obligations under the Convention on Biological Diversity. However, the sanctions under the former that permit, e.g., cross retaliation in any area of trade are much stronger compared to the weak enforcement mechanisms of international environmental laws. Indian NGOs along with transnational networks like GRAIN[4] and RAFI[5], for example, have been using this plurality of transnational legal regimes to question the legitimacy of the WTO TRIPs framework. They claim that this framework contravenes provisions of the Biodiversity Convention or the Protocol on Biosafety on genetically modified life forms and does not conform to the earlier International Undertaking of the FAO, which explicitly recognizes Farmer's Rights to seeds.

A plurality of norms at the national and international levels and their collision may not necessarily be detrimental to the protection of the rights of local communities. It could afford a space for states, if they are politically inclined to use it, to protect the rights of their vulnerable citizens. The question is whether within the constraints imposed by the processes of neoliberal globalization and its new institutional architecture, a state has the political will to use all the available legal space to further and protect the interests of the poor and marginalized sections of its population. Or does the national political elite gain instead by

---

4. GRAIN is an international non-governmental organization that promotes the sustainable management and use of agricultural biodiversity based on local knowledge and on people's control over genetic resources.
5. The international NGO, Rural Advancement Foundation International (RAFI), now renamed ETC group, addresses issues of conservation and sustainable advancement of cultural and ecological diversity and human rights. It supports the socially responsible development of technologies useful to the poor and marginalized and addresses to this end international governance issues and corporate power at local and global fora.

pointing to the shrinking capacity of the nation-state to choose policy options and enact its own legislation by laying responsibility for its laws and policies at the door of the World Bank, the WTO or the IMF and thus divest itself of political accountability to its citizens?

2.4. NGOs as Mediators and Creators of Laws

The protracted struggle against the Dunkel Draft[6] and the TRIPs Agreement shows the variety of vital contributions to legal 'glocalization' made by transnationally linked NGOs and social movements in India. Just as they have represented the interests of the Indian farmers in international and transnational fora, they have also disseminated information on the legal complexities to the national press and local communities. Not only have their campaigns created public awareness of the issues involved, mobilized farmers and put pressure on the state but they have challenged in American and European courts the granting of patents to TNCs from the North over agricultural and pharmaceutical products and genetic resources in the South. In addition to mediating between the local and the national levels as well as representing local interests in supranational fora and contesting new legal regimes in various political and legal arenas, NGOs and advocacy groups are also engaged in the production of alternative norms weaving together norms from different sources. The Gene Campaign has drafted, for example, a Convention of Farmers and Breeders (COFaB) in 1998 as an alternative to the UPOV treaty which it considers ill-suited to conditions in India and in the South more generally. The alternative proposal recognizes both individual rights of farmers as breeders and collective community rights as well as common knowledge from oral or documented sources. It stipulates that the breeder will forfeit his right if the "productivity potential" claimed in the application is no longer valid or if he fails to meet the demand of farmers, leading to a scarcity of planting material, increased market price, and monopolies. Moreover, it advocates that each contracting state be granted the right to independent evaluation of the performance of the seed variety under diverse local conditions before

6. The Dunkel Draft (named after the then general secretary of GATT, the General Agreement on Trade and Tariffs) was finalized in December 1991 and formed part of the Uruguay Round of multilateral trade negotiations launched in 1986 which ended in 1995 leading to the setting up of the WTO. The Dunkel Draft came in for severe and sustained public criticism in many countries of the South as it canceled key concessions allowed under the GATT by the advanced capitalist countries to the underdeveloped countries. For example, its provisions prohibiting governments of developing countries from protecting home industries and agriculture for social reasons led to massive public protests by farmers all over India making Dunkel and the Uruguay Round a household name much before ordinary citizens in the North were aware of issues of trade liberalization, the intellectual property rights regime of the GATT/WTO, and its impact on their lives.

allowing patent protection. The 1999 Human Development Report of the United Nations Development Program commends the innovative draft of the Indian NGO as a "strong and coordinated international proposal" that "offers developing countries an alternative to following European legislation on needs to protect farmers' rights to save and reuse seeds and to fulfill the food and nutritional security goals of their peoples" (UNDP, 1999: 74).

Social movements and NGOs in India have long been resisting a destructive and inhumane model of development. They have recently assumed salience not only as translators of national and international law at the local level but also as channels for the assertion of customary collective rights over local commons in national and international fora. As mediators linking the global with the local, social movements and grassroots NGOs with transnational connections are an important interface between nation-states, supranational institutions, and local communities. Their entry into the national legal domain has been facilitated by the growth of judicial activism and public interest litigation but it has not been without its costs in terms of protracted legal battles with uncertain outcomes and the risk of depoliticizing an issue in the legal arena. Despite their equivocal experience with state law courts and supranational instances, social movements and NGOs across the country continue to use these arenas in their struggles for social justice. But after extensive consultations at the grassroots, they have also formulated alternative peoples' laws and policies on land acquisition, forests, rehabilitation or intellectual property rights in addition to holding public hearings on these issues (Randeria, 2001; 2002a). They have thus challenged not merely the monopoly of the state over the production of law but also its exclusive claim to represent the greater common good.

2.5 Fragmentation of State Law and Fractured Sovereignty

Transnationalization of law is accompanied by an increasing fragmentation of law and a fracturing of state sovereignty. State action becomes increasingly heterogeneous with state law losing its unitary and coherent character. For example, Indian patent laws have to be brought into conformity with several supranational legal regimes which may contravene one another like the WTO TRIPs regime and the Convention on Biological Diversity. Or Indian population policy, which is strongly influenced by the UNFPA (United Nations Family Planning Agency) and the USAID (United States Aid for International Development), has to be in tune both with the UN Cairo Conference Action Program with its emphasis on reproductive rights and with the Tirhat Amendment in the US Congress, prohibiting American financial assistance to any national population program which permits abortion. The IMF and the World Bank loan conditionalities in the 1990s required far reaching changes in Indian tax laws, industrial licensing laws, trade liberalization. The dilution of labor laws demanded by them would contravene constitutional guarantees but would also collide with ILO (International Labour Organisation) agreements and ICESCR (International Convention on Economic, Social, and Cultural Rights) provisions. The coexistence of these different logics of regulation by different institutions of the state, or in different areas of regulation, and sometimes within the same area of regulation results in a new kind of legal pluralism, a pluralism within state law. This legal pluralism is linked, on the one hand, to the transnationalization of law (cf. Santos, 1995: 118) and, on the other hand, to the simultaneous operation of multiple transnational norms without their incorporation into domestic law.

2.6 Post-Colonial Continuities?

Let us return for a moment to the Sri Lankan farmer Ranjith de Silva who appeared as a witness for the transnational coalition of petitioners in the European Patent Office in Munich to challenge an American patent on a product of the Neem tree. His grandparents would certainly have been astonished to hear that products of a tree in their backyard could become, by the stroke of a European pen, the intellectual property of an American corporation and the US Department of Agriculture. But neither legal pluralism nor transnational law or jurisdiction would have been unfamiliar to south Asians of his grandparents' generation. The Privy Council in London, for example, had the ultimate authority to decide over their property disputes for they were subjects of the British Empire. And the family law, which applied to de Silva's family as members of the Catholic community, always had a transnational dimension being a hybrid mixture of the prescriptions of the Roman Catholic Church and a variety of local practices codified by the colonial state into a homogenous Christian personal law. In disputes concerning land, British ideas of individual property and of 'eminent domain' would have collided with traditional norms of community access to natural resources and collective usufructuary rights throughout the colonial period, a point I shall return to below. So that in the South, for many critics of the current corporate driven neoliberal globalization it represents a *recolonization* of their future, which signals the end of a short interlude of post-colonial national autonomy and sovereignty.

A sensitivity to the history of colonialism would be an important corrective to the presentism and Eurocentrism of most analyses of globalization with their propensity to overstate the singularity of the present and to posit a radical discontinuity between contemporary social life and that in the recent past. For example, when in the globalization literature references are made to an erosion of the sovereignty of the nation-state, or an increasing legal pluralism (both supranational and subnational), or a new hybridity of laws in the wake of their transnational export, transplantation, and domestication in different cultural contexts, these may represent new developments for societies in the West. From the perspective of the non-Western world, however, it may seem like an irony of history that, turning Karl Marx on the head, one could argue that today the former colonies mirror in many ways the legal future of Europe. This is especially striking with regard to phenomena such as transnational law and jurisdiction, supranational and subnational legal pluralism, the role of private actors in legal diffusion as well as the emergence of multiple and shared sovereignties. Like transnational corporations in the contemporary world, the British East India Company, which began the process of introducing British law into India prior to its becoming a Crown colony, was a private trading company. The relationship between the state and private trading companies in European countries has not been clearly delineated in the past and present. Powerful, partly autonomous from the state, and seeking to escape from government control and metropolitan law, private trading companies in the 19th century, like their transnational counterparts today, have always relied on their respective governments to further their interests abroad. The "post-sovereign states" (Scholte, 1999) of the industrialized world increasingly resemble (post-)colonial ones in which the state has never enjoyed a monopoly over the production of law and has always had to contend with competition from within and beyond its borders. Critics of neoliberal globalization in the South fear that like the colonial state, the post-structural-adjustment state today may have be simply reduced to implementing policies conceived of abroad.

3. Contesting the Lion's Share:
Pastoral Communities, Biodiversity, and the World Bank

International organizations like the World Bank introduce into the national legal arena concepts and principles which may be seen as 'proto-law' as they do not have the formal status of law yet but in practice often obtain the same degree of obligation. Moreover, through their credit agreements with the state they also introduce what may be described as 'project law' as an additional set of norms. Similarly, concepts like 'good governance', 'co-management', 'sustainability' etc. have all been elaborated in various international treaties, conventions, protocols though they are neither fully developed principles nor show internal coherence (Benda-Beckmann, K. von, 2001). At the national and local levels various sets of actors invoke them as competing with, or overriding, national laws, or use them to ground the legitimacy of national law as well as to advance claims against traditional rights and customary law.

Some of the paradoxes and contradictions of the possibilities of the coexistence of multiple and overlapping legal orders are evident, for example, in the controversy between environmentalist NGOs and the human rights groups which have been at odds with one another over the protection of the rights of lions versus those of the pastoralists in the Gir forest. Whereas the environmentalists champion the cause of wild life protection, the human rights NGOs have been concerned with securing the livelihood and cultural survival of the pastoral communities in the area. The powerful NGO, the Worldwide Fund for Nature–India (WWF–India) with its transnational linkages, draws its moral legitimation as representative of global stakeholders in the environment. It has used its financial resources and media connections to make a case for the displacement of the pastoralists who in its view endanger the survival of the lions. For example, as part of its campaign for the protection of biodiversity, it filed a case in the Supreme Court against the Government of India for failing to implement national environmental laws and policies. Against such a narrow environmentalist agenda, which pits peoples' rights to access commons against conservationist goals, human rights NGOs and the local peoples' movement, supported by a South Asian and Southeast Asian network, have mobilized for the protection of traditional rights of access to, and use of, natural resources based on the customary rights of the pastoral communities. But instead of relying entirely on local norms to make their case, they have also invoked the doctrine of public trust, borrowing from its elaboration in recent American court decisions on environment. They invoke the principle of regarding the state as a trustee rather than as the owner of natural resources that are seen to belong to local communities dependent on them. The American doctrine of public trust is thus used by civil society actors in India to challenge the validity of the continued reliance by the Indian state on the colonial doctrine of 'eminent domain' which secures its sole control of forests, water, and mineral resources (Randeria, 2002a).

Issues relating to both biodiversity conservation and displacement have been at the center of the controversy surrounding the ecodevelopment project of the World Bank in the Gir forest.[7] The Gir sanctuary and National Park are locat-

7. I am grateful to Varsha Ganguly and Ashok Shrimali (SETU, Ahmedabad) for their generosity in sharing with me their experience of the struggle against the displacement of Maldharis from the Gir forest in the context of the World Bank ecodevelopment project and for giving me access to their material on the project and the campaign.

ed in Junagadh district with the Protected Area covering 1,412 square kilometers, out of which 258 square kilometers constitute the National Park with restricted access and complete displacement of the local population. The protected area is the last intact habitat of the Asian lion in the wild with about 284 lions estimated to be living in the area. According to the Forest department's own figures, there are 54 traditional hamlets of pastoralists (*nes*) with an estimated population of 2,540 within the area demarcated for the sanctuary (Ganguly, 2000). These families which belong to several Hindu castes of Rabari, Charan, and Bharwad, including two Muslim communities of Makrani and Siddi, raise livestock and sell milk products. They are collectively known by the occupational term Maldhari (owners of cattle).

In 1972 over 800 families of Maldhari were forcibly displaced from the area defined as the National Park. 600 of these families were resettled under an inadequate rehabilitation program that gave them land in villages near the sanctuary. This half-hearted attempt to turn pastoralists into farmers failed due to the poor quality of land made available to families which had no knowledge of agriculture and no access to the inputs required for cultivation. Within a few years, many successful pastoralists, who had been selling milk and milk products over long distances, were reduced to wage labor. In a survey conducted by the Forest Department in 1971, the families living within the area demarcated for the sanctuary as a Protected Area were divided into residents recognized as 'permanent', those deemed to be 'non-permanent', and those considered to be 'illegal'. Only the 'permanent' residents were granted a so-called 'Maswadi' pass, which entitles them to live with their families and graze their cattle within the Protected Area. This completely arbitrary division of the Maldhari communities has created families, and family members, with differential rights to residence and to carry on their traditional livelihood. It has also ruptured the social fabric making it difficult for those living outside the borders demarcated by the Forest Department to visit the sacred sites of their communities within the Gir forest. Daughters and sisters married into villages on the periphery of the sanctuary, for example, now have the status of 'tourists' who are required to pay for a daily pass to visit their natal kin living in the Protected Area.

The rights of the pastoralists to forest products, grazing land and water resources are sought to be overridden in the name of the greater common good by WWF–India and the state government of Gujarat. They argue that both the local ecological system and the lions are endangered by the traditional grazing methods for the large herds of livestock as well as by the Maldharis' increasing demands for the provision of modern infrastructure and other facilities in the area (such as tarred roads, electricity, schools, and health centers). Following the interim order of the Supreme Court in 1997 in the case filed by WWF–India, the Collector of Junagadh issued a notice evicting the Maldhari families from the Gir sanctuary in view of the proposed conversion of the entire area into a National Park. Human rights NGOs and people's organizations in the Gir area have so far been able to prevent forced displacement as it contradicts the terms of the ecodevelopment project agreement between the World Bank and the government of India. In terms of the overriding commitments accepted by the Government of India in its agreement with the World Bank (World Bank, 1996), for the limited duration of the project and within the six biodiversity project areas, World Bank policies safeguarding the rights of indigenous peoples and protecting those affected by a project from involuntary resettlement prevail over state laws. However, it is far from clear whether these conditionalities will have any permanent or pervasive impact on national resettlement policies or environmental laws.

The Wildlife Protection Act drafted with the expert advice of the Smithsonian Institute (USA) in the 1970s and adopted by the Indian Parliament has provisions for declaring certain areas as 'protected areas' for purposes of setting up national parks or wildlife sanctuaries. Aimed at environmental conservation, it also contains procedures that work in practice to the detriment of the rights of local communities in these areas. WWF–India has found an ally in the Gujarat government and the two have teamed up to protect the environment using national legislation, whereas human rights activists have found an ally in the World Bank—which is committed to the standards laid down in its own operational directives and policies that protect project-affected persons from forced eviction and guarantee the traditional rights of indigenous communities. These also provide for a participatory resettlement and rehabilitation of families affected by a project in a manner which protects their living standards, earning capacity and production potential and further stipulates that these should not deteriorate as a result of a World Bank project. So that ironically, the displacement envisaged by the Gujarat government and the WWF–India in consonance with national law has been temporarily averted by NGOs invoking World Bank norms. As the displacement would have contravened credit conditionalities accepted by the Government of India as signatory to the agreement with the World Bank, the federal government prevailed on the regional government to stop all forced eviction. But this fine balance is likely to last only as long as the World Bank project does.

In order, therefore, to anchor peoples' rights to natural resources in a more permanent policy framework beyond the short-term validity of the project law of the World Bank, human rights NGOs have advocated more systematic changes. They would like a program of joint participatory management of national parks and sanctuaries modeled on the Joint Forestry Management programs in which local communities and the state act together to preserve the forests. These joint conservation programs are premised on the assumption that local communities, especially indigenous people, are the best protectors of their environment. Having lived in a symbiotic relationship with nature since centuries, they are assumed to have a traditional way of life and alternative local knowledge that enables them to live in harmony with their environment. Apart from the tendency to romanticize indigenous people within a global anti-statist environmental discourse that valorizes local knowledge (Benda-Beckmann, F. von, 1997), a primarily ecological view makes the local community's access to commons contingent on their conservation skills and intentions (Benda-Beckmann, K. von, 1997) rather than framing the question in terms of their rights to land, forests, and water for their livelihood. It may thus freeze the cultures and lifestyles of these communities in time, so that an obligation to continue with their traditional way of life is a price they may have to pay for their non-displacement from their ancestral lands and forests. Demands by Maldhari communities in the Gir forest for modern amenities like electricity, or metalled roads linking their settlements *(nes)* with the markets for their dairy produce outside the protected area, are rejected by the WWF–India and the Forest Department in the name of wildlife conservation. What appears at first sight to be the autonomy to pursue their own way of life may turn out to be an obligation to do so, an "enforced primitivism" (Wilder, 1997: 217) in the interests of biodiversity and the Asiatic lion.

4. Civic Alliances Contest State Control over Natural Resources

Human rights NGOs present a case for peoples' rights over natural resources which goes much beyond the highly limited protective approach to displacement outlined in the World Bank policy as well as the sympathy for the mere participation of local communities as conservationists in the global environmental discourse. An all-India network of NGOs has recently challenged the very basis of such a policy, and of national laws, which recognize only individual rights for purposes of compensation disregarding the collective rights of communities to access natural resources. The Campaign for Peoples' Control Over Natural Resources is a large new nationwide coalition of NGOs, including one from Gujarat, which seeks to reassert and protect the collective customary rights of local communities (e.g. pastoralists, fishing communities, marginal and poor farmers, landless laborers, and indigenous peoples) to land, water, and forests. Apart from court battles, many of the NGOs involved in the new network have been involved in local mobilization and resistance on these issues for several years.

The entire problem of access to, and use of common property resources, has acquired a new urgency due to the policies of liberalization and privatization introduced by the Indian state under the directive of the IMF and the World Bank. The central government itself admits in the new draft National Policy for Rehabilitation of Persons Displaced as a Consequence of Acquisition of Land that economic liberalization and an increase in private investment will generate a greater demand for land as well as for mineral resources and reserves located in regions inhabited primarily by tribal communities. Yet instead of a just and humane rehabilitation policy (based on a process of consultation and respect for democratic rights of the displaced, which would take into account the ground-level realities and complexities of land use and traditional rights to commons) the new policy only seeks to ensure efficient expropriation and legal security in the interest of investors. Increasingly, areas seen as 'wasteland', forests, and coastal areas under special environmental protection through the Coastal Area Zonal Plan are being acquired by the state and made over to industries at nominal prices. That such iniquitous development destroys the traditional agricultural, pastoral or other patterns of livelihood of those who are forcibly displaced, economically marginalized, and rendered assetless seems to be an acceptable price for inexorable industrial growth and progress. Here is where the 'enabling state', representing the sectional interests of the rich in the name of 'national interest', comes increasingly into conflict with those of its citizens living in poverty who are dependent on common property resources of land, water, and forests for their survival. Paradoxically, the proliferation of national and supranational environmental and human rights law, and an expansion of its scope, goes hand in hand with the erosion of the collective rights of communities, their traditional access to the commons and their right to determine for themselves a vision of the good life. Ecologically sustainable agriculture or pastoralism, which is either at the level of subsistence or produces for the market without large-scale commercialization, finds no place in official plans and policies. In the view of capitalist development shared by the state and the World Bank, 'backward' peasants, pastoralists, and tribal communities are to be modernized through integration into the 'national mainstream' and the market economy. The promise of industrial wage labor is held out as a stepping stone to higher income and skills for setting up independent business, a mirage of mobility into the middle classes which is no more than "a myth inspired by wishful thinking" as Jan Breman in his trenchant critique of the 1995 World Bank Development Report has argued (Breman, 1997: 88).

Liberalization has meant a shrinking of state responsibilities but not a shrinking of state apparatus just as it has not led to less state interventionism but rather to state intervention in favor of capital (Randeria, 1999). Through a combination of legislative and executive measures, the Indian state has been seeking to undermine the access of local communities to their natural resources and their control over them. As the Campaign for People's Control Over Natural Resources[8] has pointed out in its appeal published in November 2000, the increasing pressure of privatization and industrialization under the neoliberal regime is eroding people's rights to land, water, and forests, turning theses common resources into sources for private profit. The Campaign has drawn attention to two extremely worrying recent developments in this regard—the proposed amendments to the Land Acquisition Act of 1894 and the proposed amendments to the Schedule V of the Constitution.

Of colonial provenance, the Land Acquisition Act of 1894 (revised in 1986) enables the state to acquire land for a public purpose without recognition and protection of people's right to their natural resources and without consulting them beforehand. The post-colonial state has so far used it to dispossess and displace some 30 million people for large-scale dams and irrigation projects, urban development schemes, wildlife parks and sanctuaries. Most of those forcibly evicted have been the rural poor and about 40 percent of the displaced belong to indigenous communities whose rights the government of India as a signatory to the ILO Convention 107 is obliged to protect. They have hardly received any adequate compensation in the absence of a national law or policy on resettlement and rehabilitation which has been a long-standing demand of NGO networks who have presented an alternative draft peoples' policy on rehabilitation for public discussion.

Under the new policies of economic liberalization, there has been a rapid increase in land alienation by the state on behalf of private industries and mining companies. Simultaneously, there has been an increase in both spontaneous, sporadic, unorganized local resistance to these developments as well as more organized protest through networks of NGOs and social movements throughout the country. As the Land Acquisition Act of 1894 only enables the state to acquire land for a *public purpose*, the central government is now proposing to amend the law to allow confiscation of land by the state on behalf of private

8. My thanks to Achyut Yagnik (SETU, Ahmedabad) for clarifying many of the issues raised in this paper in the course of discussions about the network and the campaign as well as for providing me documents relating to it.

industries and to introduce only cash compensation instead of providing new land for resettlement and cultivation. Ruling in a case where farmers had challenged such acquisition, the Supreme Court recently defined the setting up of private industry to constitute 'public purpose' thus permitting land acquisition by the state for use by private companies. A network of NGOs has started a nationwide campaign to protest against the proposed amendments and have drafted an alternative new Land Acquisition Act. Challenging this redrawing of the boundary between the public and the private, they advocate a participatory process of legislative amendment and a right to information rather than the shrouding of these new laws and policies in secrecy.

In September 1997, the Supreme Court had given an important judgment restraining state action and upholding the rights of Adivasi communities (indigenous peoples) to life and livelihood and to land and forests in Scheduled Areas reserved for them by the constitution. Responding to a case filed by Samata, an advocacy group for Adivasi rights in Andhra Pradesh on the issue of mining in Scheduled Areas, the Court had held that government or tribal community-owned forests and lands in these areas cannot be leased out to non-tribal or to private companies for mining or industrial purposes. It declared all such leases by various state governments to be null and void as they contravene Schedule V of the Constitution. It decreed that mining activity in these areas could only be carried out by the state Mineral Development Corporation or a cooperative of the tribal communities subject to their being in compliance with the Forest Conservation Act and the Environment Protection Act (SETU, 1999). The Supreme Court also recognized that under the 73rd Amendment to the Constitution, organs of local self-government at the village level like the Gram Sabha and Panchayats are competent to preserve and safeguard the natural resources of the community and thus once again it reiterated the right of self-governance of Adivasi communities.

This landmark judgment, known as the Samata judgment, was an important check on the illegal practices of the state that encouraged an uncontrolled commercialization of land, forests and water. The Supreme Court dismissed the subsequent appeals by both the regional state government and the federal government that tried to overturn this decision against an environmentally unsustainable and economically inequitable industrialization. Under pressure from multinational corporations and Indian industry, the federal government has been seeking avenues to circumvent the judgment. The Ministry of Mines proposed, for example, an amendment to Schedule V of the Constitution with a view to remove all restrictions on the transfer of tribal and government lands in Schedule Areas. The proposed amendment of the Schedule V, was to be brought to discussion in Parliament during the winter session of 2000–2001, and would have permitted land acquisition by the state on behalf of private companies not only for public purposes but also for engaging in production for private profit. The amendment did not foresee any participatory process in which public purpose could be determined jointly by those communities whose rights to land, forests, and water, and rights to a traditional way of life and livelihood are to be affected adversely. NGOs and social movements, who had been demanding such a consultative process and guarantees of protection since many years, have succeeded so far in blocking the legislation from entering the national legislature.

5. Transnational Coalition Against the Narmada Dam: Global Victories, Local Failures

Given the fact that more and more citizens are now directly affected in their daily lives by the working of international institutions and their policies, it is not surprising that they choose to address these institutions directly with their protests, bypassing the national parliamentary arena in an attempt to transnationalize an issue. However, leapfrogging the national political arena through the use of campaign coalitions focusing on a transnational arena of action and jurisdiction comes at a price. Many of the ambivalences of this emerging global civil society are well illustrated by the long drawn-out struggle against the building of the Sardar Sarovar dam on the river Narmada by the Narmada Bachao Andolan (NBA, Save Narmada Movement) in Gujarat, together with a network of national and transnational NGOs in Europe and the USA. The World Bank was eventually forced to withdraw its financial support comprising some 18 percent of the costs of the dam and 30 percent of the expenditure on the canals. Highly detrimental to the environment, the project was originally expected to displace 70,000 people (an estimate which had to subsequently officially revised to 120,000) from a submergence area of approximately 370 square kilometers (Morse and Berger, 1992). The World Bank itself conceded that it was later discovered that the construction of the canal network of 75,000 km would lead to the eviction and resettlement of at least about another 120,000 people which had neither been planned for in the project nor taken into account at the time of its appraisal by the Bank (Shihata, 2000).[9]

9. Estimates of the number of people to be displaced vary widely and is a highly contested issue between the state and the movement. Irrespective of these competing claims, the Indian state has a dismal record of development induced displacement and the failure to rehabilitate those forcibly evicted. Large dams alone have displaced 16–38 million Indians since 1947, 75 percent of whom are still to be rehabilitated. See the report of the World Commission on Large Dams (2000: 104, 108).

Protest among the displaced communities had initially concentrated on issues of just compensation for the loss of land and livelihood, fair resettlement and rehabilitation policies and their implementation. Transnational linkages with the campaign against multilateral banks led over time to a shift of agendas and priorities. As local mobilization and strategic action came to be focused increasingly on ending the World Bank funding for the project, local grievances came to be articulated increasingly in terms of an environmental discourse which would have international legitimacy and legibility. Gradually a radical 'no large dams' agenda, for which there was growing transnational support, eclipsed concerns about appropriate technological safeguards, displacement, equity, and justice. The vocabulary of the movement as much as the timing of local action was determined by the demands of the global arena and transnational constituency-building instead of seeking to work through regional and national political institutions. Some of the complexities and contradictions of the campaign involving several Indian NGOs, environmental rights groups in the USA, development aid groups in Europe (especially Germany), Japan, and Australia are explored in Jai Sen's (1999) excellent ethnography of the struggle against the dam. It traces the emergence of a new modality of transnational social action, the transnational advocacy network (Keck and Sikkink, 1998), and delineates how the dynamics of local resistance came increasingly to be shaped by the choice of the arenas of negotiation and the structures of the international institutions used as levers of power. The successful strategy whereby social movements and NGOs in the South link up with powerful Northern and especially North American NGOs to use U.S. Congressional hearings as a forum to reform multilateral development banks in general, and the World Bank in particular, has some unintended consequences. It not only reinforces existing asymmetries in power between the North and the South, both at the level of NGOs and national legislatures, but also lends greater legitimacy to these international institutions and the US Congress. Leapfrogging the national parliamentary arena and addressing directly the World Bank, and putting pressure on it through the US Congress and the executive directors of industrial countries, further diminishes the legitimacy of subaltern states in the South.

The movement in the Narmada valley, and the transnational campaign supporting it, led to several unintended long-term structural changes but these were in Washington, DC rather than in India. Jai Sen (1999) argues that, paradoxically, the campaign thus reduced democratic control over the structures of the World Bank by increasing the control of the US Congress and the concentration of power of the major share-holding states of the North (G–7 members control about 60 percent of the vote) over the staff of the World Bank. However, the campaign also resulted in internal changes of control and review mechanisms at the World Bank. Among the latter is the revised information disclosure policy which lays down that specific project information pertaining to environment and resettlement be made known to those affected by the project prior to its appraisal (Udall, 1998). It also contributed to the setting up of the Inspection Panel at the World Bank, which is discussed in the next section, as well as of the World Commission on Large Dams, a forum for the negotiation of a new set of international ecological and human rights standards for large dams in which all stakeholders could participate (World Commission on Large Dams, 2000).

The experience of Indian citizens at a transnational fora like the Inspection Panel have been disappointing, as I will discuss in the next section. But developments at the national level after the withdrawal of the World Bank from the project have not been encouraging either. The Narmada Bachao Andolan's failed attempt to seek judicial remedy in the Supreme Court of India exposed some of the limitations of the use of national courts as arena for social justice as well. It has been as difficult to make an international institution like the World Bank conform to its own resettlement norms and environmental standards as it has been to get judicial remedy against a state which has constantly flouted its own laws and policies. Despite a controversial and prolonged public debate in India the issue has neither been seriously debated in the national parliament nor have any legal or policy changes taken place with respect to mega-dams, land acquisition, involuntary displacement, or resettlement and rehabilitation. The movement in the Narmada valley sought to radicalize the 'damn-the-dams' agenda into a critique of the ideology of gigantism in developmental practice and to broaden national policy to include models of an alternative future, based on small local autonomous projects. But having decided to go to court, it was caught up for years in the Supreme Court negotiating technicalities like the height of the dam. And the government could justify its inaction with respect to policy changes by pointing to the sub judice status of all the issues before the court. In retrospect, the withdrawal of the World Bank from the project may seem like a mixed blessing as under pressure from NGOs in Gujarat, some Bank staff and missions had sought to enforce rehabilitation policies and their implementation. The relative improvement in policies and their enforcement in Gujarat as compared to Madhya Pradesh and Maharashtra can be traced to this donor pressure.

In its writ petition filed by the Narmada Bachao Andolan (NBA) against the federal government in 1994 the movement had asked for a ban on the construction on the dam. It sought this judicial remedy under Article 32 of the Indian Constitution that guarantees every citizen the right to appeal to the Supreme Court in defense of the enforcement of his or her fundamental rights. The NBA contended that the magnitude of displacement caused by the dam was such that a total rehabilitation of those whose land was to be submerged by the project was impossible. More fundamentally, the NBA raised the question of who has the right to define the greater common good and according to which criteria. Whose interest may be defined as the national interest when the interests of the displaced collide with those of future beneficiaries? Can a merely utilitarian calculus (a larger number of potential beneficiaries as compared to the victims) be used to deny poor and vulnerable communities their right to life and livelihood? Is it legitimate for the state to declare one set of partial interests, those of the rich farmer lobby, industrialists, and contractors, to be synonymous with the public good? The NBA thus challenged the very assumption that the state, by definition, acts in public interest and asked for an independent judicial review of the entire project, including its environmental, economic, and human costs.

In response to the petition, the Supreme Court halted further construction on the dam from 1995 to 1999 while asking for reports from the three state governments on the progress in the rehabilitation of 'oustees' as well as on future provisions for them along with expeditious environmental surveys and plans to overcome hazards. In the hearings in 1999, the counsels for the state government of Gujarat had asked the Court to give a clear signal in favor of the dam so that foreign investors would be encouraged to invest in it (Sathe, 2000). It is difficult to judge how much weight the argument carried in the Court's decision to allow construction to be resumed although not much progress had been made on either rehabilitation or environmental assessment. But the argument reflects the priorities and concerns of the government of Gujarat, which chose to privilege the right to security of foreign investment over the fundamental rights of its own citizens.

The final verdict of the Indian Supreme Court in October 2000 was a grave denial of justice as well as a severe blow to people's movements. Moreover, it raised fundamental questions about the very limitations of the use of law courts by social movements in their struggle for social justice. For it took the apex court six and a half years to come to the conclusion that the judiciary should have no role in such decisions! The majority judgment dismissed all the objections regarding environmental and rehabilitation issues relying entirely on the affidavits given by the state governments. It merely asked the Narmada Control Authority to draw up an action plan on relief and rehabilitation within four weeks. As critics of the judgment pointed out, it is hardly likely that the state government will do in four weeks what it had failed to do in 13 years. The majority judgment, which praised large dams and their benefits for the nation, permitted not merely the construction of the Narmada dam but by questioning the *locus standi* of social movements as public interest petitioners, it also sets limits on the future legal options for collective action by citizens against the state. Despite decades of resistance by the victims of development in the Narmada valley, who have borne the brunt of state repression and violence, there has not been much rethinking in state policy on the basic issues raised by the movement—forced displacement; ecological destruction in the interest of industrial development; the search for more environmentally sustainable and socially just alternative models of development which respect cultural diversity; and the right of communities to determine their own way of life.

6. Governance Beyond and Within the State: The World Bank Inspection Panel

A major achievement of the transnational campaign against the Narmada dam was the establishment of an independent Inspection Panel at the World Bank in 1993. It was set up in response to pressure from NGOs for more transparency and accountability as well as to threats from influential members of the United States House of Representatives to block further American contributions to the International Development Association (Udall, 1998). The Panel is by no means a full-fledged body for adjudication, but provides a forum for an appeal by any party adversely affected by a World Bank funded project. The primary purpose of the Inspection Panel is to examine whether the Bank staff has complied with its own rules and procedures and its influence on policy formation within the World Bank is probably limited (Kingsbury, 1999). Barring a couple of exceptions, claims before the Panel so far have only had limited success as Bank staff has usually teamed up with the borrowing country in question to deny any violations. Together they have subverted full-fledged field investigations by the Panel by hastily drawing up remedial action plans for the future. The larger and powerful borrowing countries have supported each other on the Executive Board of the World Bank in resisting investigations that they regard as an infringement into national sovereignty. So the Panel has been increasingly used by civil society actors, as much to publicize the violation of international environmental and human rights norms by their own governments and to pressurize these into compliance as to seek remedy against the World Bank's non-implementation of its own operational policies.

Among the 17 requests entertained by the Panel until mid-1999,[10] two were related to projects in India: the National Thermal Power Corporation (NTPC)

10. For a detailed analysis of the history of the Panel, its procedures and of the cases before it so far, see Randeria (2001).

power generation project in Singrauli in 1997 and the ecodevelopment project (of which the Gir project discussed earlier is a part) in the Nagarhole National park in Karnataka in 1998 (Umaña, 1998). In both cases it was alleged that the Bank management had failed to comply with its own policies on environmental assessment, the displacement of indigenous people, and involuntary resettlement. The request regarding serious flaws in the design and implementation of the ecodevelopment project was submitted by an Indian NGO representing indigenous people living in the Nagarhole National Park. It submitted that no development plans had been prepared with their participation as laid down in Bank guidelines because the project had simply not recognized the fact that they resided within the core project area. The forced displacement of these Adivasi communities from their forest habitat would not only disrupt their socio-cultural life but also destroy their means of livelihood. Although the Bank staff denied any breach of policies and procedures, the Panel, after studying the written documents and a brief field visit, recommended that the Bank's Board authorize an investigation. The Panel felt that "a significant potential for serious harm existed" (Shihata, 2000: 135) as key premises in the design of the project appeared to be flawed. In view of the meager information available to the Bank staff, the Panel felt that the staff could not have been able to foresee during the project appraisal how the project could harm the Adivasi population in the park. Rather than consultations with them *prior to* the project as required by the operational procedures, Bank management stated that it was envisaged to ensure their participation in the implementation stage. Shihata, the then Chief Counsel of the World Bank and a senior Vice President, himself admits that such an approach involves the risk of non-compliance with the World Bank policy of consultation and participatory planning, a "feature, though apparent, was not explained at the time the project was presented to the Board for approval" (Shihata, 2000: 134)!

The Panel noted that in violation of the guidelines on involuntary resettlement, no separate indigenous people's development plan was prepared at the appraisal stage and no 'micro plans'—through which individual families and groups in the protected area can express their needs and get financial support—were under preparation for the Adivasi families, 97 percent of whom wished to remain in the National Park (Umaña, 1998). Despite these findings, and the potential of serious negative impact of the project on the indigenous communities in the area, the Bank's Board decided not to authorize any investigation in 1998. Instead it merely asked the management, together with the government of Karnataka and the affected people, to address the issues raised in the Panel's report and intensify project implementation and micro-planning. Given the long history of non-compliance with Bank guidelines both by its own staff and by the government of Gujarat in the case of the Narmada Dam project, as amply documented in the Morse Commission report commissioned by the World Bank, the Board's decision is a cause for concern. Besides the power of the Bank staff, it reflects the success of executive directors from borrowing countries, including India, as a bloc in thwarting Panel investigations which they regard as an infringement of their national sovereignty. Under these circumstances, NGOs continue to be skeptical about the independence of the Panel, of its limited mandate, and of the difficulties of access to it for people affected adversely by World Bank projects all over the world (Udall, 1997).

In response to the request to the Panel for looking into the NTPC power generation project in Singrauli, the World Bank management conceded, for the first and only time in its history so far, its partial failure to implement some of the Bank's policies. It submitted to the Panel a detailed action plan of corrective measures agreed upon with the government of India. After a review of the records and a brief preliminary field visit, the Panel concluded that although the guidelines regarding indigenous people had not been breached, the possibility of serious violations by the Bank of policies and procedures relating to involuntary resettlement and environmental assessment need investigation. The Panel's investigations confirmed these violations and it noted in its report that the failure "appear[ed] more serious than previously assumed" (Shihata, 2000: 132). The Indian government, however, denied permission to the Panel for a full field-based investigation into the complaints leading the World Bank Board to allow only a desk review of the project. And the Panel watched helplessly as the World Bank remained inactive in the face of a backlash in Singrauli as reprisals against the villagers, harassment and intimidation by local police and project authorities increased.

One is rather surprised to learn from Shihata's account that after this the "Management concluded that 'valuable lessons were learned' from intensive reflection on the request (in the NTPC case) and continued to place emphasis on the implementation of the action plan" (Shihata, 2000: 132)! A decade after the World Bank's and the Government of India's serious violations of environmental and resettlement policies led to the withdrawal of the Bank from the Sardar Sarovar project, one is surprised by the poor institutional memory of the World Bank. Even in the absence of legal liability, what surprises is the World Bank's continued lack of responsibility towards those affected adversely by its projects as well as its infinite faith in the borrowing government's political will and capacity to implement environmental and human rights conditionalities. It is difficult to understand why the World Bank defers supervision of project implementation and, more generally, why it remains insensitive to the social and ecological costs of the kind of development it advocates and finances. Despite the failure of the government of India to issue a national resettlement and rehabilitation policy since decades, the World Bank surprisingly continues to advance credits to it for development projects involving forced displacement. This raises doubts as to the World Bank's seriousness in ensuring compliance with its own credit conditionalities and operational policies. It is not as if the Bank as an institution has not learnt from its past mistakes. Many of the norms enshrined in operational policies reflect the experience of the Bank with the adverse effects of its earlier projects and are the result of sustained lobbying by, and consultations with, civil society actors and representatives of affected communities in many countries. So that World Bank standards often emerge from local sources and are then globally diffused to other international and bilateral development institutions and borrowing countries through their incorporation into Bank policies and practices. A good example of such a process is the norm of land-for-land compensation for those families being displaced by a World Bank project instead of the earlier cash compensation for land acquired by the state. This standard was introduced after the experience of forced displacement and the struggle against the Narmada Dam. But instead of ensuring compliance with it, it is being given up by the World Bank under pressure from borrowing governments and private industries.

Although the World Bank continues to claim immunity from legal liability for the adverse impacts of its projects, parallel to the setting up of the Panel, Bank management began to convert operational directives and policies which were binding on the staff into 'non-mandatory recommendations' or 'Best Practices'—which would render them 'Panel-proof' by placing them beyond the jurisdiction of the Inspection Panel. So that instead of the existence of the Panel affecting greater compliance by the Bank staff with the institution's own standards, the limited desk investigations by the Panel are already leading to a watering down of standards to make them conform to the Bank and borrower's common practice of non-compliance.

7. Conclusion

The empirical material analyzed here demonstrates the uneasy coexistence of several contradictory facets of processes of globalization and resistance to them. If financial and technical aid for the gigantic Narmada project is organized transnationally, so is the protest against human rights abuses, ecological destruction, and state violence. The World Bank simultaneously advocates economic policies in support of privatization and advances credits for large dams and polluting industries that *infringe* on environmental and human rights along with directives to *uphold* those rights. But states eager to follow its directives to create an enabling environment for capital are likely to be brought under the scrutiny of the Bank's Inspection Panel for non-implementation of environment conditionalities and failure to comply with rehabilitation standards. Paradoxically, a proliferation of supra-state governance and an increasing 'juridification' of social life go hand in hand with the erosion of customary rights of the poor to common property resources. However, it may be easier to protect these rights by invoking international norms, the World Bank project law, or credit conditionalities than by relying on national courts and domestic policies.

In any case, the existence of multiple and overlapping transnational legal orders within a particular field may also present a third option for states with a political will and strong democratic institutions; an option between the unrealistic hope of restoring national legal autonomy and the equally utopian dream of an all-encompassing global regulation. National norms could be supplemented and strengthened through a multi-layered approach that could envisage various public and private actors acting within and beyond national borders to establish multi-level public and private regulatory regimes. Rather than pinning one's hopes on the state as a unitary source of normative order, it is important to see the new role of private actors, such as transnationally networked movements and advocacy coalitions, which create, mediate, and weave together norms from different systems into new regulatory webs. Instead of posing the problem in terms of a stark binary choice between national or global regulation, or between state law as opposed to community law, this paper has tried to sketch the contours of an emerging new landscape of "interlegality" (Santos, 1995), a mosaic of supranational regulation, national legislation, alternative people's treaties and policies, project law, traditional rights, and international laws. Any mapping of the changing contours of governance within and beyond the nation-state must trace these complex and contradictory connections between local actors and global discourses, between micro-practices and macro-structures.

As I have tried to show, in such a context the protection of the rights, lives and livelihoods of the most vulnerable citizens in the South will need shifting alliances between their representatives and the states or international institutions. Faced by cunning states and non-accountable international institutions, civic alliances in the 21st century will probably have neither permanent friends nor permanent enemies, but only permanent interests. Changing coalitions according to context, rather than ideological affinities, are thus likely to characterize the politics of civil society actors protesting pauperization and exclusion as they attempt to (re)claim rights to local and global commons.

References

Benda-Beckmann, Franz von (1997) "Citizens, Strangers and Indigenous Peoples: Conceptual Politics and Legal Pluralism." In René Kuppe and Richard Potz (eds.) *Law and Anthropology*. International Yearbook for Legal Anthropology, No.9. The Hague: Martinus Nijhoff Publishers, pp.1–42.

Benda-Beckmann, Keebet von (1997) "Environmental Protection and Human Rights of Indigenous Peoples: A Tricky Alliance." In René Kuppe and Richard Potz (eds.) *Law and Anthropology*. International Yearbook for Legal Anthropology, No.9. The Hague: Martinus Nijhoff Publishers, pp.302–323.

Benda-Beckmann, Keebet von (2001) "Transnational dimensions of legal pluralism." In Wolfgang Fikentscher (ed.) *Begegnung und Konflikt. Eine kultur-anthropologische Bestandsaufnahme*. Abhandlungen der Bayerischen Akademie der Wissenschaften, Neue Folge Heft 120. München: Verlag der Bayerischen Akademie der Wissenschaften, in Kommission beim Verlag C.H. Beck, pp.33–48.

Breman, Jan (1997) "Labour Get Lost: A Late-Capitalist Manifesto. A Stylized Summary and a Critique." *Zeitschrift für Sozialgeschichte des 20. und 21. Jahrhunderts*, 12(1): 83–104.

Ganguly, Varsha (2000) *Impact of Displacement on Quality of life of Maldhari (Pastoral) Women of Gir Forest*. PhD Thesis, South Gujarat University, Surat.

Gill, Stephen (1999) "The New Constitutionalism of Disciplinary Neoliberalism in an Age of Globalization." Paper presented at the Heinrich Boell Foundation Conference 'Feminist Perspectives on the Paradoxes of Globalization', November 5–6, Berlin.

Günther, Klaus and Shalini Randeria (2002) *Recht im Prozess der Globalisierung*. Frankfurt am Main: Suhrkamp Verlag.

Krastev, Ivan (2002) "The Balkans: Democracy without Choices." *Journal of Democracy*, 13(3): 39–53.

Keck, Margaret and Kathryn Sikkink (1998) *Activists Beyond Borders. Advocacy Networks in International Politics*. Ithaca and London: Cornell University Press.

Kingsbury, Benedict (1999) "Operational Policies of International Institutions as Part of the Law-Making Process: The World Bank and Indigenous

People." In G.S. Goodwin-Gill and S. Talmon (eds.) *The Reality of International Law: Essays in Honour of Ian Brownlie*. Oxford: Clarendon.

Kumar, Navleen and Shilpa Shivalkar (2001) "Impact of Land Alienation on Adivasi Women and Children." Paper presented at the Minority Rights Group (London) and SETU (Ahmedabad) seminar 'Development, Equity and Justice: Impact of Globalization on Adivasi Women and Children of India', Hyderabad, September 2001 (to be published by the organizers).

Morse, Bradford and Thomas Berger (1992) *Sardar Sarovar: Report of the Independent Review*. Ottawa: Resource Futures International.

Moore, Sally Falk (2000) "An international Legal Regime and the Context of Conditionality." (Manuscript.)

Santos, Boaventura de Sousa Santos (1995) *Towards a New Common Sense: the Paradigmatic Transition in Science Politics and Law*. London: Routledge.

Randeria, Shalini (1999) "Globalization, Modernity and the Nation-State." In Katja Füllberg-Stollberg *et al.* (eds.) *Dissociation and Appropriation: Responses to Globalization in Asia and Africa*. Zentrum Moderner Orient Studien 10. Berlin: Das Arabische Buch.

Randeria, Shalini (2001) *Local Refractions of Global Governance: Legal Plurality, International Institutions, NGOs and the Post-Colonial State in India*. Habilitation, Faculty of Political and Social Sciences, Free University of Berlin.

Randeria, Shalini (2002a) "Legal Pluralism, Fractured Sovereignty and Differential Citizenship Rights: International Institutions, Social Movements, and the Post-Colonial State in India." In Boaventura de Sousa Santos (ed.) *Another Knowledge is Possible: Beyond Northern Epistemologies*. London: Verso.

Randeria, Shalini (2002b) "Entangled Histories of Uneven Modernities: Civil Society, Caste Solidarities and Legal Pluralism in (post) Colonial India." In Yehuda Elkana *et al.* (eds.) *Unraveling Ties: From Social Cohesion to New Practices of Connectedness*. Frankfurt am Main: Campus, pp.284–311.

Randeria, Shalini (2002c) "Protecting the Rights of Indigenous Communities in the New Architecture of Global Governance: the Interplay of International Institutions, Cunning States and NGOs." Proceedings of the Conference of the Commission on Folk Law and Legal Pluralism, Chiang Mai, April 2002.

Randeria, Shalini (2003) "Domesticating Neoliberal Discipline: Transnationalization of Law, Fractured States and Legal Pluralism in the South." In Wolf Lepenies (ed.) *Shared Histories and Negotiated Universals*. Frankfurt am Main and New York: Campus Verlag and St. Martin's Press.

Sathe, S. P. (2000) "Supreme Court and NBA." *Economic and Political Weekly*, 35(46): 3990–3994.

Sen, Jai (1999) "A World to Win—But Whose World is it, Anyway? Civil Society and the World Bank, the View from the 'Front': Case Studies." In John W. Foster and Anita Anand (eds.) *Whose World Is It Anyway? Civil Society, the United Nations and the Multilateral Future.* Ottawa: United Nations Association in Canada.

SETU (Center for Social Knowledge and Action) (1999) *Development, Equity, and Justice. Adivasi Communities in India in the Era of Liberalisation and Globalisation.* Report on a Roundtable, 6–9 April, 1998. New Delhi: Minority Rights Group.

Shihata, Abraham F. I. (2000) *The World Bank Inspection Panel in Practice.* Washington, DC: The World Bank Information Center.

Udall, Lori (1997) *The World Bank Inspection Panel: A Three-Year Review.* Washington, DC: The World Bank Information Center.

Udall, Lori (1998) "The World Bank and Public Accountability: Has Anything Changed?" In Jonathan Fox and L. David Brown (eds.) *The Struggle for Accountability: The World Bank, NGOs and Grassroots Movements.* Cambridge: MIT Press.

Umaña, Alvaro, (ed.) (1998) *The World Bank Inspection Panel: The First Four Years (1994–1998)* . Washington DC: The World Bank Information Center.

Wilder, Lisa (1997) "Local Futures? From Denunciation to Revalorization of the Indigenous Other." In Günter Teubner (ed.) *Global Law Without a State.* Aldershot: Dartmouth.

World Bank (1996) *Staff Appraisal Report: India. Ecodevelopment Project.* Report No. 4914-IN, August 3.

World Bank (1997) *World Development Report 1997: The State in a Changing World.* New York: Oxford University Press.

World Commission on Large Dams Report (2000) *Dams and Development: a New Framework for Decision-Making.* London: Earthscan.

Corruption, Anti-Corruption Sentiments, and the Rule of Law

Ivan Krastev

D73
H11
K42

1. Introduction

In the unpublished Dictionary of Globalization "C" stands for corruption. It is impossible to understand the strife for global governance without properly interpreting the meaning of the new anti-corruption sensitivity of the last decade. And Eastern Europe is the proper place to study this new anti-corruption sensitivity. Postcommunist societies are simply obsessed with corruption. Corruption is the most powerful policy narrative in the time of transition. It explains why industries that were once the jewels of the communist economies have bankrupted. Corruption explains why the poor are poor and the rich are rich. For the postcommunist citizen, blaming corruption is the only way to express his disappointment with the present political elite, to mourn the death of his 1989 expectations for better life, and to reject any responsibility for his present well-being. Talking about corruption is the way the postcommunist public talks about politics and economy, about past and future.

Outsiders are even more obsessed with postcommunist corruption. For many observers corruption explains why some transition countries succeed and others fail, why reforms are endangered and democracy is at risk, why people are unhappy and the Mafia is powerful. Rose, Mishler and Haerpfer argue that "corruption has replaced repression as the main threat to the rule of law" (Rose, Mishler, Haerpfer, 1997). Their multiple regression analysis suggests that the level of corruption is a more important determinant of attitudes towards "undemocratic alternatives" than the country's democratic tradition, its current level of freedom, or its current economic performance. Corruption steals economic growth, erodes democracy, degrades society, and dooms the chances for the establishment of rule-of-law societies in Eastern Europe.

Corruption is the explanation of last resort for all failures and disappointments of the first postcommunist decade. It is thus the 'black myth' of transition. Rule of law, on the other hand, is the 'white myth' of transition. After some years of flirting with the ideas of democracy and market economy, rule of law is now the magic phrase in Eastern Europe. It is rule of law and not democracy that

135

lures foreign investors, it is rule of law that secures development and protects rights. It is the lack of rule of law that explains the spread of corruption and it is the march of rule of law that will guarantee success in the fight against corruption. What strikes in this new rule of law orthodoxy are the formalistic and anti-political overtones. Rule of law is not portrayed as a society in which rules of the game are respected and the rights of the citizens are protected but as a set of institutional devices and capacity building programs that should free people from the imperfection of democratic politics. And in this rule of law building exercise the special role is reserved for anti-corruption campaigns. Anti-corruption campaigns designed as achieving transparent institutions, raising public awareness and building institutional capacities are viewed by the World Bank and other external policy makers as the critical strategy for promoting the rule of law. But are the anti-corruption campaigns the shortest cut to the rule of law culture and are we aware of the hidden risks of such campaign. The major argument of this article is that the current policy thinking misunderstands the effects of anti-corruption campaigns and by this blurs the prospects for the establishment of rule of law culture in Eastern Europe. The central reason for this misunderstanding is the misreading of the nature of the public's anti-corruption sentiments.

It is a close reading of the attempts to create a state-socialist rule of law in the early 1980s and the analysis of the moral economy of the anti-corruption sentiments in the period of transition that can enlighten us on the dark side of the current obsession with fighting corruption.

The present paper is neither a study of corruption, nor a study of rule of law politics; it is an interpretation of the anxieties of transition. It is a reflection on the popular discourse on corruption and its role in making postcommunist society. Anti-corruption discourse is not simply a discourse on the real or alleged acts of bribery or other forms of misusing public office for private gains. It can not be reduced to the unarticulated public disappointment with the status quo. It is a discourse expressing the painful process of social stratification in the transition societies. It is a discourse on social equality and fairness. It is thus a set of discourses, conflicting with each other and re-constituting the meaning of postcommunist transition.

The anti-corruption pronouncements of the international financial institutions have almost nothing in common with the anti-corruption outcries hosted in the tabloid media, heard on the streets, or captured in focus groups selected by pollsters. What is corruption, who corrupts whom, what are the reasons for the rise of corruption, what should be done to curb it—these are among the questions that will be answered differently depending on whom you ask in a postcommunist society.

"It would be impossible for an historian to write a history of political corruption in the United States," noted Walter Lippmann in 1930. "What we could write is the history of the exposure of corruption." It would be also impossible for a historian to write a history of political corruption in postcommunist Eastern Europe. What we could write is the history of policy responses to corruption and what we can speculate on is the long-term effects of these responses.

2. The Corruption Paradox

It was a commonplace among the ordinary citizens of the Soviet bloc to view corruption and special privileges as the most disgusting features of 'really existing socialism'. Privileges were for the nomenclature; corruption was for the people. People complained about it, lived with it, and protested against it—but dependence on bribes and contacts was notorious. Communism was also described as highly corrupted by various scholars. Towards the end of the communist regime, a majority of respondents in DiFranceisco and Gitelman's survey of Soviet *émigrés* suggested that bribery or connections could be used, among other things, to change an unwelcome work assignment or to get a dull child into a good university department (cited in Miller, Grødeland, Koshechkina, 2001).

A decade ago both the academic community and the wider public and scholars would have been shocked to learn that one day postcommunism would be seen as more corrupt than communism. It is this transformation of the 'unexpected' into 'unproblematic' in the perception of corruption that I refer to as 'corruption paradox'.

3. The 'Non-Banality' of Postcommunist Corruption

What is common between the successful Polish transition, the semi-successful Bulgarian transition, and the unsuccessful Russian transition? Not much, except that the majority of Poles, Bulgarians, and Russians are convinced that in their country there is more corruption today than in the days of communism.

The similarity of this interpretation is striking because the opinions of the Polish, Bulgarian, and Russian public sharply differ in the way they judge the success, direction, and desirability of the economic and political changes, and assess their personal benefits and losses in the period of transition. The result is striking also because in the rankings of the Corruption Perception Index published by Transparency International for 1999, Poland is 44th, Bulgaria is 66th, and Russia 82th, and because corruption is perceived as a major social problem in Bulgaria and Poland, but not in Russia (Sajó, 1998).

The claim that postcommunism is more corrupt than communism can not be explained simply with the failure of market reforms. The success or failure of reforms can be a working explanatory model when we compare the scale of corruption in different countries, but it is a weak explanation when we compare 'now' with 'then'. Culture, religion, the length of the communist rule also do not explain corruption. Poland is a catholic society; Bulgaria and Russia are Orthodox countries. Russia has lived much longer under communism than Bulgaria and Poland. The countries differ significantly in their size and ethnic homogeneity—two other factors that affect the spread of corruption. They differ in GDP, attractiveness to foreign investment, availability of natural resources, and level of economic optimism with respect to the future. The finding that Bulgarians, Poles, and Russian share a common view of postcommunism being more corrupt than communism is an unexpected finding, a non-trivial one. It is worth closer exploration.

Corruption can not be studied directly. The indirect studies of corruption are also problematic. What do we claim when we assert that a certain regime or certain period is more corrupt than the other? Do we claim that during this period the number of corrupt transactions has increased? Do we claim that the number of people involved in corrupt transactions has increased? Do we claim that corruption has reached the highest places of power? Do we claim that the social costs of corruption have increased? Do we claim that society as a whole is more tolerant to corruption? Or do we claim all these together?

How can we know what exactly the respondent wants to tell us when judging that postcommunism is more corrupt than communism? Does he refer to the cost of corruption, to the ugliness of grand political corruption, or to pervasive bureaucratic corruption? Is his judgment based on his personal experience with petty corruption or is his claim based on the media stories about the scale of political corruption? It is also well known that the popularity of corruption practices increase the level of their acceptability. If almost everybody is a practicing 'corrupter' or 'corruptee', then corruption is the rule and not a deviation from the rule. Does it mean that communism look less corrupt because everybody was part of corruption games?

And finally, is really postcommunism more corrupt than communism? The empirical data is controversial and incomplete to sustain such a claim. In most of the communist countries corruption was a taboo topic, so the reliable data on perceptions of corruption or well-documented reports on the spread of corruption acts are not available. The court and police records can not be a source of valid information. Most of them are silent about corruption when it comes to the high ranking communist officials. Communism was a political system based on virtue, so the regime was unwilling to demonstrate the human vulnerability of its outstanding members.

And what kind of definition will be adopted for the purpose of comparison? Should we consider only the corrupt acts that are criminalized in the given period? Should we count only acts that are perceived as corrupt by public opinion, what Heidenheimer called "white corruption" (Heidenheimer, 1989), or should we adopt a more general public interest definition that will define as corruption all those acts that are viewed as corruption today? In interpreting corruption we should face all these and many other constrains.

4. The Debate

In the current debate various approaches compete in explaining and constructing the corruption phenomenon. They legislate how to think about corruption, what to think about corruption, and how to act against corruption. The dominant anti-corruption discourse of IMF and World Bank is institutional in its nature. For this institutional discourse, the claim that one political regime is more corrupt than other is not an empirical claim. It is a normative claim. This hegemonic discourse measures corruption through the corruption incentives created by various institutional environments. In the context of this approach, regime A is more corrupt than regime B if the discretionary power of public officials and the level of state intervention is higher in regime A in comparison with regime B.

The dissident or perceptionalist view on the rise of corruption is limited in its influence and is perceived by many as the last incarnation of the 'apologists' of corruption. This discourse is not interested in the incentives for corruption behavior that are made available by different political regimes. It starts with the assumption that there is no necessary link between the perception of the public that corruption is pervasive and the actual level of corruption. In the context of this school of thought corruption perception is a product of a given media reality (in the broader sense) and not of any significant changes in the actual spread of corruption. Perception change in Germany in the wake of the 'Kohl affair' is a powerful illustration of the fact that it is the corruption that we know about and not the actual level of corruption that governs public sentiments. Germany after the brake of the Kohl scandal is not more corrupt than Germany in the day before the story was revealed, but the perception of the cleanness of the Berlin Republic has declined dramatically both inside and outside the country. The perceptionalist argument distrusts the consensus that corruption is in the rise. In their seminal study of street-level corruption in four East European countries, Miller, Grødeland, and Koshechkina documented that citizens' actual experience of dealing with street-level corruption is far less negative than their perceptions (Miller, Grødeland, Koshechkina, 2001).

My interpretation of the boom of corruption perceptions in Eastern Europe does not side either with the institutionalists or with perceptionalists. It agrees that the link between corruption perceptions and the actual levels of corruption is highly problematic. But it suggests that when the public compares corruption 'now' and 'then' it does not simply 'count' corrupt acts, nor does it 'count' corruption-related media materials. The judgment on the rise or decline of corruption is mediated by reflections on its social functions. Interpreting the claim reflected in diverse public opinion polls that postcommunism is more corrupt than communism needs to bring in the broader context of actors' experience of social change. Numbers and correlations are not enough for reading public mind. It is in the course of the endless talks about corruption, corrupted and the government's failure to resist corruption that postcommunist citizens negotiate their attitude to the phenomenon. And in the course of these unsanctioned negotiation processes, the consensus that postcommunism is more corrupt than communism is being reached.

5. When Less State Does Not Mean Less Corruption

In arguing that the actual corruption in Eastern Europe has increased, political scientists and economists point to several recent developments. The globalization of trade and financial transactions during the last decade and the end of grand ideological divide count as external reasons for the 'eruption of corruption'. But there are also several 'transition' arguments for the rise of corruption.

From the communist past, particularly the legacy of the interventionist state is singled out as the critical domestic precondition for the rise of corruption. Postcommunist regimes as a rule have inherited a complex system of licenses, permissions, and discretionary powers for state officials. The existence of these discretionary regimes is at the core of the institutional explanation for the eruption of corruption.

The crisis of legitimacy and the eroded trust in public institutions is another part of the explanation. The existence of corruption incentives can not be directly translated into claims for more corruption. Values do matter. The Nordic countries that are known for the significant presence of the state in the economy are among the most corruption-free countries in the world. Corruption incentives increase the actual level of corruption only when they are reinforced by public tolerance to corruption and the absence of professional bureaucracy and rule of law. Social norms are the independent variable in the corruption equation that constrains the ambitions of institutional reductionism.

Not only big governments but also weak states contribute to the pervasive corruption in Eastern Europe. A weak state lacks the capacity to enforce rules and dramatically diminishes the risks connected with corrupt behavior. Weak state is at the heart of the argument developed by Shleifer and Vishny (see Shleifer and Vishny, 1993). In their article titled "Corruption" they suggest that postcommunist corruption is more inefficient than the communist one and as a result, it is more costly. Communist corruption was a centralized one. It was enough to bribe the boss in order to set the chain in action. The model of postcommunist corruption is the model of the independent monopolists. In order to make the transaction happen the corrupter should bribe almost everybody in the chain.

Another argument explaining the rise of corruption in the transition period is the argument of the Hungarian constitutional law professor András Sajó (Sajó, 1998). He suggests that postcommunist corruption is clientelistic in its nature and is closely connected with the forming of new political parties and the redistribution of state assets. Corruption is the hidden tax that society pays for the functioning of the multiparty system. Misrecognition of clientelism for corruption and Western pressure for transparency is the reasons for over-dramatization of the East European corruption problem.

But it is the large-scale privatization that dominates popular explanations for the rise of corruption in the time of transition. Theoretically, and in a long run, privatization is advertised as a corruption-reducing policy. But practically and in a short run privatization increases the level of corruption. The incentives for quick enrichment are so high that corrupt behavior is unavoidable. Polish Minister of Privatization Janusz Lewandowski gave one of the best descriptions of the internal controversy of the process. "Privatization," wrote Lewandowski, "is when someone who does not know who the real owner is and does not know what it is really worth sells something to someone who does not have any money" (quoted by Dunn, 1999).

Lewandowski's definition touches on the three types of trouble with postcommunist privatization. The first is *the pricing of ex-socialist property*. The prices of the socialist enterprises differ dramatically in the eyes of the market and in the eyes of society. The complaint that the state is selling 'cheap' is the most popular complaint in the time of transition. In her study of workers' perception of privatization in one Polish food producing factory Elizabeth Dunn underlines that "the idea of the 'bribe' here is the difference between two distinct measures of value: the supposedly 'objective' measure set by Western accounting or by the market, and Alima workers' subjective opinion of the value of their lives and work under socialism, which were crystallized in the firm" (Dunn, 1999).

The second trouble concerns *the buyers of the former state property*. Domestic buyers for the big and even middle-sized enterprises did not exist in Eastern Europe. State socialism as it existed was not a society of equal prosperity; indeed, at the beginning of the political and economic transition many people still believed that it was the society of equal poverty. It was in the initial years of transition that some got access to credit and became investors and others remained on the side of the selling state. The past of the new owners intrigued public imagination much more than the future of the privatized enterprises.

And the third trouble with privatization is that the very process of privatization was *conceived by many as corruption per se*. The absence of effective control on the black and gray privatization practices acted as a catalyst in rising anti-corruption and anti-elite sentiments. One Czech study identified 33 cases of personal gain in the area of privatization for a 12-month period, totaling 25 billion Czech crowns, but it resulted in only two cases of indictment (Miller, Grødeland, Koshechkina, 2001). And Bulgarian economist Rumen Avramov defined "privatization of the profits and nationalization of losses" as the major formula for creating the private sector in postcommunist Eastern Europe (Avramov, 2001).

The perceptionalist school in explaining 'the eruption of corruption' suggests different readings of the postcommunist obsession with corruption. A number of studies stress the fact that there is low correlation between respondents' personal experience with corruption and their judgment on the level of corruption in the country (Miller, Grødeland, and Koshechkina, 2001). The regular newspaper readers in Bulgaria estimate the country as more corrupt than those who do not regularly read newspapers. Miller, Grødeland, and Koshechkina documented that contrary to the proverb, familiarity bred trust rather than contempt. People tend to view as less corrupt those institutions that they know personally and as more corrupt those institutions that are far away from their daily experience. As a result the Parliament as a rule is viewed as more corrupt than the police. In a paradoxical way, free media is an instrument for controlling and reducing corruption but at the same time it increases corruption perceptions in the society.

The perceptionalist argument suggests that the boom in corruption perceptions is a result of the media's obsession with corruption and the role of corruption accusations in postcommunist politics. Corruption stories sell well. The public loves reading stories of degradation. But commercial explanation is not sufficient. In the time of transition when grand ideological divide is already in history and when policy differences between main political parties are negligible, corruption accusations are the major weapons of the opposition. To accuse the government of being corrupt saves the need to offer alternatives to its policies. In Eastern Europe today there is a distinct prejudice in favor of those who make the accusations. The number of court verdicts on corruption charges is ridiculously small all over the region. The inefficient legal system allows the media to take the roles of both prosecutor and judge. In the postcommunist world, anti-corruption rhetoric is the favorite weapon for anybody seeking power.

In the context of the institutional paradigm transition period creates high incentives for corrupt behavior and the weak postcommunist state constantly fails to respond efficiently. The perceptionalist argument presents the rise of corruption as a media phenomenon. Both arguments are vulnerable in their explanations as to why postcommunist public opinion is convinced that 'today' is more corrupt than 'yesterday'.

Institutional arguments underestimate the role of social and cultural norms in restraining corruption. The perceptionalist argument overestimates the lack of genuine information in the time of late communism. The fact that official channels of information were blocked does not mean that people were ignorant about the spread of corruption in their society. The unofficial discourse has recorded many corruption stories. Thus, we need to include the perspective of the participant in order to offer more convincing interpretations to the corruption paradox. The real question is not whether postcommunism is more corrupt than communism, the real question is why public opinion judges postcommunism to be more corrupt than communism.

6. The Moral Economy of Corruption—'Now' and 'Then'

The introduction of the actors' perspective in interpreting public opinion's view on corruption is the only alternative to institutional and perceptionalist explanations. But the introduction of the actor's perspective is not an easy task. The data provided by anthropological studies and pollsters' assembled focus groups is contextual and heterogeneous, and the risks for misinterpretations are grave. Respondents claiming that postcommunism is more corrupt than communism do not share a common view on what should be and should not be defined as corruption. They come from various social backgrounds and their tolerance with respect to corruption varies. Reconstructing individual motivations for blaming postcommunism for being more corrupt than communism is 'mission impossible'.

The general hypothesis in my essay is that the claim expressed by the respondents that postcommunism is more corrupt than communism is not a factual claim. It is a value statement that includes in itself a reflection on the social function of corruption.

Respondents do not simply 'register' corruption, they judge the result of its work. The key factor explaining the new corruption sensitivity is that a new type of corruption replaced the earlier type, characteristic of state socialist times: bribery replaced *'Blat'*.

Interpretation of the 'corruption paradox' necessarily pre-supposes comparison of respondents' perception of *'blat'* and 'bribe' as the dominant forms of corruption respectively in the communist and postcommunist periods. When they are asked about corruption in the communist period, respondents interpret corruption as *blat*; when the same respondents refer to postcommunist corruption, they mean bribe.

7. "Do-Me-A-Favor Society" Versus "Give-Me-A-Bribe Society"

The mysterious and at the same time prosaic practices that Russians called *blat*, Bulgarians called 'connections', and Poles called *załatwić sprawy (settling things)* are known to be the secret key for understanding the communist society. It is a society in which, according to Guardian reporter Martin Walker, "nothing is legal but everything is possible" (quoted in Ledeneva, 1998).

In her enlightening book *Russia's Economy of Favors*, Alena Ledeneva defines *blat* as "the use of personal networks and informal contacts to obtain goods and services in short supply and to find a way around formal procedures" (Ledeneva, 1998). All authors agree that *blat* is a typically Soviet (communist) phenomenon. *Blat* shares many similarities to pre-modern practices of gift giving and many theorists (like most of the citizens) are unenthusiastic of classifying *blat* as corruption. Among the general public, it is a widely shared view that 'adultery is not a crime and *blat* is not a corruption'. But in essence, *blat* is a classical form of misuse of public position for private or group gains. *Blat* works to the extent to which certain public officials betray their duties in order to favor their friends or friends of their friends.

In her remarkable book, Ledeneva presents a complex analysis of the phenomenon and its role for the survival and erosion of the Soviet system. In the context of my interest in revealing the moral economy of anti-corruption sentiments in Eastern Europe several characteristics of *blat* are of critical importance. *Blat* was a widespread phenomenon all over the Soviet bloc. Living out of *blat* was a form of asocial behavior. *Blat* was an exchange of favors. Even when some gifts and money were involved in the *blat* relations it was the exchange of favors and not the bribe that were the driving force of the relations. In the words of Ledeneva "*blat* is distinctive form of non-monetary exchange, a kind of barter based on personal relations" (Ledeneva, 1998). *Blat* was totally conditioned on the economy of shortages. It was "survival kit reducing uncertainty in conditions of shortage, exigency and perpetual emergency, in which formal criteria and formal rights are insufficient to operate" (Ledeneva, 1998). *Blat* was condemned in the official discourse but it was not criminalized (with the exception of extreme cases). *Blat* relations were not simple barter; they were not necessary dyadic. *Blat* transactions could be circular: A provides a favor to B, B to C, C to D, and D to A, and the last chain might not have taken place. *Blat* exchange is mediated and covered by the rhetoric of friendship. In contrast, the relationship between corrupter and corruptee is centered on bribe.

In the days of communism *blat* coexisted with bribe and other classical forms of corruption. But *blat* was the most popular type of surviving strategy. *Blat* was the paradigmatic form of corruption. Communism was totalitarianism moderated by the spread of *blat* and petty bribery. When respondents reflect on their communist experience *blat* comes as the form of corruption they associate with the old regime. Participants in different focus groups insist that the practice of 'connections' was widely spread in the old days, but the acts of 'real corruption' were much limited than now.

In her book Ledeneva even argues that *blat* should not be classified as corruption. Such a view can be found also when people tell their own *blat* experience. Personal friendship and readiness to help colored participants' *blat* memories. Ledeneva's argument is valuable in distinguishing *blat* from other forms of informal transactions. But it is also true that *blat* was perceived as corruption and that *blat* involves abuse of public office for private gains. Corruption was simply other peoples' *blat*. In the popular discourse 'other people's *blat*' was commented and viewed as a corruption. When a mother explained why her kid failed to enter a university, when a customer complained about not 'obtaining' valuable goods, privileges, and 'connections' were the explanations and they were judged as corruption.

The anti-corruption campaigns that were common feature of the late days of the communist regimes best illustrate the fact that *blat* was perceived as a specific form of corruption and as a practice which erodes public good. The citizen of communist society was aware of the social price of *blat* but he was also aware of the lack of any other realistic alternative for surviving.

The disappearance of *blat* is the key development for understanding the post-communist corruption reality. "Market conditions have changed personal relations and ruined many friendships," stated one of the Russians interviewed by Ledeneva, "there is no room for *blat* as it used to be. It looks like *blat* won't be the same and the very word is going into oblivion." Results of the opinion polls show that *blat* is loosing its significance (Ledeneva, 1998; Miller, Grødeland, Koshechkina, 2001).

The end of the economy of shortage and the rise of the 'real money' changed the rules of the game. The major process observed in all transition countries is the monetarization of the *blat* relations and replacement of *blat* by bribe. The economy of favors was replaced by the economy of paid services. The transition rediscovered the unrestricted power of money. So, it is not surprising that former communist societies reacted to the monetarization of *blat* in the same way the premodern societies reacted in their earlier encounters with modernity (Avramov, 2001).

In my interpretation the perception inside the transition societies that post-communism is more corrupt than communism is linked to the fact that bribes replaced *blat* as the dominant form of corruption. *Blat* networks are reorganized on market principles. *Blat* networks are transformed into classical corruption networks involved in the redistribution of the state assets while other *blat* networks simply disappeared. Personal interests have become business interests. In the view of one of the participants in Ledeneva's survey "finance, licenses, privileged loans, access to business information are the shortages of today" (Ledeneva, 1998).

The critical question is what makes *blat* and bribe so different in the perception of the postcommunist public. Umit Berkman has stressed that corruption behavior is conditioned by the nature of the corrupt act (Miller, Grødeland, Koshechkina, 2001).

The non-monetary character of *blat* is critical in understanding its social acceptability. Citizens are easier to offer presents than money. And officials are more easily asking for favors than for money (Miller, Grødeland, Koshechkina, 2001). But the social acceptability of *blat* can not be reduced to its non-monetary character. In the last years of socialism bribe money was making its carrier in the *blat* relations. It is the latent functions of *blat* and bribes in respectively the communist and the postcommunist system that explain the distinction.

Blat is a socially acceptable form of corruption not simply because it is a non-monetary form of corruption but because it increases social equality in the communist society. It 'allows' participants in *blat* transactions to misrecognize their activities as 'help' and to cover it in the rhetoric of friendship. In most of the studies *blat* is analyzed as an exchange of services and information. *Blat* was the only channel for the unprivileged to obtain deficit goods. It was viewed as a form of protest against the communist regime. But what is even more important is that *blat* was also an exchange of social statuses. In the economy of deficit the power status of the person was defined on one side by his position on the power vertical (being in or out the nomenclature) but on the other side by the access to deficit goods or information. *Blat* destroyed the dependence of consumption on the place in hierarchy. On the queue for a popular but deficit book, it is not the professor or the senior official but the friend of the bookseller who usually won the bid.

In its radical form *blat* has replaced the relations between public roles with relations between people. This redistribution of power sustained and subverted the system in the same time. It made life bearable but it undermined the power relations. Loyalty to one's *blat* network was higher than loyalty to the state. Using the present jargon *blat* empowered the powerless. In the discourse of the majority of the people, 'connections' were unfair but they were the only way to 'give a human face' to the bureaucratic nature of the regime. The word 'bureaucracy' had a connotation more negative than connections. The discourse on corruption under the communist regime was a discourse of *inclusion*.

The social functions of bribe in the postcommunist reality are contrary to the functions of *blat*. Bribe caused the inflation of the social capital defined as *blat*. Monetization of social relations led to the inflation of social investments that ordinary citizen had put in their *blat* networks. Only *blat* networks of the powerful survived in the new conditions. The market deprived the socialist bookseller from his power. The end of the shortage economy inflated bookseller's shares in the *blat* cooperative. Now he has nothing to offer except his friendship. It is also much costly to sustain previous *blat* networks. *Blat* was conditioned not only on the economy of shortages but also on the low costs of communications, coffee and the unrestricted availability of free time. Now it is not possible any more to spend long hours on telephone talking about nothing and to leave the office any time your friend wants to see you.

The transition from *blat* to bribery was painful for postcommunist societies. Bribery can not be covered under the rhetoric of friendship and this makes people feel morally uncomfortable. Bribe contributes to the social stratification making it easier for the rich to obtain what they want. "Corruption causes a distinction where in reality there should not exist difference," stated a participant in a focus group discussion in Sofia. Inequalities of wealth provide the means to pay bribes, while inequalities of power provide the means to extort them (Miller, Grødeland, Koshechkina, 2001).

Why public opinion in Eastern Europe perceives postcommunism as more corrupt than communism? This essay argues for a complex answer. Public judges about corruption not by counting corruption acts or corruption-related media stories. Judgment on corruption is mediated by the social functions of corruption in society. The dramatic change of corruption perception in Eastern Europe in the last decade can not be explained simply with the actual rise of corruption or the boom of media's interest in corruption. Anti-corruption sentiments in Eastern Europe were provoked by the fact that bribe has replaced *blat* as a paradigmatic form of corruption. *Blat* is viewed by the public as a socially more acceptable form of corruption. It was the non-monetary character of *blat* and its role in redistributing goods and power positions that made it look more legitimate in the eyes of the public opinion. Bribery is less acceptable not only because it is more ugly (aesthetically), or because it is more risky (in legal terms). Bribery is less acceptable because it is a mechanism for producing social inequality. A World Bank report states that "inequality within the transition countries has increased in alarming pace. In some countries of the region inequality has now reached levels on par with the most unequal Latin American countries" (World Bank, 2000).

The popular anti-corruption discourse is not a discourse on transparency or good government; it is a discourse on the rise of inequality. This is the reason why anti-corruption discourse is the most popular discourse to criticize market economy and democracy in a society in which market economy and democracy do not have an alternative.

8. The Rule of Law Paradox

In the early 1980s three strange 'criminals' shared a cell in Lefortovo prison in Moscow. They perfectly well symbolized the three most dangerous enemies of the communist system. Lev Timofeev was dissident and economist writing on corruption as institutional problem in communist society. Vahab Usmanov was a top Soviet official, former minister of cotton in Uzbekistan, who in 1986 was executed for corruption and abuse of power. The third inhabitant of the cell was of less importance. He was a former University professor who was arrested for currency speculations and money extraction from his foreign students (Timofeev, 2000). All three stayed in prison at the time when Soviet authorities inspired by Andropov tried to use anti-corruption campaigns and anti-corruption rhetoric as an instrument for replacing the ideological legitimization of the regime with a rational-legal legitimization. The ultimate goal was the creation of a socialist legal state (Holmes, 1993). All three were skeptical about the chances of the undertaking. The ex-minister was struggling to understand why somebody should be put in prison for doing what all senior party officials usually do. It was true that Usmanov was taking bribes and he did not deny it, but was it possible not to take bribes when you should give bribes? The success or failures of Uzbek cotton production depended on the success of the bribe-mediated bargains in the Plan Committee and other federal institutions. For Usmanov, the anti-corruption campaign was a form of the leadership war.

Timofeev was also unable to grasp the logic of the undertaking. For him it was a mystery how Soviet leadership was planning to fight corruption when the very existence of the Soviet system depended on workings of the black markets. Black markets made the life in the Soviet system bearable. The third prisoner did not have a specific argument for mistrusting the anti-corruption campaign but he had a general argument: he mistrusted *anything* that the government did.

The prisoners were right in their skepticism. The Andropov-initiated anti-corruption campaign and the officially tolerated anti-corruption rhetoric did not increase the trust in the government; on the contrary, they contributed to the de-legitimization and the collapse of the communist system. After Andropov's attempt to clean up the system, it became legitimate to claim that the system is corrupt.

In my view there is also room for skepticism that anti-corruption campaigns are the shortest path to rule of law culture in Eastern Europe. An unavoidable trait of the anti-corruption campaign is the constantly expanding definition of corruption. If in the beginning of the campaign the suspicion is that corruption is almost everywhere, already in the middle of the campaign the suspicion is that corruption is almost everything. The final stage is the conviction that almost everybody is corrupt. The fear of corruption accusation paralyses the energy of the government officials and the major objective of the policy makers to opt for solutions that look clean nevertheless of what other disadvantages they can have. Making 'transparency' the ultimate policy incentive explains why Bulgarian government in the last two years became in favor of the auction type of privatization. The criticism that such type of privatization is not the best option for attracting strategic investors and preventing criminal money to enter the process have been ignored. For the government it was more important to prove cleanness than to go for better economic option.

The second disadvantage of the anti-corruption campaigns is that focusing on corruption contributes to the blurring of the lines between different political options. Corruption-centered politics in a way is the end of politics. It moralizes the policy choices to the extent that politics is reduced to the choice between corrupt government and clean opposition. Corruption-centered politics is one of the explanations for the transformation of East-European democracy into protest vote democracies.

The third disadvantage of the anti-corruption campaigning is the increasing unattractiveness of politics as a vocation. A number of young and talented people, who in different environments would likely choose politics or public administration as their vocation, prefer to stay away from these spheres under the present conditions. The claim that politicians are corrupt, by definition, is supported by the majority of respondents in the public opinion polls in countries like Bulgaria, Romania, and Macedonia.

Corruption is a crime very difficult to be proved in courts. This creates specific problems for the political system. It is difficult to understand when anti-corruption investigations of leading politicians are quest for justice and when there are instruments of power struggle. Anti-corruption campaigns as a rule increase the powers of investigating agencies. Loyal to the principles of the rule of law courts face difficulty to produce corruption sentences. There is a huge difference between the politicians accused in the media and the politicians sentenced in the court. The pressure for spectacular verdicts in the war against corruption comes into conflict with the fact that corruption is one of the most difficult crimes to be proved in court. In Bulgaria, practically all ministers that have been in office for the last ten years are investigated or have been prosecuted for corruption-related allegations—but there is no single minister in prison. The result is growing mistrust in the judicial system and growing accusations that the judicial system is totally corrupt.

Contrary to the expectations and intentions of the architects of the postcommunist anti-corruption campaigns, crusade against corruption can be as harmful to the emergence of rule of law culture in Eastern Europe as corruption itself. The anti-corruption rhetoric creates expectations that can not be met by the results of the anti-corruption policies and the major reason for the vicious circle that emerge is the nature of the anti-corruption sentiments in the period of transition. Anti-corruption sentiments are driven not by the actual level of corruption but by the general disappointment with the social and economic changes and rising social inequality. It is this weak correlation between the world of corruption and the world of anti-corruption sentiments that questions the usefulness of the anti-corruption campaigns. What postcommunist societies need are policies that reduce corruption but not a rhetoric that leads to corruption-centered politics.

References

Avramov, Rumen (2001) *Stopanskia XX vek na Bulgaria*. Sofia: Centre for Liberal Strategies.

Coulloudon, Virginie (1997) "The Criminalization of Russia's Political Elite." *East European Constitutional Review*, 6: 73–78.

Dunn, Elizabeth (1999) "Audit, Corruption, and the Problem of Personhood: Scenes from Postsocialist Poland." Manuscript; lecture held at the Wissenchaftskolleg in Berlin, Germany.

Grødeland, Åse B., Tatyana Y. Koshechkina, and William L. Miller (1998) "'Foolish to Give and Yet More Foolish Not to Take.' In-Depth Interviews with postcommunist Citizens on Their Everyday Use of Bribes and Contacts." *Europe-Asia Studies*, 50: 651–677.

Hellman, Joel S., Geraint Jones, and Daniel Kaufmann (2000) *'Seize the State, Seize the Day': State Capture, Corruption, and Influence in Transition*. Policy Research Working Paper, No. 2444. Washington, DC: The World Bank.

Holmes, Leslie (1993) *The End of Communist Power: Anti-Corruption Campaigns and Legitimation Crisis*. Cambridge, UK: Polity Press.

Ledeneva, Alena V. (1998) *Russia's Economy of Favors: Blat, Networking, and Informal Exchanges*. Cambridge, UK: Cambridge University Press.

Meny, Yves (2000) "*Fin-de-siècle* Corruption: Change, Crisis, and Shifting Values." In Robert Williams (ed.) *Explaining Corruption* (*The Politics of Corruption* series, Volume 1). Cheltenham, UK: Edward Elgar.

Miller, William L., Åse B. Grødeland, and Tatyana Y. Koshechkina (2001) *A Culture of Corruption: Coping with Government in Postcommunist Europe*. Budapest: Central European University Press.

Mishler, William and Richard Rose (1997) "Trust, Distrust, and Skepticism: Popular Evaluation of Civil and Political Institutions in Postcommunist Societies." *Journal of Politics*, 59(2): 418–451.

Mishler, William and Richard Rose (1998) *Trust in Untrustworthy Institutions: Culture and Institutional Performance in Postcommunist Societies*. Studies in Public Policy, No. 310. Glasgow: Centre for the Study of Public Policy, University of Strathclyde.

Rose, Richard and Christian Haerpfer (1998b) *Trends in Democracies and Markets: New Democracies Barometer, 1991–1998*. Studies in Pubic Policy, No. 308. Glasgow: Centre for the Study of Public Policy, University of Strathclyde.

Rose, Richard, William Mishler, and Christian Haerpfer (1997) *Getting Real: Social Capital in Postcommunist Societies*. Studies in Pubic Policy, No. 278. Glasgow: Centre for the Study of Public Policy, University of Strathclyde.

Rose-Ackerman, Susan (1994) "Reducing Bribery in the Public Sector." In Duc V. Trang (ed.) *Corruption and Democracy*. Budapest: Institute for Constitutional and Legislative Policy, 21–28.

Rose-Ackerman, Susan (1999) *Corruption and Government: Causes, Consequences, and Reform*. Cambridge UK: Cambridge University Press.

Sajó, András (1998) "Corruption, Clientelism, and the Future of Constitutional State in Eastern Europe." *East European Constitutional Review*, 7(2): 37–46.

Shleifer, Andrey and Robert Vishny (1993) "Corruption." *Quarterly Journal of Economics*, 108: 599–617.

Timofeev, Lev (2000) *Institutcionalnata Korupcia*. Moscow: Moskovskiy Gosudarstveniy Universitet.

World Bank (2000) *Anticorruption in Transition: A Contribution to the Policy Debate*. Washington, DC: The World Bank.

III.

The Global Trade System
and Development

Why Trade Must Triumph in the 21st Century: Lessons from the Past[1]

Jean-Pierre Lehmann

F10

1. The Market

The market is undoubtedly one of man's greatest achievements. It is also universal: markets are found in all countries in all continents. In the early stages of human development, men were self-sufficient. They would hunt and gather for themselves and their family. As agriculture developed and human society became more complex, the recognition that men and women could share and benefit from their respective advantages arose. The market is the venue for people to exchange. The market is where people bring produce, but also skills. The 'letter-writer', or scribe, was, for a long time, a prominent feature of the market: someone who could read and write and thus help those who could not, to write to their loved ones, fill out legal forms, etc. This feature of the market still exists in countries with high levels of illiteracy, for example in Brazil, as witnessed in that magnificent film *Central do Brasil* by Walter Salles.

The market, especially in ages and places that had not yet experienced mass means of communication, education and entertainment, was where people also engaged in communication, education and entertainment. In the great market town of Córdoba in Andalucía, southern Spain, under Arab rule in the eleventh and twelfth centuries, where Muslims, Jews, and Christians lived prosperously and peacefully side-by-side, philosophers such as the Muslim Averroës, the Jew Maimonides, and their followers exchanged ideas.

In his very moving novel on the history of Bosnia and Herzegovina, *The Bridge on the Drina*, Ivo Andrić traces the impact on a village and its bridge of the vicissitudes resulting from different invasions, annexations, occupations, main-

1. Many of the thoughts that emerge here have featured in discussions at Evian Group meetings. Gratitude and recognition must be given to the Chairman of the Evian Group, Mike Garrett, and to the intellectual wealth, depth and generosity of all its members. From the Evian team, I also wish to acknowledge a strong debt to Rachel Thompson, who has in particular stressed the link between trade and human rights; to Maria de la Fuente, for posing probing questions on trade and social responsibility; to Marc Laperrouza for his many contributions, including the impacts of technology on governance and the impact of China; and to Valerie Engammare for all her research assistance. Of course I bear sole responsibility for the contents of these pages.

ly between the Christian Austro-Hungarian Empire, Serbia, and the Muslim Ottoman Empire. This history created the religious composition of Bosnia and Herzegovina that survives—even if with difficulty—until today. Throughout these vicissitudes, the market on the bridge was constant, one place where the whole village and its constituent parts could congregate. That is why, among the many atrocities that occurred during the war in Bosnia and Herzegovina, while the death toll and the number of injured (sixty-eight and two hundred respectively) were by no means among the highest, the massacre of the Markale market in Sarajevo on February 4, 1994 nevertheless stands out as especially heinous. It was not just the blood, but also the symbol.

Going to market as a reflection of a natural human aspiration can also be illustrated from the abysmal and extremely costly failures of Stalin in Russia, Mao in China, and Pol Pot in Cambodia (among others) in the collectivization or communization of agriculture and the abolition of the market. When the murderous madness of the Cultural Revolution ended in China in the mid-1970s, peasants returned to the market with alacrity and enthusiasm. The market corresponds not just to a human physical aspiration, but also to a spiritual aspiration. Although most of the conversation will not be at the level of Averroës or Maimonides, it's the right place to exchange gossip, to cultivate relations, to flirt, and so on.

The idea that the market is synonymous with the jungle—perpetrated by such 'luminaries' as former French Prime Minister Edouard Balladur—is total nonsense. The market can only function if rules are properly observed and there are ample doses of mutual respect not only between buyers and sellers, but also, of course, among-sellers. It is quite striking how even in countries easily given to disorderly chaos, the market-place tends to stand out as a model of exceptional orderliness. The market—hustle, bustle, and noise notwithstanding—is a highly civilized place.

The very fundamental attraction of the market is also evidenced by the fact that even in the most developed societies with high levels of internet penetration, open-air markets—for fish, furniture, flowers, canaries, hats, antiques, and so on—remain highly popular. Especially in those societies blessed with multi-ethnic populations, the market is where one is likely to find the highest degree of heterogeneity, as, for example, a Sunday stroll down Lincoln Road in Miami Beach reveals.

The global market of the 21st century is—or should be!—an extension of the village market through time and space. But in order for the global market to achieve and sustain its potential impact and myriad benefits, three very important points must be remembered:

1. There is a very close association between the market and the village. Thus if there is to be a global market that will be both dynamic and sustainable, there must be a global village. And for the village to function, respect, communication, and education are essential. Markets do not operate in isolation from their cultural habitat. Cultures are dynamic and subject to change, but cultures remain distinct. The idea that the global market will become one vast homogenous place where all cultures and people will be alike, and therefore no effort is called for to understand the diverse cultures that compose the market, is (fortunately!) as much nonsense as Edouard Balladur's equation of the market and the jungle.

2. Markets are the antonym of monopoly. There is no market with a single stall. The best markets are those from which one can choose one's oranges or mussels from several stalls. Thus markets are about healthy competition, but also about tolerance and compromise. A strong market position must not be abused, as ultimately it might risk destroying the market. This is true of goods or technologies, but also of cultural and linguistic attributes. It is indeed fantastic that the global market of the 21st century should have a global *lingua franca*, and that it should be English—a very rich, creative, and reasonably (grammar-wise) simple language. Everyone operating in the global market should learn to speak English, but native English speakers should not abuse their linguistic market position. For English language speakers to learn how to speak other languages provides the respect, understanding, communication, tolerance and compromise that will make the global market function dynamically and in sustained fashion. Native English language speakers must avoid being arrogant and imperialistic.

3. As has been mentioned, but must constantly be stressed, though the market may appear dominated by hustle-and-bustle, in reality no market operates properly without rules. The market must embody the principles and practice of a level playing field. Free and fair are congruent.

There is another point that needs to be stressed. Though the market is a central dynamic hub of the village, it is not, of course, the village's only institution. A proper village needs a school to educate the young, a hospital to care for the sick, a nodal point for transport in-and-out of the village—in the modern age, generally a train station—a garrison, or some form of *gendarmerie*, to ensure security, etc. As Soros has written, a distinction in respect to human needs must be drawn between private goods and public goods (Soros, 2002). The market, so long as it properly observes rules, will function best in response to basic laws of supply and demand, and thus is the ideal provider of private goods. If the villagers are not at all *aficionados* of olives and peppers, then ultimately the olive and pepper stall will disappear. The minority who liked olives and peppers will feel deprived, but life will go on and they will survive. The same, however, cannot and *must not* apply to the school, the hospital, the transport station or the garrison. It is not up to the market, but to the political authority (in whatever form) to ensure the proper provision of these public goods. This is not the same as saying that the state must control or monopolize the provision of these public goods—indeed provision of some public goods by the private sector may be less costly and more efficient—but it is to say that the provision of these goods cannot be left entirely to the market.

It is emphatically wrong, therefore, to say that the state and the market are forces of opposition. When both are functioning properly, they are complementary and indeed reinforce each other. South Korea in the 1960s was one of the poorest countries in the world. The South Korean state undertook to provide its citizens with ample and strong public goods—one of the world's best primary and secondary education systems, a good national and international transport infrastructure, good medical care ensuring the strong health and longevity of the population and, of course, a strong garrison to defend the country from the lunatics inhabiting the northern part of the Korean peninsula. South Korea was transformed from being a third-world basket case to one of the global market's most active players. Conversely, the United Kingdom is today in danger of slipping seriously in the global market primarily because three of the four providers of key public goods—education, health, and transport—are seriously deficient.

2. Trade

To trade literally means to engage in the exchange, sale, or purchase of goods. Trade initially—and in many places still today—consisted of barter. "In exchange for six eggs and a small pot of honey, you will write a letter to my son who lives four villages away telling him that all the family is well and that Mathilda is expecting another baby for June." In her interventions in Evian Group meetings, Rachel Thompson has insisted that trade should be seen as a basic human right. Certainly it is a natural human impulse, driven by a combination of ambition and curiosity. As the village market developed, greater profit and learning might be gained from going to the next village, then the village beyond, etc. Marketers, driven by ambition and curiosity, traveled their universe and returned laden with gold and knowledge—if not always the former, at least the latter. Those who stayed in the village were a much duller lot. The former made the world go round, the latter believed it was flat.

For a good deal of history, trade is associated with learning and discovery—discovery not only of ever more distant lands, but also of other forms of

158

resources, produces and skills. Marco Polo, as legend has it, returned to Venice from China not only with noodles, but also with magnificent stories of Cathay. It also tends to be associated with learning and understanding and conjures up romantic images.

In ancient and medieval times, the great silk road linking China and Europe, passing through Bokhara, Samarkand, Tashkent, Urumchi, and so on, until reaching Ch'ang-an (Sian) in China, saw silk coming west, in exchange for wool, gold, and silver going east. Simultaneously, teachings derived from Christianity went east and ones derived from Buddhism and Confucianism came west. Prior to the rise of the European (Portuguese, Dutch, English, and French) sea-borne empires, in the later Middle Ages trade between Europe and South-East Asia (e.g. spices from Indonesia) was dominated by Muslim traders from the Levant. The spread of Islam across great swathes of maritime South-East Asia occurred as a result of trade.

To say that trading activity is exclusively a peaceful activity is, of course, wrong. Trade, however, inclines towards peace. The savagery of the Crusades or of the Spanish *Conquista* in Latin America, to cite two examples, had nothing to do with trade. Both were driven by the desire for spoils, by fanaticism and by militaristic adventurism: for God, Gold, and Glory. One must also be very careful not to imply that trade is a moral activity: it is neither moral, nor immoral; it depends on how it is conducted and what is traded. Thus, though trade in silks, spices, and herbs will generally benefit all parties concerned—producers, traders and users—this is of course not true of the trade in arms or in drugs. The slave trade is one of the ugliest pages of human history. This point again emphasizes the one made earlier, namely that the market and trade need to be subjected to regulation, whether to uphold principles of fairness or, even more so, to uphold principles of basic humanity.

The role of trade as a driver of history, in the rise and fall of nations, deserves strong emphasis, not only for the interest it presents as an intellectual exercise, but also for the lessons to be derived in the emotional contemporary debates about globalization. The strong correlation between trade and curiosity is evident in China's decline three centuries ago. There was no doubt that China was a very advanced civilization, not only in the arts, but also in science and engineering. The Chinese invented the printing press, suspended bridges, gunpowder, and many other things. The Chinese also gained great power. However, at a time when China had reached greatness and its fleets circumnavigated a good deal of the globe and it stood on the threshold of achieving the status of global power, in fact its sense of economic and cultural self-sufficiency led it to display power, rather than gather knowledge. Having traveled the distant seas, but seeing no material or intellectual benefit to derive, China turned in upon itself and more than two centuries of decline set in, from which the country is only beginning to recover now.

In contrast, the European sea-borne empires, especially the Dutch, the British, and subsequently the French, tended to be composed of both avid traders and avid learners. For example, during some two centuries, Japan remained closed to the outside world with the exception of a tiny trading station operated by the Dutch in the Bay of Nagasaki. The minute detail with which the Dutch recorded the customs, flora, and fauna of Japan made their writings major sources of reference.

2.1 Trade and Empire

European superiority in cartography, naval construction, military strategy and industry, ultimately drove a handful of European nations to dominate the planet. Historians have debated extensively the question whether Empire was driven by the flag following trade or trade following the flag: was it the governments of nation-states that engaged in imperialism for whatever reason—national glory, demography, and so on—who then encouraged their traders to follow, or was it merchants engaged in opening markets and needing the state (and its armies and navies) to impose itself on recalcitrant governments? In any case, trade loomed as a very large dimension in the history of Empire. As the European powers rose, however, bloodshed and deprivations ensued. Thus, while the early settlers in North America initially came to trade with the Amerindians, soon afterwards they slaughtered them in order to take their land. The development of the slave trade as an adjunct of the rise of the European powers has been noted. The arrival of the British in India was supposed to be about commerce—even if initially dominated by a state enterprise, the East India Co.—but culminated in colonization that lasted 190 years. As to China, again though the initial objective was to engage in peaceful trade, the British resorted to trade in opium, which led to the Opium Wars (1839–1841 and 1856–1860). The Opium Wars, apart from the slaughter of human beings, also degenerated, through the sacking and pillaging of the Summer Palace in Beijing in 1860—so much for learning!

Though it is said that trade is not a zero-sum game, but a win-win situation for all sides concerned, the 'package' that the European powers presented to the world in the age of Empire had rather different results. In this package, trade was one component; but other components included military clout, political authority, scientific advance and industrial superiority. With the exceptions of the

160

United States and Japan, which by the end of the 19th and early 20th centuries were beginning to emerge as economic powers in their own right, most of the rest of the world served as Europe's economic satellites—whether as markets for Western industrial goods; sources of raw materials for European factories and households; sources of labor (slave, indentured, or just cheap); or as destinations of European emigration.

There can be no doubt that this tremendous European upsurge has had lasting consequences and, even if not necessarily by design, has resulted in what may seem a tremendous injustice. Thus, with the age of discovery and the rise of the European sea-borne empires, its rivals, such as China, India, and the entire world of Islam, went into eclipse. Though there has been some redistribution between the principal players, the world economy today is a consequence of the centuries of uneven economic development that ensued. The 16 percent of the world population that is of European extraction produces about 75 percent of world GDP.

In the course of the last half-century, there has been a degree of shift, but only a marginal one. The Netherlands, with a population of 16 million people has almost the same proportion of world exports of merchandise products (3.6%) as the People's Republic of China (3.7%) with its population of 1,280 million. The advantages of history are obviously quite overwhelming. Countries with a head-start in the game of international trade possess the know-how, the infrastructure, all the trade related institutions and activities (insurance, law firms, shipping, education, and so on) and of course key players in the global market. The Netherlands may be a small country, but Shell, Unilever, Philips, Heineken, Akzo, are (or have) globally known brand names. Hong Kong's (3.5% of world merchandise exports) traditional role as a center of *entrepôt* trade ensures it will continue as a forceful global actor despite its relatively small size (7.2 million people).

Looking at the world's 20 leading exporting nations in 2000 and comparing the list with the one from 1900, the only major players to have totally disappeared from the league are Argentina and Portugal. Otherwise, all of the former European sea-borne colonial powers are still prominent there, as are some of the smaller European states, namely Belgium, Switzerland, and Sweden. The three emerging economic powers of the early 20th century, the United States, Germany, and Japan, are, in the early 21st century, respectively in first, second, and third positions as the world's leading exporting nations. The most noticeable 'newcomers' are the four Asian 'NIEs'—newly industrialized economies—South Korea, Taiwan, Hong Kong, and Singapore. The only two other newcomers are Mexico and Malaysia, both of which have become major export platforms for foreign investors. Malaysia is one of the world's most important hubs of semiconductor manufacturing, while trade from Mexico has been in great part driven by investments following the country's joining NAFTA.

In the course of the first half of the 20th century, two very big problems developed in respect to the international trading situation, the legacies of both of which remain in the early 21st century. One was the use of trade as a tool of offensive nationalist policy. The second was the disparity between the metropolitan industrial powers and the 'satellite' commodity suppliers, with the latter seemingly doomed to dependence on the former.

2.2 Trade and Nationalism

The century following the defeat of Napoleon (1815) until the outbreak of the First World War (1914) was Western Europe's grand apogee, when the Europeans, in Victor Kiernan's phrase, perceived themselves as "the lords of human kind" (Kiernan, 1969). Generally peaceful conditions in Western Europe prevailed over an extraordinary demographic, economic, industrial, social, cultural, scientific, and military boom. However, simultaneously with the flourishing expansion of the Western European states occurred the disintegration of the Central and Eastern European Empires (Austria-Hungary and Russia), as well as that of the Ottoman Empire. In Asia, the emergence of Japan contrasted with the submergence of China. Whereas economic forces had been driving forces in establishing Empires in their initial stages, by the latter part of the century, nationalism and militarism came increasingly into play. Nationalism was also rising as a powerful force throughout Europe—notably in the Balkans—and indeed across the planet. The chemistry that blew up in the First World War had been made of various explosive compounds.

The 'settlement' at the end of the war was motivated by retribution, indeed revenge, and the determination on the part of the victors to emasculate the vanquished. The war exhausted Europe; the peace settlement crippled it. All over the world, the decades following the First World War witnessed the spread of nationalism, racism, and chauvinism. Then, with the Great Depression of 1929, the international economic order collapsed. Resulting from the growing strength of totalitarian doctrines—fortified by the Revolution in Russia and the establishment of fascism in Italy, Germany, Spain, and Portugal—and the virulent crescendo of xenophobia, but also by the apparent bankruptcy of capitalism, liberalism was jettisoned. In this awful climate of the 1930's, trade became a weapon of nationalist confrontation and discrimination. Thus the 1930s witnessed all forms of 'trade warfare': protectionism, dumping, 'beggar-thy-neighbor', boycotts, and competitive devaluation after the abandonment of the gold standard. Trade war did not cause the Second World War, but it preceded and precipitated it.

Going against the tide, indeed the tidal wave, of economic nationalism, in 1937, Cordell Hull, at the time Franklin Roosevelt's Secretary of State, wrote: "I have never faltered and will never falter, in my belief that enduring peace and the prosperity of nations are indissolubly connected with friendliness, fairness, equality and the maximum practicable degree of freedom in international trade" (Hull, 1948: 355).

The position of Cordell Hull and other statesmen who have espoused the principles of free and non-discriminatory trade is partly, of course, based on theory, but also on a basic and empirically verifiable fact. In a trade war, there is no victor. If, for example, country A goes to war with country B over.a piece of territory and country A wins, in spite of some losses of men, it wins: it gets the territory, its riches, its resources, its strategic position, etc. If, however, country A forbids the import of products from country B, then while country B will lose in foreign revenue, the citizens of country A who depend on or even simply have a predilection for the imports from country B will be deprived. This in itself is not a case for never using trade sanctions, but it does nevertheless provide a powerful argument of why it should be used rarely and selectively and that it should be done in the full realization that while one may be aiming one's gun at the 'enemy', in trade battles one almost invariably ends up shooting oneself in the foot—or worse! An open trade policy is not about altruism, but is perhaps one the best and most blatant manifestations of enlightened self-interest.

It was in that spirit that Roosevelt and Churchill met in mid-Atlantic on August 14, 1941; there they drew up the *Atlantic Charter*, in which they gave prominence to the concept of freedom of trade. In the fourth clause of the Charter, they proclaimed that in the peace settlement and the new order that would follow the end of the war, "all States, great or small, victor or vanquished, [should enjoy] access, on equal terms, to the trade and raw materials of the world, which are needed for their economic prosperity" (*Atlantic Charter*, August 14. 1941). These principles were embedded in the spirit and letter of the Bretton Woods institutions that were established at the end of the war. In total contrast with the settlement after the First World War, when harsh punitive measures were imposed on the vanquished, the objective in 1945 was economic reconstruction.

The cardinal principle, indeed very foundation, of the international trading system as institutionalized in the General Agreement of Tariffs and Trade (GATT) was that of non-discrimination. And what an outstanding success it has been! The member-nations of the GATT that espoused its principles and engaged in open trade enjoyed unprecedented prosperity and peace. Prosperity accrued not only in material terms, but also in terms of welfare and social and political well-being. Trade freedom provides greater scope for social freedom and ultimately impetus to greater political freedom. Thus, it is not an exaggeration to say that: "The principle of 'non-discrimination' between nations, proclaimed in the Atlantic Charter and embodied in the GATT, is arguably one of the most enlightened achievements of the 20th century" (Lehmann and Thompson, 2001).

The contrast between the great benefits that were derived by citizens of countries with open economic systems and the deprivations imposed on those living in closed economic systems became increasingly so glaring that by the late eighties and nineties the latter were no longer sustainable. The closed economic world imploded. The Soviet system, clearly ideologically and economically bankrupt, collapsed. Countries that had pursued nationalist economic ideologies and protectionist import-substitution policies, such as Mexico, Brazil, Argentina, India, and China, undertook sweeping trade liberalization reforms. A nation such as Japan, which had been cheating for decades by having a dual policy of competing externally with select industries, but protecting a very wide spectrum of inefficient industries in the domestic market, began to pay a heavy toll for its past.

With the completion of the Uruguay Round (1986–1994) and the establishment of the World Trade Organization (WTO) in 1995, it seemed as though the world on the trade front at least was back on track.

2.3 Trade and the Third World

Many, possibly most, places in the world never really got a chance. The superiority that Northwestern Europe and its offshoots—Australia, New Zealand, the United States, and Canada—got from the industrial revolution has been overwhelming. This is true not only in technology, industry, manufacturing, but also in all the ancillary activities: law, accounting, academe, insurance, banking, the media, communications, and so on. The economies of the industrialized countries are in fact increasingly referred to as 'post-industrial' countries, because, among other reasons, of the growing proportion of the service sectors in their GDP. The West's competitiveness and strength in these service sectors arise from their origins in serving industry and manufacturing. The international accounting firm Andersen may have collapsed, but its place will be taken by one (or several) of the established 'western' international accounting firms and not, say, by a sudden upstart from Senegal or Paraguay.

In the two decades or so that followed the end of the Second World War, a considerable amount of turbulence occurred in respect to what came to be called the Third World.

1. Movements of independence galvanized the populations of colonies throughout the continents of Asia and Africa, resulting in some cases in war (for example, Vietnam and Algeria) or in less virulent forms of struggle. But the 'struggle' was nonetheless an important ingredient virtually everywhere; and charismatic popular nationalist heroes generally led the struggles.

2. Soviet Russia, albeit exhausted and devastated by the war, came out well, not only in terms of its prominent position in determining the post-war settlement, but also as an emblem of courage (the battle of Stalingrad), a symbol of revolution, and 'friend' of the oppressed. The symbolism of Soviet defiance and leadership was further emblazoned by initially beating—and ridiculing—the US in space with the Sputnik. There emerged the image of a powerful 'Russian model'.

3. The political left dominated western universities in the social sciences. This was true of the European intellectual climate in general, and writers, such as Jean-Paul Sartre, earned prominence. While fascism had failed, capitalism and liberalism had by no means been restored to positions of intellectual legitimacy, let alone respect. The market and capital had to be controlled, it was widely believed, lest their natural rapaciousness should continue to exploit the weak. Control had to be exercised by the state. Theories of economic development, also influenced by left-wing political ideologies, sought to identify means by which recently developing countries might accelerate development, indeed, make a miraculous leap forward. Here again the state was thrust onto the 'commanding heights'.

4. While Europe was leaning towards the left, the United States veered to the extreme right under the impulse of McCarthyism. The McCarthyist smear extended not only to any and all Americans suspected of harboring 'leftish' thoughts, but also to any political leader in the developing world who had liberal inclinations or—heaven forbid!—socialist inclinations. The McCarthy meteor eventually plunged, albeit unfortunately not into oblivion. For decades, America's 'friends' in developing countries were gun-toting, corrupt, human rights violating, often militarist dictators—Trujillo of the Dominican Republic was a good example. These were the fellows who constituted the leadership of what the United States quite amazingly and brazenly called 'the free world'. The McCarthyist legacy has left a great credibility gap abroad in respect to US policy, a strong residue of suspicion and resentment on the part of many people in developing countries, and an atavistic blinkered vision in Washington, manifested most blatantly in the puerility of American policy *vis-à-vis* Cuba.

It was under these circumstances that the Third World came about, not only as a categorization of states that belonged neither to the First World of capitalist industrialized states, nor to the Second World of advanced socialist economies, but also as an economic condition, a frame of mind, a political statement. This was also a period rife with economic nationalism. Many political leaders and economists deemed the role of the state in driving the economy crucial at the time. This in turn gave rise to the idea of leap-frogging through political interventionism, economic planning, and social engineering. The need of post-independence political leaders to maintain popular support further fueled the doctrines of economic nationalism.

Throughout the fifties, sixties, and seventies, Third World countries were for the most part under the hegemonic doctrinal thumb of a structuralist developmentalist ideology that favored state-driven import-substitution industrialization. A leading academic figure of this era and movement was Raúl Prebisch, the Argentinean economist who, among his many accomplishments, introduced and developed the 'dependency' theory. Essentially, Prebisch argued that as a result of imperialism the institutional, industrial, and socio-economic structures of developing countries had been geared towards serving the First World. This created a set of structural problems in these countries—namely, export-orientated dependence and unbalanced growth. Third World countries were not as much 'underdeveloped' as they were 'badly developed'. Prebisch's protectionist advocacy resided in the view that international trade would reinforce and thus perpetuate this 'bad development' path. Third World countries, Prebisch argued, were being dragged into a state of 'dependency' upon the First World, becoming the producers of raw material for First World manufacturing development, constituting what he described as a 'center–periphery' relationship. Thus trade protectionism and import-substitution strategies were necessary to escape dependency and enter a self-sustaining development path (Prebisch, 1964; 1965; and 1981).

Countries throughout the Third World embarked on policies of economic nationalism, state-driven industrial policy, protectionism, and import-substitution. Within this in fact quite broad spectrum, there were various degrees. Maoist China was an extreme form, while countries such as Brazil, Indonesia, Egypt, Argentina, Mexico, etc., were more moderate: all of the latter, for example, were members of the GATT. It is true, however, to say that not a single developing country adopted an open liberal trade policy. The two exceptions to this pretty overwhelming rule might be Hong Kong—which in any case was a colony—and eventually Singapore. Though South Korea and Taiwan—and later other Asian countries—abandoned import substitution in favor of export-oriented strategies, they did not adopt liberal import regimes, and South Korea was also not open to foreign direct investment.

By the 1980s, the great tragedy of the second half of the 20th century became blatantly manifest. The economic policies of Third World countries, with only a very small handful of exceptions, had failed. The failures ranged from unmitigated disasters (most of Sub-Saharan Africa) to acute disappointments, with Brazil and India, the two countries credited with 'eternal potential', as prominent examples of the latter. Contrary to contemporary conventional wisdom, corruption is not a major cause of this failure. Corruption should probably more properly be seen as a symptom, rather than a cause, of Third World economic decline.

Julius Nyerere of Tanzania, for example, is credited with having been a man of exceptional probity. He was also a hero, not only in developing countries, but also in the West. In his 'Arusha Declaration' in 1967, he committed himself to the creation of an egalitarian socialist society based on cooperative agriculture. Nyerere understood the importance of social development, as a result of which he carried out mass literacy campaigns, and instituted free and universal education. He also emphasized Tanzania's need to become economically self-sufficient rather than remain dependent on foreign aid and foreign investment. The Arusha Declaration was hailed for its enlightenment. Thirty-five years later, Tanzania ranks among the world's least developed countries.

After half-a-century of experience and many disappointments, we are not that much the wiser. Notwithstanding the often seemingly visceral arrogance of economists, there are many things—indeed most things—we do not understand. Two things, however, seem to be pretty clear.

The first is the imperative of *investing in human capital formation*. Among the very few countries that have succeeded, all of them invested heavily in education *as a means* of achieving economic growth—*not as a result* of economic growth! South Korea is the most remarkable example. In the mid–1960s its GDP *per capita* was lower than that of most Sub-Saharan African countries; today it provides aid to these countries. South Korea understood that the educational horse—and indeed a robust and healthy horse—must be put in front of the developmental cart. South Korea also understood the imperative of having an educational pyramid with a solid base. India has some of the most educated people at the very top, but a very weak base, something that today is its biggest handicap.

Education is a prerequisite, but not a guarantee. It is not enough. Cuba has a higher level of education than most of Latin America, yet one of its lower GDP *per capita*. Russia and many of the Central and Eastern European countries had high educational levels, yet that did not prevent them from wallowing in socio-economic mire.

This leads to the second thing we should know: countries that have done reasonably well economically (bearing in mind what has been overall a very dismal record among most countries of the Third World) are those that have been *more open*—to trade, to investments, to technology transfer, and to foreign sources of learning. This is true across continents, cultures, and comparable levels of education: e.g. West Germany versus East Germany, South Korea versus North Korea. Burma (Myanmar) started off much wealthier and better educated than Thailand, but now falls far behind not only in economic rankings but also in the Human Development Index: Thailand is 66th, Myanmar 118th. The contrast can also be drawn from the same country embarking on radically different policies. Maoist China witnessed the creation of misery on an unprecedented scale—most dramatically in the famines that accompanied the 'Great Leap Forward'—while Dengist and post-Dengist China have seen the eradication of poverty on an unprecedented scale.

Thus, while there may continue to be uncertainty and controversy about many aspects of economic growth policy, especially in the area of finance, there should be no controversy that education is a *sine qua non*, and that, on balance, open economies do substantially better than closed economies. While stressing these points, perhaps the third lesson from the last fifty years is that *there is no quick fix*. One of the challenges of the 21st century, while aiming to generate growth and development, should also be to manage expectations.

3. Trade Obstacles and Visions
for the 21st Century

It has taken a century for policy-making and intellectual consensus to return to the ideas and principles of progressive liberalism that had been developed and espoused, but were interrupted, indeed aborted, by various forces—ranging from the truly destructive of the human condition and the human spirit (fascism and communism) to the ineffective, even if well-intentioned (e.g. the Arusha Declaration). It has taken a long time for recognition to be given, even if often grudgingly, to the fact that trade and the market are dynamic and powerful forces of human wealth, human welfare, and human well-being. In this context, from a perspective of economic history, the establishment of the WTO—and the quasi-universal adherence and/or application among states for membership—could be considered 'the end of history'. We stand at the threshold of what could conceivably be a tremendously dynamic and progressive next few decades.

But we are certainly not there yet! A number of major obstacles remain before trade can triumph, as it should. A critical, but unfortunately not exhaustive, list of obstacles includes the following:
- atavistic nationalism, mercantilism, and imperialism;
- the absence of leadership and vision;
- hypocrisy and double-standards; and
- the legacies of 'Third Worldism'.

Let us look at each in turn.

3.1 Atavistic Nationalism, Mercantilism, and Imperialism

Japan is the world's second biggest economy and third biggest trading power. For several decades, until its economic collapse in the early 1990s, many countries, especially in Asia, looked upon Japan as a 'model'. Yet Japan has never adopted a liberal trade policy; its blunt mercantilism stands as an antithesis of liberalism. Its market has been closed, not only to the products of industrialized countries, which is no more than a minor problem, but to the products of developing countries, which is a major problem.

If Japan is obsessively mercantilist, the United States is schizophrenic. Although the principal architect and often champion of the remarkable post-war multilateral trading system, the US can also be its biggest threat. The schizophrenia is reflected in the tremendous lobbying power of sectorial vested interests, notably, for example, the steel industry, the agriculture lobby, textiles, cotton growers, lumber, and so on. The fact that the United States government panders to different sectors for political gain does not make it any different from other industrialized nations. The problem with the US is the speed of turnarounds, which has given its trade policy the appearance—and reality!—of inconsistency.

It is also an extraordinary fact that while the United States is, with the exception of the few Amerindians who remain, a nation entirely composed of immigrants, it retains a visceral suspicion—or worse—of 'foreigners'. George W Bush's famous lament in a CNN television interview during his campaign that "most of our imports come from overseas" (!) touches a national raw nerve. The suspicion of foreigners extends to deep suspicion of international organizations, and especially ones not on American soil.

Though the principle of non-discrimination was invented and promoted by the United States, many Americans are uncomfortable with the obligation that arises in which trade should not be used as a foreign policy instrument. America has repeatedly engaged in trade sanctions, in trade retaliation, in trade discrimination, and in trade conflict. This issue also splits the right. While institutions such as the Cato Institute and the Hudson Institute, to name only two, remain fervently in favor of free trade, many American conservative politicians have supported offensive trade nationalism. A recent letter from William R. Hawkins, Senior Fellow for National Security Studies, of the US Business and Industry Council, to the *Financial Times* illustrates the point. In response to criticism that George W. Bush's steel import tariff policy was discriminating in favor of certain countries, notably the UK, Mr Hawkins begins by decrying the view that the abstract doctrine of free trade should prevail over political realism as nonsense. Friends and enemies should not be treated alike. The problem arises when defining 'the enemy':

> Trade between allies makes both parties stronger, whereas trade with an enemy creates a security diseconomy. This is clearly seen in China, where trade and investment are transforming Beijing's capabilities in ways that are shaking the entire region (Hawkins, 2002).

In what sense and according to what legal basis should China be labeled an 'enemy'? Mr Hawkins could—probably should—be dismissed as a xenophobic crank, except that unfortunately a lot of American political thinking on trade is along these lines. Many American political leaders, even those who should know better, rather than responding forcefully in favor of the many benefits accruing to the nation from a liberal trade regime, actually pander to these views.

The EU has only in the last few years developed a unified trade policy. In so doing, it has had difficulty reconciling the differences between generally liberal trade oriented regimes in the north (UK, Netherlands, Belgium, Germany, and the Scandinavian countries) and the protectionists of the south, notably France, Italy, and Spain. Economic nationalism in some European countries was manifested by the desire to promote and protect 'national champions'—for example, in the automotive, electronic, or computer industries. Things have changed, or at least been attenuated, with the result that, with the important exception of agriculture, European trade policy and European trade ideology have become more liberal. Having said that things have improved, by no means can one deduce that the European Union is going to be a global driving force for trade liberalism. Furthermore, European inflexibility on its protectionist and trade-distorting agricultural policies may seriously jeopardize the entire global trade system.

Whatever is arrived at in trade policy settlements is the result of murky deals, concessions, threats, and so on. The self-proclaimed 'trade policy champion' is the one who returns home bragging that s/he has imposed market opening on a third party and preserved protection at home. Neither the US nor the EU has provided leadership, while 'Japanese leadership' remains the ultimate oxymoron. Nor have any of the West's political leaders provided any vision. The perspective of an open global market and an open global society is the most exciting, uplifting thing that has happened since the creation of the United Nations. The material and cultural benefits that should accrue to all nations that participate are potentially immense. With the rapidly growing populations of young people in the developing economies—with 700 million about to join the labor market in the next decade—the opening of markets and minds may be our only real chance for a peaceful, prosperous, and dynamic 21st century. There is a very grave risk that the new world economic order might degenerate, as was the case with the new political order after the Second World War.

The United Nations was born in exuberance and has degenerated into generally cynical inertia, though under the leadership of Kofi Annan it may enjoy a degree of resurgence. In the course of the immediate postwar decades, however, the spirit of the UN was extinguished as it was seen, on the one hand, to have become a gravy-train for well-heeled bureaucrats and, on the other, a battle-ground for political brinkmanship, as opposed to the ideals of collective cooperation for which it had been established. The UN was seen as either a travesty of what it was supposed to be, or simply ineffectual. There is a very grave risk that a similar cynicism may come to envelop the World Trade Organization, which, in turn, may also be perceived as an arena for trade conflict, or, as with the UN, as irrelevant and ineffectual.

Worse than the absence of leadership and vision has been the brinkmanship that has characterized trade relations, especially between the United States and the European Union. The fact that the public should be at best confused by or, worse, strongly antipathetic to the international trading system is hardly surprising when one thinks of all the fire and thunder that have attended trade battles, ranging from bananas to steel, between these two giants!

No western political leader, to my knowledge, has spoken out in favor of imports, especially in stressing the correlation between an open import regime and welfare. Protectionism rarely affects wealthy consumers: the import tariff on a Ferrari or a Cartier watch is pretty irrelevant. Protectionism in developed countries is primarily directed at cheaper goods and necessities, typically clothes, shoes, and food.

In developing countries, protectionism also favors the rich. The very skewed income differentials in most Latin American countries—a tiny minority of extremely wealthy, a big majority of extremely poor—is in great part caused by the absence of land reform, but also by the rent that oligopolistic business oligarchs have been able to extract from their markets when protected by thick protectionist walls. When Brazil, for example, liberalized its import regime, among other consequences was a drop by more than 60 precent in the price of pencils, thus allowing kids in the *favelas* to have much easier access to the most basic instrument necessary for achieving literacy.

The last example illustrates how vital it is that trade liberalization should proceed rapidly. The demographic boom of the early 21st century in developing countries is a time-bomb ticking away. It needs to be defused. Political leadership and vision are urgently needed.

3.3 Hypocrisy, Double-Standards . . .

The biggest indictment of the trade policy regime in the beginning of the 21st century is that it strongly discriminates against developing countries. The point need not be belabored here, partly because it has been stressed so often that there is not much scope for saying anything new on the subject—even though the problem remains acute.

Agriculture, agriculture, agriculture, . . . and agriculture! The discriminatory regimes practiced by Japan, the EU, the US, Switzerland, Norway, or Korea are terrible. As in any protectionist policy, they are of course detrimental to the interests of their own citizens. The EU's agricultural subsidies are equivalent to *seven percent* of total EU GDP, which is equivalent to the size of the entire Spanish economy. In the meantime, many parts of Europe suffer from increasingly poor education, health services, and transport. But the worst effect of course is on developing economies. Competitive agricultural producers in Latin America, Africa, the Middle East, and Asia are severely handicapped. The potential losses of revenue incurred are astronomic.

A similar litany may be made about textiles and garments. In theory, the restrictive textiles and garments regime is to be abolished by 2005. In practice, it remains to be seen. Equally discriminatory has been the abuse by industrialized countries, especially the US, of anti-dumping—though some developing countries have also joined the unholy fray. There are a few other egregious examples of the hypocrisy and double-standards of the developed countries *vis-à-vis* developing countries that deserve to be highlighted.

The Japanese admiral Isoroku Yamamoto, famous for having planned the attack on Pearl Harbor, said in 1931, the year that Japan invaded and colonized Manchuria and was indignantly lambasted by the League of Nations: "the Western powers taught us how to play poker, now that they have all the chips they have taken up contract bridge." By no means, of course, should this read as an endorsement on my part of the Japanese invasion of Manchuria! The point Yamamoto was making, however, was that with the British in India, Burma, Malaysia, three-quarters of Africa, and so on, the French in most of the remaining bits of Africa, as well as Indochina, the Dutch in Indonesia, the United States in the Philippines, the Belgians in the Congo, it was really a bit rich on their part to be criticizing Japan for seeking its place under the sun.

Even if sometimes motivated by good intentions, the West is often seen to be suddenly changing the goal posts. When in 1848 the French Second Republic abolished slavery on all French soil—that is, including French colonial soil—the impact on the economy of Senegal was devastating. This is of course not to say that slavery should not have been abolished; indeed it should have been abolished well before, and, even better, never initiated. The point is, however, that in 1848 French interests and motives dictated the abolition of slavery. It may have been 'evil' on the part of Senegalese leaders and traders to have connived in the slave trade. But nevertheless they had—and the economy was highly dependent on it. The French, however, responding to the lofty principles embodied in the revolutions of 1848, just suddenly abandoned their erstwhile allies and partners. Of course it is a good thing that slavery was abolished on French soil; it would have been an even better thing if French leaders had then contributed to helping Senegal adjust to the economic shock and develop alternative productive economic activities.

A similar point applies today to the controversy over labor standards and environment. So far as the former is concerned, for example, there is absolutely no doubt that the conditions in many factories and workshops in developing countries are 'Dickensian'. There are lots and lots of abuses: the exploitation of child labor, brutal sexual harassment, intimidation against worker representatives, unsanitary and dangerous work environments, long hours for minimal pay, etc. These abuses need to be terminated. But there is, understandably, on the part of people in the developing countries a strong degree of irritation when holier-than-thou self-appointed Western apostles of labor rights come preaching. The conditions, as we said, are 'Dickensian'. Dickens described conditions as they existed in Britain as it was in the throes of its industrial revolution, not the conditions in Cambodia. Thus, the perspective from developing countries easily arises that while it was OK for us to exploit labor when we were busy industrializing, it is not OK for others and we will prevent them from doing so. Changing the goal posts: poker to contract bridge!

A vision of the 21st century *must* include labor standards dramatically improving, such as children being kept away from factories and put into schools. Proper recognition must be given to the *absolute imperative* of ensuring a sustainable development that will preserve the planet and provide well-being not only to the current generation, but also to future generations.

It is also necessary to find the best means to achieve these ends. Imposing trade sanctions is emphatically not the best means; in fact it is probably the worst means. A very important means of not only achieving the objectives, but also reducing the friction arising from the perceptions of hypocrisy is to revert to the fundamental principles of the market and talk about it.

Probably the most blatant form of double-standards and the one whose implications are the most complex is that of migration. When Western Europe was going through its phase of rapid development in the 19th century, as with developing countries today, this involved booming demographics. With land reform, industrialization, greatly improved medicine and hygiene, it was no longer possible for Europe to contain all its excess population. Throughout the century, European migration took place on an enormous scale. Not only did this provide tremendous economic activity and opportunity, but it also acted as an essential socio-political safety valve. Had there not been the migration there was, Europe would have been even far more plagued with war and revolution. European countries might have, to use contemporary jargon, 'imploded'.

Today, Europe and Japan, Australia, New Zealand, Canada, and the US are prosperous and some are plagued by rapidly aging populations. They must open their doors far more widely to immigration. This is partly out of self-interest, because domestic demographic conditions will require the 'importing' of young people, but also as a means of providing all the things that Europe benefited from—economic activity, economic prosperity, political safety valves—when its immigrants were populating the earth.

A final example, out of many others that could still be given, refers to the current fuss over intellectual property rights. There are, of course, very sound and convincing reasons why intellectual property must be respected. True. Yet, it is impossible to name a single industrialized nation that did not initially arrive at its position of wealth and power without stealing intellectual property! Perpetuating theft is no doubt not the answer, but while intellectual property protection may be a reasonably worthy goal, it must be accompanied by means of ensuring greater and cheaper technology and scientific transfer to those developing economies capable of absorption.

Though I have often referred in this chapter to the 'Third World', in fact it never existed, and does so even less today, except as a state of mind. The differences in every respect between booming and dynamic developing countries with reasonable institutional foundations and forms of governance, such as Mexico or Thailand, at one end, and poverty-disease infested tin-pot dictatorships, at the other, are generally far greater than the differences between top-end developing countries and the First World. And these distinctions need to be made clear.

It must also be recognized that this is indeed an unjust world. Current generations of Europeans do not deserve to be so much more prosperous than their counterparts in Africa, Asia, or Latin America. Their prosperity derives in good part from good luck; and the poverty of Africans, Asians, and Latin Americans in great part from bad luck. Their respective conditions arise not from individual merits, but from the actions of their great-great grandparents (or thereabouts!). This is true. And it is true that the deplorable conditions in which many countries—notably in Africa—find themselves in today are due to past colonial exploitation. The Democratic Republic of Congo (alias Zaire, former Belgian Congo) is one of the most flagrant examples.

For the past several decades it has been common discourse among many Third World leaders to blame the West. That's fine, except it does not get one anywhere. It is an unfortunate truism that one cannot undo the past. Though the West is—without doubt, in good part—to blame, it does not have a monopoly of responsibility for the travails many countries find themselves in. In many cases the evils of colonialism have been perpetrated—or even worsened—by abysmal indigenous governance.

It is disconcerting, for example, as occurred to me in March 2002, to be sitting in a hall at a UN Conference on Financing Development and seeing Third World delegates euphorically cheering and clapping the empty populist 'anti-imperialist' rhetoric of Hugo Chavez. Venezuela is a quite glaring example of a country whose wounds have been self-inflicted, arising from deplorable governance and a greedy, pathetic political class.

The same point applies to trade regimes. Of course, leaders of developing countries are entirely correct to attack the protectionist policies of industrialized countries. But they must also recognize that a lot of the harm is also being caused by protectionist discriminatory trade policies and practices directed by developing countries against developing countries.

Greater maturity is needed. And this greater maturity must also be exhibited in the realization—note: the realization, not the resignation—that the accumulated baggage of history will make it unlikely that big leaps can be quickly achieved. There is no instant formula, no *panacea*.

There is of course the example of China that has quadrupled income in two decades. And that is great. But before becoming too euphoric about China's future, one should remember that all past extrapolations based on growth have proved to be false in the long term; that China in many ways has over the last couple of decades been making up for the entrepreneurship that was so disastrously stifled in the three decades of Mao's reign, and that it remains to be seen how sustainable the Chinese economic model is.

The road from underdevelopment to prosperity is likely to be a long one. It will be based on incremental improvements, rather than sudden leaps and bounds. But it is important to embark on that road now.

Why Trade Must Triumph?

The lessons from the past are quite clear. Trade must triumph not just because it is the best means, but because it is arguably the only means, for humanity to develop materially and spiritually through active participation in the global market. The global market in the global village is one of the most exciting possible visions and goals for the 21st century. The benefits must be propagated, abuses curtailed, leadership exercised.

References

Andrić, Ivo (1959) *The Bridge over the Drina*. London: Macmillan.
Atlantic Charter, 14 August 1941, http://www.internet-esq.com/ussaugusta/atlantic1.htm.
Hawkins, William R. (2002) "Political Realism of Trading with Allies." *Financial Times*, April 19, 2002
Hull, Cordell (1948) *The Memoirs of Cordell Hull*. Volume I. London: Hodder and Stoughton.
Kiernan, V.G. (1969) *The Lords of Human Kind*. London: Weidenfeld and Nicholson.
Lehmann, Jean-Pierre and Rachel Thompson (2001): *The Evian Manifesto*, www.eviangroup.org.
Prebisch, Raúl (1981) *Capitalismo Periférico: Crisis y Transformación*. México: Fondo de Cultura Económica.

Prebisch, Raúl (1965) *Transformación y Desarrollo*. México: Fondo de Cultura Económica.

Prebisch, Raúl (1964) *Una Nueva Politica Comercial para el Desarrollo*. New York: United Nations.

Soros, George (2002) *On Globalization*. New York: Public Affairs.

The WTO and the New Development-Oriented Trade Round[1]

John Whalley

F13

1. Introduction

This paper discusses the new WTO Trade Round launched in Qatar in November 2001, focusing on its development component.[2] It takes as background the state of play in the WTO since the end of the Uruguay Round, with both incomplete implementation of and developing country dissatisfaction with the Uruguay Round agreements, a developing country unwillingness to launch a new round in Seattle, and the calls at the time of the launch of a round to pay close attention to developing country concerns.[3] Some EU foreign ministers suggested that the round be launched as a "development round,"[4] a label also used by the UK development minister some two years earlier (see Short, 1999).

Its main themes are twofold. The first is that the WTO is by its structure not primarily a development-oriented organization. The predecessor of the WTO, the GATT, was set up in 1947 to establish a rule regime to keep markets open and to foster exchanges of concessions to reduce barriers through rounds of trade negotiations. Its central principles are non-discrimination and equal treatment of member countries. Preferential arrangements for a subset of countries (developing countries) thus runs counter to the spirit of the original organization and there has been continuous tension between the basic principles of the system, and the development objectives of poorer countries. Developing countries continuously argued from the 1960s on that they should receive varying forms of special treatment both under GATT rules and in negotiation, and typically they have been dissatisfied with the outcome. Grand sounding statements of how the trading system should be focused to achieve development objectives, and the reality of a system based on nondiscrimination over the years have repeatedly run directly counter to each other.

1. This is based on a presentation at a CEU conference on globalization held in Budapest in November 2001, and draws on an earlier paper Whalley (2001)
2. See also the discussion of the new trade round in Third World Network (2001).
3. See *Financial Times* (2001a).
4. See *Financial Times* (2001b).

Making development the focal point of the new WTO Round seems to imply either that the WTO will devote much or all of its negotiating capital to an enterprise that logically does not fit its central mandate, or that the word development will be used as a fig leaf for OECD countries to continue with a negotiating agenda which in the main is non-developmental, while nonetheless keeping the developing country majority at the negotiating table. By being disappointed with the Uruguay Round outcome and acting as a blocking coalition in Seattle, and forcing the OECD countries to recognize that they are a clear minority in the multilateral process, the developing countries may well earn more than a fig leaf, but perhaps not much more. If so, this may point to further conflict over a cosmetic adherence to development, and the aspirations of developing countries for genuine developmental content in the WTO.

The second theme is that irrespective of whether the negotiating outcome is more cosmetic or substantive, what constitutes appropriate developmental content in a new WTO Round is not clear. The issues involve less the technical details of, say, what kinds of changes in the detailed application of anti-dumping laws are good or bad for the developing countries, than the broad sweep of policy and its effects on development. This is the case because what the appropriate trade policy stance is in developing countries, and what is good or bad for them is in many areas unclear. Improved access abroad is generally agreed to be good, but protection at home may be either good or bad in traditional economic welfare terms. If broader human development considerations enter the equation, the effects of increased openness on the relative positions of the rich and poor are unclear, and issues of impacts on absolute and relative poverty arise. Adjustment costs from increased openness, and their impacts on the poor are a further issue.

Economists have long argued that for small open price taking economies, the best policy is one of complete openness and free trade. Trade interventions distort and misallocate resources. And yet developing countries have sought autonomy and flexibility in their use of various trade interventions, which some economists say are nonetheless bad for their development. And as if this were not confusing enough, another branch of more modern economic theory focused on endogenous growth, and 'uninternalized externalities'—implicitly highlighting the virtues of protection in certain instances. And wider goals of human development, poverty alleviation, and sustainability face the equally perplexing situation that whether or not particular trade interventions improve or worsen on these grounds is typically unknown. Thus, substantively, how a Development Round should be structured to foster both development in its narrower sense and human development more broadly is not an issue on which there is uniform agreement.

2. The Background to a New Development Round

2.1 Trade and Development in the WTO System

While far from having a completely common WTO position, developing countries have generally thought for some decades that global trade arrangements should be designed to foster their own growth and development, not simply to yield gains from trade through exchanges of trade concessions between members (see Whalley, 1989; 1999a). They have also argued that the developed countries committed themselves to such goals in the 1960s in the form of Part IV of the GATT[5] and have not met the agreed standard since. They also tend to view trade institutions (the WTO) as a rich man's club in which developing country interests play little role. The developed countries generally take a different position on these issues; claiming they have met their commitments and take a different line on the role of trade policy in development, stressing openness and freedom in trade.

The most recent disagreements over the participation of developing countries in the WTO have stemmed from the Uruguay Round decisions of 1994. Developing countries generally believe that they have benefited little from the Uruguay Round decisions, and point to WTO Uruguay Round studies claiming annual global benefits of around 500 billion USD (Francois, McDonald, and Nordström, 1994; 1995; 1996) asking where is their share that these studies projected. The sense that they were misled over the Uruguay Round is one key reason for developing country skepticism over a new round.

They point to the complexity of the decisions and the limits they place on what they see as their policy flexibility as key, requesting exemptions and implementation delays in a number of areas, including Trade-Related Investment Measures (TRIMs). The term 'implementation' is now widely used to refer to this set of issues in discussion of a future round. Finally, developing countries point to cosmetic implementation of the early stages of some of the Uruguay Round decisions (such as textiles and apparel) where they claim the developed countries have not acted in good faith.

Conflicts over these issues escalated at the 1999 Seattle ministerial meeting where large numbers of developing countries concluded the process offered them little and effectively withdrew. Most had come into the Uruguay Round with a positive approach and pursued national rather than bloc-wide interests by

---

5. Part IV of the GATT added in 1965 refers to Articles 36, 37, and 38, which set out the developmental needs of developing countries in the trading system.

attempting to exchange concessions (as they had been requested for several decades). The final stages became embroiled in developed country issues (agriculture) with the final text of the agreement largely presented to developing countries to sign, with little input. Since Seattle developing country issues have continued to have high profile in the WTO because launching a new a multilateral trade round without 80 percent of the membership makes little sense. Key developed countries (and especially the EU) have thus made resolving these issues the top agenda item.

As things moved towards Qatar in November of 2001, the fundamentals of the situation did not change much from what they had been in Seattle. So one might ask why the outcome should have been any different. One response is that the developing countries may have believed that they have received relatively little from the WTO process in the positive sense of achieving a further lowering of barriers they face, but they also had an interest in preserving and strengthening multilateral rules and disciplines which kept the trading system open. They thus supported a new launch to underpin present trade openness through ongoing negotiations even if they were critical of what happened in the Uruguay Round. A second factor was that the developed countries had, at least at a rhetorical level, made developing country issues top WTO agenda items. The test was whether substance supported rhetoric. One positive indicator was the seeming softening of tone by developed countries on the two issues of labor standards and the environment relative to Seattle, and the message this sent to the developing countries.

Whether it will really be a development round in substance, more than in rhetoric, is thus the issue. The GATT system as cast in 1947 was one of agreed rules restraining the trade policy actions of contracting parties, and progressive liberalization to be achieved through mutual exchanges of concessions. To pretend that this system provided instruments for achieving development objectives is, in my view, to fly in the face of logic. Developing countries do have developmental aspirations, and these can, in principle, be accommodated in the WTO system by various special arrangements for them, but at the same time these run counter to the non-discrimination principles on which the system was founded.

In addition, developed countries had their own issues to pursue in a new round. But believing that a new WTO negotiation can fundamentally deal with poverty and malnutrition in the developing world, negative growth in Africa, and other ills more effectively than, say, major increases in aid flows, technical assistance, nutritional, educational, and infrastructure support to the poor, seems unrealistic. Developing countries will clearly seek pro-development changes in global trade rules and WTO procedures in a new round, but how large the contribution of such changes will be to their own growth and development remains unclear.

All in all, a new trade round is perhaps likely and even inevitable by some calculations due to the joint interest of all countries in preserving the system and preventing the erosion that would follow a further stalling of progress towards negotiations. It may be called a development round, and on that basis the developing countries may embrace it. But the proof of this development pudding will be very much in the eating.

2.2 The Uruguay Launch Pad for a New Round

A new development round will also build directly on the last WTO Trade Round, the Uruguay Round (1986–1994), the longest and most complex of the eight negotiating rounds conducted under GATT/WTO auspices in the postwar years. While this covered a number of elements of key interest to developing countries, its significance for the new round is that it provides its launch pad through built-in negotiations and review processes in a number of areas. Understanding the Uruguay Round is thus key to understanding much of a new WTO Round.

Therefore, let us take the Uruguay Round component by component. In *agriculture*, the agreements brought agricultural trade within WTO rules and disciplines for the first time and conceptualized agricultural reform as a long-term process covering four main component areas: (1) market access; (2) domestic support; (3) export subsidies; and (4) sanitary and phytosanitary measures. It contained special arrangements for the least-developed and net food-importing developing countries. The implementation period was six years for the developed countries and ten years for the developing countries; the least-developed countries were exempt.

Under the *market-access provisions* in agriculture participants agreed to convert all non-tariff barriers to equivalent tariffs,[6] to be reduced by an average of 36 percent by developed countries and 24 percent by developing countries. Developed countries agreed to decrease their *domestic agricultural support* by 20 percent from a base period level of 1986–1988. Special provisions apply for the developing countries that only committed to 13.3 percent reductions and least-developed countries that were exempt.

---

6. But see Ingco's (1996) discussion of so called 'dirty tariffication' in agriculture, substituting higher tariffs for existing measures.

Developed countries also committed to reduce the value of their *direct export subsidies* by 36 percent below the 1986–1990 base period over six years and their volume of subsidized exports by 21 percent. Developing countries committed to reductions equal to two-thirds of those of developed countries over 10 years. Developing countries were also exempt from commitments to reduce the costs of marketing exports of agricultural products or internal transport subsidies. Least-developed countries were again exempt.

The agricultural agreement further recognized that the least-developed and net food-importing developing countries could face higher prices for food imports. It set out objectives for providing food aid and for ensuring that increasing proportions of basic foodstuffs would be financed by grants so as to offset any negative effects of the decisions from the round on net food importing countries.

The *textiles and apparel agreement* in the Uruguay Round had as its aim to integrate textile and clothing sectors into the WTO by phasing out the Multi-Fiber Arrangement (MFA). Ultimately, all non-MFA restrictions not justified by a WTO provision were to be phased out or brought into conformity with the WTO. The agreements were to be implemented over four stages. Stage One (January 1, 1995 to December 31, 1997) required each importing country to liberalize products representing 16 percent of the total volume of 1990 imports. Also, annual MFA quota growth rates were to be at least 16 percent higher than those allowed under the MFA. In Stage Two (January 1, 1998 to December 31, 2001), a further 17 percent of 1990 imports were to be integrated into WTO disciplines and annual MFA growth rates increased by 25 percent. In Stage Three (January 1, 2002 to December 31, 2004), a further 18 percent of 1990 imports are to be integrated and annual growth rates increased by 27 percent. In the final stage (from January 1, 2005), all the remaining products are to be fully integrated. A new safeguard mechanism was set up to cover textile and apparel products not integrated into the WTO at any stage.

The agreement in this area reflected a central developing country demand when the round was launched to repair a major erosion in the trading system relative to its central principles. However, while it is an achievement from a developing country perspective, the cosmetic compliance with the terms of the phase-out by the larger developed countries has been a concern, as has what may replace the MFA in 2004.

New agreements involving *intellectual property rights* (Trade-Related Intellectual Property Rights or TRIPs) and *investment* (TRIMs) were a further part of the Uruguay Round decisions key to the developing countries. The TRIPs agreement set out basic principles, including national treatment for intellectual property and Most Favored Nation (MFN) treatment, and addressed copyright, computer programs, trademarks and service marks, geographical indications, patents, integrated circuits, and antidumping practice in contractual licenses. In these agreements Members were required to adhere to the Bern Convention (1971) on *copyrights* and the Paris Convention (1967) on *patents*, and also grant product and process inventions. The agreement defined types of trademarks and copyright eligible for protection and the minimum rights to be accorded to them, with protection guidelines set for geographical indicators.

The agreement also established a Council for Trade-Related Aspects of Intellectual Property Rights, with disputes arising from the agreement to be settled under new WTO dispute settlement procedures, which allow for retaliation in the goods sectors. Developed countries were given a year to comply with the agreement, developing countries were allowed five years, and least-developed countries ten years. Developing countries with no system in place for protecting product patents were given ten years to introduce one, but were required to accept a mandatory filing of patent applications in the areas of pharmaceutical and agricultural chemicals.

Trade Related Investment Measures (TRIMs) agreements required members not to use any domestic measures inconsistent with GATT Article III (on National Treatment) and Article XI (on Quantitative Restrictions). A list of TRIMs was agreed, including local content requirements and trade-balancing requirements extensively used in the developing world. The agreement requires notification of TRIMs and their elimination within two years for developed countries, and five years for developing countries; least-developed countries had a seven-year period.

The Uruguay Round Agreements also included *services* for the first time. A Framework Agreement contained basic obligations of all members, while the National Schedules of Commitment contained specific national commitments, the subject of future negotiations. A final part included a number of annexes that addressed individual service sectors, such as telecommunications, audiovisual, financial, and maritime services. There were six key annexes. The annex on Article II Exemptions dealt with exemptions from MFN treatment, while the annex on the Movement of Natural Persons Supplying Services under the Agreement allowed for free movement of service providers under specific commitments. An "Annex on Financial Services" set out the rights of parties to protect investors and deposit holders, and to ensure the stability of the financial system. An "Annex on Telecommunications" dealt with access to and use of public telecommunications and services. An "Annex on Air Transportation" excluded traffic rights and directly related activities for the agreement. An

"Annex on Basic Telecommunications" set out exemptions from MFN obligations for basic telecommunications. Developing countries were resistant to including services in the Uruguay Round at its launch, but by the end of the round some had come to see services liberalization as an opportunity to be taken.

A further and major change the Uruguay Round yielded was the creation of the World Trade Organization (WTO) to replace the GATT. The WTO was established to encompass all agreements and arrangements previously concluded under GATT, and other agreements and ministerial decisions resulting from the Uruguay Round. As established, the WTO was to take on a range of functions. It was to facilitate the implementation, administration, and operation of the agreement establishing the WTO and related plurilateral agreements. The WTO was also to be the forum for further multilateral trade negotiation and was to administer both the procedures for the settlement of disputes and the trade policy review mechanism (TPRM). The organization was to be lead by biannual ministerial conferences, a process that led to the Qatar meeting.

A General Council was established to oversee the operation of the WTO and to act as a Dispute Settlement and Trade Policy Review Body. A Goods Council, a Services Council, and a TRIPs Council were established. The organization required members to have schedules of market-access concessions and specific services commitments; least-developed countries had an additional year to submit their schedules. The round also changed the dispute settlement procedures. Its decisions build in more automaticity into procedures. Members must enter into consultations within 30 days of another member's request for them. If a dispute is not resolved after 60 days of the request for consultation, the complaining party can request a panel. But if the request for a consultation is turned down, the complaining party can immediately request a panel. Panel reports are adopted unless the DSB (Dispute Settlement Body) rejects it by consensus.

The creation of the WTO, while at the time largely cosmetic in relabeling the GATT, has had a major effect on trade policy and negotiation, and has engaged the developing countries further than ever before in global trade debate. It has become a permanent body and the developing countries form a majority in it. They have become more vocal, and more prepared to act than before as the Seattle experience indicates. The WTO is now once again a body in which the majority plays a key role, and hence offers leverage to the developing countries.

Not only are the Uruguay Round decisions complex, they also remain little quantified in terms of their impacts in general, let alone their impacts on developing countries—either as a group or individual countries. It is generally believed that developing countries benefit from the elimination of restraints on the textile agreement (but even here there are arguments the other way), while they lose from the intellectual property provisions. In other areas, such as agriculture, certain groups of developing countries probably gain and others lose; no bloc-wide effect occurs across all countries. Other areas, such as services, investment, safeguards, dispute settlement, and institutional reform are viewed as wholly unclear.

Whalley (2000) discusses the results from general equilibrium trade models built to analyze the impacts of the round. These include those used within the WTO and executed towards the end of the round, and which report the large global gains in which the developing countries thought they would share. These models only cover those Uruguay Round changes that can be readily quantified, such as tariff changes, agriculture, and textile trade. The model results generated some five years ago were important to the debates at the end of the Uruguay Round: they provided comparative information on the impact of concluding or not concluding the round, specifically on the developing countries.

However, despite the extensive agency involvement with these model results, there are substantial inconsistencies between them, some of which are difficult to explain. One model shows that most of the gains are coming from agricultural liberalization, another from textiles, and yet another from tariff cuts. One shows that developing countries account for around 10 percent of the total gain, another shows them gaining by over 50 percent. One model shows developing countries losing from elimination of the MFA, another shows them as large gainers. One model shows that imperfectly competitive and scale economy effects double global gains, another shows almost no impact. These differences in results occur even where similar data sets and benchmark years are used, and are seemingly hard to explain on the basis of parametric specifications for models used, even though these are frequently poorly exposited.

For all these reasons, there is relatively little guidance from existing studies concerning the impacts of the decisions from the Uruguay Round on developing countries, although many believe them to have gained little. Early model results generated under WTO auspices projected global annual gains of 500 billion USD, and in the Seattle meeting developing countries repeatedly asked where their share of these gains were. Unfortunately, both the size and the country composition (including sign for the latter) are ambiguous in the full set of model based analyses, clouding the picture for the developing countries both as to what they have obtained from the round and what they might gain from a future negotiation. This all makes formulating their negotiating position for a new round that much more difficult.[7]

In addition, assessing developing country gains and losses from the Uruguay Round decisions is complicated by disagreements as to what is desirable for them on developmental grounds. As mentioned earlier, many economists believe that as small open economies, the development process in these countries is best served by an open trade regime. If this is the case, anything that allows for recurring trade intervention is bad. But developing countries saw new limits on their policy autonomy from the Uruguay Round decisions (in TRIMs, for example) as bad, and tried to resist such pressures. Also, newer theories of development stress the role that externalities can play in growth, and—if these go uninternalized—how development suffers. If protection plays a role in internalization (albeit as an inefficient instrument), surrendering protection, as many developing countries have done unilaterally over the last 15 years, may be bad for development. The absence of clearly agreed yardsticks of what is good or bad for development thus also makes assessments of gain or loss for developing countries from the Uruguay Round decisions difficult.

3. Framing a Development Round

The WTO Seattle Ministerial Meeting between November 30 and December 3, 1999 had been widely expected to launch a new WTO Trade Round but failed to do so for a number of reasons; one being that the launch did not have widespread support from the developing countries. The issues that were supposed to emerge from Seattle in the declaration to launch a new Round included the implementation of existing Uruguay Round agreements, new negotiations in agriculture and services (as required by the Uruguay Round), and the opening of new negotiating areas, such as *environment* and *labor standards*. The failure to launch a round in Seattle, and the role that the developing countries played in blocking a launch is in large part the reason for proposals (mentioned in the introduction) to make the new round a development round. This then becomes a window of opportunity for the developing countries, and one they may choose to seize.

7. Also see the discussion in Perroni (1998).

A new WTO Round, even if labeled a development round, will likely build on the same broad elements that defined the possible agenda for a launch earlier. It would, however, almost certainly exclude as central elements the two new issues of labor standards and environment that the developing countries successfully blocked in Seattle.

The first element reflects the so-called Built-in-Agenda (BIA) of negotiations stemming directly from the Uruguay Round decisions. This contains the implementation issues mentioned above, which reflect delayed entry into force of some of the Uruguay Round decisions, and negotiations committed to in the Uruguay Round decisions. The former include the introduction of the TRIPs and TRIMs agreements in ways that developing countries find acceptable as two central elements. The latter include mini-negotiations in agriculture and services, originally committed to by the end of 1999, and were slow to be kick-started in a new round.

Overseeing and completing the implementation of Uruguay round decisions, including sectoral negotiations in agriculture and services, might be a first step at what could potentially yield a package sufficient to constitute a round. The development component would then principally lie in the implementation part of the package. This would seemingly be of small (if symbolically important) substance for the developing countries on the development front since the more fundamental issues of harnessing the system to fuel their growth and development would go unaddressed.

The elements that could be added to this Built-in-Agenda include new issues (environment, labor standards), new negotiations on barrier reductions (in tariffs, including agriculture), and a generalized refocusing of special and differential treatment under WTO (see Whalley, 1999b). It would be the last of these that would inject the genuinely new development material into the round, although with issues in agriculture, services, textiles, and TRIPs from the Uruguay Round, there would be many other areas of interest for the developing countries.

New issues such as environment and labor standards took on profile after earlier new issues such as services were first discussed in the Uruguay Round. These were discussed as part of a new trade negotiation package in Seattle, but there was a backing away from concrete negotiation. Developing countries were successful in the 1996 Singapore Ministerial Meeting in largely removing from any future negotiating agenda the *trade and environment* issue—which would focus on the rights of importing countries to use trade restrictions for environmental purposes—even though it continues to circulate as a potential negotiating issue in the new round. As custodians of environmental assets, developing countries want to be compensated for environmental restraint, rather than to face environmentally driven trade actions.

Trade and labor standards is another new issue (rights of importing countries to use trade restrictions on imports of products which have been produced in ways that violate core labor standards, such as child or prison labor). Developing countries were again successful in both earlier WTO Ministerial Meetings and at Seattle in resisting pressures to commit to start such a negotiation. But pressures on these two fronts will likely continue. The developing countries will likely once again view the exclusion of these topics from the agenda of a launch as central to a development round.

Other new issues may arise in the round, but strong opposition is not so much a problem here as lack of concreteness concerning what is it to be negotiated. Broad ranging negotiations on *investment* remain a possibility even after Seattle, although there will be resistance from some OECD countries after the failed Multilateral Agreement on Investment initiative (MAI) in the OECD. *Competition policy* (Lloyd and Sampson, 1995) is a further topic that was included in the Qatar discussions on a new WTO Round in November, 2001. The aim would be to move some way towards harmonization of country competition policies, but some countries, and especially many developing countries, have no competition policy statutes. There are also issues like the lack of extraterritoriality of country competition policies, a concern of developing countries. Broadly speaking, the problems here lie in defining the precise focus of such a negotiation, more so than overcoming opposition to it. Electronic commerce and the growth of the Internet as a vehicle for conducting international trade may be a further item for negotiation, where some (including the WTO) have argued that developing countries have much to gain, but what concretely will be negotiated again remains unclear.

A new round could also be the venue for negotiations seeking to achieve further exchanges of concessions on trade barriers beyond what had been achieved by the end of the Uruguay Round. The possibilities would likely be portrayed as positive for development and hence central to a development round, and this could indeed be the case—depending on what was included and how one interprets benefits for developing countries. The list begins with agriculture, where existing quantitative and other restrictions were converted into visible tariffs by the Uruguay Round—many at high levels, such as tariffs of over 1,000 percent on certain types of rice in Japan. It is very much possible that the new WTO reciprocal exchanges will focus on agriculture, thus moving away from manufacturing, which was more central in the past. The problem here is that the barriers developing country exporters face involve also other issues besides tariffs, including health and phytosanitary restrictions.

Other elements of the post-Uruguay-Round, post-Seattle environment could also provide opportunities for new negotiated barrier reductions beneficial to developing countries. The commitment to eliminate MFA quotas on textiles and apparel in the year 2004 will leave tariffs in place on these items in many OECD countries, which are among the highest on manufactured products. Possibilities of new reciprocal exchange between both developed and developing countries arise here whose effects now become larger on trade, due to the quota elimination. Developing countries, however, remain fearful of what a post-MFA regime could bring them (new dumping duties is their fear) and would want restrictions over the use of any new trade restricting measures in this area.

The extensive tariff bindings undertaken by the developing countries in the Uruguay Round—with product coverage of bindings moving from around 20 percent before the launch of the Uruguay Round to around 80 percent at the end of it—also widens the scope for negotiated barrier reductions. Some observers have argued that if services are added to this, in case a new round is launched, it could offer possibilities for a considerable broadening of reciprocal exchange beyond that achieved in either the Uruguay Round or in earlier trade rounds. For the developing countries, opportunities may be there to aggressively pursue new access-related opportunities. These opportunities might well be portrayed as a central development element in a new round, and if pursued through to the end of a round this may indeed turn out to be the case.

Discussion of the potential development content of a round will also centrally involve the issue of special and differential treatment for developing countries under the WTO. This was an issue brought up repeatedly before Seattle, and it has not gone away but instead become even higher profile because of the perceived need to obtain agreement from developing countries on the content of a new round.

The Uruguay Round decisions contain multiple elaborations on the earlier, more restricted (Tokyo Round) notions of special and differential treatment, focusing on special rights to protect domestic markets, and preferential access to foreign markets. In the preamble to most Uruguay Round decisions there was a reference to special and differential treatment, acknowledging it as a central part of the GATT/WTO system of disciplines, but a wide range of new arrangements (some more of detail rather than of major substance) came into being in its name in a range of areas. New arrangements can be found in agriculture, textiles and clothing, technical barriers to trade, TRIMs, customs valuation, import licensing, subsidies/countervail, safeguards, services, TRIPs, dispute settlement, and measures for the least developed countries. These areas can be grouped into a number of categories: exceptions and delays in implementation; special flexibility in WTO disciplines and procedures; indications of best efforts on various issues by developed countries; technical assistance commitments; and specific commitments in services. Many of these arrangements were explicitly tailored to the needs of the least developed countries.

Most of these elaborations on earlier notions of special and differential treatment were seemingly offered as a response to perceived problems posed by new Uruguay Round rules for the developing countries. One problem was their limited capability to implement any new arrangements. It seemed clear the developing countries needed both time and special help in dealing with complex new areas such as intellectual property. Another problem was that with their fragile and small manufacturing sectors, the adjustment costs they faced in adapting to a new post-Uruguay-Round environment were disproportionately large. More generally, it was perceived that in exchange for agreeing to new WTO disciplines, some form of compensation in the form of special arrangements should be offered to developing countries.

However, by acknowledging that there were special developmental problems in the developing countries, developed countries also opened the door to a wider debate on how they are best dealt with under the WTO. And as most of the development benefits concerned the least developed countries, it opened ground for introducing the concept of 'tiering' development benefits in the WTO across types of countries. Many developing countries still view the special Uruguay Round provisions as largely 'tokenesque', and as such, not fundamental developmental assistance. But whether new negotiated arrangements emerging from a new round can be more substantive in development impact, remains a topic of discussion. The new Uruguay Round provisions may be *ad hoc* in design, and are for now little used, but the room for discussion of changes in special and differential treatment beyond the Uruguay Round and in a new development round is certainly there.

A further issue in a new WTO development round will likely be *technical assistance* on the trade front for the developing countries. Even though this has not been an element for negotiation in any previous trade round, it is now widely accepted that it makes little sense talking of a new multilateral trade negotiation if the majority of the countries involved in the negotiations simply do not have the resources and technical training to follow and effectively participate in the negotiation. The issues here involve both the level of resources devoted to technical assistance for lower income countries, and the form that assistance takes; and whether they are more like a response to donor interests than to genuine developing country interests.

This was particularly manifest in the agricultural area with the formation of the Cairns Group and the active participation of Argentina, Brazil, and Thailand, all of whom had clear trade negotiating objectives of enhancing their own export access rather than that of developing countries in general. On the other hand, developing countries who were net importers of food (Jamaica, Egypt, Peru) fore-saw losses from limits on export subsidies used by major food exporters (the EU, in particular), and argued strongly against liberalization in agriculture. In the agri-cultural area, negotiating developing countries took different sides on the same issue. The change to country rather than bloc-wide interest from earlier rounds raised the level of participation, but in a 'once-off' manner.

By blocking the launch of a new WTO Round in Seattle, and making OECD countries return with proposals for significant development content in Qatar, devel-oping countries have positioned themselves for new negotiating opportunities. They, however, remain skeptical that the WTO is able to get rid of the image of a rich man's club which serves the interests of others, and 50 years of negotiation experience in GATT/WTO suggests to them that dramatic change is unlikely.

The developing countries would participate in the WTO process more effec-tively if they shared a genuine belief that they could successfully negotiate to their own benefit and that their active participation will influence the outcome. The Uruguay Round in 1986 was largely sold to the developing countries as an opportunity for them to repair the erosion in the trading system in such areas as textiles, agriculture, and voluntary export restrictions. They have been disap-pointed by the outcome. A new Development Round at first sight offers them the chance of real developmental assistance through barrier reduction, rule rewriting, and technical assistance. Success at Qatar thus hinged on whether developing countries could be persuaded that there is more at stake than simply preserving a system they see as largely in the interests of developed countries, but that instead their growth and development will be advanced by negotiating, and that positive benefits for them can result.

The new Round has been launched at the Qatar meeting in November, 2001 under the heading of a Development Round, and it is to conclude in 2005. Time will tell what the outcome is from a developing country point of view.

References

Financial Times (2001a) "Zoellnick Promises New Trade Talks." *Financial Times*, May 17, 2001, p.1.

Financial Times (2001b) "Big Push for Start of a New Trade Round." *Financial Times*, May 18, 2001, p.10.

Francois, Joseph F., Bradley McDonald, and Håkan Nordström (1994) "The Uruguay Round: A Global General Equilibrium Assessment." CEPR Discussion Paper. London: Centre for Economic Policy Research.

Francois, Joseph F., Bradley McDonald, and Håkan Nordström (1995) "Assessing the Uruguay Round." In Will H. Martin and Alan Winters (eds.) *The Uruguay Round and the Developing Economies*, World Bank Discussion Paper No.307. Washington: World Bank.

Francois, Joseph F., Bradley McDonald, and Håkan Nordström (1996) "A User's Guide to Uruguay Round Assessments." CEPR Discussion Paper No.1410. London: Centre for Economic Policy Research.

Ingco, Merlinda (1996) "Tariffication in the Uruguay Round: How Much Liberalization?" *World Economy*, 19(4): 425–446.

Lloyd, Peter J. and Gary Sampson (1995) "Competition and Trade Policy: Identifying the Issues after the Uruguay Round." *World Economy* 18(5): 681–705.

Perroni, Carlo (1998) "The Uruguay Round and Its Impact on Developing Countries: An Overview of Model Results." In H. Thomas and J. Whalley (eds.) *Uruguay Round Results and the Emerging Trade Agenda*. Geneva: UNCTAD.

Short, Clare, Rt. Hon. (1999) "Future Multilateral Trade Negotiations: A 'Development Round'?" March 2, 1999, Department for International Development; UK Government.

Third World Network (2001) *The Multilateral Trading System: A Development Perspective*. New York: United Nations Development Program.

Whalley, John (1989) *The Uruguay Round and Beyond: The Final Report from the Ford Foundation Project on Developing Countries and the Global Trading System*. London: MacMillan.

Whalley, John (1990) "Non-Discriminatory Discrimination: Special and Differential Treatment Under the GATT for Developing Countries." *Economic Journal*, 100(403): 1318–1328.

Whalley, John (1999a) "Building Poor Countries Trade Capacity." Report prepared for an OECD Informal Experts Group, and *Centre for the Study of Globalization and Regionalization Working Paper* No.25/99. Warwick, UK: University of Warwick.

Whalley, John (1999b) "Special and Differential Treatment in the Millennium Round." *World Economy*, 22(8): 1065–1093.

Whalley, John (2000) "What Can the Developing Countries Infer from the Uruguay Round Models for Future Negotiations." *UNCTAD Discussion Paper* No. 4, October 2000.

Whalley, John (2001) "The WTO Ministerial and the Launch of a Development Round" (mimeo). London: University of Western Ontario.

WTO (1998a) "Implementation of WTO Provisions In Favor of Developing Country Members." Note by the WTO Secretariat, Geneva.

Globalization and Economic Systems:
A Homogeneity Test

László Csaba

Fo2

1. Introduction

It would be hard to find an issue that is more controversial among social scientists and the public than globalization. While some analysts' hail it as the apotheosis of the final victory of the market over the state (Yergin and Stanislaw, 1998) or praise it as a way of overcoming an antiquated and dangerous construct of socio-economic organization, the nation-state (Ohmae, 1995), others strike a more skeptical tone. Leaving old-style ideologues apart, some leading contemporary political economists sound alarm over the potentially destabilizing influences of globalization, which, allegedly, upsets social norms and welfare systems that had lent capitalism a human face in many advanced countries (see, for example, Rodrik, 1997). Other critical observers highlight the parallel processes of disintegration and tribalization, as well as the spread of various (economic, criminal, political, and other) networks that may reinforce each other in a way that potentially results in the undermining of representative democracy and controlled power (Barber, 1995).

The distinct trend of leftist-critical analysis, which has emerged in the critical tradition within the social sciences, is documented richly in the volumes edited by Higgott and Payne (Higgott and Payne, eds., 2000). Besides this intellectual, academic critique, also various social movements, relying to a large degree on the new networking opportunities provided by the Internet and diminished travel costs, organized themselves in a colorful protest movement across the globe. Those raising their serious doubts over the state of the contemporary world and many of its complexities and ills, from environmental pollution to child labor, formed a mass movement around the various critical issues, and expressed their concerns in a recurring series of mass protests.[1] Whenever the perceived or real 'captains' of globalization and the world economy convened, at G–8 summits or WTO meetings, anti-globalization

---

1. These groups were later dubbed in the British press as the "people of Seattle."

protests followed. In other words, concerns about the perceived or real dangers of globalization have become a social fact that needs to be analyzed and tackled.

In the present contribution I do not aim at an exhaustive analysis of these social and intellectual movements, that in itself could be topic of a whole monograph. My focus is on a single, though rather comprehensive, question: Do the intermingling processes of globalization lead to a uniformity of economic systems along the lines of the Anglo-American model of capitalism? (Cf. e.g. Lányi, 2001.) Is it true that the universalism inherent in the modern analytical economic approach would imply a descriptive and normative conclusion favoring a single 'proper' model of market economy for all countries that wish to be successful in the international arena? If the answer was negative it would also signal that although the emotional and massive protests—that came to a temporary halt only as a consequence of the September 11 attacks—raise serious issues, they often are falsely addressed, as the protesters choose WTO, IMF, G-8, or World Economic Forum meetings to articulate these legitimate concerns. For if no uniformity is in the making, the fora of international coordination cannot be blamed for imposing their straightjackets on the vulnerable or defenseless societies of the globe.

2. What Do We Talk About?

There is no single, universally accepted definition of globalization in the social sciences. According to some of the foremost experts on the subject (see e.g. Lechner and Boli, eds., 2000), we find at least four, only partly overlapping dimensions: economic globalization, political globalization, cultural globalization, and the globalization of social problems—that is, issues pertaining to the changing world society, including environmental concerns. This approach to the subject is obviously so broad that it does not allow any single analytical framework to grapple with the issue, thus I will confine myself only to economic globalization.

In a narrower approach we may conceive the expansion of markets; the challenges to the nation state as a basic unit of economic regulation; and the rise of new social movements as the defining features of globalization. The most visible outcome of this process is that the strong states become stronger, while the weak ones become weaker (Woods, 2000: 3–6). In a still narrower approach we may see globalization in terms of trade and international economic policies, where multilateralism, regionalism, and unilateralism are the relevant dimensions of comparison (Lahiri, 2001: xix).

In the following I shall adopt a 'medium-broad' approach. This involves problems (not just issues) the solution of which requires the cooperation of all mankind, since their scope and nature is such that neither (sub)national, nor regional approaches can be satisfactory. It is clear that urgent action is needed in the interest of all humankind, if we think of such challenges as epidemic diseases (where the spread of an epidemic may be conditional on the expenditures of those caring the least); the shortage of water (especially clean water); contagion and volatility stemming from and through innovations in the international financial system; organized crime; urbanization crises; unregulated mass migration; disregard for human rights, among others women's rights; the steady growth (and non-attendance) of the millions of disposed persons; the consequences of failed states (from Afghanistan to Eritrea); famines and deforestation; the 'digital divide'; the lack of participative growth in most of the world; the lack of religious and ethnic tolerance and its dire consequences; and many more.[2]

This non-exhaustive list of the major issues on the agenda demonstrates that action is required at the macro level, which needs to be coordinated across continents. These are rarely, however, representative of the wide variety of issues often emotionally raised by critics of the globalization process. While they bring up weighty issues such as income disparities or environmental concerns, these often fall under what Paul Krugman discusses as an "illusion of conflict" in international economic relations (Krugman, 1997: 69–84). In other words, legitimate concerns are being discussed under false headings and in an economic framework of "pop internationalism" that has little if anything in common with the established body of knowledge in general economics. The concept, for instance, of macroeconomics being like corporations competing with one another for a limited market; or the idea of a zero-sum international economy; or the fear of less developed participants losing out 'inevitably' in competition are, as Krugman shows, much more vague than the convincing points raised in the debate on globalization.

Therefore I shall define the process of globalization in standard economic terms, in order to underscore the peculiar features that characterize the Internet age—as opposed to the times of the Roman Empire or the colonial era, when sizable flows of international exchanges had also occurred. The economic concept of globalization thus outlined encompasses the worldwide intermingling among markets, among organizations, norms, and standards and forms of communication.

---

2. The notion/category of global problems is what we borrow from Bognár (1976), whilst the concrete examples are naturally different: in his time digital divide or organized crime networks were nowhere comparable to what is experienced nowadays.

2.1 The Globalization of Markets

The globalization of markets has at least three dimensions. The first is the increasingly unhampered, and by-and-large free flow of most commodities across borders, regulated by the disciplines of the World Trade Organization and its constituting multilateral agreements. Here there are industries where international flows are limited—such as in the sectors of farm products or in audiovisual products—and in some cases even classical command economy methods survive, such as in the various commodity agreements. Still, the bulk of international trade is transacted in industrial commodities, where both tariff and non-tariff barriers have seen a steady decline over the last half-century or so.

Second, capital used to be controlled in the Bretton Woods system. However, with the introduction of the flexible exchange-rate regimes in 1971, the ever growing importance of capital transactions, starting from the need to recycle large surpluses that emerged from the two oil price hikes of the 1970s, was followed by the gradual capital market liberalization of the 1980s. It should be stressed that this liberalization was only partly induced by the changes in the economic philosophies and the resulting turning away from the Keynesian approach of managed economy concepts. Technological innovation and financial innovation played a much more decisive role: in a truly Hayekian manner, the spread of information technology made possible a better utilization of decentralized knowledge. It allowed for a never-before-seen number of people involved in 24-hour financial transactions across the globe. In a way, the central controllability of the process has been irrevocably lost, since the size and dimensions of financial transactions, the channels of operation and the final outcomes have all become too complex to allow for the oversight by any national, let alone international, supervising or controlling agency.

This state of affairs has filled many people with unease or 'shivering', despite the overall welfare-enhancing nature of the process (Csontos, Király, and László, 1997). The fundamental concern voiced by the opponents has been caused by the dematerialization of wealth creation as well as by the lack of oversight over these processes by governments and the public alike. The latter rendered Keynesian demand management and prearranged controls over macroeconomic outcomes, targeted by the widespread neocorporatist arrangements, next to impossible to sustain. Although these claims about and fears of an uncontrolled and unbridled financial capitalism—exerting a dictatorship over everything from consumer needs to democracies—could be relatively easily proven wrong (Pete, 1999), the challenges to established patterns of welfare states and of economic

198

arrangements remained to a large degree unanswered (an issue we shall come back to later).

Third, not only commodities and capital, but also services can and increasingly do flow across borders, which is represented, for example, in the GATS (General Agreement on Trade-Related Services), one of the new multilateral agreements constituting the WTO. This should not come as a surprise since most of the advanced economies have long ago entered the post-industrial age, in which wealth creation is increasingly concentrated in the non-tradable services industries. On the one hand, the tendency of trade localization diminishes the share of tradables in wealth creation and leads to a stagnant or declining international 'openness' (external trade per production ratio) among major economic powers such as the US (Krugman, 1997: 205–214). On the other hand, services become increasingly internationalized, which is particularly visible in, though by no means constrained to, the financial sector.

2.2 The Globalization of Organizations

The second major dimension of economic globalization takes place among organizations. This process has at least three layers. First, the emergence of supranational agencies—especially in the post-Second World War period—have set new and effective limits to governmental sovereignty, traditionally postulated to be unconstrained in post-Westphalian theories. While some of the supranational arrangements, like the IMF or the EU, have emerged as a result of conscious self-limitations by the sovereign states, this is only part of the story. The emergence of multinational business, and especially of huge corporations transacting more than the total GDP of many developing nations—whose operations enhance the limitations on governmental freedoms to regulate, allocate, and redistribute—has been manifest.

Another layer of structures constraining governmental authority is that of intergovernmental organizations and agreements, such as the United Nations, the Council of Europe, and the WTO. Similar effects are being exerted by international conventions and agreements, like those on preserving biodiversity, the (recently modified) Kyoto protocol, the Geneva convention on refugees and prisoners of war, and the Hague Tribunal on international war crimes. In these cases, instead of developing supranational governance, compliance is being monitored and gradually enforced by the international community. The Milošević trial demonstrates that the appropriate and cooperative behavior of governments is enforced neither by force nor by a supranational authority, but via voluntary compliance brought about by the spread of norms and expectations of the international community. The pariah status of such countries as Belarus under Lukashenka, or of the North Cyprus 'Republic' are also points in case.

Last but not least, a third layer of organizations has emerged that can be labeled as meso-economic forms of coordination. These include such formal institutions as the ever more powerful regional municipalities in the European Union, the still quite powerful chambers of trade and industry, the trade unions, and the ever more vocal NGO sector (the latter, for example, by limiting governmental discretion in such cases as Chechnya or Kosovo). But aside from these formal institutions, such informal actors as the Mafia, the international networks of trafficking human beings, the terrorist networks, and the money-laundering establishments also put severe limits on how law and order can be enforced. The economic implications of these are so all-embracing that they need no further elaboration, since even international agencies routinely work to mitigate their negative effects.

2.3 The Globalization of Standards

A third dimension of economic globalization is traceable in the ever-growing role of uniform standards and norms. These include not only such points as the proscription of slave and child labor, but also the enforcement of such arrangements as international accounting and disclosure standards. While many transnational corporations are obliged to produce statistical figures in line with the regulations of local laws, none of them can spare producing the same types of statistics according to the international rules for their own headquarters. But the discussion of other issues, like quality standards, have also been spreading throughout the world.

2.4 The Globalization of Communication

Finally, the fourth formative dimension of economic globalization is the increasingly important channel of communication. The information technology revolution has made clandestine processing of information increasingly difficult, especially for authorities of various sorts that are in dire need of new cryptography technologies. Societies can be less and less isolated from the external world; governments, official ideologies, or traditions are less and less able to influence and form expectations, priorities, tastes, perceptions, and other cultural characteristics. This process, which is probably the greatest emancipatory step for the individual since the invention of book printing or contraceptives, makes at the same time various self-nominated vanguards see red: those who pose as guardians of controlled societies or traditions or those who intend to make decisions for millions, in issues ranging from state security to consumption patterns, savings habits, and investment decisions.

Ramifications of the IT revolution make various statist propositions—from introducing the Tobin tax to creating new institutions to limit volatility in the international financial system, such as an international bankruptcy court, or a lender of last resort, or an international liquidity control agency—not feasible (Rogoff, 1999). What remains is basically a set of unilateral reform measures to be instituted by developing countries to improve the solidity of their banking system, their reputation, and quality of regulatory frameworks. The ghost of international capital flows has been let out of the bottle and there is no way to force it back again. This, in turn, does put limit on what formally sovereign, especially small and open economies may or may not rationally do. As has been evidenced by the slowdown and stagnation in the US economy in 2000–2001, as well as the ensuing slowdown in the EU, there is no way for economic policies to set and attain prefixed quantitative plan, growth or income targets—even in the largest economic units of the globe. And conversely, if the slowdown is global, there is no way to opt for isolationist but growth-promoting policies in the longer run. The capital controls of Chile, often invoked as a good example of interventionism supplanting market friendly overall policies, has been shown to be both procyclical and ineffective (increasing cyclical crises of the economy, as opposed to mitigating their effects; see Edwards, 1999).

It is important to bear in mind that information technology has the potential to spread rapidly in societies, above the control of national governments, often much to their dismay. The Chinese government may switch off the broadcast of CNN in Beijing, or the Iranian government may prohibit women to follow Paris fashion, nevertheless with today's diversity of international intercourse there are fewer ways to stop news, products and people from getting where they wish to. In a different way, the terrorist attack on the US and the resultant 'war on terror' has supplied more than sufficient evidence for the changed modus operandi of the globe. Likewise, the organization of the million-strong protests against globalization in Genoa in 2001 via e-mails, and despite extreme police and border control measures, has sent a clear signal to the limits of even combined and joint governmental efforts.

This implies, *inter alia*, that only such patterns of reforming the international financial architecture can be considered as non-utopian and policy-relevant that take the ensuing decentralization and decontrol of processes for granted. These advocate measures which view the dominance of market processes as a given, and suggest modifications that enhance their transparency (by good fiscal practice code and by the imposition of international accounting and disclosure standards). This may be complemented by those that aim to bail out the private sector rather than replacing its activities in the old-styled Keynesian fashion (for more on this see Fischer, 1999).

2.5 Why Globalization Is a Dominant Trend?

Finally we need to address the issue of why globalization is a dominant trend even in the view of those who would like to tame it or domesticate it, because they perceive it as something like a wild animal. The answer is certainly in line with mainstream international economic theory: that it is a welfare-enhancing process, which must be beneficial to all participants involved, at the macro and micro levels. And indeed, long-term reviews of the developments in the world economy (Maddison, 1995; Craft, 2001) are clearly indicative of an overlooked fact: namely, the big differences in current per-capita GDP and per-capita consumption (and even more in terms of other human development indicators, like life expectancy or health) that emerge between the countries that have been incorporated into the global economy and those that have been left out of the process. Thus while traditional, say Sub-Saharan African economies stagnate, wealth creation explodes in the countries that participate in and are the driving forces of globalization.

There are two ways of how we can support this insight. First, if the combination of factors of production is not hindered, it can be maximally efficient in intertemporal, intersectoral, and international terms. If we look, however, at the mechanics of growth, this must translate into a productivity-enhancing measure of more globalization, since at the bottom line, it is national productivity that sets the pace of welfare improvement. And indeed empirical studies of sectoral impacts of "more globalization" (Gersbach, 2002: 227–228) have indicated that there is a strong empirical correlation between more globalization and higher productivity (although with a time lag), and that the differences between the local and the globally most efficient producers are declining. Therefore the payoffs, in terms of welfare, from more globalization can be shown to be significant (with the numbers, of course, varying across countries and sectors, but the trend being unequivocal).

Even with reference to the simplest neoclassical Solow-model, it can be expected and demonstrated that less developed countries can benefit disproportionately: by importing more advanced technologies, by relying on more advanced forms of management knowledge and by improving their capacity to process information. This requires a degree of domestic social capital (in the sense of Amartya Sen) and supportive institutions. Thus the causal link is a non-automatic one.

Last but not least it is hard to overlook that once a centrally uncontrollable global market has emerged, by and large spontaneously from technological innovations, its structure, organization, and modus operandi is unlikely to be reducible to previously known and tested forms of societal organization, such as the Bretton Woods system, or the interwar bilateralism and state trading. The only way national governments may rationally react to this is by redefining their roles and perceptions as well as their regulatory instruments to be in line with the new challenges—an issue we shall revisit in the concluding part of this study.

3. Globalization and Macro Systems

3.1 An Historical Perspective

As indicated above, it would be misleading to identify globalization with one of its features—such as financial globalization or the global flow of information technologies, that have, indeed, been salient features of the developments in the last fifteen years or so. All in all, most other features of the process have already been unfolding with the emergence of capitalism as a global system, that is, ever since the 16th and 17th centuries.

As we know from Max Weber (1982: 43–87) there is a world of difference between profit maximizing as an individual or stratum-specific behavior, and a capitalist market economy, where the entire macro system is organized around the "commercial spirit," with formal and informal institutions serving the same purpose. From this perspective, starting with colonialism, the geographical spread and the parallel 'deepening' of capitalist institutions have also been the features of what we may call globalization. As Marx highlighted in many of his writings, capitalism is unlike all other previous forms of human organizations in its universalist, cosmopolitan, and expansionary nature. Thus the history of the modern market economy is also a history of extending the peculiar logic of economic calculation to the whole earth. Let us list very shortly, how this has taken place by the factors of production.

a) Colonialism followed national and religious ideologies, but also resulted in incorporating all, previously dispersed, and differently organized societies in the dominant mode of production. Most visibly, land and natural resources—primarily in the Americas, Africa, and Asia—were included into the sourcing of inputs for states and companies of the core colonial powers. In the colonial system, trade barriers had been demoted, traditional societies disrupted, new production lines introduced to serve the world markets. Improving transport facilities, coupled with their falling costs following the invention of the steam engine, all contributed to the intensification of the process.

b) It has been particularly important for the global economy to channel surplus labor and thereby solve a major puzzle of overpopulation and social strains in contemporary Europe. It is quite well known that the overpopulation of Ireland, Italy, Austria-Hungary, and the United Kingdom was partially remedied by emigration to the New World. Conversely, the sparse population and the labor shortages of the new states were relieved through immigration to those countries. Immigration played a major role in the lasting economic boom in the Austro-Hungarian Monarchy in the second half of the 19th century (O'Rourke, 2002). Labor mobility thus has been an entirely realistic common assumption of classical economics.

c) With the consolidation of the colonial system and with the strengthening of the post-revolutionary systems in nineteenth-century Europe, the spread of industrial and corporate organization following capitalist principles became unstoppable. International corporations in trade, banking, and insurance, together with the emergence of the global commodity and stock markets and the invention of the telegraph, extended the profit principle as the basic way of social organization across the world.

d) Closely related to the above transformations we can observe several waves of industrial revolution. The defining moment in these is the wide-scale industrial use of innovations, in other words, the unprecedented spread of technological skills and inventions in society. This has to do with social improvements, like universal schooling; but still, it is hard to oversee the importance of market conditions for this outcome. For it is common knowledge that many technical inventions, such as printing, had already long been known in non-European cultures. Still, these were not heavily used before the competitive spirit started to dominate the entire social fabric. It is hardly surprising that inventions and publications (as scientific output) emerge from all quarters of the globe, still most applications, patenting and embodied technological innovations are registered in the United States. Technological leadership is not unrelated to social organization.

e) It is hard to disregard that the flow of capital reached its peak in the years preceding the First World War, and that net flows of trade measured against GDP recovered to their 1914 levels only in 1995 (Williamson, 1998).

f) Lastly, mention should be made of the role of the gold standard that implied full current and capital account convertibility coupled with zero exchange rate risks. Since credit has not been fiat money, the expansion needed to service an ever-growing economy has been constrained by the quantities of gold production or irresponsible emission. Still, monetary stability and the ensuing calculability allowed for a truly global flow of scarce finances according to considerations of best return.

It is common knowledge that the restoration of the global economy based on the gold standard was only partial in the 1920–1929 period, and the Great Depression of 1929–1933 introduced a paradigmatic change in economic theory and policy. Up until about 1989, various state-led models of management dominated economic theory and practice alike. With the benefit of hindsight, it may be legitimate to ask whether this represented a mainstream human development, or a mere digression, despite the considerable variation of national models.

In the following I try to survey the major economic models of this period. By relying on the recent textbook of the Budapest University of Economics (Bara and Szabó, eds., 2000)[3] and some supplementary materials I try to address the decisive issue of sustainability of the respective alternatives. For it is common knowledge that if an economic model is a non-sustainable, it must be seen as a mere digression, even if it is extremely popular. The stop-go cycles observed under populist Latin American regimes may serve as a yardstick: no matter how popular the expansionary phase is with voters, it cannot be sustained as it creates inflation and, in the end, balance of payments crises. Thus, once global embeddedness is given, the re-emergence of stop-go cycles is a sign of notorious miscalculation. Or else: our question is directed at the sustainability of alternative arrangements that emerged in response to the Great Depression, alternatives aiming at national economic policy autonomy.

a) The most decisive alternative to the free market has been the centrally administered economy, in its Nazi Germany and Soviet variants. In the first, though property rights were formally observed, decisions on major investments and price calculations, on resource allocation and foreign trade were under the control of the state administration. In the second variant, full nationalization and a constant mobilization along a few priority investments dominated all horizontal forms of coordination. Sustaining each of these systems required oppressive politics and expansionary ideology that led to the belligerence of Germany and explosive economic development in the Soviet Union. While solving imminent

---

3. This is the only textbook available on comparative economic systems in the post-communist world, and to my knowledge, the only textbook (rather than reader) covering post-communist transition (besides discussing Latin American and East Asian models) and globalization, beyond the usual opposition of centralized and market systems.

social and economic problems, these arrangements proved self-defeating in the long run.

b) The social market economy then emerged as a search for a third way between *laissez-faire* capitalism and the centrally administered economy. It proved to be a tremendous success in the 1950s and 1960s, with seven to eight percent annual growth rates in the German Wirtschaftswunder, and the absorption of twelve million refugees in a country of 50 million. However, following the oil price hikes the German consensual model proved unable to adjust to the challenges of world economic changes. When in the 1990s it was confronted with reunification, the process thwarted all reforms and postponed organizational adjustment further. As an authoritative analysis (Cassel and Rauhut, 1998) pinpoints, the improvised nature of the construct as well as its inability to innovate resulted in a stagnant economy, where state expenditures exceed 50 percent of the GDP. What was conceived as a competitive order turned into a bargaining society where defending the status quo remained a dominant concern.

c) In Hungary and Yugoslavia market socialism was beginning in the 1960s. These changes of policy and of organizational structure have tried to combine plan and market, self-management and free prices, and political centralization with economic decentralization. While better performing than those countries that adopted the Soviet model, lagging behind the Western countries proved a lasting trend. Moreover, when more radical reforms were introduced, Hungary turned to a market economy without adjective in 1990, while Yugoslavia disintegrated along the lines of winners and losers of the similarly market-economy-type Marković-reforms of the same period. In sum, none of these attempts proved sustainable when geopolitical constraints derived from bipolarism were lifted.

d) Following decolonialization the idea of non-capitalist developmentalism emerged as a dominant paradigm both in theory and policy-making. The emphasis was put on capital accumulation, on import substitution, on state management of macroprocesses, and on defending autochthonous structures from the swings in international markets. In hindsight (Stiglitz and Hoff, 2001), these attempts appear to have failed, both in terms of generating growth in the long run, and even more in delivering for the poor. The wider scope of human development indicators we invoke, the more dismal this performance is. And while the survey quoted above provides insightful feedback and inferences to general economic theory on the role of institutions and good governance, the failure of the original paradigm is hardly a discussion issue any longer. As a matter of fact, failed forms of nationalism and industrialization often contributed to the heart of social problems and even partially induced the Islamic revolution of the late

1970s. Lacking institutions and governmental structures that developmentalism tended to presume as a given, many states were confronted with trends they were unable to deal with and radical solutions were often the result.[4]

e) Mention should be made of the changing nature of technological progress. If in the previous centuries economies of scale and scope seemed to be the name of the game, this situation has dramatically changed, not least due to the 'intrusion' of IT into the conventional activities of various sorts. While large scale investment was previously needed for any new business, and industrial forms of mass production were dominant, currently IT individualizes both producers and consumers. Individual sourcing, lean organization, outsourcing, subcontractor networking, and tailor-made production are now dominant. It is no longer fixed capital, but the ability to absorb and utilize information that constitutes the major competitive edge (a leading corporation's major asset is its loyal and motivated workforce in the new management paradigm).

3.2 New Trends

These changes have triggered wide-ranging consequences. Small states, once relegated to the status of anachronistic historical formations, have gained new viability, not least due to the sharply diminishing costs of producing various necessities, including symbols and national language cultural outputs (Brada, 2000). The growing importance of the meso-level—summed up in the concept of the 'Europe of Regions'—is yet another sign, supported by the wide-ranging decentralizations affecting the formerly highly centralized, uniform states such as France, Italy, Spain, the United Kingdom and Belgium.

In sum, inward-looking and state-led models have not proven sustainable, while globalization and new trends in technology and industrial organization all move towards a new direction. Thus while the future, as always, is open-ended, the solutions managed in the 1929–1989 period are no longer applicable.

The only question that remains to be addressed in closing this section relates to the mechanism, through which globalization affects the evolution of macro systems. This takes place in the competition among various solutions that emerge in a variety of layers.

---

4. This has emerged, alas, as one of the very few consensus points from the discussions at the University of Warwick conference entitled "Globalisation, Growth, and (In)equality," held on March 15–17, 2002.

The competition among commodities is trivially valid in a system of open trade regimes and under WTO disciplines. Hence, arrangements protecting non-viable or inferior producers tend to be crowed out. Technologies also compete, with more advanced ones being not only often cheaper but creating indirect spillovers, especially via the IT sector. Also the growing concern for the environment and the related change in priorities and self-perception of leading firms creates a competition for excellence.

The latter implies the massive flow of people. The more a society proves unable to cope with multiculturalism, the less it is able to profit from the major factor of long term growth, i.e. human capital. It is worth mentioning that current trends of migration are nowhere close to what had been the case at the *fin-de-siècle*, or to those in the USA during the past century.

Similarly important are the application of new organizational techniques and management skills. The more some stick to the outdated Taylorist-Fordist solutions, the higher the likelihood of these losing out to those familiar with more sophisticated technologies of coordinating activities of physically disconnected people.

Last but not least secularly divergent trends in living standards penalize those societies which stick to antiquated, non-performance related remuneration, over taxation and oppressive societal arrangements. This creates a vicious circle of stagnation, while others continue to generate new momentum. Only Cubas and North Koreas are able to seal off their frontiers.

4. Does Globalization Homogenize or Differentiate?

The methodological universalism built into modern analytical economics, like the standard McDonald hamburger or the standard Hilton room, leads many people to fear the unifying influence of globalization. True, some observers talk of unification of the mindset and denationalization of production and organizations alike (Ohmae, 1995); nevertheless, analytical economists have emphatically called our attention to the market as a creative process, where non-linearities are typically present. This means that even small changes may trigger large effects, thus indeterminism of future states is an inherent feature of evolution (Buchanan and Vanberg, 2001: 101–102).

In the following, I try to contrast the unifying and differentiating features of contemporary developments so as to be able to answer the question raised in the subtitle.

a) As we have seen above, the unstoppable spread of IT has already been revolutionizing management and industrial organization. Those wanting to profit from new technologies must be involved in global sourcing, in networking and in the processes leading to organizations without boundaries, since those sticking to Taylorism and self-sufficiency inevitably lag behind. In a non-factory type of production and marketing organization long hierarchies are counterproductive. The same holds for individual remuneration in overseeing and managing tasks requiring cooperation and a conscientious effort even in the lack of constant observance or without policing private e-mails and phone calls. These innovations have already penetrated many traditional sectors and thus this trend is not conditional upon the recovery of the IT sector as reflected in NASDAQ indices.

b) Large-scale corporations raise additional funding from capital markets. The more one is interested or reliant on non-bound equity financing, the more one needs to observe the accounting rules and disclosure requirements. Following the bad experiences of 1997–1999 in East Asia and more recently with the collapse of Enron and its auditor, Andersen, market participants might be even more concerned about solidity and adhering to conservative behavior. The emerging Basle Two Accord on Sound Banking Principles will decentralize risk assessment and impose more burden on those involved in emerging markets. This might, indeed, reduce available amounts for less developed countries (Griffith-Jones, 2002), but in the meantime it may mean better screening functions in the use of available money. And similarly, awareness raising about the real costs of additional funding might be the best way to discourage developing country politicians from engaging in yet another wasteful mega-project. Thus capital market discipline may indeed be severed, but this may be good news for both sides. Still, the overall validity of solid financial practices can hardly be doubted any longer.

c) As we have seen above, environmental concerns tend to be growingly endogenized by the leading corporations, or a growing segment of them. This has to do with the spread of the green agenda, with the presence of green parties (or like-minded value conservatives) in many governments, enforcement of ever-stiffer environmental legislation, and the extremely negative publicity of environmental scandals that loom for culpable companies.

One of the oldest wisdoms is that an attack is the best defense; thus leading firms have already been engaged in building up their corporate image as a green and clean organization. This may have to do with their activity area, their use of computers, their emphasis on high value added and many similar features. And nobody should underestimate the deterrent effect of the recurring environmental scandals on any management with a long-term strategy concerned with corporate image (not to speak of his own). The bigger and the more multinational a company, the stronger both positive and negative incentives are for it to adopt a modern profile.

d) Last but not least is the growing use of international standards and codes of conduct, be that the Code of Good Fiscal Practices of the IMF or the TRIM agreement of the WTO. The latter, limiting the use of local contents, minimum export requirements, and obligations to export, have limited the use of these as a redistributory measure, although it equally limited the distortion of markets and the resulting welfare losses in a dynamic perspective (Greenaway and Milner, 2001: 157). In rejecting customary, non-efficient and welfare reducing policies, poor countries though sacrificed their 'sovereign rights', still improved their policy quality and the welfare of their populations. Similarly, by renouncing fiscal misreporting, though freedom of administration to cheat is diminished, still by the same token, the ability of the public to check its government in a democratic fashion improves. The same goes for the 'outlawing' of corruption or the disregard for women's and children's rights with reference to cultural specificities. The more often the non-representative nature of governments is raised, the higher is the possibility of Pareto-improvements,[5] should these criticisms be heeded, since that would diminish policy-induced distortions (like prestige projects) common in the developing world.

4.2 Factors Inducing Diversity

a) Modern management literature is supportive of insights from industrial organization literature and economics over the paramount importance of culture in shaping forms of corporate governance. When Japanese carmakers attempted in Britain to induce the workforce to start the day by singing the corporate anthem, they were met with stiff resistance. Similar rebukes were experienced by Americans wanting to introduce individual remuneration schemes or individual initiative projects in Korea. German and Italian managers still dislike the idea of going to the capital market, and the British government still is terrified by the EU idea to introduce some form of 'employee co-decision' in the Statute on the European corporations.

5. This means a state in which improving the welfare position of one actor does not deteriorate the position of anybody else.

b) Equally dissimilar are the arrangements of the labor markets. If we only look at the best performers, the diversity is already astounding. In Japan, the life-long employment scheme, or the practice of re-employing 'heavenly envoys' (former high ranking bureaucrats in business positions) is still not buried. In Switzerland, guild-like arrangements produce outcomes where an unemployment rate over two percent is already a cause for concern. Meanwhile in Britain, Blair's New Labour has vigorously deregulated; in the Netherlands, part-time working has halved the army of unemployed; and Hungary leads transition economies via a practically liberalized labor market. In sum, there is no sign of any uniform arrangement.

c) One of the longest observations of comparative studies has been the differences in the performance and orientation of civil service. While in some countries this is seen as a property of the political class to support its clients, in other cases non-partisan public administration ensures high professionalism across stormy party politics. In some countries the 'high tax, high service' ideal is still popular, as in Scandinavia; in other cases public distrust is deeply seated, thus free market options are selling better. There is no 'iron law' prescribing, say thirty percent, as an ideal benchmark for the optimal level of public spending. Some analyses pointed to the marked diversity of public dues across the OECD countries and concluded that a big government may actually be quite attractive for big business. The reason is that big government provides more law and order, more externalities in terms of public service, and generally a more amenable business environment including better human capital (Garrett, 2000: 114; cf. also Rodrik, 1998). By contrast, low taxes or tax holidays may be seen as a way to try to compensate for a lack of institutional infrastructure or rule of law. These may be deterrents just as too low prices may indicate theft or inferior quality.

d) Lastly, we may reiterate one of the basic qualities of any competitive arrangement. Those following some standards, like benchmarking or market leaders, though opt for a low risk, also accept a low premium. Those going after a high return take more risks by innovating in various dimensions, or looking for yet untested markets, uncharted waters, and may, though by no means will, be rewarded lavishly. This Schumpeterian nature of any market implies a constant trial and error, but also ensures a diversity of competing options and strategies as the fundamental feature of the arrangement. If market entry cannot be blocked, and public power ensures this, then diversity will remain the defining feature of the market game.

In sum, we find both diversity and uniformity as lasting features in the globalization process. Uniformity relates basically to features that form the rules of the game. Diversity relates to the concrete steps that yield the best outcomes.

5. Conclusion

Thus we come to a conclusion that converges to what we observe in any game that is being played globally, like soccer. While the general rules of the game are the same everywhere, individual strategies may continue to differ just as much as the styles of the Brazilian and German teams tend to differ. The more we believe that general rules require different solutions under different contextual settings, the less we are surprised to see this outcome. Good governance these days thus implies facing sovereignty constraints, but also taking up public policy goals such as creating solid institutions and good quality regulatory environments that favor investors, foreign and domestic alike (Prakash, 2001: 560). This means nothing less that the open-ended nature of market economy and the principal indeterminacy of outcomes seems to be dominant over any fashionable concept of maximization. The latter can not even be postulated, since the global welfare function is even less definable than the social welfare function according to Kenneth Arrow, for much the same reasons (Arrow, 1950). Even if we accept his (mathematically proven) classic claim that in a nation-state it would take a dictator to order individual preferences according to a fiat social preference, this insight lends itself to easy generalization at the level of the world community. Therefore globalization is likely to increase, rather than diminish, the diversity of economic arrangements of the world.

References

Aoki, Masikiko (2001) *Toward a Comparative Institutional Analysis*. Cambridge, MA and London: MIT Press.

Arrow, Kenneth (1950) "A Difficulty in the Concept of Social Welfare." *The Journal of Political Economy*, 58(2): 328–346.

Bara, Zoltán and Katalin Szabó (eds.) (2000) *Gazdasági intézmények, országok, rendszerek. Bevezetés az összehasonlító gazdaságtanba.* (Economic Institutions, Countries, Systems. An Introduction to Comparative Economics.) Budapest: Aula.

Barber, Benjamin (1995) *Jihad versus McWorld*. New York: Free Press.

Bognár, József (1976) *Világgazdasági korszakváltás.* (A Change of Epoch in the World Economy). Budapest: Gondolat Könyvkiadó.

Brada, Josef C. (2000) "Technology, New Globalisation, Old Cultural Identities, and the Emergence of New Small Countries." In Zoltán Bara and László Csaba (eds.) *Small Economies' Adjustment to Global Tendencies*. Budapest: Aula, pp.17–30.

Buchanan, James and Viktor Vanberg (2001) "The Market As A Creative Process." In Viktor Vanberg (ed.) *The Constitution of Markets. Essays in Political Economy*. London and New York: Routledge, pp.101–113.

Cassel, Dieter and Sigismund Rauhut (1998) "Soziale Markwirtschaft: eine wirtschaftspolitische Konzeption auf dem Prüfstand." In Dieter Cassel (ed.) *50 Jahre Soziale Marktwirtschaft*. Stuttgart: Lucius und Lucius Verlag, pp.3–52.

Craft, Nicholas (2001) "Historical Perspectives on Development." In Gerald Meier and Joseph Stiglitz (eds.) *Frontiers of Development Economics. The Future in Perspective*. Oxford: Oxford University Press and Washington, D.C.: The World Bank, pp.301–334.

Csontos, László, Júlia Király, and Géza László (1997–98) "The Great Shivering Around the Millennium." *Acta Oeconomica*, 49(1–2): 1–34.

Edwards, Sebastian (1999) "How Effective Are Capital Controls?" *The Journal of Economic Perspectives*, 13(4): 65–84.

Fischer, Stanley (1999) "Reforming the International Financial System." *The Economic Journal*, 109(459) (Nov): 557–576.

Garrett, Geoffrey (2000) "Shrinking States? Globalization and National Autonomy." In Ngaire Woods (ed.) *The Political Economy of Globalization*. Houndsmill and London: MacMillan and New York: St.Martin's Press, pp.107–146.

Gersbach, Hans (2002) "Does and How Does Globalization Matter at the Industry Level?" *The World Economy*, 25(2): 209–229.

Greenaway, David and Chris Milner (2001) "Multilateral Trade Reform, Regionalization and Developing Countries." In Sajal Lahiri (ed.) *Regionalism and Globalisation. Theory and Practice*. London and New York: Routledge, pp.144–169.

Griffith-Jones, Stephanie (2002) "The new financial architecture as a global public good." Paper presented at the international conference at the University of Warwick entitled "Globalisation, Growth and (In)equality", the 5th CSGR conference, March 15–17, 2002.

Higgott, Richard and Alan Payne (eds.) (2000) *The New Political Economy of Globalisation*, Vols.I–II. Cheltenham and Northampton, MA: Edward Elgar.

Krugman, Paul (1997a) "The Illusion of Conflict in International Trade." In Paul Krugman, *Pop Internationalism*. Cambridge, MA and London: The MIT Press, pp.69–84.

213

Krugman, Paul (1997b) *The Localization of the World Economy*. In Paul Krugman, *Pop Internationalism*. Cambridge, MA and London: The MIT Press, pp.205–214.

Lahiri, Sajal (2001) "Preface." In Sajal Lahiri (ed.) *Regionalism and Globalisation: Theory and Practice*. London and New York: Routledge, pp.xvi–xx.

Lányi, Kamilla (2001) "Európa választásai (Choices of Europe)." *Valóság*, 45(6): 17–35.

Lechner, Frank and John Boli (eds.) (2000) *The Globalisation Reader*. Oxford and Malden, MA: Basil Blackwell.

Maddison, Angus (1995) *Monitoring the World Economy, 1820–1992*. Paris: OECD.

Ohmae, Kenichi (1995) *The End of the Nation State*. New York: The Free Press.

O'Rourke, Kevin (2002) "Globalisation and Inequality: Historical Trends." Paper presented at the 5th CSGR conference, University of Warwick, March 15–17.

Pete, Péter (1999) "Some Thoughts about 'The World Ruled by Money'. The Increased Role of the Financial Ssystem." *Acta Oeconomica*, 50(3–4): 239–255.

Prakash, Aseem (2001) "Grappling with Globalisation: Challenges for Economic Governance." *The World Economy*, 24(4): 543–565.

Rodrik, Dani (1997) *Has Globalization Gone Too Far?* Washington, D.C.: The Institute of International Economics.

Rodrik, Dani (1998) "Why Do Open Economies Have Bigger Government?" *The Journal of Political Economy*, 106(5): 997–1032.

Rogoff, Kenneth (1999) "International Institutions for Reducing Global Financial Instability." *The Journal of Economic Perspectives*, 13(4): 21–42.

Stiglitz, Joseph and Karla Hoff (2001) "Modern Economic Theory and Development." In Gerald Meier and Joseph Stiglitz (eds.) *Frontiers of Development Economics. The Future in Perspective*. Oxford: Oxford University Press and Washington, D.C.: The World Bank, pp.389–459.

Yergin, Daniel and Joseph Stanislaw (1998) *The Commanding Heights: The Battle Between Government and the Market that Is Remaking the Modern World*. New York: Simon and Shuster.

Weber, Max (1982) *A protestáns etika és a kapitalizmus szelleme* (The Protestant Ethic and the Spirit of Capitalism). Budapest: Gondolat Könyvkiadó.

Williamson, Jeffrey (1998) "Globalization, Labour Markets, and the Policy Backlash." *The Journal of Economic Perspectives*, 12(4): 51–72.

Woods, Ngaire (2000) "The Political Economy of Globalization." In Ngaire Woods (ed.) *The Political Economy of Globalization*. Houndsmill and London: MacMillan and New York: St.Martin's Press, pp.1–19.

IV.

New Sources of Founding
and Reforming the Aid System

Strengthening the Aid System

Jonathan T. Fried and Bruce Rayfuse

(africa)   F35

519

1. Introduction

The issue of foreign aid effectiveness has gained considerable prominence in recent years. Much of the increased emphasis has come about as a result of pressure on aid budgets. Through most of the 1990s, donor countries reduced their development assistance in relation to their GNPs and sometimes even in absolute terms (OECD, 2000). In one sense then, the emphasis on increasing the effectiveness of aid resources was a response by development agencies and institutions to the necessity to make do with fewer resources.

More fundamentally, perhaps, aid agencies and institutions recognized that being able to demonstrate that aid does indeed promote development and make a significant difference in the lives of citizens of recipient countries was critical to winning public support for it in donor countries.

The pressure on donor country aid budgets through the 1990s reflected both international and domestic factors. On the international side, the end of the Cold War affected not only the volume of aid but also the direction of aid flows. On the one hand, there was less perceived need to use aid to win or to support ideological allies in the developing world. On the other hand, Western governments saw great benefit and urgency in using aid to help the states of the former Soviet bloc to build democratic societies and market economies.

The 1990s also saw tremendous growth in private capital flows to developing countries. By the mid-1990s, private investment flows to developing countries dwarfed official aid flows (World Bank, 1997a). While much of this investment was concentrated in a relatively small group of developing countries, the fact that it was taking place contributed to the perception in some donor countries that by improving the climate for investment, developing countries could attract private flows that would more than compensate for any reduction in official development assistance (ODA).

On the other hand, the governments in many donor countries found themselves under severe budget pressures in the 1990s. In times of fiscal restraint, reducing international assistance is often one of the most politically expedient measures that governments can take. Cutting aid budgets was made even easier by a general disenchantment or fatigue among donor country publics about the perceived results that development assistance was achieving. According to polling information, many citizens in donor countries thought much of their aid was wasted, either skimmed off by corrupt elites in developing countries or wasted in white elephant development projects (see Kull, 2001 or Stackhouse, 2000).

The most prominent policy-maker questioning the value of aid in recent months has been former US Treasury Secretary Paul O'Neill, who has openly and eloquently asked what "the hundreds of billions spent in the name of economic development" has achieved (O'Neill, 2002). He has called for development institutions to be able to demonstrate measurable results to justify their efforts and expenditures. He has argued that demonstrable success in development assistance will increase public support for future increases in development assistance.

This argument is entirely plausible. It is noteworthy that at the same time as public disenchantment with official aid programs was growing, so too was willingness among the publics in developed countries to try to help developing countries (Kull, 2001). Polling data in donor countries consistently shows a widespread desire to assist developing countries. One need only look at the success of the international effort led mainly by non-governmental organizations to forgive the debts of poor countries to see this desire in operation. Popular pressure through movements such as Jubilee 2000 were instrumental in the development of the Heavily Indebted Poor Countries (HIPC) Initiative in 1996 and its enhanced version adopted in 1999.[1] This initiative, with accompanying measures by bilateral donors, will see the debt burdens of HIPCs reduced by almost two-thirds, or about US $40 billion in 2001 net present value terms.[2]

The issue of aid effectiveness and of the willingness to increase aid resources is of enormous significance to the people of the developing world. The United Nations Millennium Summit in held in New York in September 2000 helped to set the agenda for development efforts when it established the Millennium Development Goals. In his report leading up to the United Nations Financing

1. Jubilee 2000 was an international campaign that began in the early 1990s aiming to have creditors "cancel the unpayable debts of the poorest countries by the year 2000, under a fair and transparent process." Eventually, Jubilee 2000 campaigns were active in over 60 countries. An international petition circulated by the campaign gathered more than 24 million signatures. For more information, see www.jubilee2000uk.org.
2. The data on the amount of debt to be forgiven comes from IMF/World Bank (2002). For information on how the HIPC Initiative works, see Andrews et al. (1999).

for Development Conference in Monterrey, Mexico, former Mexican President Ernesto Zedillo estimated that achieving the Millennium Development Goals would require a doubling of development assistance from current levels (Zedillo *et al.*, 2001). The United Nations Conference on Financing for Development called for a substantial increase in ODA to meet internationally agreed development goals and objectives. But as noted above, however, enhancing aid effectiveness is crucial to building support for increased development assistance. The Monterrey consensus therefore included commitments by developing countries to improve governance and the climate for investment in order to stimulate long-term growth (see United Nations, 2002).

The question of development effectiveness was one of the key issues the G–8 Finance Ministers discussed at their meeting in Halifax in June 2002. In their Africa Action Plan, which emerged out of the G–8 Summit held in Kananaskis, Canada, later in June, G–8 Leaders stressed that their commitment to increased assistance to Africa was dependant on a reciprocal commitment by Africans to undertake the governance and economic reforms necessary to make aid effective (see G–8 [2002], especially paragraph 4).

2. Development and Aid Effectiveness—Uneven Progress

Development economics as a field is not much more than 50 years old, but the literature on development effectiveness has grown significantly in recent years. The passage of time has led to an accumulation of evidence and experience that has enabled some judgements to be made on what works to promote development and what does not. Over the last 50 years there have been development successes, most notably the economies of the 'Asian tigers'. Hong Kong, Taiwan, Korea, and Singapore were able to make the leap from poor country to developed country status. Other Asian economies, such as China, Indonesia, Thailand, and Malaysia, also made enormous progress in development and poverty reduction. The crises that hit some of these economies in the late 1990s, while certainly serious, have not come close to erasing these gains.

At their meeting in Ottawa in November 2001, the G–20 Finance Ministers asked the World Bank to prepare a report on development assistance, with a focus on what worked, what did not, and why. The research report, titled *The Role and Effectiveness of Development Assistance: Lessons from World Bank Experience*, was prepared for the April 2002 meeting of the Development Committee of the IMF and World Bank (see Goldin *et al.*, 2002). The report catalogues a number of clear development successes:

- Over the past 40 years, life expectancy at birth in developing countries increased by 20 years, an increase as large as had been achieved in all human history up to that point.
- Over the last 30 years, the illiteracy rate in the developing world was almost cut in half, from 47 percent to 25 percent.
- Over the last 35 years, the per capita GDP of the developing world increased at an average annual rate of 2.2 percent.
- Over the last 20 years, the number of people subsisting on less than $1 per day has been falling after two centuries of increase. Since 1980, the number of poor has fallen by about 200 million, even as the world's population increased by 1.6 billion.

While there have been development successes, however, there have also been spectacular failures. Nowhere is this more evident than in Sub-Saharan Africa:

- This region as a whole saw no increase in per capita incomes between 1965 and 1999. In some countries in the region, per capita incomes fell 50 percent or more.
- Half the population of Sub-Saharan Africa lives on less than $1 per day, and this proportion is rising.
- One in five people in this region live in a country severely disrupted by conflict.
- The AIDS pandemic is having a disastrous effect on development in Africa. As a result of the AIDS epidemic, life expectancies in Africa declined over the 1990s.
- In the year of 2000, 2.4 million people, many in their productive primes, died of AIDS. The disease has already orphaned 12 million children in Africa; that figure could increase to 40 million by the end of this decade unless more effective control measures are taken (World Health Organization, 2002).

The failure of development in much of sub-Saharan Africa has come despite sizable development assistance flows. Net transfers from foreign assistance amount to nine percent of GDP of countries in the region or to about half of public spending (World Bank, 2000a). Obviously, much work remains to be done on how development assistance could contribute more effectively to development.

3. The Goal of Development Assistance

In considering how to improve aid effectiveness, it may be worth taking a step back to remind ourselves about the underlying objectives of ODA, so that we might better consider how and where we can best achieve these goals.

We would suggest that the overarching goal of ODA is to enable the recipient countries to achieve sustainable development, by which we mean creating the conditions for sustained economic activity—an environment where savings can be generated, and investments made, thereby permitting an economy to grow and generate more prosperity. As we explain below, the ability to generate savings and attract investment depends on a broad set of factors that can be considered the social and physical infrastructure of a country. Aid can make a contribution to development by helping to provide this infrastructure sooner than the recipient country would be able to out of its own resources.

In the rest of this paper, we make *ten observations*, grouped under three broad headings, regarding (1) what in our view aid policy should be focused on; (2) how we can go about strengthening the aid system to this end; and (3) where this must be pursued.

3.1 What Should Aid Policy Be About?

(Observation 1.) Despite 50 years of development experience, there is still a lot that donors and recipients do not know about what promotes development. More often than not, the experience gained has been to show what is it that does *not* work (see, for example, Easterly, 2001).

Experience, however, has not been entirely negative; those concerned about aid have learned some things about what is necessary to promote development. To start with what is perhaps the most obvious: it is now beyond dispute that growth is necessary to reduce poverty. Poverty reduction is not just or even primarily a question of redistributing income and wealth. Economic growth is required to generate additional income and wealth to redistribute. We know of no case where poverty indicators, such as incomes or health and education standards, have improved during years of negative economic growth.

By the same token, the experience of the last 50 years confirms that growth benefits the poor (see for example Dollar and Kraay, 2000). Summing up the experience of developing countries, Stiglitz and Squire (1998) wrote:

[T]he record of the last quarter century demonstrates two points: Aggregate economic growth benefits most of the people most of the time; and it is usually associated with progress in other, social dimensions of development.

Stimulating growth, however, is a complex task. Aid communities have learned that a healthy vibrant private sector is necessary for growth. Collectivist models of development have been thoroughly discredited. Autarchic models of growth, while they may have generated growth for short periods of time, also ultimately failed (Yergin and Stanislaw, 1998).

Private sector-led investment and economic development in a relatively liberal trading environment must, ultimately, be the engine for growth to meet developing country needs, and development policies need to recognize this. Development policy must therefore address the issue of what makes private markets work. It must work with the societies in developing countries as they focus on strengthening their institutions. Domestic residents will not leave their savings at home and foreign investors will not send in their capital if a country's institutions do not inspire confidence that they will be able to benefit from the return on those assets. Without the required savings and investment, economic growth is unlikely to be initiated.

Macroeconomic stability is also critical for investment and growth. This includes low inflation, a sustainable exchange rate regime, and sustainable fiscal and monetary policies.

In addition to healthy rates of domestic savings and investment, a strong financial sector to mobilize the supply of savings also seems to be an important contributor to growth. And indeed building strong financial sectors, and creating the conditions for deeper capital markets in developing countries, is gaining increased priority in the allocation of technical assistance by the World Bank (through, for example, its financial sector adjustment lending) and regional development banks.

Foreign savings can sometimes substitute if the level of domestic savings is inadequate. Experience has shown, however, that relying on foreign savings can be a risky strategy. Empirical literature dating back to Feldstein and Horioka (1980) has demonstrated that capital is not as mobile internationally as had commonly been supposed. For most countries, investment is closely correlated with domestic savings. Moreover, capital from abroad can be risky, particularly if it is short-term and the capacity of the domestic financial sector to manage rapid reversals is weak.

In any event, access to foreign savings depends to a considerable extent on the achievement of macroeconomic stability. If we look at the widening range of spreads on various emerging market bonds, it is clear that investors are now able to—and do—differentiate between those countries that pursue good economic policies and those that do not.

If this section sounds a lot like the so-called Washington Consensus[3], it should. The Washington consensus has been criticized in recent years for not having generated growth in many developing countries. In our view, however, it is not that the Washington Consensus is wrong, but rather that it is incomplete.

(Observation 2.) As reflected in the Montreal Consensus promulgated in October, 2000 by G–20 Finance Ministers, private markets, liberal trade, and a solid macroeconomic framework must be accompanied by the necessary social investments. Human capital must be built through investments in health and education, and through ensuring that social safety nets are adequate to facilitate the process of adjustment to a global economy.[4] At the same time, the quality of growth—that is, where the benefits of growth are shared equitably—matters, too: a society cannot afford to have a large proportion of its population excluded from growth, marginalized and resentful of the benefits flowing to those able to participate in the global economy. Investment in human capital, especially education and healthcare, as well as some level of social protection and inclusion is therefore vital.

The good news is that, as noted above, development does not generally lead to greater inequality of income, let alone necessitate it, as some of the early literature on development had suggested (see World Bank, 2000b). The evidence is that growth is associated with improvements in most social indicators. It is also the case, however, that targeted social investment can significantly improve equality in developing countries.

Nor is it the case that sound social spending discourages investment and growth. Rather, growth and social investments tend to be "complementary and mutually reinforcing" (Stiglitz and Squire, 1998). Investment in people generates growth, which in turn generates resources to increase and improve social investments. The relative equality in access to educational opportunities, for example, was one of the major contributors to the success of the Asian 'miracle' economies in the last quarter century. One of the lessons of those economies is that support for equality in social investments like education, in fact encourages investment. Improving health is another social investment that can pay huge div-

---

3. The term 'Washington Consensus' was coined by John Williamson (1990). In his essay, Williamson set out the elements that the political (i.e Congress and senior members of the administration) and technocratic (i.e., staffs of the international financial institutions, agencies of the US government, the Federal Reserve, and the major think tanks) elites in Washington appeared to believe were necessary for effective reform. The policy prescriptions of the Washington consensus included reducing fiscal deficits, establishing a competitive exchange rate, practicing monetary discipline, and undertaking 'market-friendly' reforms—such as privatization, deregulation, and increasing openness to trade.
4. To be fair to the Washington Consensus, it did stress the importance of government spending on health and education. It did not, however, put much emphasis on social protection and income redistribution. Indeed, it was generally hostile to redistributive measures.

223

idends in terms of aggregate growth (World Health Organization, 2002). In Africa, as we indicated earlier, effective action against AIDS will be a crucial determinant of growth in the coming years.

(Observation 3.) It follows from the first two observations that, ultimately, priority must be put on a 'good governance' agenda. A governance agenda is one that encompasses political and social, in addition to economic, dimensions. Although concern with governance was never entirely absent, it was often underestimated both in the development literature and in practice by development institutions. Many development agencies and institutions were prepared to overlook shortcomings in governance or were reluctant to be seen to be interfering in the politics of recipient countries. More recently, however, the importance of governance in development has come to the fore. As Collier *et al.* (2000) wrote:

> The challenges of improving governance and the provision of public services, and their focus on the poor, highlight the importance in development of institutions, norms, and behaviors. *If we had to single out one key idea that has risen to prominence in development thinking in the 1990s, that would be it* (our italics).

The increased importance of governance and the better appreciation of the complementary roles of the public and private sectors is evident in the World Bank's own work. The World Bank's 1997 World Development Report, for example, was centered on the role of the state in development. The 2002 World Development Report was entitled *Building Institutions for Markets*.

While markets and private business are the chief engines of growth in the medium to long-term, they in turn rely on an institutional infrastructure to ensure their functioning. Business will go to places where there is a regulatory environment conducive to doing business—one characterized by the transparency and predictability sought, one where governments do invest in human capital by way of both social safety nets and education permitting workers to keep pace with structural adjustment, and one where participants in the economy—those who are governed—have a say in how they are governed.

When we say, with no particular claim to originality, that good economic governance is vital for development and growth, and thus for poverty reduction, what do we mean? We mean a fair and effective legal and institutional framework, reinforced by a culture of competent, transparent, and accountable public management, committed to eradicating corrupt practices. It necessarily features governance based on the principles of inclusion, whereby all those potentially affected by regulation, domestic and foreign alike, can provide input, and can know the rules of the game. Good economic governance thus helps to ensure that market participants, the local population, and potential foreign investors, have confidence in the government and in its development policies, in the rule of law—so that contracts can be relied on—and in the country's financial institutions.

And governance is critical not only in attracting foreign investment, but also in mobilizing a society's own resources for its development. It is noteworthy, for example, that almost 40 percent of Africa's wealth is held abroad. Similarly, one of the results of the Russian government's failure to establish the rule of law in the 1990s were outflows of over 20 billion USD a year.

The problem is that while recognizing the importance of governance and institutions in the development process is a helpful first step, one has to see that it is exactly that, only a first step. Institutions, norms, and behaviors develop over time. They reflect a complex interplay of historical, cultural, economic, and political factors. They cannot be grown overnight, nor is transplanting institutions from one society to another an easy task.

3.2 How Can We Strengthen Aid Policy to This End?

(Observation 4.) As we have stressed above, development is a lengthy, complex process that touches almost all aspects of a society. Something so integral to a society cannot be imposed from outside. The society itself must be committed to development. Country ownership therefore is key. 'Staying the course' with reforms that can have unsettling consequences in the early stages, particularly for entrenched interests, requires genuine buy-in on the part of recipient countries. And this means all key ministers in government, as well as the citizenry, must strive for meaningful domestic consensus on development priorities. Vested special interests championing less productive expenditures need not, and should not, dictate political choices.

The process that arose out of the G–8 Summit in Cologne in 1999 and the IMF/World Bank meetings in Washington the following September—whereby countries receiving debt relief under the enhanced HIPC Initiative were to prepare Poverty Reduction Strategy Papers (PRSPs)—embodies this approach of putting developing countries themselves in the lead in arriving at development strategies. Moreover, the process requires governments to consult with a broad cross-section of civil society interests. This approach is still in its early stages, and there is no guarantee that it will succeed. It does, however, represent a sincere attempt to encourage and accommodate country ownership.

In 2002, the Canadian Prime Minister and his colleagues decided to look at this challenge through the eyes of the peoples of Africa. At their 2001 Summit in Genoa, Italy, G–8 Leaders made a commitment to respond to a remarkable

African initiative called the *New Partnership for Africa's Development* (NePAD), which was presented to them by a number of Leaders from Africa in attendance at the Summit (see the Appendix). What is perhaps most remarkable and most encouraging about the NePAD is the extent to which African leaders recognized and admitted that problems of poor governance and lack of capacity were the source of many (but certainly not all) of Africa's present difficulties.

NePAD is not a document, however, that seeks to place blame; rather, it is a statement of determination to reform and to become part of the global economy. It provides a vision to address the governance gap, a vision founded on the essential principle that Africa's present circumstances and Africa's destiny are the responsibility of Africans. Africans must take the lead in shaping their own futures. Donors can help but they, the Africans must lead.

At Kananaskis in June 2002, G–8 Leaders published the *G–8 Africa Action Plan* in which they pledged to help build and expand on the NePAD by working with committed African Leaders to achieve the goals set out in NePAD (G–8, 2002). The G–8, however, cannot make it work in the absence of a commitment by all Africans.

Accordingly, one of the challenges that African leaders must face if they are going to make NePAD work is to ensure that their societies share the vision of NePAD. While no one doubts the sincerity of the framers of NePAD, it is nevertheless true that at present it is a document drawn up by elites. Relatively few outside the leadership circles have even heard of NePAD, let alone had a role in drafting it or implementing it. If it is to be a development strategy that works as opposed to a statement of pious intentions, then the leaders who drafted it will have to communicate their vision to, and win the allegiance of, their own citizens.

(Observation 5.) If we in donor countries are going to ask developing countries to develop their own strategies for reducing poverty, then our behavior is in many cases going to have to change. We are going to have to 'get with the program', so to speak. We are going to have to shift the manner and the forms in which we deliver our aid to be coherent with the recipient country's strategy.

For development assistance to be truly effective in bringing about development, then, its purpose must be development. In the past, many other factors have influenced the distribution of development assistance, from geo-strategic considerations to industrial or agricultural policy in the donor countries (Boone, 1996; Alesina and Weder, 1999; Alesina and Dollar, 1998). This has too often led donors to direct their aid to countries where it was not used for development; indeed some aid may even have been antithetical to development.

Moreover, donors will have to work together more than they have in the past. Donor coordination does appear to be improving. This may be the primary contribution of approaches like the Comprehensive Development Framework, the PRSP process, by bringing bilateral and multilateral donors together for a common cause. A newly revitalized Integrated Framework (IF) for trade-related technical assistance may well be a model in this regard. And Sector-Wide Approaches to development assistance (SWAps), serve a similar purpose.[5]

Donors are increasingly prepared to accept a commitment to mobilize ODA and other resource flows, to get maximum 'bang for the buck' by enhancing donor coordination, by attaching fewer but more focused (i.e. streamlined) conditions to their assistance, and by liberating financial resources for productive expenditures through debt relief.

(Observation 6.) Conditionality must be streamlined and harmonized. Donors have begun moving away from insistence on process to measuring outcomes. While much additional work is required to improve our ability to measure through the development of social indicators, good work is being done at the United Nations, the World Bank, and the OECD's Development Assistance Committee. And greater flexibility is reflected in adjustment lending by the international financial institutions and in increasing use of 'floating tranches', which allow donors and recipients to distinguish those reforms absolutely essential within set time-frames from those that may be managed across a longer time period.

Developing countries have highlighted the problem of onerous reporting requirements. Tanzania, for example, was required to receive 1,000 missions from donors each year, and to file 2,400 reports each quarter (Wolfensohn, 1999). Such a reporting burden can obviously distort the priorities of the recipient government and absorb administrative resources that are often in short supply. Donors should therefore be prepared to adopt common standards that recognize the limited administrative capacities of some of the recipient countries. More generally, bilateral and multilateral donors have to make concerted efforts to streamline and consolidate reporting requirements and thereby reduce transactional costs.

This may prove challenging given the current movement, as part of the increased attention being paid to aid effectiveness, to develop indicators of measurable outcomes. Experts and governments will have to ensure that such indi-

---

5. SWAps, as the name implies, address entire sector of an economy, such as health, education or trade, rather than individual projects. According to Schacter (2001), "The central idea of a SWAp is that in a given sector in a given developing country, all significant donor interventions should be consistent with an overall strategy and sector budget that have been developed under the leadership of the recipient country." This approach does require relatively efficient public administration on the part of the recipient country, as funds provided are not as visible or easy to track as funds provided for a specific project.

cators are meaningful and do not skew development efforts, which are necessarily long-term in nature, to meeting short-term targets.

(Observation 7.) One of the main areas where donor countries are going to have to 'get with the program' is in facilitating developing country access to the world trading system. While debates may exist about the importance of trade to a country's growth (see, for example, Rodrik, 2000), there is no instance of a country successfully achieving sustainable growth without it. Growth has usually been associated with an increasing trade to GDP ratio. Increased exports are the vehicle by which hard currency is earned, capital equipment imported and productivity, income, and wealth increased. In countries where domestic savings are low, as is the case in almost all developing countries, foreign direct investment is also a critical ingredient.

A few developing countries, including such countries as Bangladesh and Cambodia, have had important successes in participating in the world trading system. But most have not. Africa in particular has been unable to use trade as a source of growth. Its already small share of world trade fell by a third between the 1950s and the mid-1990s. African countries were singularly unsuccessful in reducing their reliance on single commodity exports. It is for this reason that greater integration of the developing world into the global trading system is a key goal, as well as a critical component, in the new round of multilateral trade negotiations.

This is the notion of 'mainstreaming trade'. What does it mean? It is not solely about teaching people how to understand and interpret WTO agreements. This is only a small part of the story.

First, it must mean action on the part of developed countries to open their markets to more goods and services from developing countries. It must also mean ending expensive subsidies that so distort trade in many agricultural products, to the detriment of developing countries. Subsidies to their agricultural sectors by OECD governments amount to some 300 billion USD annually, which is approximately the size of GDP for all of Sub-Saharan Africa. It is also almost six times the annual amount of global official development assistance.

Mainstreaming trade, however, also encompasses building the necessary institutional capacity in developing countries to permit them to participate in the international trading system. For example, a developing country's Finance Minister should ensure that his or her country's financial sector is well-regulated. The sector does not have to be the most sophisticated in the world to permit participation in the global economy, but it has to be sound. Mainstreaming trade means looking at other parts of economic regulation in a similar way: being able to ensure that goods meet internationally agreed standards for safety; being capable of proving that agricultural products come from a pest or disease-free area; and supporting the ability of developing country exporters to market goods and services abroad in a timely and effective manner.

Mainstreaming trade also means that governments need to reflect on how to use most efficiently the limited resources they can devote to trade issues. Many aspects of developing countries' institutions can usefully be enhanced to improve their ability to trade with the developed world, including customs facilitation measures, intellectual property rules, private commercial regulation, as well as administrative and judicial review procedures for commercial disputes between private parties and the government. As with all other aspects of development, however, it is the governments of developing countries themselves that must take responsibility—ownership, if you will—for the implementation of these policies if they are to be effective. Country ownership of development plans means that the country itself needs to make the decisions.

For example, a country may consider that the expense of putting together a developed-world-consistent inspection system is too great, given the expected increase in the volume of agricultural exports to developed countries in the short run. It may be more worthwhile, instead, for that country to focus on greater economic integration with neighboring countries as a means of increasing trade and promoting economic growth, provided that this is done in a manner that is consistent with the principles underlying the world trading system. It is encouraging in this regard to see the recent progress in efforts to rebuild the East African Community, capitalizing on the useful work done by Uganda in the trade area in its development planning. In sum, strategies for mainstreaming trade need to be country-specific and 'country-owned' to be viable and successful.

Ultimately, mainstreaming trade means giving greater visibility to the linkages between trade and all other related policy areas. The creation of an environment that encourages trade will require changes to the financial and commercial institutional infrastructure, including changes in areas such as accounting, corporate governance, and supervision of financial institutions. Development planning therefore must consider the needs associated with these changes alongside improvements in health, education, general social conditions, and the creation of adequate social safety nets.

The Integrated Framework (IF) can be an important mechanism to mainstream trade concerns in development strategies. The IF was conceived as an instrument of coordination, to ensure that institutions involved in trade-related technical assistance were aware of each others' activities.[6] The IF is grounded on assessing individual country needs and priorities. The IF can help to integrate country-defined trade-related technical assistance and capacity building needs into broader development and economic planning frameworks.

How can this be accomplished? One vehicle is the PRSP process, to which we referred earlier. PRSPs, supported by the regular World Bank Country Assistance Strategies (CAS) reports[7], are increasingly becoming blueprints for national development and poverty reduction strategies in the least developed countries, as well as being mechanisms for coordinating donor development assistance.

In the rush to get as many countries into the HIPC process (i.e., to their HIPC decision points)[8] as possible, countries were permitted to develop temporary or 'interim PRSPs'. Countries were expected to continue working toward a full PRSP. The interim PRSP obviously could not and did not focus on all aspects of development and poverty reduction. For example, few countries have identified trade as a policy priority in their interim PRSPs, although Uganda has done good work on trade in its full PRSP. As the process develops, the PRSPs and the CAS are supposed to be developed in tandem. Given their significance in development policy, it is important that trade policy issues figure prominently in their formulation and implementation.

3.3 Where Should We Pursue This Agenda?

(Observation 8.) We began this paper by pointing out the importance of building public support in the donor countries for international assistance. Broadening the understanding of the core objectives of development assistance, and of how we can better achieve these objectives, is a responsibility shared not

6. The IF was inaugurated at the Singapore Ministerial Conference in December 1996 and revamped in July 2000. Six core agencies are associated with it—the World Bank, the IMF, the United Nations Conference on Trade and Development (UNCTAD), the United Nations Development Program (UNDP), the World Trade Organization (WTO), and the International Trade Centre (ITC).
7. The CAS is the principal vehicle for developing the World Bank Group's assistance to developing countries. The CAS document outlines the Bank Group's strategy based on an assessment of priorities in the country as well as the level and form of assistance to be provided. Since July 1998, CAS Reports can, at the government request, be publicly disclosed.
8. The decision point is the point at which the indebted country enters the HIPC process and begins to receive debt relief. In early 2000, G-8 Finance Ministers set a goal of having at least 20 countries reach their decision points by the end of the year. In fact, 22 countries reached their decision point by the end of 2000. As of September 2002, 26 countries have reached their decision points. For more information on the workings of the HIPC Initiative, see Andrews et al. (1999).

only between donor and recipient countries, but also among finance, development, and other domestic ministries of government, and as we mentioned earlier, by society more generally. Among donors, better communication about the role of ODA as an investment in future prosperity is required.

At present there are, in many donor countries, some fairly serious misperceptions about foreign aid. Recent surveys in the United States, for example, showed that whereas foreign aid accounted for less than one percent of the US budget, the public thought it accounted for 20 percent (Kull, 2001).

In Canada over the past year, the Canadian International Development Agency circulated a discussion paper, *Strengthening Aid Effectiveness*, and undertook a cross-country series of consultations with all interested Canadians (CIDA, 2001). These consultations have been used to frame discussions in Canada of new approaches to enhancing development effectiveness.

On the recipient side, government cabinets and legislators, and key stakeholders in the society, must be engaged, as well, of course, as the citizens concerned. As noted earlier, efforts are being made within the PRSP process to ensure that development strategies are formulated by the recipient countries themselves and based on broad societal support. These efforts must succeed if this approach is to work.

(Observation 9.) In the international context, strengthening aid is a subject appropriate not only for the OECD's Development Assistance Committee, nor solely for the UN's development family (ECOSOC, UNDP, UNCTAD, etc.), but also for a range of individual country ministers. Thus, finance ministers of the G–20 are concerned about aid effectiveness. Foreign ministers and development ministers focused their attention on this and related issues at the recent United Nations conference on Financing for Development in Monterrey. And as already mentioned, aid effectiveness was a major theme of the Africa Action Plan at the 2002 Kananaskis G–8 Leaders' Summit.

(Observation 10.) And one last element to add to the mix: mainstreaming governance internationally. Strengthening aid effectiveness demands greater coordination, or 'coherence', among international institutions themselves, including in particular those within the UN family, among international and regional development banks, and between the UN, the international financial institutions, and the WTO.

Accepting our premise that a comprehensive development framework requires addressing the challenge of sound economic governance, social investment, and trade in a coherent way, then the international institutions responsible should also be acting in a coherent manner. Consider trade as an example.

While the IMF is concerned with stable macroeconomic environments that are necessary conditions for an effective and successful trade regime, it should, for example, also consider the potential impact of the required changes in trade policies on government revenues, and devise methods to compensate for any losses. UNCTAD and the UNDP should provide policy assistance in managing the domestic adjustment to a more open trade environment.

In the WTO, technical assistance is admittedly limited by budgetary and institutional constraints. However, a more integrated approach means that existing mechanisms could be levered to achieve the desired results. For example, the periodic trade policy reviews called for under WTO Agreements could be used to build up the capacity of developing countries to understand the rights and responsibilities of being a WTO member.

The World Bank, in preparing a Country Assistance Strategy, should be more active in engaging with national trade policy-makers to determine the nature and extent of the trade-related technical assistance and capacity building needed in the country. At the same time, trade ministers and trade ministries of developing countries need to become more involved in national debates on the elaboration of full PRSPs so that informed decisions can be made about the allocation of scarce resources.

4. Some Conclusions

Increasing the effectiveness of development assistance is, as the foregoing has argued, the responsibility of a wide range of actors in developing countries, donor countries, and multilateral institutions. It is not surprising that much of the recent discussion of increasing aid effectiveness is framed in terms of a 'global development pact' where the responsibilities of each party to react to constructive measures taken by other parties are openly acknowledged.

Clearly, developing countries have a primary responsibility for their own development. They have to take ownership of the development process. They have to build the institutions necessary to sustain development. They have to implement the policies that underlie successful growth. To do this, they must engage all elements of their societies. They are going to have to develop responsible and accountable governments.

Donor countries must help to create the conditions in which developing countries pursuing good policies can prosper. Aid from donor countries can play a critical role in getting sustainable development off the ground. Donor countries must be prepared to make development the goal of their international assistance programs. They have to work with societies who have taken ownership of their own development. They have a responsibility to direct increased assistance to countries that have shown a determination and an ability to use those resources wisely. And perhaps the most fundamental additional contribution they can make is the creation of a world trading regime that is more open to the products of developing countries. The governments of donors owe this responsibility not only to the recipient countries, but also to their own taxpayers.

The multilateral development institutions have a responsibility to continue to work with both donor and recipient countries to improve the effectiveness of aid resources. They too have to work as part of a coordinated development effort.

Appendix:
The New Partnership for Africa's Development

The New Partnership for Africa's Development (NePAD) seeks to place African countries on a path of sustainable growth and poverty-reducing development. To accomplish this, global leaders undertake to end the marginalization of Africa in the globalization process; indeed, the intention of the framers of NePAD is to participate in and harness the process of globalization.

Broadly speaking, there are three components in NePAD:

- The first component sets out commitments to provide the preconditions for sustainable development—these include initiatives to establish peace, security, and democracy; initiatives to strengthen economic and corporate governance; as well as initiatives to promote regional and sub-regional approaches to development.
- The second sets out sectoral priorities, including building needed infrastructure; and initiatives in human resource development, agriculture, environment, culture and science and technology.
- The third concerns the mobilization of resources, and contains initiatives to increase capital flows and improve the access of African products to world markets.

The text of NePAD and considerable background information about it is available on the Republic of South Africa Department of Foreign Affairs website (www.dfa.gov.za).

References

Alesina, Alberto and Beatrice Weder (1999) "Do Corrupt Governments Receive Less Foreign Aid." *NBER Working Paper*, No. 7108. Cambridge, MA.: National Bureau of Economic Research, May 1999.

Alesina, Alberto and David Dollar (1998) "Who Gives Foreign Aid to Whom and Why?" *NBER Working Paper*, No. 6612. Cambridge, MA: National Bureau of Economic Research, June 1998.

Andrews, David, Anthony R. Boote, Syed S. Rivazi, and Sukhwinder Singh (1999) *Debt Relief for Low-Income Countries: The Enhanced HIPC Initiative*. IMF Pamphlet Series, Number 51. Washington, DC: International Monetary Fund.

Boone, Peter (1996) "Politics and the Effectiveness of Foreign Aid." *European Economic Review*, 40(2): 289–329.

Canadian International Development Agency (CIDA) (2001) *Strengthening Aid Effectiveness: New Approaches to Canada's International Assistance Program*. Ottawa: CIDA.

Collier, Paul, David Dollar, and Nicholas Stern (2000) "Fifty Years of Development." Paper presented at the Annual Bank Conference on Development Economics, Paris, June 26, 2000. World Bank mimeo.

Dollar, David and Aart Kraay (2000) *Growth Is Good for the Poor*. World Bank mimeo. Available at http://www.worldbank.org/research/growth/index.htm.

Easterly, William (2001) *The Elusive Search for Growth: Economists' Adventures and Misadventures in the Tropics*. Cambridge, MA: MIT Press.

Feldstein, Martin and Charles Horioka (1980) "Domestic Saving and International Capital Flows." *Economic Journal*, 90(358): 314–329.

G–8 (2002) *Africa Action Plan*. Available at www.g8.gc.ca.

Goldin, Ian, Halsey Rogers, and Nicholas Stern (2002) "The Role and Effectiveness of Development Assistance." Research Paper from the Development Economics Vice Presidency of the World Bank, April 2002.

IMF–World Bank (2002) *Heavily Indebted Poor Countries (HIPC) Initiative: Status of Implementation*. April 2002. http.//www.imf.org/external/np/hipc/2002/status/041202.htm

Kull, Steven (2001) "Vox Americani." *Foreign Policy*, 126(September/October, 2001): 29–38.

OECD (2000) *OECD in Figures: Statistics on the Member Countries*. Paris: OECD.

O'Neill, Paul (2002) *Remarks at the World Economic Forum*. New York, February 1, 2002. http://www.weforum.org/site/knowledgenavigator.nsf/Content/World Economic Brainstorming (WEB) Restoring Global Growth.

Rodrik, Dani (1999) "Institutions for High-Quality Growth: What They Are and How to Acquire Them." Paper delivered at IMF Conference on Second Generation Reforms, Washington, November 8, 1999. Available at http://www.imf.org/external/pubs/ft/seminar/1999/reforms.

Rodrik, Dani (2000) "Can Integration into the World Economy Substitute for a Development Strategy?" Paper delivered at the Annual Bank Conference on Development Economics, Paris, June 28, 2000.

Schacter, Mark (2001) "Sector-Wide Approaches, Accountability, and CIDA: Issues and Recommendations." Paper prepared for Policy Branch, Canadian International Development Agency, June 2001. Available at www.iog.ca.

Stackhouse, John (2000) *Out of Poverty and into Something More Comfortable*. Toronto: Vintage Canada.

Stiglitz, Joseph and Lyn Squire (1998) "International Development: Is It Possible?" *Foreign Policy*, 110(Spring, 1998): 138–152.

United Nations (2002) *Monterrey Consensus, Financing for Development Themes*. Available at www.un.org/ffd.

Williamson, John (1990) "What Washington Means by Policy Reform." In John Williamson (ed.) *Latin American Adjustment: How Much Has Happened*. Washington: Institute for International Economics.

Wolfensohn, James D. (1999) "Coalitions for Change." Speech made to the IMF/World Bank Annual Meetings, September 28, 1999.

World Bank (1997a) *Private Capital Flows to Developing Countries: The Road to Financial Integration*. New York: Oxford University Press.

World Bank (1997b) *The State in a Changing World: World Development Report, 1997*. Washington: The World Bank.

World Bank (2000a) *Can Africa Claim the 21st Century?* Washington: The World Bank.

World Bank (2000b) *Entering the 21st Century: World Development Report, 1999/2000*. Washington: The World Bank.

World Health Organization (2002) *Report of the Commission on Macroeconomics and Health*. New York: United Nations.

Yergin, Daniel, and Joseph Stanislaw (1998) *The Commanding Heights: The Battle Between Governments and the Marketplace that is Remaking the Modern World*. New York: Simon and Schuster.

Zedillo, Ernesto *et al.* (2001) *Report to the UN Secretary General by the High-Level Panel on Financing for Development*. New York, June 28, 2001. Available at http://www.un.org/reports/financing.

Can Aid Help Globalization Work?

Vira Nanivska

1. Introduction

Globalization, which is not a new phenomenon, offers a mixed package of possibilities. Although global networking took different forms in the past, in each instance it shared similar features: intensive migration; great geographic discoveries; life-changing social and technological revolutions; and political upheaval. These waves of changes brought breakthroughs in development that altered the lives of a lucky few, but lavished wide-scale destruction for scores of peoples, countries, and cultures. Unless reshaped, today's global movement, like those of the past, also embodies the potential to produce development and demise, creation and destruction. Thus, it can be safely observed that globalization is a challenging and dangerous process for those who are willingly, or unwillingly, caught in its web.

2. Globalization: The Problem of Diversity

In a world that increasingly celebrates diversity and promotes inter-cultural recognition and awareness, globalization stands out as a leveling process that undercuts difference in its movement towards economic 'sameness'. Humankind's challenge, then, is to protect diversity, through enabling societies and countries to sustain their uniqueness under this pressure for economic transformation. At the same time, this process of unifying the international landscape works contrary to the development principles emerging in the twenty-first century among the world's largest donors, which foregrounds respecting difference as a key to human development and the reduction of global poverty. If these two trends, globalization and development, remain pitted against each other, the losers will be those most in need of support, that is, the poor countries undergoing transformation. Therefore, it is critically important that a dialogue be opened up, which overviews the situation and creates a flexible environment that will facilitate creative solutions and lead the way towards mitigating the destructive effects of globalization.

It is the task of all those involved in technical assistance and development work to insist that governments and the private sector are brought to the table to discuss ways to minimize the destructive impact of globalization. Diversity must be preserved against the monolithic leveling of globalization.

3. The Demands of Globalization

Countries in which democracy is institutionalized have systems that regulate and thereby control the relationships within and between nation-states. These democracy-oriented market economies have the upper hand in all other global relationships because the systems that produce a positive effect from globalization are in place and the rules that regulate the destructive side of globalization are also potent and working. However, these components and skills do not exist in the developing world and therefore it is strongly disadvantaged when negotiating with the developed world. Today's world is not one of equal partners debating free trade—it is arranged in a fashion reminiscent of the way the unskilled workers were exploited by the early capitalists.

The globalization process is advantageous for the countries that are able to cope with the emerging world of competition and openness, because it extends their market capacity and produces new opportunities for economic success. At the same time, globalization is harmful for those nations lagging behind in building democracy and market economies, however rich they are culturally, educationally, and/or in philosophical thought. The disadvantage created by lack of experience and dearth of skills weakens their capacity to protect their own interests, negotiate fair deals and competitively enter the global marketplace. Yet, in spite of the lack of preparedness, developing countries are pressured to enter the competitive market even though they are unable to compete with any hope of success. They are preyed upon by developed nations that are interested in exploiting their resources, labor force, and lack of regulations.

What role does the donor community play in this situation? Could technical assistance ameliorate the dark side of development and regulate the emerging global market-economy? It seems highly possible that technical assistance could cooperate with the process that would enable developed and developing countries to coexist productively within the environment of globalization. Through building the capacity of governments and civil society to implement the mechanisms of democracy and market economies and provide skills-based training, developing countries are increasingly able to participate in the global marketplace. Empowered by this training, they are able to negotiate fair trade.

It should be noted, however, that there is a difference between building the capacity for collaboration and the redistribution of wealth through charity donations to developing countries. Charity ultimately fails for simple and well-established reasons: 'teach a person how to fish, don't just give them a fish' has been the development watchword since the 1960s. Further, charity may produce a backlash effect; it can provoke resentment against a world order that increases the difference between the rich and poor, and limits the poor's involvement to simply receiving handouts. The anger incited by such circumstances calls for a radical redistribution of global resources and wealth, as rage is not an ideal environment for negotiation. This scenario leaves all of us vulnerable.

4. Lessons from History

These problems can be avoided. Examples from the past reveal that there have been two different approaches to donor assistance in support of transformation: 'results-based management' and 'non-results-based charity'. The effectiveness of these approaches is a matter of historical fact, so is the international benefit derived from strong countries participating as equals in the global marketplace.

The first approach emphasizes a kind of 'results-based management' paradigm with a goal of building institutions and infrastructure comparable to that in developed countries. By introducing rigorous standards that are translated into benchmarks and through careful monitoring in consonance with a calendar-plan, real and sustainable democratic changes can emerge. In spite of the success of this model, its application has been restricted to the countries identified as future members of the 'developed world': for instance, Western Europe and Japan after the Second World War. This strategy is at work today with the candidate countries for European Union membership. The realization of the Copenhagen Criteria is being achieved through a systemic approach. The EU accession approach includes a binding framework of strategy and vision for the transformation process. Candidate countries are required to adopt EU institutional standards and develop necessary infrastructures. Finally, the distribution of aid is directly tied to accession performance and must further the country's strategy towards EU membership.

The implementation of this first approach, as history reveals, is an arbitrary political decision and is not based on such concerns as historical or cultural similarity; preparedness for change; internal political determination; level of wealth. It is well known, for example, that a World Bank report on Japan in 1948 stated that this country—due to its cultural tradition, history, and work habits—would never become a developed market economy and democracy.[1] Upon the application of the first strategy, however, Japan is now a fierce competitor in the global economy. History reveals that this approach is consistently successful and that these positive developments are repeatable in a variety of environments. In short, the strategy for democracy-building is known, has been applied, and has been seen to work.

The second development strategy is much more like charity and as such it does not stipulate any sustained responsibility for results from any of the stakeholders. This type of assistance is intended for all the rest of the poor and transition countries that are not envisioned as members of any existing democratic union in the near future. Without specific goals and objectives to shape the development program, or a time schedule against which to assess progress, these countries are trapped in non-systemic processes that delimit their chances for democratic transformation and for setting their feet in the global market economy. This strategy always fails in achieving beneficial and sustainable results and leaves the state weakened, dependent, and therefore disabled from moving towards active participation in today's world.

5. Globalization Affects Two Different Systems

To further complicate the situation, it needs to be noted that in today's world the process of globalization engages two different scenarios. One is found in countries in need of democratic and market transformation. These states are typically emerging from a totalitarian system that has been non-accountable and non-transparent. These types of government are secured by impunity and provide no room for the kind of public dialogue that is fundamental to a healthy democracy. As a result of unchecked government operation, these countries are open to unregulated power and unfettered corruption. In this environment, globalization does not provide a democratically realized good but benefits a select few, at the expense of the majority.

On the other hand, there are the states that have institutionalized democracy. For centuries democracy has developed as a means of public restraint that imposes boundaries on government discretion and power. These democratic constraints are implemented by sophisticated political, governmental, and societal institutions such as constitutions, legislation, governmental green and white policy papers, public service delivery surveys, public budget hearings, and ethical codes

1. Daniel Kaufmann, a resident representative of the World Bank in Ukraine between 1992 and 1996 quoted the World Bank report on Japan at a World Bank weekly roundtable.

for public servants. All these components are targeted to ensure public control over state power. The rich countries of the developed world are also in the position to dictate democratization and economic transformation processes in other countries (for instance, in the EU candidate countries) by providing technical assistance that supports the accession design. Further, they are the key players in the globalization game and possess the know-how to make it work in their favor.

6. Ukraine: A Case Study

Ukraine, along with other transition and developing countries, is now undergoing a manufactured transformation from totalitarianism to democracy, as opposed to the evolutionary democratization process seen in the countries of the West. Because this process is being guided through donor assistance, the quality of the management provided by the West becomes a crucial variable in the success of the reforms. This invites the following questions that seek to assess the progress being made towards democratic transformation:

- What is the design of the process and what kind of guidance is being implemented?
- Do the reforms produce working democratic institutions? In other words, are their structure, procedures, standards, and skills appropriate?
- What new informational and technical resources have been made available by the donor community for the country in transition?
- Are new skills provided for the key actors in democracy, such as the government, private business, and civil society?

These questions are touchstones that invite an assessment of the process of transformation, in order to evaluate whether it is effectively achieving the country's stated objectives.

Further, they provide the opportunity for all stakeholders to measure the effectiveness of their part in the transformation process. For instance, are donors connecting the declared goals of providing aid to practical outputs in the context of the country's expected performance?

The transformation strategy currently at work in Ukraine's case, which is of the non-results-based type, had been designed on the basis of certain assumptions about what key focuses, actors, and processes were required. The implementation of this strategy has produced concrete, observable results—although not all of them are positive. Further, these questions uncover which type of donor scheme is being utilized: institution building or charity. For instance, con-

cerning government reforms in Ukraine, the donor community obviously assumed that once the pressure of totalitarianism was removed the government would accept good advice; would make good decisions to achieve liberalization, privatization, and financial stabilization, and would automatically:
- acquire the new role of public policy-maker;
- stop interfering in business operations;
- begin providing quality public services; and
- manage public finance in an effective and transparent way.

However, very little changed because the Soviet-style government machinery was left intact after gaining independence and Ukrainian politicians and the public service lacked the needed skills required to run democratic institutions. Ukrainian power structures did not have the capacity or skills to deal with the new, legitimate forces in society.

The main problem is that a new, professional class of democratic government bureaucracy has not emerged yet. As the government officials were untrained in the practice of formulating and implementing public policy, the government was unable to deal systematically with balancing the conflicting voices that are a necessary part of democracy, or provide services that it was never previously required to provide. Instead, practically all government actions were 'manually' managed.

Ukraine continues to suffer from the burden of the lost time and opportunities of the first ten years of independence. When compared to the progress made by the EU candidate countries, which were recipients of effective aid assistance following the pattern of the first strategy, the lack of progress in Ukraine becomes very stark indeed.

The situation is further exacerbated by assumptions made by the donor community concerning civil society reform. In this case, it was predicted that once the pressure of totalitarianism was removed, it would only be a matter of personal will to commence with public participation in policy processes, citizens rights movements, and public monitoring of government and its management of public finance. But in reality, Ukrainian citizens are without the democratic skills that make such public engagement possible. Such methods as institutionalized public feedback, public service delivery surveys, citizens' charters, and public budget hearings have not been established in Ukraine. As a result, participatory democracy, which extends past the ballot box and survives the full parliamentary term, was neglected, although it is both a skill and an institution critically needed in a transforming country. Results-based aid management could have facilitated its introduction; in the lack of which the skills that have been gained over the past decade developed haphazardly. Ukraine has only had *ad hoc*, one-off projects similar to those philanthropic activities supporting civil society in developed democracies, where the system is already in place. In fact, without the Soros Network and the systemic approach of the Open Society Institute to create and support independent NGOs, Ukraine today would not be able to discuss civil society problems.

Democracy in Ukraine is lame. Only one part of the democratic political system was established; the formal political institutions ensuring the transfer of power—a constitution providing for human rights, elections, and political parties—are essentially in place. The other vital part of democracy, that which ensures public control over the elected power between elections, has not been established. The democratic institutions ensuring smooth everyday public–private interactions are also missing. The public policy process, a cornerstone of institutionalized democracy, is not a focus of technical assistance programs in the fSU and developing countries.

In Western democracies, public policy is ubiquitous, and understood to be an integral aspect of sustaining democratic values. There are university departments that specialize in public policy; governments with policy analysts and policy managers; procedures and standards of policy consultations and policy communication; guidelines, policy document templates, green books, white books; and citizen participation procedures and institutions. This system enables the government–citizen partnership upon which healthy, effective states can be built and it provides all aspects of society with a voice to discuss the issues. In such a context of empowerment, it is possible to regulate such potentially overpowering situations as globalization.

7. Consequences

In Ukraine, as in other transition and developing countries, the consequences of the donor community applying the second approach to aid, the charity system, are everywhere evident. Across the globe, there is growing dissatisfaction among developing countries with ineffective aid implementation. This unhappiness is caused by the growing social and economic failures and the observation that the gap between the developing and developed worlds is widening. It is also becoming bitterly apparent that this application of aid has often worsened the situation for developing states. Few fSU states, for instance, could show sustained transparency or openness, effective government reforms, growing market economies, or other stable democratic indicators.

As a result, Ukraine and other transition and developing countries are unable to compete successfully in the context of globalization. In these countries, aid has failed, partly because the donor community has neglected to impart what has been repeatedly shown to be a learnable skill: implementing democracy by attending to the ways that it has become institutionalized and sustainable in the West. The social impact of these failures are disastrous: populations have become discouraged by their country's downward economic spiral and psychologically excluded from the process of reforms. The West enjoys the advantage of globalization: it can benefit from entering a market ill-prepared to protect itself from a monolithic influence. The developing countries on the other hand experience the disadvantages of globalization: they are once again unevenly exploited by this new, twenty-first century incarnation of colonization.

8. Conclusion

After receiving over five billion dollars of aid, Ukraine is still in the situation of lacking an effective government administration and civil society, and the necessary infrastructure and capacity to negotiate the terrain of globalization. The implementation of the charity paradigm is a betrayal of both the donor countries' taxpayers and of Ukraine's citizens. The abuse of resources is staggering. Nevertheless, it is fundamentally good news that democracy is not a mystery but a skill that can be taught and learned. The world community and all the stakeholders must therefore begin to hold donors accountable for applying what has already been proven an effective democracy-building model. The strong must bear their burden of responsibility for the consequences of their interventions.

Once again, in today's world, Central European countries have been successful at mastering this craft of democracy. The donors should find ways to repeat this accomplishment in other countries and thereby make effective use of the more-than-enough money that is available in the aid system. Otherwise, globalization will remain an adversary of developing and transforming nations. Unless the transforming and developing world is equipped with the machinery and the capacity to enter the process fairly and skillfully, empowered by their growing skill in applying the tools of democracy both at home and in the global environment, globalization will simply reinforce the prevailing injustices.

Innovative Sources of Financing for Development

Jean-Pierre Landau[1]

Mobilizing resources for development has been a major objective of the international community for several decades. However, the search for 'innovative' sources of financing is more recent. Most of these efforts, up to now, have been focused on achieving debt relief for poor and middle income countries. Significant progress has been made, most recently through the Highly Indebted Poor Countries (HIPC) Initiative.[2] Based on that success, a 'new agenda' for development is now being discussed. One major component—together with increased market access for exports of developing countries—is a search for development finance which would be both quantitatively more important and qualitatively different.

Many ideas have been put forward to that end, some of them very controversial. This paper examines and discusses the issues raised by those proposals.

1. Is There a Need for Innovative Sources of Financing?

There are at least four reasons why new ways of financing development deserve to be explored. There is a need (1) to finance 'global public goods'; (2) to complement traditional mechanisms of Official Development Assistance (ODA); (3) to achieve predictability and consistency in development financing; and, finally, (4) to combine the search for new financing with changes in economic mechanisms and behavior (the so-called 'double dividend').

---

1. These remarks are strictly personal and do not represent the views of any institution I might be associated with.
2. This is an initiative by developed countries, the World Bank, and the International Monetary Fund to provide grants to the highly indebted and poor countries in order to help them service their debt owned to international financial institutions.

1.1 Global Public Goods

What is a public good? Economists have a strict and narrow definition. To qualify as 'public', goods must have both of the following characteristics: first, *non-rivalry*, which means that use by an individual does not preclude use by any other individual. The standard examples are defense and police. Second, *non-exclusivity*, that is, it is technically impossible to prevent usage of the good by setting a price: this is the case for fresh air, for instance. As a result of these two attributes, nobody is prepared to pay for public goods and, since their production cannot be normally financed, they are chronically under-supplied. For these two reasons, it is justified to pay for them through public resources, including taxes.

As the examples show, some public goods, even with this strict definition, are global by nature. But other goods may be considered 'public', if the international community is prepared to consider that they are both necessary and chronically under-supplied. Examples would include knowledge, health, and international financial stability.

Thus, we are faced with two possible definitions of public goods: one narrowly technical; the other broader and political. One can assume that the more we depart from the technical definition, the more difficult it will be to reach a consensus on what is a public good and, as a consequence, to find new sources of financing.

1.2 Traditional Mechanisms of Official Development Assistance May Be Insufficient

If the current trends continue, the international community will not be able to mobilize the resources necessary to meet the international development goals for 2015. The gap between the goals set and the resources likely available has been estimated in the Zedillo Report at 20 billion USD.

New commitments were made at the United Nations Conference on financing for development held in Monterrey (Mexico) in March, 2002. One must hope that the years ahead will see a significant increase in ODA. However, most developed countries will continue to face significant budget constraints. This will limit their ability to fund ODA from national budgets. There is also a risk of countries 'free riding' on other countries' bilateral efforts in the financing of public goods.

Money coming from international financial institutions, such as the World bank and regional development banks, when available, cannot fully substitute for bilateral aid. In most cases—although this has been a matter of considerable debate recently—they come as loans, which must be repaid. These instruments are not always the best suited for the financing of public goods such as health and education.

1.3 The Need for Consistency and Predictability in Development Financing

Such actions as fighting AIDS or increasing the level of education for women in low-income countries will mobilize important amounts of money for significant periods of time. This will be best achieved by earmarking specific resources to finance those actions. By contrast, financing coming from national budgets is highly variable and uncertain, which often compromises the efficiency of international actions.

1.4 The Possibility of a 'Double Dividend'

This is the idea behind most proposals for the creation of new international taxes, such as the 'Tobin Tax' or the tax on carbon emissions. One might try and achieve two objectives at the same time: first, eliminate economic distortions; and second, finance international development programs. Thus, these new international taxes could yield a 'double dividend'. The Tobin Tax could help both to reduce destabilizing financial speculation and finance development. The carbon tax would reduce pollution and generate additional financial resources for development. The ensuing 'double dividend', however, cannot be taken for granted and depends heavily on the practicalities, which we now turn to.

2. Questions and Difficulties

Creating innovative sources of financing is not easy. There is no *political* consensus on the need for radical changes in the way development is financed. Furthermore, each of the proposals can be discussed and their merits challenged on purely *technical* grounds.

The *political* obstacles are enormous. Creating international taxes, for instance, would mean a leap forward in international integration and further limits to national sovereignty. Consensus will not be easy, as illustrated by the debate taking place in the European Union on the creation of some kind of 'federal' resources. As noted, there is a trade-off between the scope of the definition of public goods and our ability to agree on their financing: the more ambitious the goals are, the more difficult it will prove to depart from traditional instruments. Even if agreement could be reached, one would have to insure the 'additionality' of the new resources. There is no use of creating new taxes if the revenues they produce simply substitute for existing ODA. How to insure additionality is a difficult question: some kind of international monitoring mechanism would be necessary, thus further reducing the political acceptability of the whole scheme.

As for the *technicalities*, nothing really definitive can be said. One has to keep an open mind and look at the plusses and minuses of all suggestions.

2.1 The Tobin Tax

Amongst all the proposals, the Tobin Tax has the strongest political appeal.

The economic argument is well known. Even if capital mobility brings huge benefits, it is also a source of undesirable shocks for developing countries. Creating a (very) small tax on foreign exchange transactions would reduce the destabilizing effect of speculation by 'throwing sand in the wheels of international finance'. But it would not deter long term capital flows, which are necessary for development.

The tax is also based on strong moral ground. Mobility helps capital to benefit from the advantages of tax competition, thus reducing its level of taxation as compared to other sources of income. The Tobin Tax would eliminate part of the inequality between labor and capital income, to the extent that cross-border capital flows would be subject to taxation; it would also make capital income directly contribute to development and the fight against poverty.

From a technical standpoint, it can be argued that the tax is not the best way to reduce financial instability. Short-term capital flows might not be the main source of volatility in international markets. Long term movements—which would not be deterred by the Tobin Tax—may be more destabilizing, as shown by the crisis in 1998–1999. In periods of intense volatility, when the potential benefits of speculation are huge, the tax would not act as a disincentive because of its low rate.

What is certain is that there is no double dividend attached to the Tobin Tax. Either the tax is successful in eliminating speculative capital flows—and there is no tax base left, hence no revenues—or the tax brings revenues, which means there are still speculative transactions.

Finally, one might consider a question seldom asked: who is going to bear the ultimate burden of the tax? It is a natural tendency for all intermediaries to try and pass any tax on to their final customers. Financial intermediaries are no different. It is possible that the Tobin Tax would translate into higher lending spreads. Thus the borrowers—some of whom will be developing countries—would effectively pay the tax. This is hardly a desirable outcome.

2.2 The Carbon Tax

This tax would have a clearly identified objective: industrial activities would be taxed in proportion to the carbon content of the energy resources. A possible double dividend exists here: together with the revenues raised, the tax would create an incentive to reconsider environmentally harmful production systems.

However, the transition would necessarily be long. Above all, the tax has the potential to create a big North–South divide. Developing countries would seek exemptions. But that would induce huge relocation of productions with intensive use of fossil energy—an unacceptable consequence for developed countries.

2.3 The SDR

One of the most innovative and controversial proposals has been to use the Special Drawing Rights (SDR) to help finance international development programs. The SDR is an international 'currency', in the form of accounts held in the books of the IMF by its member countries. Like any fiat money, the SDR can be created *ex nihilo* and then used for making payments between states and/or central banks. It is thus theoretically feasible to achieve a real—and apparently painless—transfer of resources between users and recipients of SDRs. The attraction of the SDR stems from its simple implementation: no tax increases, no new budgetary expenditures and, still, more money for development.

However, there are tricky technical issues to resolve. According to IMF statutory Articles, one would first have to decide a general allocation and then agree on its 'redistribution', which would, in effect, be a grant from developed to developing countries. For this reason, in many countries parliamentary approval would be necessary. This is justified in principle for reasons of political accountability since creation and redistribution of SDRs would amount to a transfer of real resources. But it would essentially remove one of the main 'advantages' of the SDR over more traditional sources of public finance.

Also, one could ask whether creating new international liquidity for the purpose of financing public expenditures is justified. Money creation to finance public budgets is prohibited in most countries and for good reasons: it creates a permanent inflationary threat; it reduces the transparency of public budgets and political accountability of governments. The same arguments could be made, at the international level, *vis-à-vis* the SDR. It has been created to help countries facing liquidity crisis; not to finance long-term development programs.

2.4 Tax on 'Common Goods'

Contrary to public goods, common goods are *rival* but *non-exclusive*. An individual cannot prevent consumption by additional users, but usage is naturally limited. Common goods are thus chronically overused, and this frequently creates congestion. Examples of international common goods are open sea lanes or air traffic space.

In my view, common goods offer the most promising avenue for the development of an international tax. If the use of sea lanes or air traffic could be taxed, it could produce a significant double dividend: less extensive—or better—use and important financial revenues. While there are obvious hurdles in implementing such an idea: a strong international agreement would be necessary, both on the principle and modalities (especially how to collect and redistribute the tax). Nevertheless it would certainly deserve further examination by the international community.

3. Conclusion

This brief review shows that there is no perfect solution to the search for new ways of financing development. All 'innovative' schemes share a common characteristic: all should have to be built on strong international agreements.

There are differences, however, between new taxes and more traditional financing mechanisms, such as the SDR. Introducing international taxes would bring significant benefits by securing a permanent and predictable flow of finance for development. But it would also mean changing the international economic and political architecture in a way most countries would probably resist. After all, the power to tax is the ultimate source of legitimacy for parliaments in most democratic regimes and it is difficult to see how it could be willingly transferred to international bodies or institutions. It is more likely that progress will be made—at least in the short run—by finding new financial mechanisms which, although less permanent and stable, could contribute significantly to meeting the urgent needs of the developing world.

V.

Need for a Global Governance?

Global Governance and Multinational Business

Cho Khong[1]

FOZ FZ3
MI4

> "Go into the London Stock Exchange ... there you will see the representa-
> tives of all nations assembled for the benefit of mankind. There the Jew, the
> Mohammedan and the Christian treat each other as if they were of the same
> religion, and they give the name of infidel only to those who are bankrupt."
>
> *Voltaire[2]*

1. The Origins of the Debate

Globalization is a process whose meaning and consequences are increasingly
ambiguous; hence it has become the object of critical debate and contestation.
During the final decade of the last century, business, and multinational enterprises in particular, came to be seen by many to be a key driver of globalization,
advancing an agenda of market liberalization, as well as being its prime beneficiary. Multinational enterprises found themselves at the center of the critical
debate on globalization. They were accused of holding a reductionist economic
view of globalization, and of believing that a rising tide of opening markets
would inevitably lift all boats. And they were attacked by those who fear the costs
and uncertainties of open economies and the strains on social fabrics that globalization appeared to impose.

Yet if we are to have a sense of where this debate might be heading, we need
to understand the roots of where we are today. The 1990s were an era of revolutions, heralded by the fall of the Berlin Wall. But it was not just a push for market deregulation that was driving change, but a whole series of forces, unleashed
by the end of the Cold War. These forces were interconnected with each other,
producing multiple consequences. Thus the ending of apartheid in South Africa
and the demise of a range of Latin American military regimes were products of
the same *zeitgeist* that also gave us the opening up of the Chinese economy and

---

1. The views expressed here are personal and do not represent a statement of company policy at Shell
International.
2. From the sixth of Voltaire's *Lettres Philosophiques*, as quoted by Fred Halliday (Halliday, 2001:
124).

market deregulation in Britain and the United States. Economic liberalization had profound social and political consequences; but while these consequences may have been destabilizing for established orders everywhere, they provided, in many instances, opportunities for people to challenge the reigning orthodoxies under which they lived, to overcome vested interests blocking change, and to advance both democracy and human rights.

Why is it important to make this point? It is because economic liberalization as it has been practiced, which has nothing to do with its theoretical cogency, has often been astonishingly *naïve* about its social and political ramifications, particularly so in countries and in areas where governance has been weak. Globalization therefore opened itself up to being caricatured as a set of powerful and impersonal forces sweeping the world, destroying cherished values and social practices. But liberalization needs to be seen as all of a piece, and it had, in many parts of the world, enormously positive social and political consequences.

Meanwhile, the domestic political debate in many countries also began to change in nature over the course of the 1990s, with the demise of a global socialist alternative. These changes were to foreshadow many of the arguments which were to surface with the anti-globalization movement, which first shot to prominence with the Seattle demonstrations at the end of the decade.[3] The old left–right political spectrum began to appear increasingly irrelevant, with the emergence of a silent majority coalescing around a libertarian consensus. The point about silent majorities, though, is that their allegiance is not committed. Instead, their allegiance is by default, because people see no alternative, but they remain critical and questioning. The consequence is a diminution in the authority of governments, and the rise of huge 'democratic deficits' between nation-states and their citizens.

What Seattle did was to openly question the libertarian consensus, particularly for those people who do not have the same stake in globalization as the educated, the moneyed, and the skilled. But the 'anti-globalizers' have, as yet, failed to articulate any cogent alternative. While public opinion at large seems unclear, there does not appear to be any large-scale rejection of globalization (though there is an element of outright rejection). Rather, what we are beginning to see is a more critical questioning of its value, by empowered and suspicious individuals, as established governance structures show an increasingly threadbare authority and legitimacy. People have real anxieties, over rising inequalities, over a global integration that seemingly destroys choice, over the

---

3. Few people foresaw the resistance that was to emerge in Seattle. An early warning shot was provided by John Gray (1998), while Raymond Vernon (1998) foresaw tensions emerging between multinational enterprises and nation-states.

concentration of power in unaccountable hands and over the trustworthiness of both governments and business. And as traditional constraints are dissolved by globalization, people are forced to construct their own lives for themselves, for better or for worse.

The most characteristic feature of our present age is the political splintering of established authority. Power has diffused beyond states to a host of other bodies, non-government organizations, markets, business, the media and those who control them, to all of whom states need to respond. This splintering process gives people more room for maneuver in the interstices between established authority.[4] While political leaders claim to be disempowered in the face of globalization, this being a very handy excuse to avoid responsibility, it also reinforces the alienation of their publics from the traditional methods of democratically representing political views. Many of these people feel increasingly compelled to seek alternative and more direct modes of political expression through the clamor of non-state entities.

In Asia, this shift in popular sentiment had actually taken place some years earlier than the Seattle demonstrations, with the onset of the regional financial crisis, which began with the crash of the Thai Baht in June 1997. Formerly, governments had justified their right to rule on the basis of the equation that globalization and economic liberalization meant growth, jobs and new income opportunities. When in the wake of the Asian crisis, this equation was no longer perceived by people to hold, many of those governments were toppled, the triumphalist proponents of the supposed superiority of Asian values fell silent, and the public mood on globalization turned embittered and critical. Yet there was no serious questioning of the need to engage with globalizing forces. Rather, what was in question was the quality of that engagement; and this was paralleled by the rise of new ethnic and religious identities that queried the motives of secular power and sought to fill the spiritual vacuum created by it.[5] People were searching for a certainty of faith to balance the sense of relentless change brought on by globalization.

---

4. Various writers have made the argument for a loss of state power. The point here though is not to deny that sovereign power no longer exists, but that while it remains 'the power of last resort', the mapping of political power is now much more complex. Susan Strange characterizes this as Pinocchio's problem (Strange, 1996: 198–199). No longer guided by strings attached to the nation-state, each individual has to make up his or her own mind what to do and whose authority to respect. The result is a range of local attitudes towards risk, the environment and valuing social concerns, and a broad variety of solutions at the local level, which do not cohere globally. It therefore becomes difficult to formulate and to enforce global rules because trust is, at least initially, local.
5. Wang Gungwu (2001) notes that the original East Asian Confucian tradition was also secular, but had to be rejuvenated by religions such as Mahayana Buddhism which came from India. The current secular domination of Asia, which derives from a western tradition, requires a similar religious counter-balance.

2. Business Responses

Where does business fit into this picture? As countries were forced through a series of wrenching social, political, economic and institutional transformations, business was seen to be a major force pushing change, and to be a new locus of power affecting people on a world-wide basis, while state structures concentrated on providing what their corporate sectors required. So when people started to look for the villains of the piece responsible for the stresses inflicted by globalization, they found them not in governments who claim to be disempowered in the face of globalization, but in international institutions such as the International Monetary Fund, the World Bank and the World Trade Organization, and in multinational enterprises as the supposed prime beneficiaries of the whole process.

While multinational enterprises certainly look to seize new opportunities from an economic liberalization agenda, with the opening up of previously restricted markets and with the lifting of regulations that had hitherto impaired their operations, yet business too, while seemingly empowered, faces an increasingly turbulent climate. It is viewed as the principal driver and prime beneficiary of open economies whose costs and uncertainties have to be borne by others. There are tensions everywhere as the business agenda is popularly seen to force a root-and-branch dismantling of established practices and the eradication of social safety nets.

Yet while multinational enterprises are demonized for constituting a corporate global governance, business finds itself facing highly competitive margins and rates of change faster than what it was previously accustomed to dealing with. Global competition constitutes an ever-quickening treadmill on which companies are in ever-increasing danger of falling off. Rather than being in charge, companies at times also feel themselves to be constantly buffeted by forces beyond their control.[6]

One response has been a wave of corporate mergers following on in the wake of globalization, as companies seek to hold strategic control points in the global market-place and to acquire the global reach necessary to capture opportunities in it. The concern over this behavior lies in the anti-competitive implications of mergers on this scale, raising the suspicion that some companies may be seeking to recover a measure of the profits that had previously accrued to them in the less competitive operating environments of the past.

---

6. Nick Butler borrows from Bertrand Russell to note that power, so far as the relationship between business and government is concerned, always seems to be somewhere else, whatever perspective one takes (Butler, 2000: 150).

Second, as companies have become more international in nature, they have developed concerns over the appropriateness of their organizational structure, the diversity of their staffing and understanding the characteristics of the different societies in which they are present. In this way, companies have begun to recognize the impact of their activity on local operating environments and, for at least some companies, to discuss the broader social and political consequences of economic liberalization. Amongst this last group, there is an increasing sensitivity for progressive adjustment and for equity concerns.

Third is a search by business for allies, through active engagement in the public debate and through seeking dialogue with its critics. This has been an informal and patchy process, the extent to which it is pursued by individual companies depending on their past history, their present perceived vulnerability and their future aspirations. And it has been largely reactive, undertaken where companies have become conscious that their reputations are at stake. But however imperfect the process and whatever the motivation may be, there has been a clear shift from a propounding of narrow corporate interests towards a much broader range of engagement and dialogue.

3. Areas of Concern

There is a sense in which globalization, especially the greater liberation of the private sector to operate freely across national borders and the growing credibility of non-government organizations as authoritative decision-making bodies, is resulting in the diffusion of legitimate authority away from national governments in three directions. The first is upwards to supranational institutions, whether organized multilaterally or regionally; the second is downwards to societal groups such as non-government organizations; and the third is outwards to the private sector. This new situation has brought about a crisis of authority, in which business is both blamed for causing problems as well as itself finding it difficult to operate in a complex and insecure environment where there are many different authorities of varying degrees of legitimacy and effective power. Debates around globalization have emerged over issues of liberalization, redistribution, regulation, democratization, and development.

We see the emergence of global markets, but markets are, by their very nature 'redistribution blind', and need to be regulated. The problem at the global level is the difficulty of formulating and enforcing global rules, because the perspectives of many people remain largely local or state-bound, and there is little sense of community at the global level. There is therefore a need at the global level to limit the arbitrary or self-serving use of power and to ensure that, at least in part, the interests of the common good are addressed.

At the national level, this concern is addressed by democracy. Originally, the concentration of power in states enabled governments to put a framework of rules around an emerging market economy. But this framework for a market economy could only be legitimized by eventually making it accountable to national democratic institutions of government. The *quid pro quo* for people to buy into the market economy was the provision of acceptable standards of public service and a measure of redistribution to mitigate its uncertainties.

There is no democratic check, however, on the workings of the global economy, leading to the fear that the workings of global markets could lead to increasing inequalities at a global level. One consequence has been the emergence of non-government organizations engaging in a politics of direct action, who seek to fill this need. But these groups are themselves self-appointed, formulate their own particularistic agendas, and are, whatever they may claim, no automatic repository of legitimacy. They too tailor their message to compete in a global market-place for the attentions of a global public.[7] In today's world, legitimacy turns out to be always 'somewhere else'.

At this point in time, it is difficult to see nation-states losing their primacy as the principal focus of people's loyalties. Only this nation-state legitimacy, which international institutions lack, enables significant resource redistribution. States and state policy are therefore central to redistribution. The problem, however, is that as value differences blur and as communications become instantaneous and barrier-free, this central position of the state in people's attentions has started to become increasingly marginalized. State legitimacy has declined in two critical respects, as an enabler of economic activity and as subject to democratic accountability. And the ability of the state to recapture its legitimacy will be key to its future survival.[8]

As for the range of pressures that have arisen against globalization, those that seek a profound 'de-globalization', rejecting technology, are impractical and will fail. However, there are other counter-pressures against globalization that tar-

---

7. Clifford Bob characterizes the agenda and actions of global non-government organizations as arbitrary, and argues that "global civil society is not an open forum marked by altruism, but a harsh, Darwinian marketplace where legions of desperate groups vie for scarce attention, sympathy, and money" (Bob, 2002: 37).

8. Simon Reich (personal communication at a workshop meeting, February 9, 2001) argues that there is a model of state legitimacy, practiced by small countries such as Singapore and such European states as Austria, Sweden, and Switzerland, which manage to combine global openness with secure welfare delivery, at the cost of a certain intolerance. These states retain their roles as 'economic enablers' and welfarists, and could provide an example to others.

get policy change in the strongest states, in the belief that they have a much greater than expected latent room for maneuver. Should this belief prove correct, we could expect to see power flowing back, especially to the most powerful states, with these states implementing a larger range of practical government policy outside of the 'golden straightjacket' of the Washington Consensus.

In this emerging debate, there are three areas of particular relevance for business. First is the argument around reform of the multilateral institutions, motivated by the increasing need for global institutions to address global problems. This concern began after the Asian financial crisis of 1997 and received further impetus after the crisis spread to affect Russia and various Latin American countries, triggering a discussion about the need to construct a new international financial architecture. This discussion has since broadened to encompass the multilateral institutions as a whole, and there are a number of proposals on reform of the international institutions together with an emerging debate over what should constitute their agenda. Various attempts have been made to engage business companies in the discussion, though so far, nothing of substance has happened, and the underlying vulnerability remains.

Second is the potential for a global civil society to emerge, with shared global concerns, to match the establishment of world markets. What are the forces driving change in national societies and how might they evolve in ways that could lead to a cosmopolitan perspective displacing national concerns?[9] The corollary of the rise of a cosmopolitan perspective is the pressure on business to take a global view not just of its operations, but also a global, rather than national, view of its social and ecological consequences.

Third is the heated discussion over the distribution of the benefits of globalization. The effects of globalization are seen to be uneven and often harmful to one or another group in society. Critics have therefore focused on the uneven distributive consequences of globalization, and have argued that business has benefited disproportionately. They have also suggested that governments have made a political choice to support business interests. Business has therefore come to be highlighted in this argument as an object of public debate and criticism.

The question really is, does globalization and liberalization generate wealth for the majority of people? And do people in general perceive themselves to be better off? In any process of change, there will always be winners and losers. The evi-

---

9. Ulrich Beck argues this point, noting for instance that "the principle that international law [which is based on national sovereignty] precedes human rights . . . is being replaced by the principle . . . that human rights precedes international law" (Beck, 2000: 83, insertion mine). The following discussion in the text draws on Beck.

dence in this area, however, suggests that, despite some significant exceptions, more globalized countries, which are integrated with the rest of the world, tend to have more civil liberties and political rights. Their governments tend to be less corrupt. And their societies enjoy more egalitarian income patterns.[10] It should be noted though, that there is no necessary causal relationship between globalization and these particular societal characteristics. Income disparities, for instance, may have more to do with past history, levels of economic growth, economic controls and attitudes to education than with globalization or trade liberalization.

4. How Might Global Governance Develop?

The simple Panglossian process which liberalization was once thought to be by some of its proponents, is now more generally recognized to be something much more complicated. Over the next few years, we will be increasingly pre-occupied with picking up its Pandoran social and political consequences. This is a moment of great unpredictability.

As has been noted, the evidence does appear to suggest that engagement with globalization, as opposed to withdrawal and protection, goes further than most other explanations to explain the difference between success and failure in today's world. Dissent over globalization shows, however, that economic liberalization is not enough. The process also needs to achieve political and economic stability, to inculcate social tolerance, and to draw people into the decision-making mechanisms that are shaping globalization and hence shaping their lives.

Global governance therefore needs to be strengthened. This is not a form of world government but a form and set of rules to govern an international system based on the present state structures—but with a common shared set of values according to which the increasing proliferation of transnational activity, including the activities of international business, are regulated. The setting up of a system of global governance, though, must not be some sort of stitch-up, agreed between the great and the supposedly good. Instead, it needs to be 'a whole new ballgame', to build new more accountable institutions, to open up and make more transparent governance processes, so as to legitimize governance in the eyes of society. How might this happen?

The first point to note, in order not to over-inflate expectations, is that if we look back over the last twenty years or so, while we see great changes in the

10. See the *Foreign Policy Magazine* Globalization Index (Kearney, 2001), on which the discussion in the text draws.

international system, global institutions have only changed marginally. By and large they have adapted to the new environment, rather than undergone a radical overhaul. There has been only one significant new global institution, the World Trade Organization, which has an increasingly wide area of authority beyond trade issues. Change in the future, if it does take place, is therefore likely to occur only over the long haul.

One possible way forwards might be through the emergence of a global civil society, as trust deepens between inter-connected cosmopolitan groups of people and as linkages develop between social movements, non-government organizations and other elements of domestic civil societies everywhere. Over time, this could form the basis on which strong rules-based regimes could be established on the global level, with global treaties upholding internationally agreed standards on a range of issues of world-wide concern, such as human rights, migration, food safety, pollution, arms control, and capital flows.

These rules-based regimes would need to be enforced by a set of strengthened global institutions, essentially the ones that we have today, but with extended areas of authority. The World Bank and International Monetary Fund could set good governance provisions alongside economic conditionality. The World Trade Organization could evolve its dispute settlement mechanism into a global commercial court to arbitrate disputes and to give greater confidence to would-be foreign investors contemplating entering uncertain investment environments.

As far as the activities of multinational enterprises are concerned, not only do market mechanisms need to be strengthened in order to integrate global markets, but they also need to be regulated in order to ensure that they function effectively. Thus there could be internationally agreed standards to ensure the effective operation of global markets, possibly enforced by a global anti-trust authority. These institutions need, though, to be made more representative of global society, addressing democratic deficits at the global level, if their decisions are to be regarded as legitimate, and hence complied with.

Another possible way forwards might be through the building of strong regional institutions, which could then begin to work to strengthen existing global institutions. This would be a looser, more fragmented process, which would recognize a variety of forms of capitalism and of economic organization. It would also help ease the tension between a single set of global aspirations and the valuing of diverse beliefs.

Whichever way we go, we are moving into a period with an increasing number of different voices seeking to shape globalization and contesting how it plays out. Business has a role to play in this process, as part of society, in seeking common areas of interest with governments, with international institutions, and particularly with the non-government organizations and other new voices emerging in the global debate. In doing so, business needs to justify its intentions and its actions to society at large. Governance structures provide the authority and legitimacy necessary for the effective functioning of the global economy. Business will need to play its part in shaping these structures, so that they maintain a commitment to an open liberal international economic order, while addressing the political and social implications of globalization both domestically and internationally.

References

Kearney, A.T. (2001) "Measuring Globalization." *Foreign Policy*, 122 (January/February): 56–65.

Beck, Ulrich (2000) "The Cosmopolitan Perspective: Sociology of the Second Age of Modernity." In John Urry (ed.) *Special issue: Sociology Facing the Next Millennium. The British Journal of Sociology*, 51(1): 79–105.

Bob, Clifford (2002) "Merchants of Morality." *Foreign Policy*, 129(March/April), 36–45.

Butler, Nick (2000) "Companies in International Relations." *Survival*, 42(1): 149–164.

Gray, John (1998) *False Dawn: The Delusions of Global Capitalism*. London: Granta Books.

Halliday, Fred (2001) *The World at 2000: Perils and Promises*. Basingstoke: Palgrave.

Strange, Susan (1996) *The Retreat of the State: The Diffusion of Power in the World Economy*. Cambridge: Cambridge University Press.

Vernon, Raymond (1998) *In the Hurricane's Eye: The Troubled Prospects of Multinational Enterprises*. Cambridge, MA: Harvard University Press.

Wang, Gungwu (2001) "Limits of Secularism." *The Sunday Times (Singapore)*, November 25, 2001, p.35.

The Global Citizens' Movement:
A New Actor for a New Politics

Susan George

1. Introduction, Bias, and Terms of Reference

The organizers have suggested that my contribution to this important conference on *Reshaping Globalization: Multilateral Dialogues and New Policy Initiatives*
deal with "key issues connected to global governance and reflect post-Seattle
debates and development." Let me begin by stating that this contribution is
biased, written as it is by someone who is not just watching from the sidelines but
is an active participant in the global citizens' movement. This movement is
increasingly international but inescapable differences in political culture exist
inside it; mine is largely that of a Western European. While I cannot pretend to
escape my political outlook—particularly as one of the Vice-Presidents of
ATTAC-France—neither can anybody else when commenting on globalization.
Any social scientist, in particular, who claims to be neutral on such a subject is
either deluded or lying—or both.

Second, allow me to clarify the terms of reference. For reasons to be explained
I'm wary of the word 'governance' and 'post-Seattle debates' strike me as virtually the same as 'pre-Seattle' ones except that they now include far more people. My
contribution will concentrate on these people because they have coalesced into a
genuine international movement with its own identity, values, and agenda.

To the 'pre- and post-Seattle' point first: The media now routinely create
these before/after distinctions once reserved for personages of immense religious
stature. 'BC' and 'AD' are basic for everyone even though they reflect Christian
and Western dominance. The Moslem and Jewish calendars start with the
Hegira and Yahweh's covenant with Abraham. In the twentieth century, 'pre-
and post-war', like the more recent 'pre- and post-Berlin-Wall', reflect momentous events. Now, however, we see cropping up everywhere, not just in this conference, the fault line of 'pre- and post-Seattle' (or Genoa, or other protest
venues, *ad libitum*). This is doubtless an accolade for the citizens' movement, but
what, exactly, does it mean?

In my view it means that before Seattle, the media paid virtually no attention
to years of hard work and organizing on all the same issues as today: if memory

263

serves, the first counter-G–7 summit was held in London in 1985. Long before Seattle, thousands of people from North and South had contributed to innumerable studies, books, films, symposia, conferences, and public demonstrations denouncing North–South inequalities and maldevelopment, structural adjustment, and debt slavery. 'IMF riots', as they are called by the people concerned, had occurred in dozens of Southern hemisphere countries with considerable loss of life. Indian farmers had marched against large dams and burned genetically modified crops; the Brazilian *sim terra* had occupied farmland; the Korean trade unions had undertaken long and dangerous strikes—one could go on and on.

A number of important international activist networks developed in the 1980s and early 1990s: such as the World Food Assembly; the Debt Crisis Network; the '50 Years is Enough' campaign trying to reform the World Bank and the IMF; protests against the patenting of life and the all-inclusive agenda of the WTO; not to mention countless environmental battles and anti-corporate struggles. In 1997–1998, a brand new French coalition with support from similar ones throughout the OECD successfully pushed the French government to withdraw from the Multilateral Agreement on Investment (hereinafter MAI), causing its collapse and subsequent formal demise. Marches of the unemployed in Europe protested the impact of financial markets and transnational corporations on jobs.

In 1998, the Jubilee 2000 campaign brought 70,000 people—far more than were later present in Seattle—to the counter-G–8 demonstration in Birmingham and nearly that many to Cologne the following year.[1] Many of them had never before participated in any public political event but were sufficiently motivated by the evils of third world debt to take the train, carry a poster and form a human chain against the 'chains of debt'. The media blinked, then yawned; as for the G–8, it made the usual promises which, as usual, were not kept.

Seattle is now seen as a watershed, first because the media finally accepted that there was another voice out there besides governments and business. Citizens might actually have something important to say and say it forcefully.

Second, however, and sadly, many North Americans in particular are convinced that the mainstream media noticed Seattle only because hundreds of poorly trained, robotic riot police confronted tens of thousands of well-trained, creative, non-violent protesters as well as a few dozen extremely marginal violent ones—some of the latter police, as we now know. It was also the first time

1. At the Denver summit in 1997, Russia became a formal participant. Since then the summit of world leaders has been officially called G–8.

264

that a determined group of people had the gall and the guts not just to protest against a major international gathering but to stop it altogether. They took the powers-that-be completely by surprise.

Now, those powers, although they have clearly learned nothing else, have learned that they can only meet in sealed-off fortresses (Prague, Quebec, Genoa), deserts (Qatar), or mountain lairs (in the Canadian Rockies).[2] Their only other response to the protests has been to repeat the same tired formulas and insist that they are sole guardians of the Truth. Refusing to hear what the movement is saying, they have chosen to insulate themselves from it. This was nicely noted in a surprising quarter, the *Financial Times*: "The response to the protests has been largely one of spluttering indignation. Instead of listening, even learning, the politicians have lectured" (Stephens, 2001).

From the protesters' side, as opposed to the media's, Seattle can also be seen retrospectively to have marked a turning point. Simply put, we are no longer on the defensive. Just as this mobilization did not start with Seattle, so it will not end with some other singular event like the police-riot in Genoa. It will assume different forms in different places but it is an increasingly international phenomenon, it has taken on a life of its own and is now an organic, permanent presence on the world stage. Although still very young, the movement is fast moving towards maturity and its participants are gaining in knowledge and confidence.

It is the nature of this movement, its history and its agenda that I understand to be under discussion here and the subject of my contribution.

2. "Who Are These People Anyway?"[3]

To the increasing irritation of the people concerned, the media constantly refer to them collectively as 'NGOs' or, worse, as 'the anti-globalization movement'. Some, though by no means all participants do belong to nongovernmental organizations with a single-issue focus, like Greenpeace, Amnesty, Jubilee, Via Campesina, etc. The movement itself is, however, multi-focus and inclusive. It is concerned with the world: omnipresence of corporate rule, the rampages of financial markets, ecological destruction, maldistribution of wealth and power,

---

2. It may well be time for the citizens' movement, to re-examine its image instead of reproducing, at the invitation of the adversary and on his terrain, the image of the medieval siege with the defenders symbolically pouring boiling oil from the battlements on the rabble beneath. Perhaps we could go even further back in history and invent a new Trojan Horse . . .

3. After the defeat of the MAI which appeared to come out of nowhere, the *Financial Times* plaintively recalled this line from Butch Cassidy and the Sundance Kid and labeled the victors "network guerillas."

international institutions constantly overstepping their mandates and lack of international democracy. The label 'anti-globalization' is at best a contradiction, at worst a slander.

As has been made clear, these forces call themselves the 'social' or 'citizens' or 'global justice movement'. They are opposed to market-driven corporate globalization but they are not 'anti-globalization' per se, which would be pointless: clearly technology and travel are bringing us closer together and this is all to the good. They are, instead, anti-inequity, anti-poverty, anti-injustice, as well as pro-solidarity, pro-environment, and pro-democracy.

Battle lines are being more clearly drawn than at any time in the past hundred years and they are being drawn internationally. Participants in the movement understand with greater or lesser sophistication that only a political project can save the planet's ecology and provide for the inclusion of everyone in the global economy on decent and dignified terms.

This is why, mostly over the last five years, people who never before worked together are shaping a common project. Some people date the new consciousness not from Seattle but from the emergence of the Zapatistas on January 1, 1995, to coincide with the transformation of the GATT process to the World Trade Organization. Some see special significance in the French public service worker strikes in the winter of 1995. All recognize the fight against the MAI, which preceded Seattle, as an unexpected, if partial, victory.[4]

Why was the defeat of the MAI significant? This treaty, negotiated in secret for the previous two and a half years, would have given blanket rights to transnational corporations and portfolio investors, including the right to sue nation-states for loss of present or future profits. States had all the obligations, corporations all the rights. Widely differing interest groups adopted the 'Dracula Strategy'—expose it to the light until it shrivels and dies. It proved effective. The media finally recognized that the MAI was not 'too technical, too complicated' for their readers and listeners to understand as they had initially argued—in fact people could not believe their ears and were outraged when they learned the actual content of the MAI.

The French coalition of citizens' organizations had a particular responsibility as Paris is the headquarters of the OECD where the negotiations were conducted. Among the activists who united were cultural industry workers and filmmakers, greens, women's organizations, immigrant rights groups, researchers

---

4. The member unions of the OECD Trade Union Advisory Committee, for example, were so sure the MAI would pass that they limited their efforts to attempting to obtain at least a 'social clause'.

and academics, trade unions, the small farmers organization, North–South development activists, some left-wing political parties, and many others. Similar coalitions sprung up in other OECD countries and links between them were quickly established. In this sense, the *Financial Times* in 1998 was correct to call the coalition "network guerillas." Ideas and information do travel faster electronically and we never would have had the funds to carry out the campaign with phone, fax and ordinary mail.

The MAI struggle was a kind of introductory course on the real nature of globalization and a trial run for what followed. People who learned to know and trust each other have remained in many informal structures and belong to the same 'list-serves' on a broad variety of issues—the Tobin Tax, the International Financial Institutions, Debt and Structural Adjustment, the WTO and the like. As the political powers that stand behind the spread of corporate globalization have continued to meet since Seattle (in Washington, Prague, Davos, Nice, Barcelona, Gothenburg, Genoa, etc.), national coalitions in each country have 'hosted' international forums and protests. The Swedish coalition preparing for Gothenburg numbered over 300 organizations, the Genoa Social Forum about 750, and so on. At the time of this writing, it will soon be the turn of the Belgians.[5]

The ATTAC movement (literally, Association for the Taxation of Financial Transactions for the Aid of Citizens) occupies a special place in this historic development. ATTAC began in France in response to an editorial in *Le Monde Diplomatique* in December 1997 following the Asian financial crisis, which called for application of the 'Tobin Tax' on currency transactions. The editorial provoked hundreds of letters from readers who wanted to become involved and the idea of creating an organization to take up the issue matured into ATTAC, founded in June 1998. ATTAC-France now has over 30,000 members and about 220 local committees.

ATTAC organizations, large and small, now exist in over 50 countries, including several in Latin America and Africa. They may be persecuted by the government as in Tunisia. For reasons we cannot entirely explain, ATTAC has not spread to the Anglo-Saxon world, although we have many counterpart organizations and working relations in Britain, the US, and Australia. Relative to the total population, ATTAC Sweden, Belgium, and Switzerland are larger than ATTAC France. While there is no formal 'ATTAC International', members from different countries meet regularly and share the same goals.

---

5. Spain saw nearly 400,000 people on the streets in the spring of 2002. The next G–8 summit will be in Evian, France in June 2003.

The Tax on Financial Transactions (the Tobin Tax title is too narrow) is still central to the agenda. But this agenda now addresses corporate-led globalization much more broadly and seeks to challenge the international financial institutions and the WTO, financial markets and pension funds, tax havens, third world debt and structural adjustment, genetically manipulated crops, mass firings by transnationals to increase their stock value, denial of vital medicines to AIDS patients, and the like.

These broad coalitions may not agree on every detail of every issue but they share the basics. They refuse the 'Washington Consensus' vision of how the world should work. Often unjustly accused of 'having nothing to propose', they are, on the contrary, constantly refining their arguments and their counter-proposals. An exceptional moment for such work is the World Social Forum of Porto Alegre in Brazil, held around the same time as the World Economic Forum in Davos. At Porto Alegre II, around 60,000 people convened to share concerns and formulate joint strategies. Several common declarations were approved, and national and continental 'social fora' are planned for 2003, including Porto Alegre III, to be held in January 2003.[6]

In Porto Alegre, but at other events as well, the emphasis is not merely on stopping the adversary from committing ever more egregious horrors, however necessary that may remain, but also on developing consensus around a more forceful agenda of proposals, solutions and devising strategies for attaining them. Although they have often been overshadowed by violence, 'counter-summits' always include forums and 'teach-ins' attracting thousands of people where recognized movement experts lead seminars and debates. In Gothenburg, there was even an encounter, via video and giant screen, between eight such experts and Romano Prodi, Joschka Fischer, Javier Solana, and two prime ministers.

These debates must also try to deal with the increasingly panicked, irresponsible and violent reactions coming from the side of the state and the corporate elites as well as the (often police-infiltrated) violence of elements claiming to be on the protesters' side. Tactics are one of the most hotly debated issues in the movement today and the answers are not simple. Yet for the participants, such problems do not seem insurmountable and the overall feeling is one of great hope and optimism.

---

6. Movement people are inspired by the participatory municipal budget of Porto Alegre (population 1.3 million) where neighborhood organizations are in charge of choosing their priorities and overseeing how the money is spent. Waste and corruption have virtually disappeared.

3. Adversarial Arguments

We have been subjected to sustained propaganda concerning the supposed benefits of 'globalization'. One tool used by neoliberal spokesmen is the constant repetition of misinformation to try to convince people that 'globalization is good for everyone'. It was thus heartening to see the results of an opinion poll ordered by *Le Monde* just before the G–8 summit in Genoa which shows that the French, at least, don't buy this line. Replying to the question "who benefits most from globalization?" 55 percent said 'transnational corporations', 47 percent 'financial markets', 32 percent 'the United States', 11 percent 'Europe', seven percent 'consumers' and only one percent 'everybody'.[7]

Another favorite argument is that over the last twenty years, more people, absolutely and proportionally, are supposed to have joined the ranks of the materially blessed. This too flies in the face of the evidence. If you can't pay you can't play. That is why it is naïve and dangerous to accept the word 'globalization' at face value; to assume that it means a process from which all the earth's inhabitants will eventually benefit, even if they must wait a very long time. This is nonsense; it is nonetheless the dogmatic view of its proponents—most recently President Bush—who never tire of repeating that the enemies of globalization are enemies of the poor.

It is not my intention to demonstrate the validity of these assertions because this has been done again and again. Studies by the Washington think-tanks Center for Economic Policy Research, Institute for Policy Studies and the Economic Policy Institute or by scholars at the United Nations University all show that inequality has worsened, growth has slowed and rewards to capital far surpass the gains of labor. To give only a few examples, in the United States, the median real wage is nearly the same as it was 28 years ago whereas it had increased by 80 percent in real terms over the previous 27 years. Globalization has not improved growth—quite the opposite. Between 1960 and 1980, growth worldwide was many percentage points higher than in the period 1980–2000, particularly in Latin America and Africa.[8]

Over the past 20 years inequalities have increased drastically both within and between countries. This skewed distribution of wealth has been more than borne out by the findings of successive UN Development Program Human Development Reports or the UNCTAD Trade and Development Reports: the top 20 percent of the world population now indeed holds more

7. Two answers were possible. See the SOFRES poll results published in *Le Monde*, July 19, 2001.
8. See in particular Weisbrot *et al.* (2001) and UNCTAD (1997).

than 80 percent of the wealth; the bottom 20 percent makes do on slightly over one percent.

Someone or something must be responsible for such marked evolution, which can no longer be denied. The citizens' movement believes that 'something' is globalization. In order to stress the perception that transnational corporations, financial markets and the holders of capital are the chief beneficiaries, movement people usually add a qualifier like 'corporate-led' or 'corporate-driven globalization'. The opposition is convinced that for the half of the world unfortunate enough to be living on less than $2.00 a day, 'globalization' means further concentration of wealth and power at the top of the social scale and their own continuing poverty and marginalization.

Nor does this movement believe, contrary to the neoliberal camp, that everyone can be included in the economic benefits of globalization although these benefits have been undoubtedly real for ten to twenty percent of any given population. The unfettered market without progressive taxation and redistribution will, as Vilfredo Pareto saw a century ago, follow a '20/80' distribution pattern in which 20 percent of the population controls 80 percent of the assets.[9]

Movement participants further affirm that this economic system has absolutely no plans for the billions left out, no matter how many years we may wait; that the global market based on the 'competition of all against all' is an engine for exclusion and will tend to freeze people, nations, and entire regions, with few exceptions, at the level at which they presently find themselves. Furthermore, as the great economic anthropologist Karl Polányi was the first to show, the market, left to itself, will destroy both society and nature.

4. Polányi's Enduring Contribution

Given that we met in Budapest, it is especially salient to refer to Polányi's enduring contribution because he refuted present-day globalization *avant la lettre*. Polányi showed that the market does not come first—society comes first and social relations are the necessary condition for a properly functioning market. The tragic mistake—but is it just a mistake?—of the 'Washington Consensus', has been to act as if one can simply introduce market relations and society will take care of itself. We have witnessed the result, clearly foreseen by Polányi, most dramatically in the former Soviet Union.

9. For a fascinating mathematical grounding of Pareto's century-old law, see Buchanan (2000).

Polányi's prophetic book *The Great Transformation* destroyed the neoliberal argument that the market can be a substitute for a genuine political project; that the market economy should dictate its rules to society and not the opposite. Such beliefs are not merely bizarre, irrational, and quasi-religious—they are lethal. To allow the market mechanism to be sole director of the fate of human beings and their natural environment . . . would result in the demolition of society.

Since, he explained, 'labor' is another name for human activity, 'land' another name for nature and 'money' comes into being through the mechanism of banking or state finance, it follows that "none of them is produced for sale. The commodity description of labor, land and money is entirely fictitious." But it is a convenient fiction for those who want nothing to stand in the way of the market mechanism (cf. Polányi, 1944: 72–73).

Writing in 1944, Polányi believed that market fundamentalists could never again gain the upper hand. As we know today, his optimism was misplaced. However, the people joining the citizens' movement in ever-increasing numbers are 'Polányians' whether they know it or not. They refuse the domination of the market over "the fate of human beings and their natural environment"—that is, they refuse present-day, actually existing, neoliberal globalization.

5. Specific Issues on the Pro-Democracy Agenda

One can be justifiably suspicious when one hears the word 'governance' emerging from this mistrusted leadership. They would like to see the notion of governance applied to those who use it so glibly for others. When the World Bank and the IMF speak of governance, for example, they mean simply another set of conditions to be added to the long list of conditions already set out in structural adjustment programs.[10]

Where is 'governance' when neoliberal globalization not only leaves out vast swathes of humanity and intentionally weakens the nation-state but also plunges even countries like the erstwhile 'tigers' Korea, Thailand or Indonesia into financial chaos, hunger, and mass unemployment? Where is governance when the Fund deliberately turns a blind eye to the looting of billions of IMF loans from Russia and their transfer to the Mafia? Over the decade of the 1990s, under

10. One can no longer politely refer to 'Structural Adjustment' but has to say instead, with the same hypocrisy as the IMF, 'Poverty Reduction and Growth Facility'.

the guidance of the IMF and the World Bank, the Russian economy shrank by more than half. The number of poor people skyrocketed from around two million to over 60 million (cf. Stiglitz, 2002). Such disasters as have occurred in Asia, Latin America and the so-called 'transition countries' show that, contrary to the neoliberal myth, freedom of capital flows, highly leveraged loans and uninhibited Portfolio Equity Investment are not the road to prosperity but to ruin.

Despite all the talk two or three years ago about a 'new financial architecture', no new safeguards have been put in place and after the collapse of Argentina we are now all waiting for other human disasters. Instead of calling a halt to its policy of safeguarding creditors' assets at all costs, the IMF has set up yet another $90 billion bail-out fund. It does not respect the legal principle of 'odious debt' and forces debtors to honor the debts contracted even by previous corrupt totalitarian, military, or apartheid regimes.

Although the IMF has lately soft-pedaled the issue, until the financial crisis of 1997–98, its only idea of 'governance' for its own account was the attempt to change its Articles of Agreement for the first time since they were adopted in 1944. The Fund wanted to drop Article VI (3) which specifically recognizes that "members may exercise such controls as are necessary to regulate international capital movements"; it wanted to make total freedom of capital circulation a condition for membership. It has also ignored its own Article VI (1) which declares that "a member may not make net use of the Fund's resources to meet a large or sustained outflow of capital . . . "[11] and indeed has caused many member-countries to do exactly the opposite. It has thus protected Western creditor assets however reckless and greedy those creditors may have been. Unrestricted capital flows and fluctuating currencies, whatever the political and economic circumstances, may be a speculator's paradise but they invariably harm ordinary people.

The movement, for its part, is demanding a genuine new financial architecture. Careless lenders and imprudent investors should be forced to take responsibility for their actions—aren't risk and responsibility what capitalism is supposed to be about? The Fund should once again become what Keynes intended it to be: a mechanism for helping countries with temporary balance of payments problems. It should advise them on how to avoid contracting future debts in hard currencies and should supervise a long-overdue debt workout: outright cancellation for the poorest (and of all odious debts); orderly bankruptcy proceedings and write-downs for many others. If it cannot be reformed, the IMF should be abolished and a new international lending institution started from scratch.

11. See www.imf.org/external/pubs/ft/aa/index.htm. Website accessed on March 5, 2003.

It may well prove necessary to have several, more local Funds as Japan proposed to create for Asia during the Asian financial crisis. The United States, however, immediately put a stop to such a plan during the Asian financial crisis, and the Fund listens closely to the US Treasury.

Sustained citizen campaigns on debt have gone on for longer than on any other global issue. The G–8 has acknowledged this movement and cannot say it has not been made aware of the problems. What has been its actual response on third world debt? Despite years of work by hundreds of thousands of people and the collection of literally tens of millions of signatures, significant debt relief for the poorest— much less the slightly better off—remains a dim hope on an ever-receding horizon. At a conference on debt strategies in Lima in 1988, I heard the well-known Peruvian economist Javier Iguiniz saying what sounded like a quip but was in fact a serious remark: "Don't cancel what we're not paying!" 'Canceling what they weren't paying' is what most 'debt relief', trumpeted by the G–8, has amounted to so far.

Since most poor countries, despite the enormous sacrifices of their peoples, are still unable to remit the total debt service theoretically due, the unpaid portion is added to the principle (the total debt owed). Canceling that portion may mean that debt grows more slowly: it does not mean that the actual burden has been lessened from year to year. And so far, in the eyes of the Bank and the IMF, only five countries have proven worthy of relief through the stiff HIPC (Highly Indebted Poor Countries) terms. Overall, less than five percent of total debt stocks has been canceled.

People who have worked on these issues for many years have frequently arrived at the conclusion that debt is not a financial or an economic problem at all but in every way a political one. It is the best instrument of power and control of North over South (and now East) ever invented; far superior to colonialism which requires an army, a public administration, and attracts a bad press. Control through debt not only requires no infrastructure but actually makes people pay for their own oppression.

Structural adjustment programs are often beneficial to local elites, providing them with such advantages as rock-bottom wages and opportunities for buy-ups of privatized companies; they are happy to cooperate. Debt has further atomized the debtor countries politically and made them far less of a threat to established Northern interests. Once significant organizations like the G–77 or third world-led initiatives in the United Nations like the 'New International Economic Order' are defunct or toothless.

The global citizens' movement sees debt relief as an essential condition of more equitable North–South relations and many people stress that it should be accompanied by restitution of the riches siphoned from the South for decades or centuries. Private banks as well as public (multilateral and bilateral) creditors should be obliged to participate: they have already been paid back many times over.

On the front of international commerce, the movement is also determined to transform the World Trade Organization. Contrary to what is often implied, everyone agrees that the world trading system needs rules. The question is who makes them and for whose benefit. One can show only too easily that transnational business is the beneficiary, to the neglect of all other sectors of society.[12]

The General Agreement on Trade in Services, GATS, is seen as particularly dangerous as it provides a broad avenue for corporate interests to invade the civic sphere. Corporations active in services sectors see public education, health care, transport, environmental services not as rights and public goods but as gigantic markets. Now that more and more citizens have understood what is at stake, the WTO is worried and accusing its "hostile and ill-informed" critics of maliciously "spreading scare stories."[13]

The fact remains that essential services for which previous generations fought and sometimes died are open to attack and, under present circumstances cannot be durably protected. The GATS limits public services not covered by its rules to those "supplied neither on a commercial basis nor in competition with one or more service suppliers" and the Services Council has established that this Article I (3.c) "should be interpreted narrowly."[14]

Furthermore, many issues have made citizens extremely wary not only of the GATS but of the WTO in its entirety: such as prescriptions against subsidies; the fact that governmental regulations in a host of areas will be open to challenge as 'unnecessary barriers to trade'; lowering of public health and food safety standards; or the patenting of life forms and universal patent protection of medicines and other vital goods for twenty years. The Dispute Resolution Body of GATS, operating in secrecy, has no obligations to place any other international law above the rules of the WTO itself: neither the Universal Declaration of Human

12. See Susan George (2001) for proof of overwhelming business involvement in establishing trade rules. The WTO has announced that 647 'NGOs' will be accredited to the Ministerial meeting in Qatar, over three-quarters of them from the rich, developed countries (502). Of the total, 328 (or 50.7 percent) will go to 'BINGOs' or business-initiated NGOs, including representatives of 35 advisory committees to the US government's trade policy bodies, which are themselves entirely made up of business interests. Only 256 of the total can be classed as 'PINGOs' or public interest NGOs; the rest are research organizations or unclassifiable. These figures do not of course include the business representatives included in official delegations. (Thanks to Vincente P.B. Yu of Friends of the Earth International for the data).
13. See, for example, the WTO's recent 16-page brochure *Fact and Fiction*. As for former Director General Mike Moore, "protesters," he said, "make me want to vomit" (cf. Hopkins, 2001).
14. Thanks for Ellen Gould for sharing with me this remark made by the Services Council.

Rights, nor Multilateral Environmental Agreements, nor ILO Labour Conventions. The WTO is entirely independent of the United Nations and therefore of the international law it has developed.

6. What To Do and How To Do It?

It is curious that, as the world slips deeper into recession, established leaders do not seem to have a clue how to come out of it. The solution to this problem is over 50 years old. It was invented by Keynes for the national context and used successfully in the international sphere after the Second World War. This post-war solution was called the Marshall Plan and it put Europe back on its feet, re-establishing it as a viable trading partner for the United States.

Today there are two Keynesian ways to kick-start the world economy. One is massive international spending on preserving and repairing the environment. The other is to start including the billions of people left out of the world economy by corporate-driven globalization. The UN Development Program claims that approximately $90 billion a year would cover a basic standard of living—enough food, clean water, shelter, basic health care and education—for everyone on earth. Let's say, generously, that the 'basics' program plus environmental clean-up and preservation would cost $200 billion a year for 10 years. In today's world, this is a paltry sum.

It is vain to hope that Official Development Aid will ever do the job. ODA from the OECD countries is dropping precipitously at about five percent yearly, proving that Northern concern for the South was largely a Cold War phenomenon and many countries simply have lost any strategic interest they might once have possessed. The UN 0.7 percent goal is a pious fiction—ODA now represents a scant 0.22 of the GDP of member countries according to the OECD Development Assistance Committee. Total aid from G–8 countries fell by a further 5 percent in the year 2000.[15]

We should stop pretending that real change will emerge from national budgetary contributions and look for the money where it really is: on international financial markets, in tax havens, and in the coffers of transnational corporations.

15. See the OECD website, "Development Assistance Committee Announces ODA Figures for 2000." Only Denmark, Luxemburg, Netherlands, Norway, and Sweden have met or surpassed the 0.7 percent target-not exactly the largest OECD members. See www.oecd.org/en/document/0,,EN-DOCUMENT-0-NODIRECTORATE-FI-12-5120,00.htm, website accessed on March 5, 2003.

One hundred years ago, inequities in the now-wealthy countries were brought to public attention by a few crusaders.[16] Health and education standards, illiteracy, appalling housing, crime, infant and child mortality rates in the poor neighborhoods of London and New York were in all respects comparable to what one finds in many third world countries today. These gross inequalities were eventually recognized as not merely scandalous but dangerous to society as a whole, including its more privileged members. Though many of the latter ranted and raved and claimed the end of the world was at hand, progressive income taxes were finally introduced so that redistribution and social inclusion could proceed.

We now stand at just such a crossroads with regard to North–South inequities. Money to deal with them is available but it will have to come from international sources, particularly taxation. Such repair and renewal is in everyone's interests. The present holders of extraordinary wealth, like the rich New York a century ago, will naturally resist. This is no reason, quite the contrary, to lessen the pressure.

7. The Future?

The global citizens' movement wants to remain exactly that: a movement. So far, it has suffered no temptations to transform itself into a political party, much less a 'revolutionary' party, and its members come from a variety of party political backgrounds or, frequently, none at all. The tacit bet is that it is still possible to work through existing political structures. How long this conviction will continue to guide the movement is anybody's guess.

It is extremely worrisome that trust in conventional politics is rapidly fraying. Thus I hope to have conveyed something of the urgency of addressing the concerns brought forward by the citizens' movement. If these concerns are not dealt with, and before soon, then we will witness even deeper social divides, increasing disgust with nominally democratic institutions, hardening of positions, confrontation and escalation of violence, mostly by the nation-state. Those who maintain that the present world system is incapable of self-regulation and reform will be proven correct.

The lessons of Genoa have not been lost on activists. We have already witnessed citizens' democratic rights being trampled and free expression denied

16. Including the great investigative reporter-photographer Jacob A. Riis, whose ground-breaking study of New York's poor led to public outrage and the beginnings of reform. The book *How the Other Half Lives* (Riis, 1897) inspired me to call my own first book *How the Other Half Dies* (George, 1976).

with unprecedented brutality. European governments which rightly protested the election of Jörg Haider in Austria and momentarily boycotted the entire country have said nothing about the outrageous police behavior in Genoa under the orders of a G–8 government.

The consequences of spreading distrust in conventional politics and governments are unforeseeable. Those who, like me, are struggling to avoid the paths of repression, upheaval, violence, and chaos and are proposing practical solutions; those who hope not for some indefinable worldwide 'revolution' but for a kind of Universal Welfare State—a perfectly feasible goal materially speaking—will be marginalized or radicalized.

There is no polite way to say this: movement people, particularly young people, are angry. Nowhere in the realms of actually existing power can they discern the slightest sign of serious recognition or responsible behavior concerning the life-threatening problems faced by human beings and the earth; neither on the part of the G–8 governments and the European Commission, nor that of the multilateral institutions like the World Bank, the IMF, the WTO; nor above all the transnational corporations, the financial markets and their numerous lobbies that have assumed unprecedented sway over human affairs.

What the citizens' movement does see is unbridled greed, the undivided reign of capital over labour and of rich over poor, rules made to insure freedom of trade in all goods and services at the expense of every human value; rampant privatization, the destruction of public services and the dismantling of welfare states where they exist and policies to make them forever impossible where they do not; massive and accelerating destruction of the earth, its climate and its creatures—all this in the name of a fraudulent 'efficiency', increased profits and so-called 'shareholder value'.

They see leaders who, once elected, are deaf and blind to the needs of ordinary citizens but attentive to those of corporations; they see an increasingly discredited political class worldwide and, with it, the discrediting of the notion of politics itself. They see that the State is prepared to use not just huge repressive 'robocop' forces, horses, dogs and tear gas against them, but live ammunition as well. They see all this, they are enraged and they are moved to fight.

I am attempting to explain to people of good will why this movement is not going to go away; also why the power of the coalition between the nation-state and the corporate world is hardening and can be expected to continue to repress, defame, and criminalize citizens exercising their democratic rights. The notion of 'dialogue' with such an adversary is becoming daily more problematic. So far, what we have witnessed is 'dialogue' which will be prolonged only so long as those in power can set the terms, name the negotiating partners, decide which subjects are on the table and which are taboo, and generally put off any genuine change.

The crystallization of anger and mistrust are at the root of the 'post-Seattle' phenomenon as well as the new confidence of the movement. Anger is legitimate when, in an age of wealth and plenty, life remains nasty, brutish and short for billions; so is the mistrust of a leadership that is at best timorous, at worst frivolous, pretentious, and mean-spirited. Repeated claims of its desire to 'help the poor' ring increasingly hollow. The Genoa G–8 proposal of a miserable 1.5 billion USD to deal with AIDS, malaria, and tuberculosis was particularly disgraceful given that Kofi Annan had, only weeks previously, asked the 'international community' for 7 to 10 billion USD to deal with AIDS alone. This 'international community', led by the G–8, has so far rejected every opportunity for remedy in every area, and listened only to a minority. Thus a new generation, not all of it young, a kind of 'trans-generational, trans-class, trans-gender, and trans-national generation' is rising internationally in opposition.

Enough people with knowledge, confidence, and organization can unmake what some have made, they can undo what some have done. This movement has made a momentous discovery and revealed a dangerous truth: the corporate *coup d'état*, the triumph of rich over poor, market over society, rapacity over nature is not inevitable. And we will be heard.

Epilogue
Clusters of Crisis and a Planetary Contract

The tragic and world-altering events of September 11, 2001 have, I believe, only reinforced the conclusions I reached in the paper above, notably in section 6. In the light of these events, I hope, however, that it may be useful to present my recommendations in a more systematic manner immediately below. I have left the rest of the above as it was at the end of August, before the terrorist attacks.

What were the major world crises before the abomination of September 11, 2001? We can identify four poles or 'crisis clusters' that are themselves, unsurprisingly, interconnected.

First is the environmental destruction cluster characterized by climate change which is in turn based essentially on excessive, crippling and foolhardy Western dependency on fossil fuels. Here, too, are to be found air and water pollution, massive species destruction, disappearance of soil fertility, deforestation, and the like.

Second is the poverty and inequality cluster, with growing disparities and maldistribution of wealth, employment and resources both between and within nations reinforcing the destabilizing North–South gap and creating a pervasive sense of injustice.

Third is the crisis of democracy and empowerment throughout the world, itself related to elite control, bred of huge inequalities. Formal democratic developments, including democratic elections, have occurred in some places, particularly since the fall of the Berlin wall, but genuine popular participation remains the exception and most people—whether from North or South—exert little if any control over the basic circumstances of their own lives.

Fourth is the looming economic crisis of recession and depression. Serious and structurally in-built over-capacity now exists in virtually all industries and services; the clear and present danger of mass unemployment and exclusion can only add to the other burdens.

As if all this were not enough, September 11 of 2001 has ushered in an age of radical insecurity and post-state conflict. We now face a clandestine, non-territorial enemy who is not fighting for traditional goals, who respects none of the 'rules of war' evolved over past centuries, and who brings the full horror of unpredictability into the homes and work places of the wealthy, the democratic, and the law-abiding.

We must at all costs avoid the "clash of civilizations" *á la* Samuel Huntington. This is this scenario Bin Laden and his fellow fanatic fundamentalists most devoutly desire, believing as they do that indiscriminate American action against Arab civilians will radicalize millions of Moslems and lead to full-scale holy war against the hated West. Egyptian President Hosni Mubarak has once described Bin Laden as "a megalomaniac who wants to take power over the world."[17] We must hand him no opportunities. Instead, it is time to recall the advice of the great Chinese general, Sun Tzu (circa 500 BC): "Do not do what you would most like to do. Do what your adversary would least like you to do" (Sun Tzu, 1963).

What does a fanatical, post-state enemy least want us to do? What paths might we choose to defeat his purposes while at the same time bringing remedy to the clusters of crisis outlined above? These paths exist, but so far our political leaders appear stunned and without vision. Once more it will be up to citizens to convince them that they must act boldly. Terrorism has brought about a moment similar—although less hopeful—to that of the 1940s when the Bretton Woods institutions and the Marshall Plan were conceived.

17. See www.theatlantic.com/issues/96may/blowback.htm.

A new, updated and globalized Keynesian strategy is now called for, not just in the United States or in Europe but throughout the world. We need vast injections of crisis-directed resources into the global economy. They must be linked to environmental renewal, poverty eradication and democratic governance.

Such a 'Planetary Contract' would include the following components:

- Environmental renewal and repair. The West should overcome its short-sighted dependence on fossil fuels, particularly as they are produced mainly in countries which could, in spite of all precautions, fall into the fundamentalist camp whose first act would be to create havoc in Western economies. We need a program to kick-start mass production of solar and other renewable energies and clean technologies, through subsidies and export credits if necessary, as well as clean-ups in the North, reforestation in the South and conservation measures everywhere.

- Anti-poverty measures insuring a dignified life for all. Various United Nations agencies have affirmed that one could supply drinking water, adequate food, basic housing, health care and education to everyone on earth for under 100 billion USD a year for ten years.

- Democratic conditionality. No one wants to see the history of past decades repeated with elites capturing virtually all the benefits of both trade and aid. Western citizens are in favor of aid to poor countries, but only if they are guaranteed that the resources will reach those in need.

Therefore, in order to receive the benefits of the Planetary Contract, governments in the South would be required to include the representatives of their own civil society in the management and distribution of these resources. All societies, no matter how poor, have organizations representing farmers, workers, women, the business community and so on, which are allowed to operate more or less freely depending on the government. Arab and/or Moslem countries wishing to join in the Planetary Contract would need to show good faith in weeding out their own dangerous fundamentalist elements.

It would often be helpful to include representatives of Northern NGOs and civil society who have already worked with the more independent groups in the South so as to make sure that government and the elite are not merely manipulating or substituting for 'civil society'. No government would be obliged to enter into the Planetary Contract, but once accepted, then democratic—and anti-fundamentalist, of whatever stripe—conditionality would have to be accepted as well, without governmental recriminations of 'interference' or 'neocolonialism'.

The model of the Porto Alegre municipal budgeting process[18] should inspire the redistribution of resources. The Planetary Contract should also provide for a corps of independent, professional auditors with the capacity to recommend an instant end to disbursement in cases of proven corruption and capture on the part of the government or elite groups.

Financing the Planetary Contract

Although far more could doubtless be found, two hundred billion dollars a year ought to be adequate to confront the clusters of crisis and, in the bargain, pull the world back from the brink of recession where it now hovers. Let us recall that after the Second World War, the United States spent nearly three percent of its GNP on the Marshall Plan, knowing that the reconstruction of Europe as its privileged trading partner was in the best interests of both. A new win/win situation can now be created at the global level, using the following elements:

- Official Development Aid (ODA) now represents about 50 billion USD: it should be pooled and Northern countries should stop trying to use it as an export-generating device. NGO bureaucracies, in many countries now dependent on their government's aid budgets would resist such a move and should be in their turn resisted.
- Debt cancellation would make a huge contribution. Democratic conditionality, as described above, would apply to the waiving of debt repayments to the North.
- Close tax havens and clamp down on money-laundering and financial crime of all kinds. Governments should find themselves with new revenues previously claimed by transnational mafias.
- A controversial proposal: legalize all drugs, sell them in drab, unglamorous 'fair price shops' under government auspices, and tax them. Would this not bring in billions in revenues while probably reducing the numbers of drug users and certainly reducing the destruction of Colombia by spraying?
- Impose Tobin-type taxes on currency and other international financial transactions. We say 'Tobin-type', because Professor Tobin's classical proposal is probably no longer perfectly adaptable to today's situation as it was designed to limit speculation rather than raise revenues.
- Apply international taxation to cross-border corporate mergers and acquisitions, which now make up some 80 percent of Foreign Direct Investment.

18. See footnote 6.

- Levy a 'Unitary Profits Tax' on transnational corporations.[19] Such a tax would be popular with citizens on grounds of tax justice because transnational corporations (TNCs) now make ample use of transfer pricing and 'creative accounting' and pay less than their fair share of governments' budgets in the North, whereas tax burdens fall increasingly on incomes and consumption. It would also reduce the pressures on third world countries to offer tax havens to these corporations. Part of the Unitary Profits Tax could be earmarked for the Planetary Contract.
- George Soros' proposal concerning Special Drawing Rights would naturally find its place in a new arsenal of financial measures.

There is no shortage of measures available to finance a Planetary Contract so long as the principle behind such a contract is recognized: for a globalized world, we need global taxation and redistribution.

Administering the Planetary Contract

As it was made clear above, the global citizens' movement has little faith in existing international institutions. The institutional void is the chief obstacle we face when we affirm that 'Another World is Possible'. International institutions with power aren't trusted; those that are trusted are powerless.

Our preference for administrating the Planetary Contract would go to a new institution rather than to a revamped World Bank or IMF which we find thoroughly discredited. This is not to say that the individuals in these institutions should be scrapped. Many of them have invaluable experience and could make a vital contribution so long as they proved willing and able to play by new rules.

The point is that we can no longer accept structures where governments and governments alone are represented. The United Nations Charter begins "We the Peoples of the United Nations" before immediately sweeping them aside: now the peoples must be brought home and civil society put back in the picture.

---

19. As proposed by Prof. Howard Wachtel of American University in several papers, if TNC worldwide profits, worldwide sales revenues, and sales revenues in each tax jurisdiction are known, then they could be taxed in each jurisdiction at a flat rate worldwide. Example: Company X makes worldwide profits of 1 billion USD and receives 40 percent of its worldwide sales revenues in the United States. The profits earned in the US are thus considered to be 400 million USD and the corporate profit tax is applied to that base.

So long as checks and balances are established, peoples' governance—as described above—in individual countries insured and flying squads of anti-corruption auditors are plentiful, various administrative structures could apply. Experts from present UN agencies should be recruited, the bureaucracy kept to a minimum, and country quotas for personnel abolished. An independent Board with real power to sanction the Administrator and top level staff should be provided for.

Conclusion

A Planetary Contract would not be a cure for human evil nor for fundamentalist fanaticism—nor would anything else. We know that the terrorists' sponsors have no interest in the poor or in justice. The fact remains that they feed on poverty and injustice, which make a rich soil for resentment. It is often remarked that the United States itself has a far from perfect record in this regard. Over only the past thirty years, the United States has itself bombed, killed, and maimed countless civilians in Vietnam and Cambodia, or helped client regimes to do so in countries as various as Panama, Grenada, the Dominican Republic, Nicaragua, Chile, East Timor, Sudan, Libya, Iraq, and now Afghanistan—and the list is not exhaustive. The 'Wretched of the Earth' know this history. They know that their lives are not valued as are those of the West and they also know exactly what is being refused to them, because globalization also means immediate and widespread dissemination of information and images, including the false images of television and its spurious promises.

To oppose the despair that breeds hatred and terrorism, it is our responsibility to establish a contract of hope and renewal. It is affordable and necessary. Citizens will stand behind it. Another world is possible.

References

Buchanan, Mark (2000) "That's the Way the Money Goes." *New Scientist*, August 19, 2000.

George, Susan (1976) *How the Other Half Dies*. Harmondsworth: Penguin.

George, Susan (2001) *Remettre l'OMC á sa Place*. Eds. Mille et une Nuits. Paris: Fayard.

Hopkins, Andrea (2001) "WTO Chief: Seatle Protestors Make Me Sick." *Independent*, February 6, 2001.

Polányi, Karl (1944) *The Great Transformation*. New York: Rinehart.

Riis, Jacob A. (1897) *How the Other Half Lives.* New York: Charles Scribner's Sons.

Stephens, Philip (2001) "A Poor Case for Globalisation." *Financial Times,* August 16, 2001.

Stiglitz, Joseph (2002) *Globalization and Its Discontents,* New York, W.W. Norton.

Sun Tzu (1963) *The Art of War.* Edited by Samuel B. Griffith. Oxford: Clarendon.

UNCTAD (1997) *Trade and Develpoment Report.* Chapter 3.

Weisbrot, Mark *et al.* (2001) *The Emperor Has No Growth.* Center for Economic Policy Research, May 2001.

Civil Society and the Governance of Global Finance

Jan Aart Scholte

1. Introduction

Civil society has figured with increasing prominence in the recent history of global governance. The Secretary-General of the United Nations, Kofi Annan, has declared that "there are few limits to what civil society can achieve," while the President of the World Bank, James Wolfensohn, has affirmed that "civil society is probably the largest single factor in development" (both cited in Edwards, 2000a). The former Managing Director of the International Monetary Fund, Michel Camdessus, has similarly applauded "the valiant efforts of NGOs" in the area of social development (see Camdessus, 1995).

Such public pronouncements are perhaps tinged with hyperbole, but it is clear that civil society matters in contemporary politics of globalization. Countless civil society organizations (CSOs) have taken initiatives to shape global rules and institutions (Smith, Chatfield, and Pagnucco, 1997; Keck and Sikkink, 1998; Boli and Thomas, 1999; Foster with Anand, 1999; Florini, 2000; Edwards and Gaventa, 2001; Khagram, Riker, and Sikkink, 2002). Most major transworld governance agencies have established special mechanisms for inter-action with civil society bodies (Weiss and Gordenker, 1996; Willetts, 1996; O'Brien et al., 2000; Scholte with Schnabel, 2002: 109–177). Various theorists of world politics have in this regard described the emergence of an 'enlarged' or 'complex' multilateralism marked by intricate networks of relationships between state, substate, suprastate, and nonstate actors (Warkentin and Mingst, 2000: 251; O'Brien et al., 2000: 1–23; Schechter, 1999).

This chapter outlines some general parameters for an investigation of civil society engagement of global finance. The first section below describes certain changes in governance, consequent upon contemporary globalization, that have encouraged the rise of civil society activity in world politics. The second and third sections review, respectively, globalization in the realm of finance and the arrangements that have emerged to govern it. The fourth section identifies the main policy challenges that currently face the governance of global finance, while the fifth section surveys the initiatives taken by civil society actors to meet these challenges. The final two sections outline potential benefits as well as possible problems of civil society activity in the area of global finance.

2. Globalization and Governance

Globalization means many things to many people, but most will agree that, broadly speaking, the trend involves a growth of social connections on a planetary scale. This greater interconnectedness has several aspects. For one thing, globalization brings increased interaction and interdependence between countries: there is more international communication, investment, trade, and travel. In addition, globalization involves reductions in statutory barriers to cross-border flows: fewer tariffs, fewer foreign exchange restrictions, fewer capital controls, and (at least for citizens of some states and certain classes of workers) fewer visa requirements. Furthermore, globalization increases the numbers of objects and experiences that spread to most if not all corners of the inhabited earth: the Gregorian calendar, McDonald's restaurants, etc. And, with globalization, people acquire various social connections that largely transcend territorial geography, for example, in regard to telecommunications and global ecological changes.

Thus globalization has several interrelated facets: internationalization, liberalization, universalization, and deterritorialization. Different commentators give one or the other of these aspects more attention. My own emphasis goes to the fourth: that is, globalization as the proliferation and expansion of relatively deterritorialized spaces. Along these lines, global relations can be characterized as 'supraterritorial', 'transworld', or 'transborder' relations (Scholte, 2000: 41–61).

This is not to discount the reality and importance of present-day internationalization, liberalization, and universalization. However, these three tendencies have appeared in substantial measure in earlier history, long before talk of 'globalization' became popular in the late twentieth century. Concepts of globality open new, distinctive and important insights about the contemporary world when they are formulated in terms of supraterritorial connectivity. In global relations of this kind, terrestrial distances can be covered in effectively no time and territorial frontiers present no particular impediment. Thus supraterritorial connections unfold in the world as a single place.

Supraterritoriality has become commonplace for hundreds of millions of people in recent decades. For example, humanity is today interconnected through over a billion telephone lines, a billion television sets, two billion radio receivers, and half a billion Internet users (Scholte, 2000: 75–76).[1] At the same time the contemporary world is marked by pervasive transborder production processes, global marketing of thousands of goods and services, unprecedented levels of anthropogenic transworld ecological changes, a substantial rise of global consciousness among people, and (as elaborated below) an immense globalization of finance.

To be sure, global relations have spread unevenly. They have concentrated more in countries of the North, in professional and wealthier classes, and in urban centers relative to rural areas. However, globalization has left few inhabitants of today's world completely untouched.

Nor does this globalization thesis maintain that territorial spaces no longer matter. On the contrary, territorial economics, territorial governments, and territorial identities continue to exert very significant influences on contemporary society. However, social geography is today no longer *wholly* territorial. We have moved from a territorialist world to one where territorial realms coexist with (rapidly expanding) global spaces.

This reconfiguration of geography has far-reaching implications for governance, that is, the ways that people manage their collective affairs. Global flows defy effective management through the statist mode of governance that prevailed during most of the twentieth century. The old model of sovereign statehood—where a centralized national government holds singular, comprehensive, supreme, and absolute authority over a given territory—is plainly not suitable for the management of transborder air traffic, transworld disease, and many other policy matters, including supraterritorial finance. Contemporary governance has to entail more than government as traditionally understood.

This is not to suggest that states are on the verge of demise. On the contrary, most states across the world are today as large and active as ever. However, it is equally clear that territorially discrete states cannot by themselves effectively handle the many and large global flows that impact upon their jurisdictions. Major innovations are necessary in the ways that we manage many problems of collective concern. Indeed, globalization has already prompted some shifts in the contours of governance, trends that seem likely to unfold further in the future.

For instance, states in the contemporary globalizing world have increasingly turned from unilateral to multilateral approaches to many policy issues. This trend has been apparent, among other things, in the expansion of interstate consultations at ministerial level, including special conferences of the United Nations (UN) since the 1960s and meetings of the Group of Seven (G–7) since

1. See also http://www.nua.ie.

the 1970s. The rise of multilateral governance has also occurred through the growth of transstate networks, where civil servants from parallel agencies in multiple states develop close regulatory collaboration in a particular policy area (Slaughter, 2000).

In addition, multilateral governance has seen considerable transfers of regulatory competence to permanent suprastate institutions. Some of these agencies, like the European Union (EU), have a regional scope. Others like the International Monetary Fund (IMF) operate on a transworld scale. 'Suprastate' does not mean 'nonstate', in the sense that these agencies have gained full independence from and control over their state members. However, like most organizations, suprastate bureaucracies have acquired some initiative and power of their own, particularly in respect of weaker states.

Globalization has not only encouraged a shift of many regulatory competences 'upwards' to suprastate bodies, but also various moves 'downwards' to substate agencies. In recent decades most states have pursued some degree of devolution from national to provincial and local authorities. Sometimes these transfers have been specifically prompted by a judgment that certain global problems (for example, transborder crime or transworld ecological degradation) can in some respects be tackled more effectively at a substate level.

Along with the dispersion of authority 'upwards' and 'downwards' from the state, globalization has also promoted 'lateral' shifts of governance from the public sector to nonofficial quarters (Cutler, Haufler, and Porter, 1999; Ronit and Schneider, 2000; Higgott, Underhill, and Bieler, 2000). This privatization of governance has transpired, for example, in increased reliance on nongovernmental organizations (NGOs) to implement development cooperation projects and several multilateral environmental agreements. As detailed below, considerable private governance has also arisen in respect of global finance.

Together, the developments just described have brought an end to the statist governance that accompanied the territorialist geography of old. Theorists have variously dubbed emergent circumstances as 'multilayered', 'post-sovereign', 'post-Westphalian', 'neo-medieval', or 'networked' regulation. Whatever label one applies to it, governance in the context of contemporary globalization is different from the territorialist-statist mode that predominated for some 300 years from seventeenth-century Europe to the mid-twentieth century world.

Much post-statist governance of global relations remains *ad hoc*, experimental, and problematic. On the technical side, the new conditions of more dispersed authority have raised major challenges of efficiency and coordination. On the normative side, globalization has raised substantial challenges to human security, social justice, and democracy. Indeed, it is widely felt that currently prevailing approaches to the regulation of global spaces are wanting on both efficiency and normative grounds.

These circumstances have spurred a notable growth of civil society involvement in the governance of global relations. As already indicated, in certain cases civil society associations have even acquired the role of direct policy executors. More often, CSOs like business forums, local community associations, NGOs, religious groups, think tanks, and trade unions have pursued advocacy campaigns to improve the capacities of governance to deliver efficiency, stability, equity, and/or democracy in respect of global flows. Frustration with these governance deficits has in recent years drawn substantial numbers of civil society critics into a so-called 'anti-globalization movement' that has attracted much media attention.[2]

This rise of civil society activism has had a mixed reception. Enthusiasts have placed high hopes on the contributions of civil society to enhance management of global issues with invaluable information and expertise as well as greater democratic credentials and more equitable policy outcomes.[3] Other commentators have been less sanguine. For the skeptics, civil society interventions in global governance tend to be disruptive, ill-informed, unrepresentative, self-serving, and unaccountable (cf. Wolf, 1999; Bolton, 2000). These potential positive and negative effects are elaborated in the final sections of this chapter.

3. Financial Globalization

Before proceeding to that step, however, we should relate the general themes just outlined concerning globalization and governance to the specific area of finance. Indeed, the financial sector has shown some of the most far-reaching globalization in recent history.[4]

For one thing, globalization has given certain monies a substantially supraterritorial character. Several national denominations like the US dollar and the Japanese yen have become global currencies. They circulate just about everywhere on earth and move instantly by electronic transfer anywhere in the world. In addition, the euro and—on a much more limited scale—the Special Drawing Right (SDR) have emerged through the EU and the IMF, respectively, as suprastate monies with transworld use. Many banking cards (such as those connected

---

2. Cf. the special issue on "Globalization and Resistance," *Mobilization*, Vol.6, No.1 (2001).
3. Cf. Susan George, "The Global Citizens Movement: A New Actor for a New Politics," in this volume, pp.261–282.
4. Unless indicated otherwise, the data below are taken from Scholte (2000), Chapters 2 and 3.

to the Cirrus network) can extract cash in local currency from over 400,000 automated teller machines across the planet. Meanwhile global credit cards like Visa and MasterCard are used to make payments at millions of establishments spread over 200 jurisdictions.

Financial globalization has also transpired in the ways that money circulates. For instance, foreign-exchange trading today occurs through a round-the-world, round-the-clock market that connects dealing rooms in London, New York, Tokyo, Zürich, Frankfurt, Hong Kong, Singapore, Paris, and Sydney. The average daily volume of foreign exchange transactions reached 1,490 billion USD in 1998, up from 15 billion USD in 1973.[5]

In global banking, the world total of bank deposits owned by nonresidents of a given country rose from 20 billion USD in 1964 to 9,600 billion USD in 2001, including an estimated five trillion dollars' worth in offshore accounts (IMF, 1993: 60–70; BIS, 2001b: 10). Electronic payments through the Society for Worldwide Interbank Financial Telecommunications (SWIFT), founded in 1977, averaged more than 6,000 billion USD per day in 2000, linking over 7,000 financial institutions in 194 countries.[6] Outstanding balances on syndicated transborder bank loans rose from under 200 billion USD in the early 1970s to well over 8,000 billion USD in 2001. New facilities of this kind totaled 1,465 billion USD in 2000, as compared with 9 billion USD in 1972 (OECD, 1996; BIS, 2001b: 68).

Other global lending has occurred on a notable scale through official financial institutions. For example, the IMF has provided balance of payments support to its member governments, occasionally (as in the cases of Korea in 1997 and Russia in 1998) to the tune of tens of billions of dollars. A number of multilateral development banks (MDBs) have emerged since the 1940s, including the World Bank Group, the Islamic Development Bank, and regional development banks for Africa, the Americas, Asia, the Caribbean, and Europe. With the huge growth of private global finance, MDB loans amount to but a tiny proportion of the total of transborder credit flows. However, the MDBs remain the principal source of global finance for many poor countries.

Contemporary securities markets have also acquired substantial supraterritorial attributes. For example, bonds, medium-term notes, and short-term credit instruments have a global character when they are denominated in a transworld money and involve borrowers, investors, managers, and/or exchanges that are spread across multiple countries. The largely supraterritorial eurobond market has grown from its inception in 1963 to a level of 371 billion USD in new bor-

5. The introduction of the euro and other developments caused turnover to drop to 1,210 billion USD per day in 2001. Figures taken from Gilpin (2001: 261) and BIS (2001a; 2001c: 98–100).
6. See http://www.swift.com.

rowings in 1995. The net issuance of all cross-border bonds and notes reached 1,246 billion USD in 2000 (BIS, 2001b: 71). In stock markets, various companies have developed global share listings, that is, on several exchanges spread across the world. Meanwhile electronic communications have enabled investors and brokers instantly to transmit and execute orders to buy and sell securities anywhere in the world. The two main clearing houses for transborder securities trading, Euroclear and Clearstream (formerly Cedel), together accumulated an annual turnover of nearly 60,000 billion USD in 1999, up from 10,000 billion USD in the late 1980s.

Additional globalization has occurred in respect of financial derivatives, an industry that has burgeoned since the early 1970s. Traditionally, instruments like forwards, futures, and options mainly 'derived' from agricultural and mineral commodities, but more recently huge global markets have developed in derivative contracts related to foreign exchange rates, interest levels, securities prices, stock market indices, and other financial indicators. Several derivatives exchanges (for example, London–Singapore and Chicago–Sydney) have established direct links to enable round-the-world, round-the-clock dealing in certain futures and options. The notional amount of outstanding over-the-counter financial derivatives contracts alone (thus excluding exchange-based derivatives) reached 99,800 billion USD at the end of 1999 (BIS, 2001d).

Finally, much contemporary insurance business has gone global. Countless insurance policies have global coverage, are denominated in a global currency, and/or are handled by global companies in global financial centers. Meanwhile insurance brokers have developed networks that allow them to transact business across the planet from their office computers.

In sum, much contemporary finance has a supraterritorial character that was barely if at all evident before 1960. Territorial places, distances, and borders are not irrelevant in today's banking, securities, derivatives, and insurance industries, but many of these activities also substantially transcend territorial geography. Moreover, the sums of business in global finance are staggering, dwarfing the numbers associated with sales turnover in other sectors of the global economy. It is understandable in this light that many worries regarding 'globalization out of control' have concerned finance.

4. Governance of Global Finance

Global finance is obviously not 'controlled,' in the sense of being ruled by a sovereign world government; nevertheless, these activities are subject to considerable if imperfect governance. Recent developments in the regulation of global finance largely conform to the general trends in contemporary governance noted earlier. In other words, states remain key, but they have increasingly adopted strategies of multilateral (both interstate and suprastate) management of transworld finance. In addition, substate actors have begun to figure in this realm, albeit still marginally. Also, regulatory mechanisms based in private-sector agencies have gained substantial significance in the governance of global finance. The following paragraphs elaborate these points in turn.

States are still, on the whole, the primary actors in the governance of finance under conditions of contemporary globalization. Any examination of the management of global finance must therefore consider the activities of national central banks, national treasuries, national securities and exchange commissions, and national insurance supervisors. Of course some states (like France and the USA) have figured more prominently and powerfully in the governance of global finance than others (like Uzbekistan and Zambia). Indeed, limited capacity for financial regulation at national level has left many states in a very weak position *vis-à-vis* global finance.

Yet even the strongest states have not tackled the governance of global finance alone. Multiple networks of intergovernmental consultation and cooperation have developed in tandem with the accelerated globalization of finance during recent decades. For example, central bank governors of the so-called Group of Ten (G–10)[7] advanced industrial countries have met regularly at Basle since 1962 to discuss monetary and financial matters of mutual concern. An Intergovernmental Group of Twenty-Four on International Monetary Affairs (G–24) was established in the early 1970s as a South-based counterpart to the G–10, though it has held far less influence (Mayobre, 1999). The G–7 summits, held annually since 1975, have also frequently discussed issues related to global finance.[8] A separate G–7 finance ministers' group was established in 1986 and normally meets 3–4 times per year. In September 1999 the G–7 finance ministers created the Group of Twenty (G–20) in order to include governments of so-called 'emerging markets' in structured discussions concerning global financial stability.[9]

Both the G–10 and the G–7 have from time to time set up working parties to

7. Actually 11: Belgium, Canada, France, Germany, Italy, Japan, the Netherlands, Sweden, Switzerland, the UK, and the USA.
8. The G–7 comprises Canada, France, Germany, Italy, Japan, the UK, and the USA. The European Community/Union has participated since 1977. Russia was added in 1998 to form the G–8. See further Hajnal (1999) and http://www.g7.utoronto.ca.
9. Membership of the G–20 is currently actually 19, comprised of the G–7 plus Argentina, Australia, Brazil, China, India, Indonesia, the Republic of Korea, Mexico, Russia, Saudi Arabia, South Africa, and Turkey, plus the EU, the IMF and the World Bank. See further http://g20.nic.in/indexe.html.

explore specific issues related to global finance. The best-known example is the Basle Committee on Banking Supervision (BCBS), formed as a standing group of the G–10 in 1975 (Dale, 1994; Kapstein, 1994; Norton, 1995). Most significantly, the BCBS has formulated the Basle Capital Accord, a framework first issued in 1988 for assessing the capital position of transborder banks, and Core Principles for Effective Banking Supervision, published in 1997. On a more specific problem, the G–7 created the Financial Action Task Force (FATF) in 1989 to combat drug-related money laundering (Reinicke, 1998).[10] More recently, the G–7 has promoted the establishment of a Financial Stability Forum (FSF), first convened in April 1999. The FSF is meant to enhance information exchange and cooperation among states in the supervision and surveillance of commercial financial institutions.[11]

As the existence of such working groups indicates, much intergovernmental collaboration on policy regarding global finance has occurred among civil servants rather than at a ministerial level. Other significant transgovernmental links among financial technocrats have developed through the so-called Paris Club (with a secretariat in the French Treasury since 1974) that convenes from time to time to reschedule the bilateral debts of Southern states.[12] Other transgovernmental groups have met under the auspices of the Organization for Economic Cooperation and Development (OECD), for example, to formulate measures in respect of financial liberalization, offshore finance centers, taxation of transborder portfolio investments, and development assistance. The OECD has also housed the secretariat of the FATF. In respect of bond and stock markets more particularly, the International Organization of Securities Commissions (IOSCO) was created as an inter-American body in 1974, went global in 1983, and now involves nearly 100 national securities authorities (Porter, 1993; Steil, 1994).[13] In addition, the International Association of Insurance Supervisors (IAIS) was formed in 1994 and has quickly grown to link authorities in over 100 countries.[14] Since 1996 the BCBS, IAIS, and IOSCO have convened a Joint Forum on Financial Conglomerates to promote cooperation between banking, securities, and insurance supervisors, given that global financial corporations increasingly operate across the three sectors.

As the work of the OECD, IOSCO, and IAIS illustrates, intergovernmental collaboration in respect of global finance is being increasingly institutionalized

10. See also http://www.oecd.org/fatf.
11. See http://www.fsforum.org.
12. See http://clubdeparis.org.
13. See also http://www.iosco.org.
14. See http://www.iaisweb.org.

in permanent suprastate bodies. The oldest such agency, the Bank for International Settlements (BIS), dates back to 1930, but it has become especially active in recent decades. The voting membership of the BIS has increased to 45 national central banks, and the institution has other dealings with several score more. The BIS convenes certain influential working groups, including the Committee on the Global Financial System and the Committee on Payment and Settlement Systems. The organization also houses secretariats for the BCBS, the IAIS, and the FSF. The BIS staff has grown to exceed 500.[15]

The IMF has undergone even more striking expansion in conjunction with the globalization of finance. Its membership has risen from 62 states in 1960 to 183 states in 2000. Its quota subscriptions have multiplied tenfold from the equivalent of 21 billion SDRs in 1965 to 212 billion SDRs in 1999. Its staff numbers have quadrupled from 750 in 1966 to 3,082 in 1999 (IMF, 1966: 133; IMF, 2000: 95). The Fund took a leading role in the management (some say *mis*management) of the Third World debt crisis in the 1980s and the emerging market financial crises since 1994. More generally, IMF surveillance of its members' macroeconomic situation has expanded since 1997 to include assessments of the financial sector (IMF, 1997: 36–37). In several countries, the Fund has taken a substantial role in restructuring the finance industry after a crisis. Since 1996 the IMF has promoted data standards that aim to make information on and for financial markets more reliable and accessible.[16] IMF management and senior staff have contributed extensively to recent discussions on the global financial architecture. The Fund's International Monetary and Financial Committee (IMFC, formerly Interim Committee) has served as an important forum for intergovernmental consultations regarding this architecture, drawing upon discussions in the FSF and the G–20.

The IMF's Bretton Woods twin, the World Bank, has played a less prominent role in the governance of global finance (as opposed to lending activity itself). The Bank's main intervention in respect of regulatory frameworks has involved loans and technical assistance for financial sector development in various countries of the South and the East. In recent years the Bank's policies in this area have focused on sector restructuring with programs of privatization and legal reform. More generally, the World Bank has had significant influence in setting the general discourse of global economic governance with its research and training activities.

Several other suprastate agencies have also served as forums for intergovern-

15. See http://www.bis.org.
16. See http://dsbb.imf.org.

mental discussion of global financial issues. The OECD has done so through its Economic Policy Committee and Working Party Three of that body, which between them meet six times per year. Within the UN system the General Assembly, the Economic and Social Council, the regional economic and social commissions, the Department of Economic Affairs, UNCTAD, UNDP and UNICEF have all addressed issues of global financial governance. However, UN intergovernmental forums have adopted mainly hortatory resolutions in this area, as opposed to formulating and implementing specific regulatory measures. The Financing for Development Initiative at the United Nations, launched in late 1997, represents an attempt to integrate wider economic and social concerns into the governance of global finance (Herman, 2002).[17]

Some further suprastate governance of global finance has emerged in recent years through the World Trade Organization (WTO). The Uruguay Round (1986–1994) produced a General Agreement on Trade in Services (GATS) that extended multilateral liberalization of international commerce *inter alia* to finance (Underhill, 1993). Since 1995 a WTO Committee on Financial Services has overseen the operation of GATS in respect of finance. In 2000 the WTO launched further multilateral negotiations on trade in services.

While contemporary globalization has often encouraged a rise of substate as well as suprastate competences in governance, devolution has been less apparent in respect of finance than in other sectors. True, various provincial and municipal governments have turned to global sources like the eurobond market for credits. However, these substate authorities have rarely participated in regulatory activities *vis-à-vis* transworld finance. A few exceptions might be noted, such as the inclusion of agencies from two Canadian provinces as Associate Members of IOSCO and the membership of bureaus from Hong Kong, Labuan, New South Wales, and Ontario in the IAIS. However, for the moment official governance of global finance remains almost entirely at state and suprastate levels.

On the other hand, the financial sector presents an outstanding example of another major trend in contemporary governance, namely, the turn to nonofficial mechanisms of regulation.[18] A number of national securities and exchange commissions have lain in the private sector for some time, of course, and IOSCO also includes over fifty securities exchanges and dealers associations as Affiliate Members. Meanwhile several industry associations have promoted the transworld harmonization of standards and devised a number of self-regulatory instruments for bond and equity business in global financial markets. These bod-

17. See the website http://www.un.org/esa/ffd.
18. For an excellent survey, see Porter and Coleman (2002).

ies include the International Council of Securities Associations (ICSA), the World Federation of Exchanges (generally known by the French acronym FIBV), the International Primary Market Association (IPMA), and the International Securities Market Association (ISMA). In addition, bond-rating agencies like Moody's Investors Service and Standard & Poor's—and the financial markets whose sentiments they reflect—have come to exercise considerable disciplining authority over many national governments (Sinclair, 1994; Friedman, 1999: 32–33 and 91–92).

Private-sector inputs to the governance of global finance have also figured outside the securities area. For example, nongovernmental groups like the Group of Thirty (composed of economists and businesspeople) and the Derivatives Policy Group (drawn from major investment banks) have taken a lead in developing rules for derivatives markets (see G–30, 1993; DPC, 1995). Two other private-sector bodies, the International Accounting Standards Committee (IASC) and the International Federation of Accountants (IFAC), have devised the main accountancy and auditing norms currently in use for global business.

In sum, then, governance of global finance is both multilayered and dispersed. It involves complex networks of state, suprastate, substate, and private-sector actors. As such, developments in respect of global finance conform to the broad patterns discerned earlier regarding post-statist governance in the context of large-scale globalization.

5. Key Issues for the Governance of Global Finance

Not only is the governance of global finance complex, but it is also particularly challenged in meeting the demands of efficiency, stability, social justice, and democracy. Almost no one argues that current regulatory arrangements for transborder finance are satisfactory, although the diagnoses of problems and the prescriptions of solutions vary widely.

In respect of efficiency, many observers have worried that global finance currently operates with substantial data deficits. Indeed, transborder financial markets are often distorted owing to missing data, rumor, and harmful manipulations of information. Limited competition has been a further efficiency concern. Market concentration in global finance has seen a progressively smaller number of corporate conglomerates come to dominate the banking, securities, and insurance industries. Some critics have also charged that global finance in its current form tends to divert investment from the 'real' economy where it would better serve general public welfare. The multifaceted character of governance arrangements for global finance raises additional efficiency concerns, as multiple forums address the same problems in an often ad hoc and loosely coordinated fashion.

In respect of stability, many commentators have argued that current global financial markets are inordinately volatile, creating insecurities that range well beyond normal investor risk to touch the basic livelihood of the public at large. Some of these harmful instabilities have arisen from large and rapid speculative swings in foreign exchange values (as occurred, for example, in the European exchange-rate mechanism in 1992). Other excessive volatility has come from enormous and swift withdrawals of transborder finance capital, especially short-term credits (as in the Asia, Latin America, and Russia crises of the late 1990s). In addition, many stock and bond markets have since the late 1980s experienced wildly unstable courses of steep climbs and precipitous downturns. Derivatives markets, too, have suffered a series of debacles: the Metallgesellschaft and Orange County affairs in 1994; Barings in 1995; Sumitomo in 1996; Long Term Capital Management in 1998; and Allied Irish Bank in 2002.

In respect of social justice, critics have worried that contemporary global finance sustains or even widens arbitrary inequalities of opportunity in the world economy. For example, people living in the North have on the whole enjoyed far better access to and far more benefits from global financial markets than people resident in the South. Meanwhile onerous transborder debt burdens have—it is now generally agreed—hampered the development efforts of poor countries. Other injustice has arisen between income groups, as the gains of transworld finance (including the 'tax efficiency' of offshore centers) have flowed largely to a wealthy minority of the world's people. As for gender equity, feminist critiques have highlighted limited access for women to global credit markets, a low representation of women in the management of global finance, and disproportionate hardships suffered by women in economic crises induced (at least partly) by global finance (van Staveren, 2002).

In respect of democracy, considerable unease has developed that current arrangements of global financial governance are insufficiently participatory, consultative, representative, transparent, and publicly accountable. For one thing, most states have been excluded from the G–7, the G–10, the G–20, and the OECD, while weighted votes have given a handful of states predominance in the Bretton Woods institutions. At the level of citizens, the vast majority of people across the world have scarce if any awareness of the rules and regulatory institutions that govern one of the most important areas of the global economy. Few governments have taken initiatives of public education to improve this sorry situation. Apart from a poll in 1992 on Switzerland's membership of the IMF and the World Bank, states have never conducted popular referenda on questions of global finance. In all countries, popularly elected bodies have had little direct involvement in, or exercised much supervision over, the transstate networks, suprastate institutions, and private regimes that have largely governed global finance. Nor have suprastate and private regulatory bodies included any representative organs of their own.

Mounting concerns about these various policy challenges have generated much discussion in recent years about change in the so-called 'global financial architecture'.[19] Innumerable suggestions have circulated to establish new principles, new policies, and new institutional mechanisms to govern global finance. Some of these proposals have promoted modest rewiring of the system (e.g. increased flexibility regarding the use of capital controls). In contrast, other recommendations have envisioned large-scale reconstruction (e.g. the creation of a fully-fledged world central bank). It is likely that the coming years will bring change in the global financial architecture, although the extent, speed, and direction of reconstruction remain to be determined.

6. Civil Society Initiatives on Global Finance

Many of the calls for change in the governance of global finance have emanated from civil society. The main sectors of civil society that have engaged with questions of global finance are business forums, development NGOs, environmental NGOs, organized labor, policy research institutes, and religious bodies (principally Protestant and Roman Catholic churches). These civil society associations have addressed five main concerns: transborder debt problems of the South; project loans by the MDBs; structural adjustment loans, mainly from the IMF and the World Bank; global commercial finance; and the shape of the overall global financial architecture. The following paragraphs review these five subjects of activism in turn.

Some of the most notable civil society involvement in global finance has come in respect of the transborder debt burdens of poor countries. Indeed, two major industry associations, the Institute of International Finance (IIF) and the Japan Center for International Finance (JCIF), were established in 1983 largely in response to the debt crisis of that day. While business forums have focused their concerns with debt on the financial interests of the creditors, other civil society

19. For contrasting perspectives, see Bond and Bullard (1999), Eichengreen (1999), and Eatwell and Taylor (2000).

bodies have highlighted the economic and social plights of the borrowers. Several think tanks like the (now disbanded) Washington-based Overseas Development Council (ODC) have given extensive attention to mechanisms for debt relief. In addition, the social costs of debt burdens in the South have occupied many Christian groups, including the Roman Catholic and Anglican churches. Numerous development NGOs have also pursued campaigns for debt relief in the South. Leading players in this regard have included the US Debt Crisis Network (which operated in 1985–1990), the Freedom from Debt Coalition in the Philippines, the European Network on Debt and Development (EURODAD), and national debt networks in several African countries like Mozambique and Uganda. The transborder Jubilee 2000 Campaign, with its demand for "the cancellation of the unpayable debt of the world's poorest countries" attracted affiliates in over 65 countries by its close at the start of the new millennium (see Collins et al., 2001). Several successor initiatives have carried the Jubilee project forward to the present day.

Other NGO-led campaigns have highlighted social and environmental questions connected to the project loans of the MDBs, especially the World Bank. Environmental NGOs have pursued some of the most highly publicized campaigns, sometimes in coalition with indigenous peoples and other local associations (O'Brien et al., 2000: 109–158; Durbin and Welch, 2002). Women's NGOs have called attention to the possible adverse gender consequences of various MDB (particularly World Bank) projects (O'Brien et al., 2000: 24–66). In addition, many development NGOs have criticized both the general paradigms and the specific conditions of MDB loans (Nelson, 1995; Fox and Brown, 1998; Tussie, 2000).

Since the early 1980s, various civil society groups have also given attention to structural adjustment lending, especially by the IMF and the World Bank. For example, certain business associations have intervened in respect of macroeconomic reform programs when proposed policy changes have touched on their members' commercial interests. In addition, a number of think tanks, trade unions, development NGOs, and environmental NGOs have argued that IMF/World Bank-sponsored structural adjustment brings unacceptable social and environmental impacts, or indeed can harm a country's overall position in the world economy. Prominent actors in these debates have included the London-based Overseas Development Institute (ODI); the former Harvard Institute for International Development (HIID); the International Confederation of Free Trade Unions (ICFTU); the global network of Oxfams; the Washington-based Development GAP; Friends of the Earth–US; and the World Wide Fund for Nature (WWF). Since 1995 the World Bank has pursued a Structural Adjustment Participatory Review Initiative (SAPRI) that has come to involve over 1,200 civil society associations in the South and the North.[20] In September 1999 the IMF and the World Bank redefined their approach to lending for low-income countries with the launch of Poverty Reduction Strategy Papers (PRSPs), whose formulation is meant to involve broad participation from civil society.[21]

In comparison with MDB and IMF lending, the governance of commercial global finance has received much less attention in civil society, apart from academic studies (mainly in the field of political economy) and self-interested initiatives by business groups. Some CSOs have in recent years supported revived proposals for a redistributive global tax on foreign exchange trading, as first advocated by James Tobin in 1971 (and hence often known as the Tobin Tax).[22] The transborder movement ATTAC, founded in France in 1998 and now spanning some thirty countries, has figured especially prominently in this campaign.[23] Certain NGOs have also promoted modest drives for so-called 'ethical investment' in global markets. Since the late 1990s several NGOs including BothENDS (Netherlands), the Fifty Years Is Enough Network (USA), and the Halifax Initiative (Canada) have organized teach-ins about the operations and consequences of global commercial financial markets. A scattering of grassroots activists in North America have advocated 'de-globalization' with a turn to local community currencies.[24] On the whole, however, NGOs, religious bodies, and trade unions have accorded little—indeed, surprisingly little—priority to commercial global finance.

A host of civil society concerns about public and private transborder finance have come together in debates regarding the overall global financial regime. Such deliberations have experienced several peaks, including calls in the 1970s for a New International Economic Order, discussions in 1994 to mark the fiftieth anniversary of the Bretton Woods accords, and recent debates on the global financial architecture. Policy think tanks and university academics have figured most prominently in these activities, through a slew of symposia and publications. Some of the more influential participants have included Washington-based bodies like the Brookings Institution, the Cato Institute, the Institute for International Economics, and the ODC. Among business groups, the Bretton

20. http://www.worldbank.org/poverty/strategies/index.htm; http://www.igc.org/dgap/saprin.
21. http://www.worldbank.org/poverty/strategies/index.htm.
22. On the Tobin tax, see *inter alia* Eichengreen and Wyplosz (1995), Felix (1995), ul-Haq *et al.* (1996), and Patomaki (2001).
23. The Association for the Taxation of Financial Transactions for the Aid of Citizens. See http://www.attac.org.
24. http://www.ratical.org/many_worlds/cc/.

Woods Committee, a Washington-based association of some 600 corporate members, in 1992–1994 sponsored a major study of the IMF and the World Bank (Bretton Woods Committee, 1994). More recently, the IIF has convened working groups on financial crises, data transparency, the liberalization of capital movements, and global standards for the soundness of banks. A few NGOs have also conducted critical examinations, in seminars and publications, of general governance arrangements for global finance. Notable activities have come in this respect from the Bangkok-based Focus on the Global South, the London-based Bretton Woods Project, and the Washington-based Center of Concern. Since the late 1990s a number of online discussion and action networks have also played a growing role in civil society engagement of global finance, particularly in the context of the so-called 'anti-globalization' protests (cf. Hill and Hughes, 1998; Ayres, 1999).

In sum, then, civil society associations have addressed various issues related to contemporary global finance. The scale of these activities should not be exaggerated, and some aspects of transworld finance have received quite limited attention. Moreover, the forms and intensity of civil society activism on global finance have varied considerably between different parts of the world (cf. Scholte with Schnabel, 2002). Nevertheless, these qualifications noted, CSOs have become active players in the politics of global finance.

7. Civil Society and Global Finance: Potential Benefits

It is important not only to describe civil society initiatives in respect of global finance, but also to assess them. To undertake such an evaluation we need explicit standards for judgment. The remainder of this chapter outlines some of the criteria that might be considered. This section identifies eight possible positive impacts, and the next section reviews eight potential negative aspects. Only a framework of evaluation is suggested here. Further empirical analysis is necessary to determine how far these potentials have been and could be realized in practice.

A first potential positive impact of civil society involvement in global finance concerns public education. Civil society activities might raise citizens' awareness and understanding of global finance and its governance. To this end, CSOs can prepare handbooks and information kits, produce audio-visual presentations, organize workshops, circulate newsletters, supply information to and attract the attention of the mass media, maintain listservs and websites on the Internet, and develop curricular materials for schools and higher education courses.

Second, civil society might make positive contributions to the governance of global finance by giving voice to stakeholders. Civil society associations can provide opportunities for concerned parties to relay information, testimonial, and analysis: to each other; to market actors; and to governance agencies. In particular, CSOs can open political space for social circles like the poor and women who tend to get a limited hearing through other channels (including constitutional representative assemblies). In this way civil society activism can empower stakeholders and indeed shift politics toward greater participatory democracy.

Third, civil society associations might fuel debate about global finance. Effective governance rests *inter alia* on vigorous, uninhibited discussion of diverse views. Inputs from civil society can put a variety of perspectives, methodologies, and proposals in the policy arena. Thanks to such contributions, policy deliberations can become more critical and creative. In addition, if we posit that openings for dissent are as necessary to democracy as securing of consent, then civil society can offer sites for objection and challenge.

Fourth, civil society might contribute positively to the governance of global finance by increasing public transparency. Greater visibility of financial market operations and their regulation allows investors and the public at large to make more informed judgments, thereby enhancing both efficiency and democracy. Pressure from civil society groups can encourage authorities in the governance of global finance to be more open about who takes decisions, what decisions they take, from what options, on what grounds, with what expected results, and with what supporting resources for implementation. Civil society actors can also interrogate the currently popular official rhetoric of 'transparency' by asking critical questions about what is made transparent, at what time, in what forms, through what channels, on whose decision, for what purpose, and in whose interest.

Fifth, civil society might promote more effective governance of global finance by increasing the public accountability of the agencies concerned. Civil society groups can monitor the implementation and effects of policies regarding global finance and press for corrective measures when the consequences are adverse. To take one specific example, civil society actors can keep a check on the social expenditure that has been promised in connection with recent debt relief packages. In addition, civil society associations can exert pressure directly on global financial corporations, for instance, by spurring consumer boycotts of their services. Through an accountability function, civil society can push authorities in the area of global finance to take greater responsibility for their actions.

Sixth, civil society might enhance the workings of global finance by improving material welfare. For example, service delivery by civil society associations can help to reduce the social fallout (unemployment, cuts in public services, etc.) that often accompanies the macroeconomic adjustments that are undertaken in response to financial crises. NGOs can also urge that global finance flows into channels (like micro-credit schemes, for instance) that may especially benefit vulnerable social groups.

Seventh, civil society might through its various positive influences enhance social cohesion. Contributions to public education, stakeholder voice, policy debate, transparent and accountable governance, and material welfare can all help to counter arbitrary social hierarchies and exclusions that global finance might otherwise encourage. As a result, global finance would contribute less to social conflict and more to social integration.

Finally, civil society might promote legitimacy in global financial governance. Legitimate rule prevails when people acknowledge that an authority has a right to govern and that they have a duty to obey its directives. Legitimate governance tends to be executed more easily, productively, and nonviolently than illegitimate authority. The IMF and the World Bank have recognized this general principle with their recent attention to issues of policy 'ownership'. Civil society can offer a means for citizens to affirm that certain rules and institutions of global finance should guide—and where necessary, constrain—their behavior. Likewise, civil society can also provide a space for the expression of discontent and the pursuit of change when existing governance arrangements are regarded as illegitimate.

In sum, civil society has considerable positive potential to improve the governance of global finance. It would be naïve to present civil society interventions as a panacea for the global financial order, particularly given the generally modest proportions of this activism to date. At the same time, the possible gains on offer are such that we would be equally foolish to dismiss the inputs of civil society out of hand. We have arguably only witnessed the early stages of a long development. Indeed, the levels of activity and contributions already far exceed the position just twenty or thirty years ago.

8. Civil Society and Global Finance: Possible Problems

None of the above fruits of civil society involvement in global finance flow automatically. The positive potentials cannot be realized in the absence of deliberate efforts and ample resources. In addition, civil society might in certain ways actually detract from effective governance of global finance. Eight general negative possibilities can be identified: some of them underdeveloped opportunities and some of them positive harms.

First, civil society actors might pursue dubious goals. Voluntary associations may not have the public interest at heart in some—or even any—of their activities. To take one striking example of 'uncivil society', transborder criminal networks have used global finance to perpetrate considerable damage. Other destructive elements such as racists, ultra-nationalists, and religious fundamentalists can seek to suppress the democratic rights of others. Business forums, professional bodies, and trade unions can focus on narrow and short-term interests of their members, possibly to the detriment of the general welfare. In their efforts to secure special interests in global finance and its governance, lobby groups may bypass—and thereby subvert—democratic processes through the state. In short, civil society is not intrinsically a virtuous force for the collective good and can in some cases do ill.

Second, civil society interventions in respect of global finance might suffer from flawed policy strategy and tactics. True, notions of 'flawed policy' are political, and care must be taken that ruling discourses of technocratic expertise do not arbitrarily suppress alternative perspectives. However, we cannot be so relativist as to argue that all policies are of equal quality. Civil society campaigns can be poorly conceived and/or ineptly executed. For example, activists may lack sufficient economic literacy to substantiate certain claims, or they may have little understanding of the mandate and *modus operandi* of institutions of global financial governance. Academics may fail to link theoretical models of global finance and its governance to empirical evidence and political practicalities. On a more specific point of strategy, it might be questioned whether civil society should focus its advocacy regarding global finance so much on the Bretton Woods institutions, to the relative neglect of commercial markets and the other governance actors mentioned earlier. As for tactics, should CSOs perhaps give more attention than hitherto to build coalitions between North and South, as well as between different sectors of civil society? True, ill-informed and misdirected civil society efforts can inadvertently produce beneficial results. More usually, however, low-quality initiatives are an unhelpful distraction and in some cases can cause actual harm, including to vulnerable social circles that well-intentioned civil society associations may be aiming to help.

Third, involving civil society might detract from the governance of global finance if the costs in efficiency outweigh the gains in equity and democracy. If taken seriously, then civil society participation in policy formulation, execution and evaluation demands a substantial commitment of resources. Democracy is not cheap. The expense is justified when it yields benefits in efficiency, security and social justice, as well as gains in democracy as a value in its own right. However, at some point the marginal returns from civil society participation are likely to decline and may even turn negative. Of course, people will disagree on how to calculate these costs and benefits—and thus on where the points of declining and negative returns lie. That said, these debates can be deferred for the moment: current levels of civil society participation in global finance are in general so modest that efficiency problems are hypothetical to all but the most dedicated technocrats. Nevertheless, it is prudent to remember, even at this early stage of development, that civil society involvement in policy cannot be run on a blank check.

Fourth, civil society engagement of global finance might have negligible or detrimental effects if the governance institutions concerned are ill-equipped to handle CSO inputs. Regulatory agencies may lack relevant staff expertise, adequate funds, suitable procedures, or the necessary receptive attitudes to take advantage of the benefits on offer from civil society. Officials can make innumerable mistakes in their dealings with civil society associations. They can treat the dialogue as a public relations exercise, or focus their contacts on sympathetic groups to the exclusion of critics, or dismiss out of hand civil society accounts that challenge 'expert' knowledge, or expect immediate results when relationships require time to mature. Needless to say, the onus for corrective action on these problems lies with official bodies rather than CSOs.

Fifth, civil society inputs to global finance might have negative consequences when CSOs become coopted, losing their previously highlighted positive potentials to stimulate debate and provide space for dissent. For example, civil society groups may come uncritically to render services to financial governance agencies or take funds from them. Campaigners may meet officials in a continual stream of convivial exchanges, without ever laying down deadlines for action. Certain civil society campaigners may even 'cross over' to work for organizations that they previously challenged. Some CSOs have engaged in what they call 'critical cooperation' with global financial institutions; however, beyond a certain point the critical element becomes diluted and eventually lost altogether. Meanwhile official institutions may coopt the language of civil society critique, subtly recasting it to their own purposes. Such captures of discourse may have occurred recently as the Bretton Woods institutions have embraced a rhetoric of 'participation', 'good governance', 'social capital', and 'poverty reduction'.

Sixth, civil society activity in respect of global finance might be undermined by undemocratic practices. Civil society groups—including those that campaign for greater democracy in global finance—can fall short of democratic criteria in their own activities. A lack of internal democracy within CSOs is not only objectionable in itself, but also contradicts civil society efforts to bring greater democracy to politics at large. For example, civil society associations might offer their members little opportunity for participation beyond the payment of subscriptions. CSOs may purport to speak on behalf of certain constituencies without adequately consulting them. The leadership or group culture of a civil society organization may impose peremptory constraints on debate. Civil society can become a realm of exclusionary cliques no less than many political parties and official circles. A CSO can also be run with top-down authoritarianism. In addition, policy making in civil society bodies can be quite opaque to outsiders—or even some insiders. Civil society groups can further lack transparency if they do not publish financial statements or declarations of objectives, let alone full-scale reports of their activities. Moreover, the leadership of CSOs can be self-selected, raising troubling questions of accountability and potential conflicts of interest. In short, the operations of civil society are no more intrinsically democratic than those in the public sector or the market. Several codes of conduct for NGOs have appeared in recent years in response to these concerns (see Cutt and Murray, 2000; Edwards, 2000b).

Seventh, civil society involvement in global finance might suffer from inadequate representation. If civil society is fully to realize its promises, then all interested parties must have access—and preferably equal opportunities to participate. Otherwise civil society can reproduce or even enlarge structural inequalities and arbitrary privileges connected with class, gender, nationality, race, religion, urban versus rural location, and so on. The capacities of civil society to advance social justice and democracy in global finance can be compromised if the participants are drawn disproportionately from middle classes, men, Northern countries, whites, Christians, and urban dwellers. To take one obvious example, civil society pressure for ethical investment in global financial markets tends to involve only those with resources to invest. Hierarchies of social power—and associated struggles of the subordinated classes, genders, races—exist in civil society no less than in other political spaces.

Eighth, and related to the problem of representation, the civil society that engages global finance might have an overly narrow cultural base. Civil society may not reflect and respond to all of the contexts for which it purports to speak. In particular there is a danger that civil society in the South and the former communist-ruled countries becomes monopolized by western-styled, western-funded NGOs led by westernized élites. For all that, such campaigners might criticize prevailing conditions of global finance, they have stronger cultural affinities with global managers than with local communities in their midst. Thus NGOs and other professionalized CSOs may—perhaps quite unintentionally—marginalize grassroots circles that could give better voice to the diverse life-worlds that global finance affects.

Given these potential problems, we do well to balance enthusiasm for civil society engagement of global finance with due caution. Much can go right, but much can also go wrong. Possible benefits can be neglected, and in some circumstances civil society involvement in global financial governance may actually detract from human security, social justice and democracy. In short, civil society can be a means to good ends, but it is not the end itself. It is quite proper to demand of civil society associations that they not merely assert, but also demonstrate their legitimacy.

9. Conclusion

This chapter has set the contemporary rise of civil society relations with global finance in the context of wider historical trends of globalization and its governance. The new geography of finance has raised opportunities for human betterment, but also major challenges for efficiency, stability, equity, and democracy. Existing governance arrangements have often failed to deliver the positive potentials of global finance and indeed sometimes have contributed to inefficiency, instability, injustice and democratic deficits. Global finance as it is has given civil society ample grounds for dissatisfaction.

Civil society can make important contributions to better governance of global finance. CSOs can advance public education, provide platforms, fuel debate, increase transparency and accountability, improve material welfare, promote social cohesion and enhance legitimacy. Of course civil society does not provide a complete answer. Improvements in global finance require not only quality inputs from CSOs, but also the will and capacity for change in official quarters and market circles. However, positive interventions from adequately resourced and suitably accountable civil society associations can bring much good to global finance, particularly in current circumstances of largely ad hoc and experimental governance arrangements.

But we must retain caution. As we have seen, the promises of civil society for global finance are not realized automatically. A sober assessment of the record to date and the possibilities for the future should help us to achieve the promises and avoid the pitfalls of civil society involvement in transworld finance.

References

Ayres, Jeffrey M. (1999) "From the Streets to the Internet: The Cyber-Diffusion of Contention." *Annals of the American Academy of Political and Social Science*, 566: 132–143.

BIS (2001a) "Central Bank Survey of Foreign Exchange and Derivatives Market Activity in April 2001: Preliminary Global Data." *Bank for International Settlements Press release*, October 9, 2001.

BIS (2001b) *Quarterly Review, December 2001*. Basle: Bank for International Settlements 2001.

BIS (2001c) *71st Annual Report*. Basle: Bank for International Settlements.

BIS (2001d) "The Global OTC Derivatives Market at End-June 2001." *Bank for International Settlements Press Release*, December 20, 2001.

Boli, John and George M. Thomas (eds.) (1999) *Constructing World Culture: International Nongovernmental Organizations since 1875*. Stanford: Stanford University Press.

Bolton, John R. (2000) "Should We Take Global Governance Seriously?" *Chicago Journal of International Law*, 1(2): 205–221.

Bond, Patrick and Nicola Bullard (1999) *Their Reform and Ours: The Balance of Forces and Economic Analysis That Inform a New Global Financial Architecture*. Bangkok: Chulalongkorn University Press.

Bretton Woods Commission (1994) *Bretton Woods: Looking to the Future*. Washington, DC: Bretton Woods Committee.

Camdessus, Michel (1995) *Address to the World Summit for Social Development*. Copenhagen, March 7, 1995. Available at http://www.imf.org.

Collins, Carole J.L., Zie Gariyo, and Tony Burdon (2001) "Jubilee 2000: Citizen Action across the North–South Divide." In Michael Edwards and John Gaventa (eds.) *Global Citizen Action*. Boulder, CO: Rienner, pp.135–148.

Cutler, A. Claire, Virginia Haufler, and Tony Porter (eds.) (1999) *Private Authority in International Affairs*. Albany: State University of New York Press.

Cutt, James and Vic Murray (2000) *Accountability and Effectiveness Evaluation in Non-Profit Organizations*. London: Routledge.

Dale, Richard (1994) "International Banking Regulation." In Benn Steil (ed.) *International Financial Market Regulation*. Chichester: Wiley, pp.167–196.

DPC (1995) *A Framework for Voluntary Oversight of the OTC Derivatives Activities of Securities Firm Activities to Promote Confidence and Stability in Financial Markets*. Washington, DC: Derivatives Policy Group.

Durbin, Andrea and Carol Welch (2002) "The Environmental Movement and Global Finance." In Jan Aart Scholte with Albrecht Schnabel (eds.) *Civil Society and Global Finance*. London: Routledge, pp.213–227.

Eatwell, John and Lance Taylor (2000) *Global Finance at Risk: The Case for International Regulation*. Cambridge: Polity Press and New York: Free Press.

Edwards, Michael (2000a) "Civil Society and Global Governance." In Ramesh Thakur and Edward Newman (eds.) *New Millennium, New Perspectives: The United Nations, Security, and Governance*. Tokyo: United Nations University Press, p.205.

Edwards, Michael (2000b) *NGO Rights and Responsibilities: A New Deal for Global Governance*. London: Foreign Policy Centre.

Edwards, Michael and John Gaventa (eds) (2001) *Global Citizen Action*. Boulder, CO: Rienner.

Eichengreen, Barry (1999) *Toward a New International Financial Architecture: A Practical Post-Asia Agenda*. Washington, DC: Institute for International Economics.

Eichengreen, Barry and Charles Wyplosz (1995) "Two Cases for Sand in the Wheels of International Finance." *Economic Journal*, 105(1): 162–172.

Felix, David (1995) *Financial Globalization versus Free Trade: The Case for the Tobin Tax*. Geneva: United Nations Conference on Trade and Development.

Florini, Ann M. (ed.) (2000) *The Third Force: The Rise of Transnational Civil Society*. Washington, DC: Carnegie Endowment for International Peace.

Foster, John W. with Anita Anand (eds.) (1999) *Whose World Is It Anyway? Civil Society, the United Nations and the Multilateral Future*. Ottawa: United Nations Association in Canada.

Fox, Jonathan A. and L. David Brown (eds.) (1998) *The Struggle for Accountability: The World Bank, NGOs, and Grassroots Movements*. Cambridge, MA: MIT Press.

Friedman, Thomas (1999) *The Lexus and the Olive Tree*. London: HarperCollins.

Gilpin, Robert (2001) *Global Political Economy: Understanding the International Economic Order*. Princeton, NJ: Princeton University Press.

G–30 (1993) *Derivatives: Practices and Principles*. Washington, DC: Group of Thirty.

Hajnal, Peter I. (1999) *The G–7/G–8 System: Evolution, Role, and Documentation*. Aldershot: Ashgate.

Herman, Barry (2002) "Civil Society and the Financing for Development Initiative at the United Nations." In Jan Aart Scholte with Albrecht Schnabel (eds.) *Civil Society and Global Finance*. London: Routledge, pp.162–177.

Higgott, Richard A., Geoffrey R.D. Underhill, and Andreas Bieler (eds.) (2000) *Non-State Actors and Authority in the Global System*. London: Routledge.

Hill, Kevin A. and John E. Hughes (1998) *Cyberpolitics: Citizen Activism in the Age of the Internet*. Lanham, MD: Rowman and Littlefield.

IMF (1966) *Annual Report 1966*. Washington, DC: International Monetary Fund.

IMF (1993) *International Financial Statistics Yearbook*. Washington, DC: International Monetary Fund.

IMF (1997) *Annual Report 1997*. Washington, DC: International Monetary Fund.

IMF (2000) *Annual Report 2000*. Washington, DC: International Monetary Fund.

Kapstein, Ethan B. (1994) *Governing the Global Economy: International Finance and the State*. Cambridge, MA: Harvard University Press.

Keck, Margaret and Kathryn Sikkink (1998) *Activists Beyond Borders: Advocacy Networks in International Politics*. Ithaca: Cornell University Press.

Khagram, Sanjeev, James V. Riker, and Kathryn Sikkink (eds.) (2002) *Restructuring World Politics: Transnational Social Movements, Networks, and Norms*. Minneapolis: University of Minnesota Press.

Mayobre, Eduardo (ed.) (1999) *G–24: The Developing Countries in the International Financial System*. Boulder, CO: Rienner.

Nelson, Paul J. (1995) *The World Bank and Non-Governmental Organizations: The Limits of Apolitical Development*. London: Macmillan.

Norton, Joseph J. (1995) *Devising International Bank Supervisory Standards*. London: Graham and Trotman.

O'Brien, Robert, Anne Marie Goetz, Jan Aart Scholte, and Marc Williams (2000) *Contesting Global Governance: Multilateral Economic Institutions and Global Social Movements*. Cambridge: Cambridge University Press.

OECD (1996) *International Capital Market Statistics 1950–1995*. Paris: Organization for Economic Cooperation and Development.

Patomaki, Heikki (2001) *Democratising Globalization: The Leverage of the Tobin Tax*. London: Zed Books.

Porter, Tony (1993) *States, Markets and Regimes in Global Finance*. Basingstoke: Macmillan.

Porter, Tony and William Coleman (2002) "Transformations in the Private Governance of Global Finance." Paper presented at the Annual Convention of the International Studies Association, New Orleans, March 23–27, 2002.

Reinicke, Wolfgang H. (1998) *Global Public Goods: Governing without Government?* Washington, DC: Brookings Institution.

Ronit, Karsten and Volker Schneider (eds.) (2000) *Private Organizations in Global Politics*. London: Routledge.

Schechter, Michael G. (ed.) (1999) *Innovation in Multilateralism*. Tokyo: United Nations University Press.

Scholte, Jan Aart (2000) *Globalization: A Critical Introduction*. Basingstoke: Palgrave.

Scholte, Jan Aart (2002) "Civil Society and the Governance of Global Finance." In Jan Aart Scholte with Albrecht Schnabel (eds.) *Civil Society and Global Finance*. London: Routledge, pp.11–32.

Scholte, Jan Aart with Albrecht Schnabel (eds.) (2002) *Civil Society and Global Finance*. London: Routledge.

Sinclair, Timothy J. (1994) "Passing Judgement: Credit Rating Processes as Regulatory Mechanisms of Governance in the Emerging World Order." *Review of International Political Economy*, 1(1): 133–159.

Slaughter, Anne-Marie (2000) "Governing the Global Economy through Government Networks." In Michael Byers (ed.) *The Role of Law in International Politics: Essays in International Relations and International Law*. Oxford: Oxford University Press, pp.177–205.

Smith, Jackie, Charles Chatfield, and Ron Pagnucco (eds.) (1997) *Transnational Social Movements and Global Politics: Solidarity beyond the State*. Syracuse: Syracuse University Press.

Steil, Benn (1994) "International Securities Markets Regulation." In Benn Steil (ed.) *International Financial Market Regulation*. Chichester: Wiley, pp.197–232.

Tussie, Diana (ed.) (2000) *Luces y sombras de una nueva relación: el Banco Interamericano de Desarrollo, el Banco Mundial y la Sociedad Civil*. Buenos Aires: Temas.

ul-Haq, Mahbub, Inge Kaul, and Isabelle Grunberg (eds.) (1996) *The Tobin Tax: Coping with Financial Volatility*. New York: Oxford University Press.

Underhill, Geoffrey R.D. (1993) "Negotiating Financial Openness: The Uruguay Round and Trade in Financial Services." In Philip G. Cerny (ed.), *Finance and World Politics: Markets, Regimes and States in the Post-Hegemonic Era*. Aldershot: Elgar, pp.114–151.

van Staveren, Irene (2002) "Global Finance and Gender." In Jan Aart Scholte with Albrecht Schnabel (eds.) *Civil Society and Global Finance*. London: Routledge, pp.228–246.

Warkentin, Craig and Karen Mingst (2000) "International Institutions, the State, and Global Civil Society in the Age of the World Wide Web." *Global Governance*, 6(2): 251.

Weiss, Thomas G. and Leon Gordenker (eds.) (1996) *NGOs, the UN, and Global Governance*. Boulder, CO: Rienner.

Willetts, Peter (ed.) (1996) *"Conscience of the World": The Influence of Non-Governmental Organizations in the UN System*. Washington, DC: Brookings Institution.

Wolf, Martin (1999) "Uncivil Society." *Financial Times*, September 1, 1999.

Index

Brazil, 85, 155, 164, 166–167, 172, 192, 268, 292n
Bretton Woods, 163, 198, 203, 279, 294, 297, 300–301, 304–305
bribe, 137, 141–142, 144–149
Britain. *See* United Kingdom
Buddhism, 159, 255n
Built-in-Agenda (BIA), 189
Bulgaria, 57, 138, 142, 150
bureaucracy/bureaucratism, 44–45, 47n, 54, 141, 242, 281, 283, 288
business associations, 295, 288–299

Cable News Network (CNN), 169, 201
CAIRNS Group, 192
Cambodia, 156, 173, 228, 283
Canada, 31, 164, 174, 219, 225, 265, 292n, 295, 300
Canadian International Development Agency (CIDA), 50, 231
capital controls, 165, 198, 201, 261, 272, 286, 298
capital markets. *See* financial markets
capitalism, 22, 165, 195, 203, 261, 272
  Anglo-American, 196
  capitalist countries, 106, 111n
  capitalist development, 119, 206
  financial, 198
  global, 19, 21
  laissez faire, 206
Cedel/Clearstream, 291
Central European University (CEU), 17–23, 29–31, 34–37, 41, 44, 61, 179n
Centre for the Study of Globalisation and Regionalisation (CSGR), 19, 75n
charity, 28, 53, 239–241, 243–244, 250

Chile, 79, 201, 283
China, 30, 33, 86, 155n, 156, 159–162, 164, 166, 168, 170, 176, 219, 292n
civic association. *See* civil society
civil society, 18, 21, 28–29, 32, 34, 36, 44, 50n, 51, 53, 55, 88, 101–103, 106–107, 115, 118–122, 126, 129–131, 225, 238, 241–244, 258n, 259, 261, 274, 280, 282, 285–308
  (*see also* global, civil society)
'clash of civilizations' theory, 20, 279
class, 306
  cross-, 75, 90, 278
  political, 175, 211, 277
  professional, 242
  See also middle class
climate change, 277–278
codes of conduct, 27, 210, 306
Cold War, 18, 217, 253, 275
colonialism, 66, 68, 90, 105, 113, 160, 173, 175, 203, 244, 273, 276 (*see also* post-colonialism)
commodification, 64–66, 68, 71–72, 271
commodity, 99, 162, 198–199, 204, 208, 228, 291
communication, 48, 64, 67, 71, 147, 155, 157, 164, 197, 200–202, 231, 258, 286, 291
community, 65, 68, 71, 97–98
  academic/intellectual, 18, 35, 41, 43, 135, 212
  access, 113
  aid, 222
  donor, 238, 241–244
  business, 32, 280
  East African, 229

314

devolution, 288, 295

discrimination, 158 (*see also* non-discrimination)

dispersion of authority, 29, 44, 254, 255, 257, 288

Dispute Settlement Body (DSB), 186

Dominican Republic, 165, 283

donor coordination, 227

donors, 27, 31, 45, 49, 56–57, 75, 79–80, 124, 192, 217–218, 221, 226–233, 237, 41, 241–244

double dividend, 28, 245, 247, 248–250

Dunkel Draft, 111

East Timor, 278, 283

Eastern Europe, 18, 23, 26, 34n, 43, 52, 56, 135–137, 140–143, 145, 148–150

ecology. *See* environment

Economic and Social Council (ECOSOC), 231, 295

economic growth, 24–27, 30–31, 85, 99, 101, 119, 135, 166–168, 176, 180–184, 188–190, 193, 201–202, 206, 208, 219, 221–224, 228–229, 232–233, 255, 260–269

economic liberalization, 119–120, 254–257

economy of shortages, 145–147

education, 30, 36, 43, 57, 68, 84, 87–88, 155, 157–158, 161, 167–168, 172, 182, 221, 223–224, 227n, 229, 247, 260, 275, 280

educational institutions, 54

educational standards, 276

in English, 65

improvements in, 28

private, 80, 87

public, 80, 301, 274, 303, 307

reform of, 35, 64

spending on, 25

efficiency, 23, 25, 31, 34, 46, 68, 119, 143, 158, 202, 210, 227n, 229, 247, 277, 288–289, 296–297, 302, 304–305, 303 (*see also* aid effectiveness)

Egypt, 166, 193

electronic commerce (e-commerce), 66–67, 190

emerging market, 209, 222, 258, 292, 294

Empire

Austro-Hungarian, 158, 162, 204

British, 113

Ottoman, 156, 162

Roman, 197

Russian, 162

sea borne, 159–160, 161

and trade, 160–162

employment/unemployment, 25, 49, 78, 85, 211, 264, 271, 279, 303

'end of history' thesis, 168

English language, 49, 64–67, 69, 157

Englishization, 64, 67

enlightenment, 167

environment, 25–27, 118, 125, 182, 196–197, 208, 255n, 264, 266, 271, 274–275

assessment, 125, 128

catastrophe of the, 52

clean, 23, 25, 33

conditionality, 128, 130

costs of the, 125

harmful production, 249, 278

justice, 102

movement, 106, 123, 299

protection, 18, 101, 117, 119

regulation, 105, 110, 117, 209, 288

renewal, 280
standards, 124, 188–189
sustainability, 29, 32, 121, 126
See also environmental conditionality; environmental movement;
environmental regulation; law,
environmental
(Environment and Development
Services) for Non Governmental
Organizations (Both ENDS), 300
equity, 75n, 77–83, 84–86, 88, 91, 99,
123, 257, 289, 297, 304, 307
Euro, 289, 290n
Eurobonds. *See* bonds
Euroclear, 291
European Network on Debt and
Development (EURODAD), 299
European Union (EU), 18, 32, 34n,
43, 47, 56–57, 76, 81, 83, 85, 89,
108, 170–172, 179, 182, 193,
199–201, 210, 239, 241–242, 247,
288–289, 292n
Euzkadi Ta Azkatasuna (ETA), 97

family planning. *See* reproduction
Federation Internationale des Bourses
de Valeurs (FIBV), 296
feminism, 297
Financial Action Task Force (FATF),
293
financial markets, 27, 33, 198, 204,
209–210, 222, 264–265, 268–270,
275, 277, 290–297, 300, 306
Financial Stability Forum (FSF), 293
Financial Times, 170, 265, 267
flexibilization, 298
Food and Agricultural Association
(FAO), 110
food security, 106

Forced displacement, 104–105,
115–117, 124, 126–127, 129
Fordism, 208
foreign aid, 27–28, 31, 167, 217, 231
foreign direct investment (FDI), 167,
228, 281
foreign exchange, 248, 286, 290–291,
297, 300
former Soviet Union (FSU), 18, 23,
34n, 205, 243, 270
fossil fuels, 278, 280
foundations, 34n, 42, 50–53, 56–57
France, 86, 170, 207, 267, 292, 300
Free Trade Agreement of the
Americas (FTAA), 76, 89
Freedom from Debt Coalition, 299
fresh air, 246

gender, 25, 278, 297, 299, 306
General Agreement on Tariffs and
Trade (GATT), 111n, 163–164,
166, 179, 181–183, 185–186, 191,
193, 266
General Agreement on Trade in
Services (GATS), 199, 274, 295
Genetic Resources Action
International (GRAIN), 110
Genoa, 201, 225, 263, 265, 267, 269,
276–278
geography, 287–288, 291, 307
Germany, 69, 78, 86, 123, 139,
161–162, 168, 170, 205, 292n
global
accounting (*see* international
accounting)
banking, 204, 290–291, 296
citizens' movement, 29, 263–284
civil society, 50–51, 106, 122,
258n, 259, 261

communication, 67
companies, 291
competition, 25, 78, 256
finance, 29, 285–312
financial architecture (*see* international financial architecture)
financial corporations, 302
lending, 290
media, 69
public goods, 25–26, 83–84, 245, 246
public policy networks, 44–46, 48, 51, 54
public policy, 24, 42–46, 48, 51–56
trade regime, 170, 188, 232
village, 157, 176
warming (*see* climate change)
Global Alliance on Vaccines and Inoculation (GAVI), 51
global governance, 28–29, 41, 63, 103, 106, 135, 253–262, 263, 285
global/world markets, 64–65, 68, 80, 84–87, 156–158, 161, 171, 176, 203–204, 233, 238, 240, 258, 256–259, 261, 270, 291, 300
Globalism and Social Policy Programme (GASPP), 77–78
gold standard, 204–205
good governance, 31, 35, 104, 114, 206, 212, 224, 261, 305
Great Britain. *See* United Kingdom
greenhouse effect. *See* climate change
Greenpeace, 42, 265
Group of 24 (G–24), 292
Group of 77 (G–77), 83, 273
Group of Eight (G–8), 23, 31, 98, 195–196, 219, 225–226, 230n, 231, 267n, 269, 273, 275, 277–278

Group of Seven (G–7), 23, 287, 123, 264, 287, 292–293, 297
Group of Ten (G–10), 292–293, 297
Group of Thirty (G–30), 296
Group of Twenty (G–20), 223, 231, 292, 294, 297
Guatemala, 34n

Haiti, 34n
harmonization. *See* standardization
Harvard Institute for International Development (HIID), 301
health, 28, 75, 77–78, 80–82, 84–85, 87–88, 90, 116, 158, 172, 190, 202, 221, 223, 227n, 229, 246–247, 274–276, 280
Heavily Indebted Poor Country Initiative (HIPC), 218, 225, 230, 245, 273
Hinduism, 116
HIV. *See* AIDS
Hong Kong, 161, 166, 219, 290, 295
Human Development Report, 112
human rights movement, 115, 117–118
human rights, 21, 23, 25, 31, 35, 83, 97, 101, 105, 110, 119, 124, 126, 128–129, 155, 165, 197, 243, 254, 259, 261
human security. *See* security
Hungary, 206, 211
hybridity/hybridization, 20

identity
of the international movement, 263
national, 68
transnational, 17

multilateralism, 17, 19, 27, 53, 123, 169, 180, 182, 186, 192, 196, 198–199, 228, 232–233, 257, 259, 274, 277, 285, 287–288, 292, 295
multilayered governance, 288, 296
multilingualism, 24, 49, 65–67, 70
multinational corporations, 54, 63, 72, 91, 101, 103, 106–107, 111, 114, 200, 269–270, 277, 282
Muslims. *See* Islam
Myanmar, 168

Narmada Bachao Andolan (NBA), 122, 124
National Association of Securities Dealers Automated Quotation system (NASDAQ), 209
National Thermal Power Corporation (NTPC), 126, 128
nationalism, 26, 162–164, 165–166, 169–170, 206, 304
nationalization, 142, 205
nation-state, 20, 24, 28, 31, 41, 46–47, 69–70, 101, 111, 114, 130, 195–196, 212, 255n, 258, 271, 276–277
neoliberalism, 22–23, 26, 75–76, 78–81, 83–84, 89–91, 101–103, 106, 110, 113–114, 120, 269–272
Netherlands, 161, 170, 211, 275n, 292n, 300
new (international) financial architecture, 259, 272
New International Economic Order, 273, 300
New Partnership for Africa's Development (NePAD), 31, 226, 233
new public management, 42, 48

New Zealand, 164, 174
newly industrializing economies (NIEs), 161
Nicaragua, 283
non-discrimination, 163–164, 169, 179, 182
nongovernmental organizations (NGOs), 17, 25, 29, 32, 36, 42–44, 50, 53, 55, 57, 77, 80, 84, 89, 101–103, 105–114, 115, 117–128, 200, 218, 243, 265, 274n, 280–281, 285, 288–289, 296, 298–301, 303, 306
North American Free Trade Agreement (NAFTA), 162
North Atlantic Treaty Organization (NATO), 18
North Korea, 208
North–South relations, 25, 76–77, 83–97, 89–91, 99, 106, 111, 123, 249, 264, 267, 273, 276, 279–280, 300, 304

odious debt, 272
Official Development Aid/Assistance (ODA), 217, 219, 221, 227, 231, 245, 246–247, 248, 275, 281
offshore arrangements, 290, 293, 297
oligopoly, 172
Open Society Institute (OSI), 19, 34–36, 39, 43, 52, 59, 243
Organization for Economic Cooperation and Development (OECD), 26, 45–49, 56, 80, 98, 180, 190–191, 193, 211, 227–228, 231, 264, 266–267, 275, 290, 293, 295, 297
Organization of African Unity (OAU), 110

reproduction, 49, 112, 265n, 306
research, 17, 41–59, 75, 81, 89, 99,
    294
  community, 98, 100
  comparative, 84–85
  linguistic, 66–67
  organization, 108n, 274n, 298
  seed, 109
  See also market, research
restructuring, 25, 30, 32, 101,
    104–105, 294
'risk society', 20
Royal Dutch/Shell, 161, 253
rule of law, 21, 26, 34, 58, 135–150,
    211, 225
Rural Advancement Foundation
    International (now named ETG
    group) (RAFI), 110
rural areas, 287
Russia, 69, 138, 144, 156, 162, 165,
    167, 259, 264, 271, 290, 292n,
    297

satellites, 69, 161–162
Saudi Arabia, 292n
science, 17, 105, 159, 165, 191–92,
    233
Seattle, 18, 29, 106, 179–195, 254–255,
    263–267, 278
Sector-Wide Approaches (SWAps),
    227
securities markets. *See* financial
    markets
security studies, 98, 170
security, 99, 157, 170, 233
  food, 106, 108n, 112
  of foreign investment, 125
  global, 19, 32, 34
  human, 29, 307

  social, 75, 78, 82, 87–88
  socio-economic, 77, 82, 85
  See also security studies
Senegal, 164, 173
Singapore, 85, 161, 166, 189, 219,
    230n, 258n, 290–291
social cohesion, 82, 303, 307
social democracy, 88–89
social geography, 287
social market economy, 206
social movements, 76, 79, 84,
    101–131, 195–196, 261
social policy, 56, 75–91
social regulation, 79, 90
social rights, 77–83, 87–88
social safety net, 34, 81, 88
socialism, 18, 79, 137, 142, 146, 206
Society for Worldwide Interbank
    Financial Telecommunications
    (SWIFT), 290
Socio-Economic Security Programme
    (ILO–SES), 75n, 82
solidarity, 77, 81, 89–91, 266
South Korea, 78, 85, 158, 161,
    166–168, 172, 210, 219, 271, 290,
    292
South Africa, 85
South Asian Association for Regional
    Cooperation (SAARC), 91
Southern African Customs Union
    (SACU), 88
Southern African Development
    Community (SADC), 77, 85,
    87–90
Southern African Development
    Coordination Conference
    (SADCC), 91
sovereignty, 20, 101–108, 112–114,
    126, 128, 199, 212, 247, 259n

Spain, 97, 155, 162, 170, 172, 207, 267n

Special Drawing Rights (SDRs), 31, 249–250, 282, 289, 294

species extinction. *See* biodiversity

Sri Lanka, 56, 85

standardization, 24, 65, 70–71, 108, 190, 295

state socialism, 18, 79, 142

stock markets. *See* financial markets

structural adjustment loans, 56, 298–300

Structural Adjustment Participatory Review Initiative (SAPRI), 300

structural adjustment programs, 224, 271–273

structural adjustment, 90, 104, 110, 114, 264, 267–268

substate agencies, 288

Sudan, 283

Support for Improvement in Governance and Management in Central and Eastern Europe (SIGMA), 47

supranational, 77, 87, 101–103, 108, 110–112, 114, 119, 130, 199, 257

suprastate, 285, 288, 292–298

supraterritorial finance, 287

supraterritoriality, 286

sustainable development, 32–33, 36, 221, 232

Sweden, 75n, 78, 81, 161, 258, 267, 275n, 292

Switzerland, 109n, 161, 172, 211, 258n, 267, 292n, 297

Tanzania, 167, 227

tax on carbon emission, 28, 33, 247, 249

taxation, 25, 28, 76, 78, 87, 208, 248, 267, 270, 276, 281–282, 293

taxpayers, 30, 233, 244

Taiwan, 161, 166, 219

Taylorism, 208–209

Technical Cooperation between Developing Countries (UNDP) (TCDC), 75n

technology, 34, 41, 51, 67, 105, 108, 110n, 155n, 164, 168, 174, 200–203, 233, 258, 266, 276 (*see also* information technology)

telecommunications, 185–186, 286, 290

telephone, 147, 209, 267, 286

television, 69, 169, 283, 286

terrorism, 19, 29, 33–34, 95–100, 200–201, 278–279, 283

Thailand, 168, 175, 192, 219, 271

think tanks, 42–43, 48–49, 51–54, 57–58, 89, 223n, 269, 289, 299

Third World, 26, 50n, 158, 164–168, 175, 264, 268, 273, 276, 282, 294

time, 43, 54, 100, 105, 156, 192–193, 202, 219, 242, 258, 269, 282

Tobin tax, 28, 201, 247, 248–249, 267–268, 281, 300

tolerance, 197, 260

trade liberalization, 99, 107–113, 164, 172, 182, 260, 295

Trade Policy Review Mechanism (TPRM), 186

trade protectionism, 166

Trade Related Investment Measures (TRIM), 181, 185

trade unions, 76, 266n

Trade-Related Aspects of Intellectual Property Rights (TRIPs), 107–112, 184–186, 189, 191